Guitar Chords for the 21st Century

This chord dictionary is for everyone. It requires no special knowledge of music theory, and guitar players of any level can start using these chords immediately. Just check out the C chords in this book. If you like how they sound,
there are 1,848 more! Use them any way that you want.

There are no boundaries – no rules – just total freedom

Play the chords in any order – any progression – any variation

Move up or down the fingerboard to create 22,176 chords

These aren't traditional chords, but new colors to add to your music.

Just randomly choose various chords from anywhere in the book. Use them to create new music or incorporate them into existing songs. Each one will lead you in a new direction.

As you play each chord, listen to its sound. Play it on a different fret, and add or take away notes to create *your own* chords.

This book is a collection of alternative chords. Each one was named for the way it was constructed. If you're interested in how this was done, or want to learn even more ways to use these chords, see the materials at the end of the book.

Otherwise – just open the book!

Pick something that looks interesting to you – and start on your journey to new sounds like you've never heard before!!

About the Author

Joe Lilore is an author, composer, arranger and teacher who has written 27 books for Warner Bros. and United Artists on the guitar, the bass, songwriting and improvising, selling over 200,000 books worldwide. He holds a Master's Degree in guitar as well as a Masters in Music History and is currently pursuing a Doctorate in Musicology. He has taught music for many years at both the high school and college level.

He has worked on this book for years in order to give guitarists unlimited resources and the ability to be free. For more info, check out www.21stcenturychords.com.

Other Books by Joe Lilore

WARNER BROS. PUBLICATIONS INC.
Bass Superstars Series

- DOKKEN
- GENESIS
- HEART
- LED ZEPPELIN
- MOTLEY CRUE
- ROLLING STONES
- R*U*S*H
- SCORPIONS
- WHITESNAKE
- YES

- CHORD DICTIONARY FOR THE MODERN BASSIST
- CLASSICAL THEMES FOR THE MODERN BASSIST
- IMPROVISING JAZZ BASS LINES AND SOLOS
- LEARNIN' THE BLUES FOR ALTO SAX
- LEARNIN' THE BLUES FOR FLUTE
- LEARNIN' THE BLUES FOR GUITAR
- LEARNIN' THE BLUES FOR PIANO
- LEARNIN' THE BLUES FOR TENOR SAX
- LEARNIN' THE BLUES FOR TROMBONE
- LEARNIN' THE BLUES FOR TRUMPET
- LEARNING THE BLUES FOR THE MODERN BASSIST
- ROCK BASS LINES FOR THE MODERN BASSIST
- SOLOS FOR THE MODERN BASSIST
- THE MODERN BASSIST - A COMPLETE METHOD

LIONHEAD PUBLISHING

- THE SONGWRITER'S GUIDE TO MELODIES
- THE SONGWRITER'S GUIDE TO CHORDS AND PROGRESSIONS
- 59 DAYS TO THE GUITAR

TABLE OF CONTENTS

LIKE INTERVALS

PAGE		PAGE		PAGE		PAGE	
1	C-MM^2 / C-mm^2	8	C-MA^3 / C-AM^3	15	C-DD^5 / C-PD^5	22	C-AM^6 / C-mA^6
2	C-Mm^2 / C-mM^2	9	C-mA^3 / C-Am^3	16	C-DP^5 / C-AA^5	23	C-Am^6 / C-MM^7
3	C-AA^2 / C-MA^2	10	C-PPP^4 / C-DDP^4	17	C-PA^5 / C-AP^5	24	C-mm^7 / C-Mm^7
4	C-AM^2 / C-mA^2	11	C-PDP^4 / C-DPP^4	18	C-DA^5 / C-AD^5	25	C-mM^7 / C-AA^7
5	C-Am^2 / C-MM^3	12	C-AAP^4 / C-PAP^4	19	C-MM^6 / C-mm^6	26	C-MA^7 / C-AM^7
6	C-mm^3 / C-Mm^3	13	C-APP^4 / C-DAP^4	20	C-Mm^6 / C-mM^6	27	C-mA^7 / C-Am^7
7	C-mM^3 / C-AA^3	14	C-ADP^4 / C-PP^5	21	C-AA^6 / C-MA^6		

LIKE INTERVALS WITH ADDED NOTES

PAGE		PAGE		PAGE		PAGE	
28	C-MM^2+ / C-mm^2+	35	C-MA^3+ / C-AM^3+	42	C-DD^5+ / C-PD^5+	50	C-Am^6+ / C-MM^7+
29	C-Mm^2+ / C-mM^2+	36	C-mA^3+ / C-Am^3+	43	C-DP^5+ / C-AA^5+	51	C-mm^7+ / C-Mm^7+
30	C-AA^2+ / C-MA^2+	37	C-PPP^4+ / C-DDP^4+	44	C-PA^5+ / C-AP^5+	52	C-mM^7+ / C-AA^7+
31	C-AM^2+ / C-mA^2+	38	C-PDP^4+ / C-DPP^4+	45	C-DA^5+ / C-AD^5+	53	C-MA^7+ / C-AM^7+
32	C-Am^2+ / C-MM^3+	39	C-AAP^4+ / C-PAP^4+	46	C-MM^6+ / C-mm^6+	54	C-mA^7+ / C-Am^7+
33	C-mm^3+ / C-Mm^3+	40	C-APP^4+ / C-DAP^4+	47	C-Mm^6+ / C-mM^6+		
34	C-mM^3+ / C-AA^3+	41	C-ADP^4+ / C-PP^5+	48	C-AA^6+ / C-MA^6+		

MIXED INTERVALS

PAGE		PAGE		PAGE	
55	C-M^2-m^3 C-M^2-M^3	72	C-m^3-m^7 C-m^3-M^7	89	C-M^6-P^4 C-M^6-D^5
56	C-M^2-P^4 C-M^2-D^5	73	C-P^4-m^2 C-P^4-M^2	90	C-M^6-P^5 C-M^6-m^7
57	C-M^2-P^5 C-M^2-m^6	74	C-P^4-m^3 C-P^4-M^3	91	C-M^6-M^7 C-m^6-m^2
58	C-M^2-M^6 C-M^2-m^7	75	C-P^4-D^5 C-P^4-P^5	92	C-m^6-M^2 C-m^6-m^3
59	C-M^2-M^7 C-m^2-m^3	76	C-P^4-m^6 C-P^4-M^6	93	C-m^6-M^3 C-m^6-P^4
60	C-m^2-M^3 C-m^2-P^4	77	C-P^4-m^7 C-P^4-M^7	94	C-m^6-D^5 C-m^6-P^5
61	C-m^2-D^5 C-m^2-P^5	78	C-P^5-m^2 C-P^5-M^2	95	C-m^6-m^7 C-m^6-M^7
62	C-m^2-m^6 C-m^2-M^6	79	C-P^5-m^3 C-P^5-M^3	96	C-M^7-m^2 C-M^7-M^2
63	C-m^2-m^7 C-m^2-M^7	80	C-P^5-P^4 C-P^5-m^6	97	C-M^7-m^3 C-M^7-M^3
64	C-M^3-m^2 C-M^3-M^2	81	C-P^5-M^6 C-P^5-m^7	98	C-M^7-P^4 C-M^7-D^5
65	C-M^3-P^4 C-M^3-D^5	82	C-P^5-M^7 C-D^5-m^2	99	C-M^7-P^5 C-M^7-m^6
66	C-M^3-P^5 C-M^3-m^6	83	C-D^5-M^2 C-D^5-m^3	100	C-M^7-M^6 C-m^7-m^2
67	C-M^3-M^6 C-M^3-m^7	84	C-D^5-M^3 C-D^5-P^4	101	C-m^7-M^2 C-m^7-m^3
68	C-M^3-M^7 C-m^3-m^2	85	C-D^5-m^6 C-D^5-M^6	102	C-m^7-M^3 C-m^7-P^4
69	C-m^3-M^2 C-m^3-P^4	86	C-D^5-m^7 C-D^5-M^7	103	C-m^7-D^5 C-m^7-P^5
70	C-m^3-D^5 C-m^3-P^5	87	C-M^6-m^2 C-M^6-M^2	104	C-m^7-m^6 C-m^7-M^6
71	C-m^3-m^6 C-m^3-M^6	88	C-M^6-m^3 C-M^6-M^3		

MIXED INTERVALS WITH ADDED NOTES

PAGE		PAGE		PAGE	
105	C-M^2-m^3+	122	C-m^3-m^7+	139	C-M^6-P^4+
	C-M^2-M^3+		C-m^3-M^7+		C-M^6-D^5+
106	C-M^2-P^4+	123	C-P^4-m^2+	140	C-M^6-P^5+
	C-M^2-D^5+		C-P^4-M^2+		C-M^6-m^7+
107	C-M^2-P^5+	124	C-P^4-m^3+	141	C-M^6-M^7+
	C-M^2-m^6+		C-P^4-M^3+		C-m^6-m^2+
108	C-M^2-M^6+	125	C-P^4-D^5+	142	C-m^6-M^2+
	C-M^2-m^7+		C-P^4-P^5+		C-m^6-m^3+
109	C-M^2-M^7+	126	C-P^4-m^6+	143	C-m^6-M^3+
	C-m^2-m^3+		C-P^4-M^6+		C-m^6-P^4+
110	C-m^2-M^3+	127	C-P^4-m^7+	144	C-m^6-D^5+
	C-m^2-P^4+		C-P^4-M^7+		C-m^6-P^5+
111	C-m^2-D^5+	128	C-P^5-m^2+	145	C-m^6-m^7+
	C-m^2-P^5+		C-P^5-M^2+		C-m^6-M^7+
112	C-m^2-m^6+	129	C-P^5-m^3+	146	C-M^7-m^2+
	C-m^2-M^6+		C-P^5-M^3+		C-M^7-M^2+
113	C-m^2-m^7+	130	C-P^5-P^4+	147	C-M^7-m^3+
	C-m^2-M^7+		C-P^5-m^6+		C-M^7-M^3+
114	C-M^3-m^2+	131	C-P^5-M^6+	148	C-M^7-P^4+
	C-M^3-M^2+		C-P^5-m^7+		C-M^7-D^5+
115	C-M^3-P^4+	132	C-P^5-M^7+	149	C-M^7-P^5+
	C-M^3-D^5+		C-D^5-m^2+		C-M^7-m^6+
116	C-M^3-P^5+	133	C-D^5-M^2+	150	C-M^7-M^6+
	C-M^3-m^6+		C-D^5-m^3+		C-m^7-m^2+
117	C-M^3-M^6+	134	C-D^5-M^3+	151	C-m^7-M^2+
	C-M^3-m^7+		C-D^5-P^4+		C-m^7-m^3+
118	C-M^3-M^7+	135	C-D^5-m^6+	152	C-m^7-M^3+
	C-m^3-m^2+		C-D^5-M^6+		C-m^7-P^4+
119	C-m^3-M^2+	136	C-D^5-m^7+	153	C-m^7-D^5+
	C-m^3-P^4+		C-D^5-M^7+		C-m^7-P^5+
120	C-m^3-D^5+	137	C-M^6-m^2+	154	C-m^7-m^6+
	C-m^3-P^5+		C-M^6-M^2+		C-m^7-M^6+
121	C-m^3-m^6+	138	C-M^6-m^3+		
	C-m^3-M^6+		C-M^6-M^3+		

Additional Resources

155   Overview

156   Chord Construction and Names
        Added-Note Chords

157   Transposition

158   Chord Melody
        Suggested Ideas
1. Substitution
2. Melody as a Guiding Force
3. Tension and Calm
4. Cycles
5. Ostinato
6. 12-Tone Row as the Guiding Force
7. Aleatoric (music by chance)
8. Bi and Tri-Tonal Groupings
9. Pedal Tones
    - Example 1: Pedal E – 6th String
    - Example 2: Pedal G – 3rd String
    - Example 3: Pedal E – 1st String
10. Parallel Chord Movement
    - Example: Parallel Major 7th over Pedal A

C-MM^2 C-mm^2

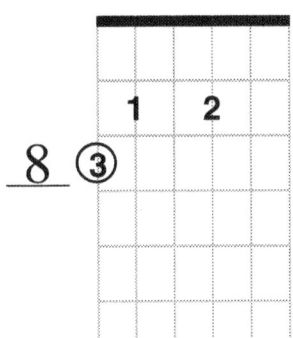
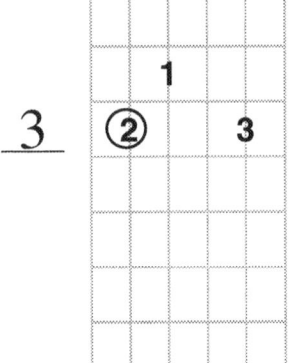
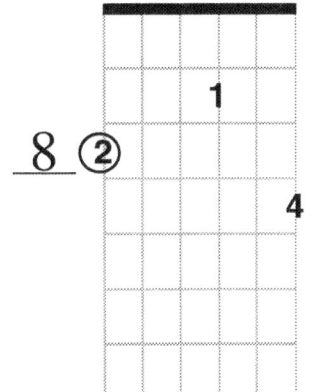
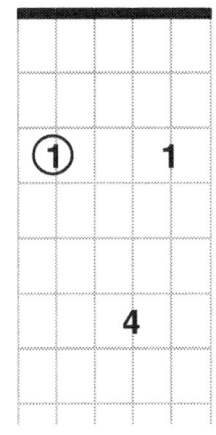

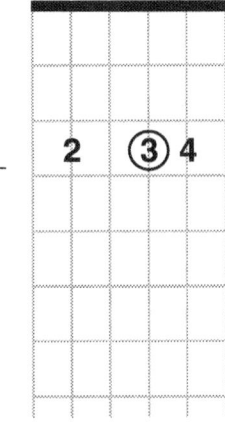
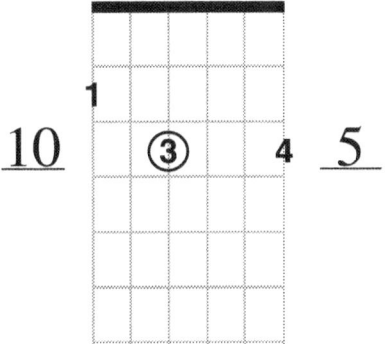
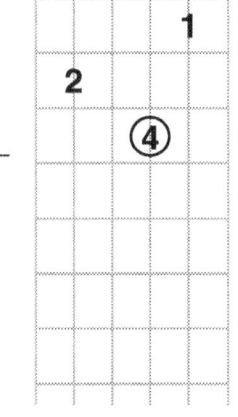

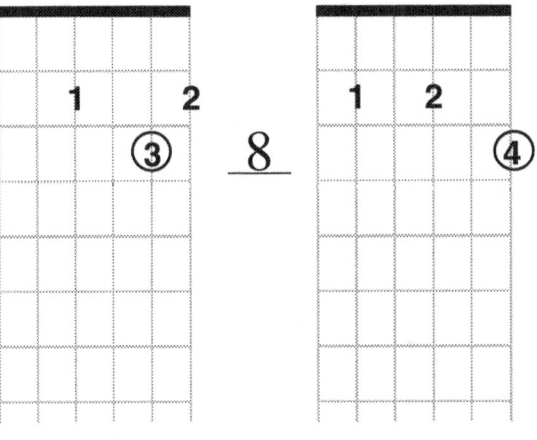
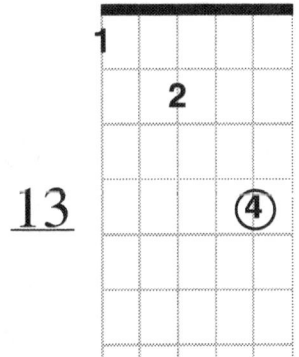
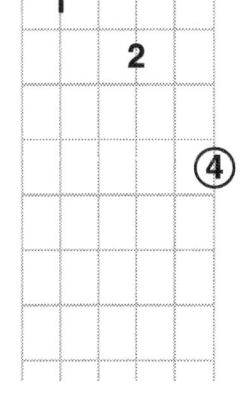

C-Mm^2 C-mM^2

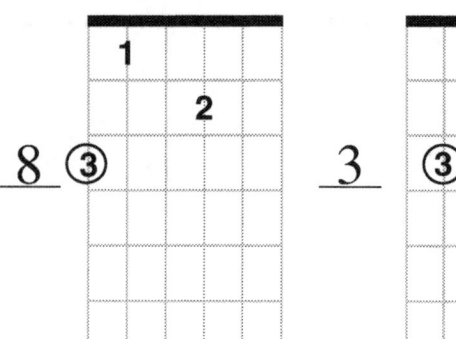 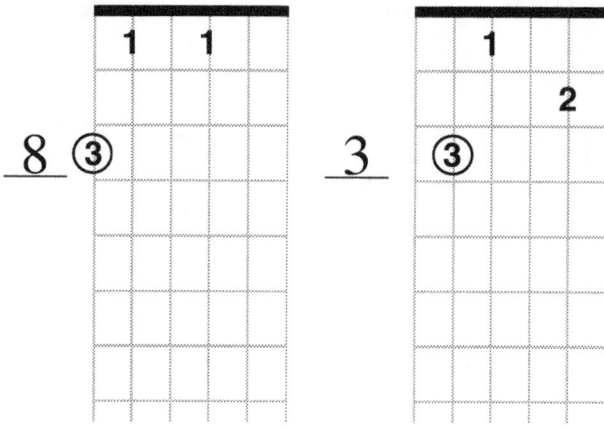

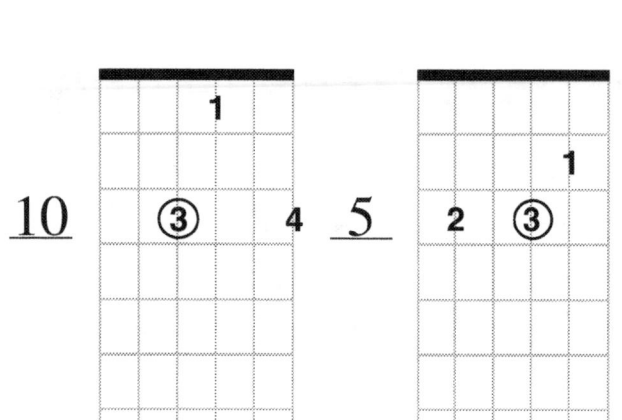 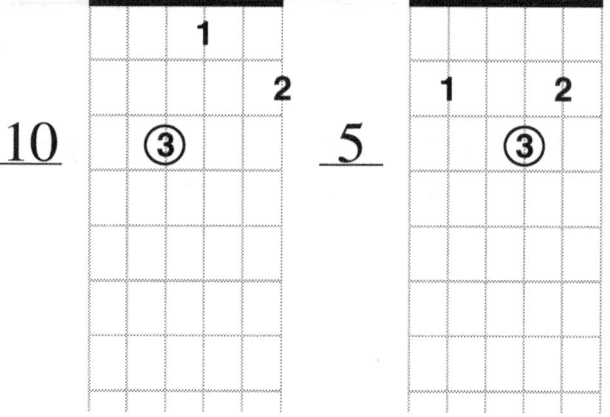

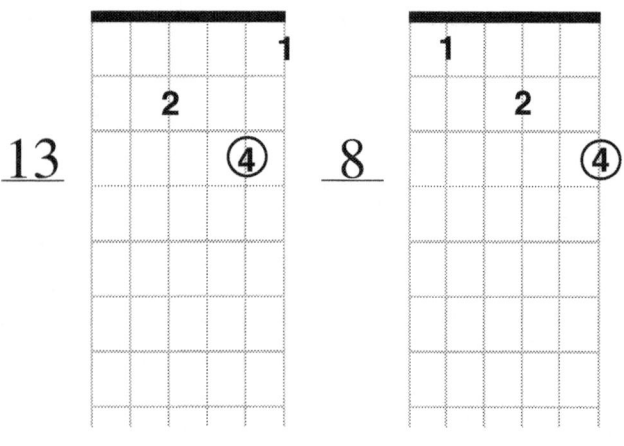 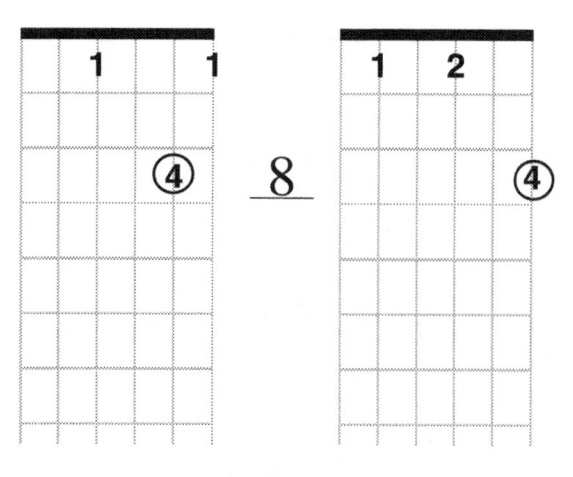

C-AA²   C-MA²

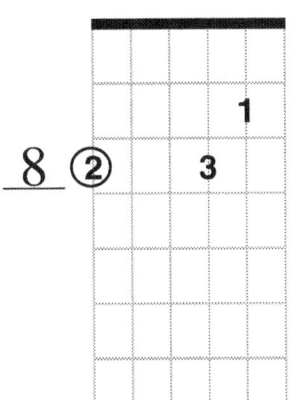
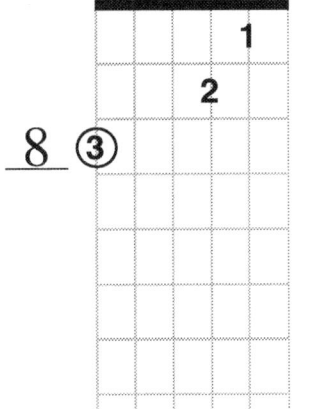
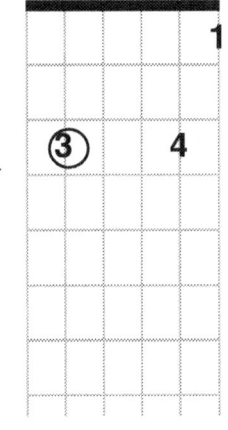
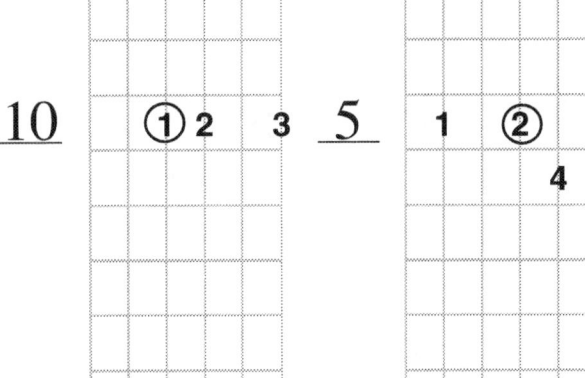
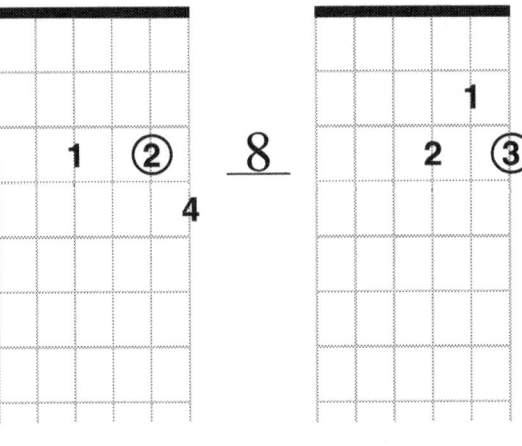
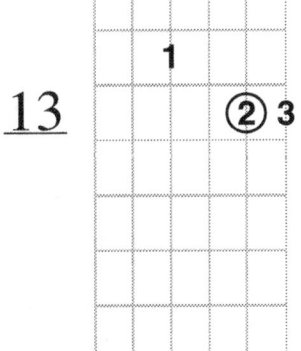
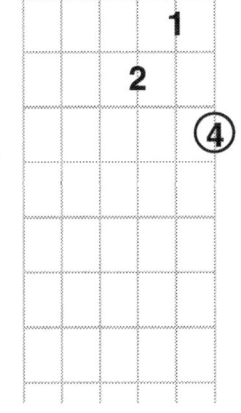

C-AM^2 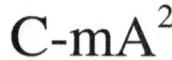 C-mA^2

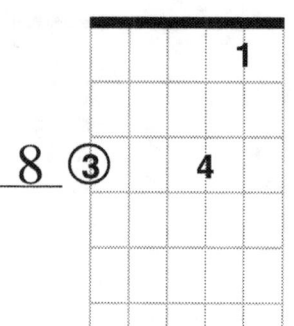 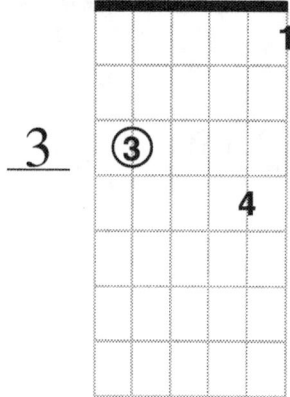 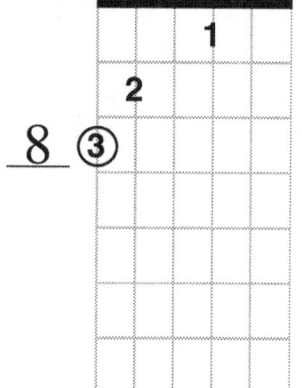 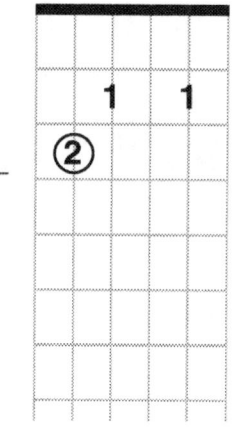

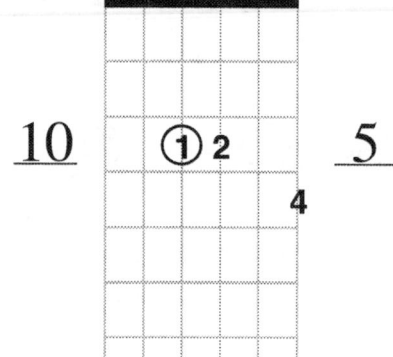 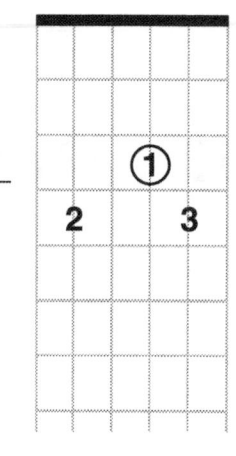 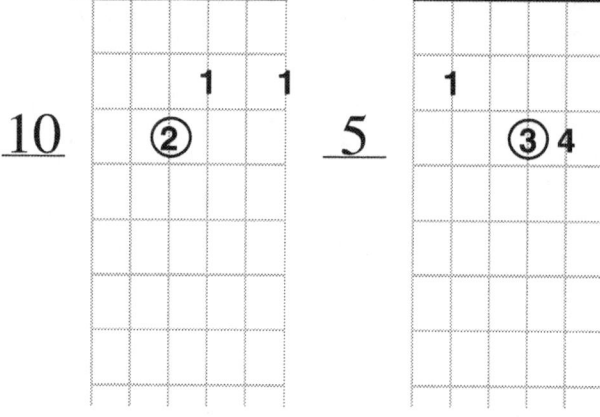

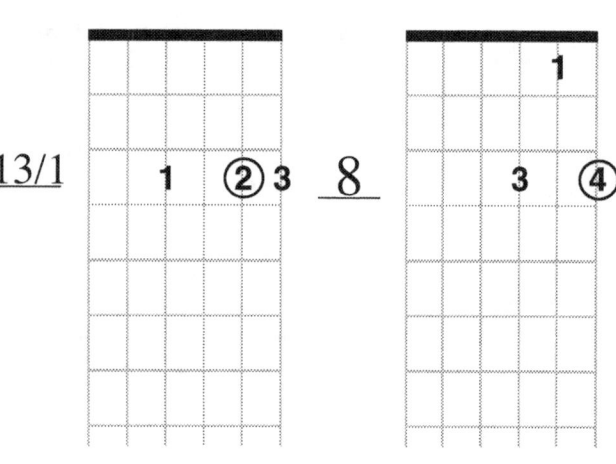 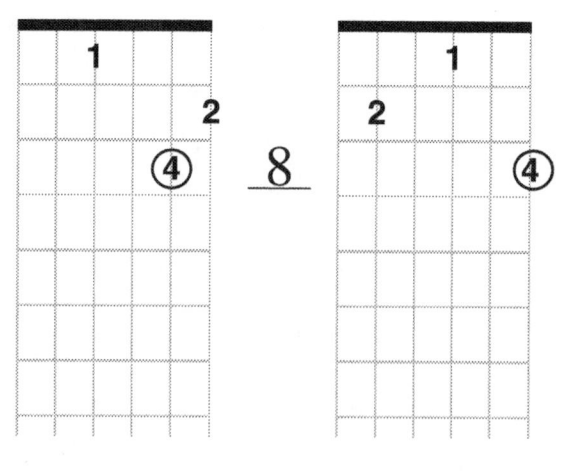

C-Am^2 C-MM^3

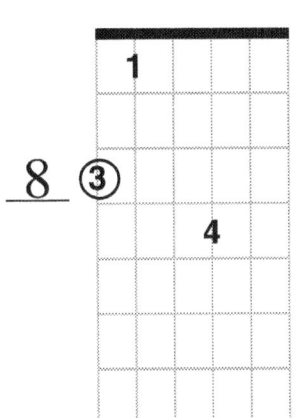 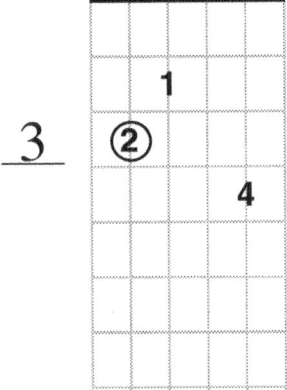 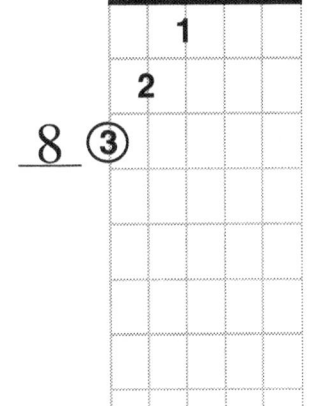 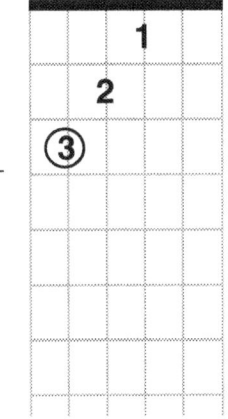

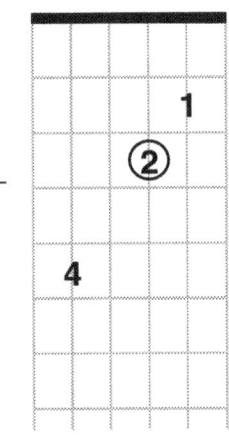 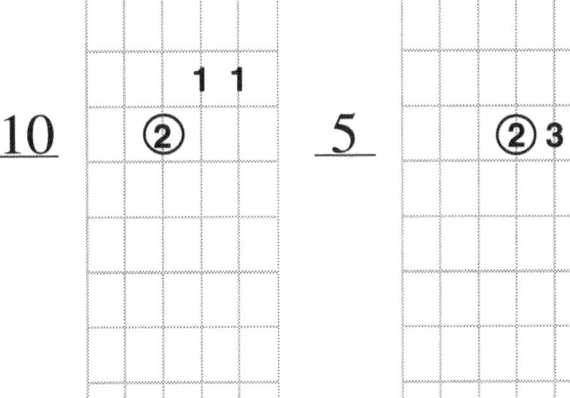

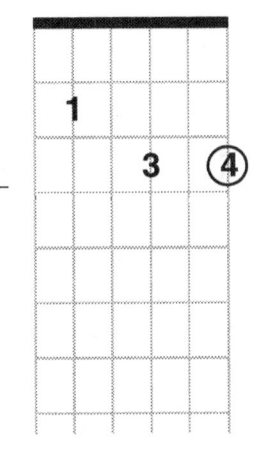 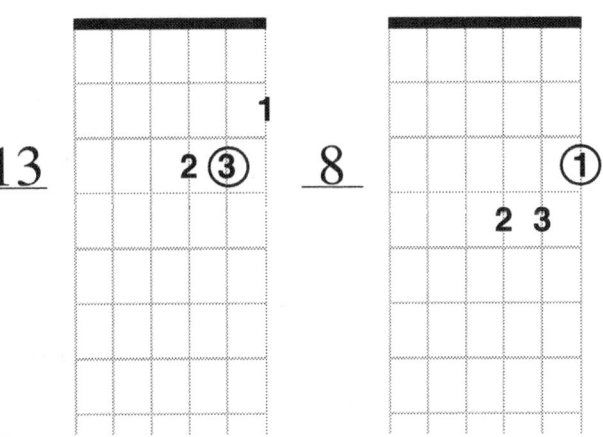

C-mm³

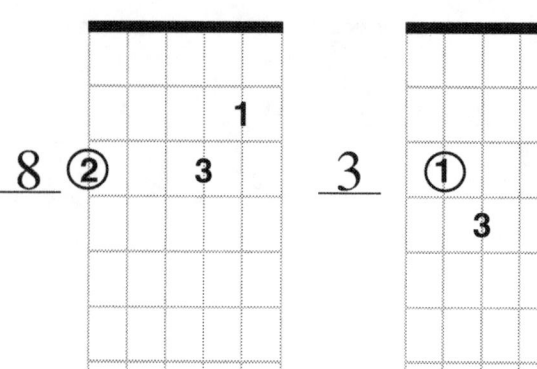

C-Mm³

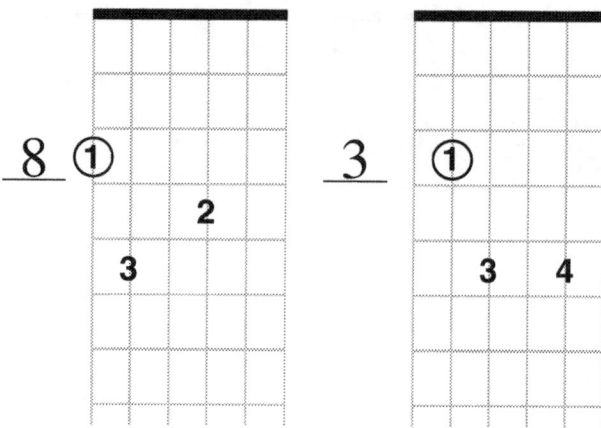

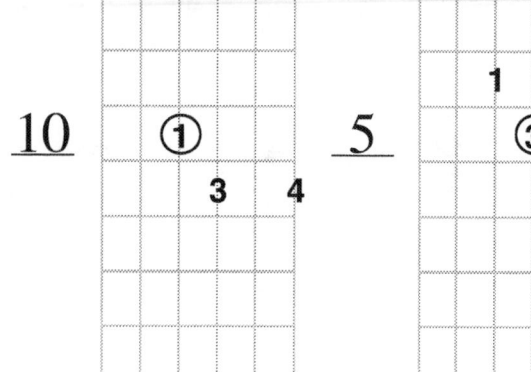

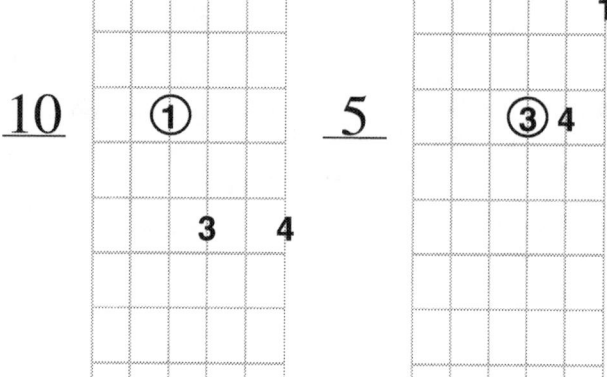

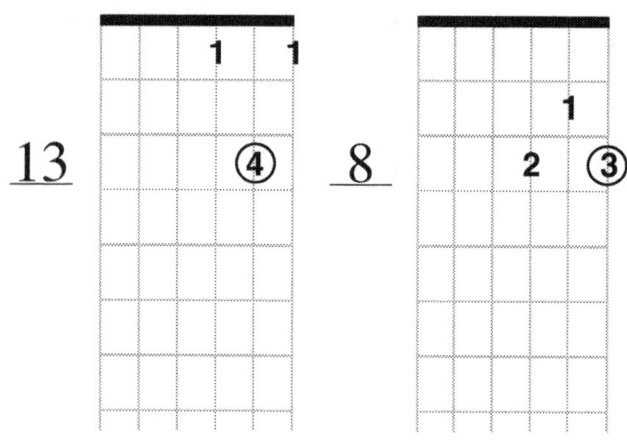

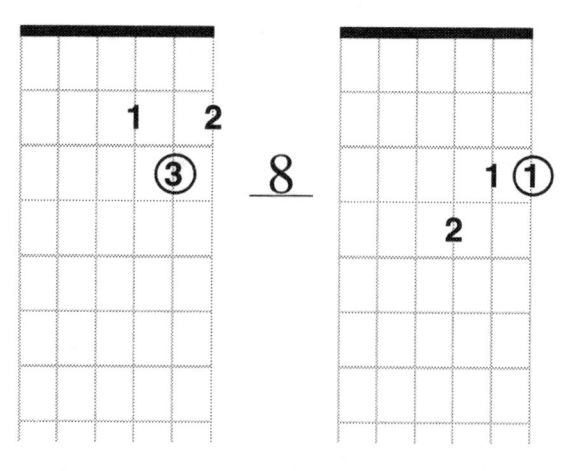

C-mM^3 | C-AA^3

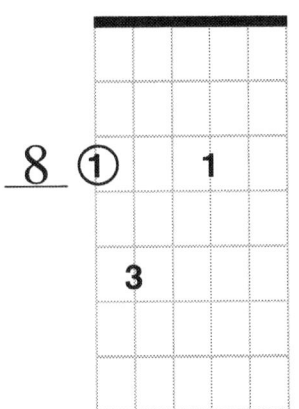 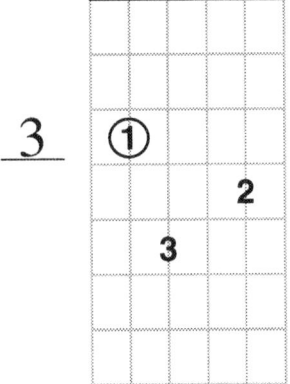 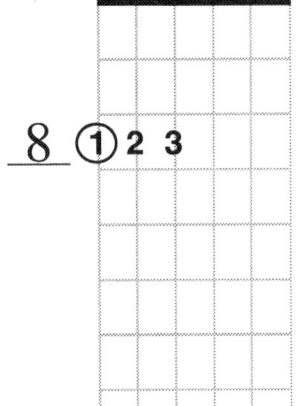 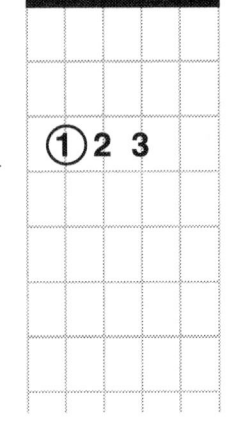

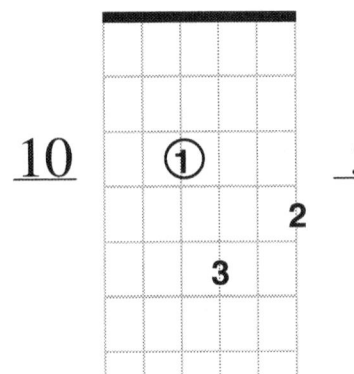 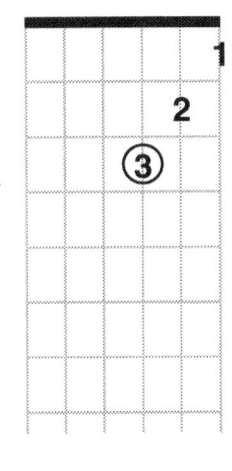 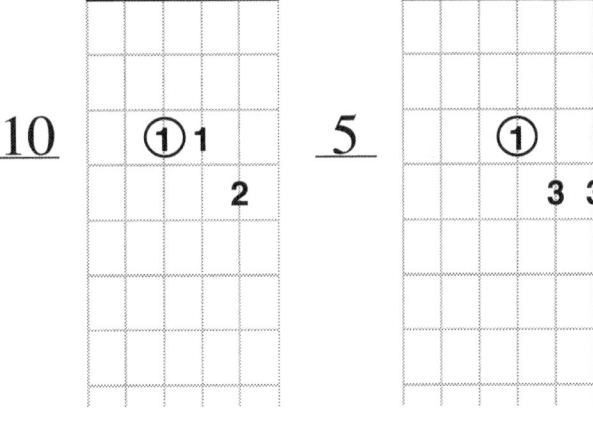

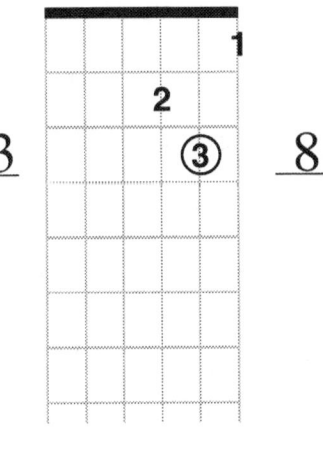 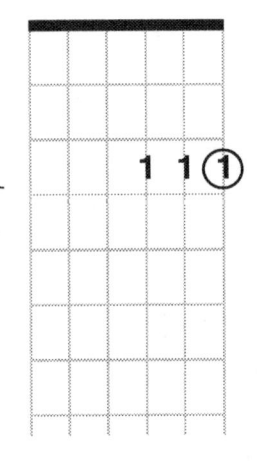 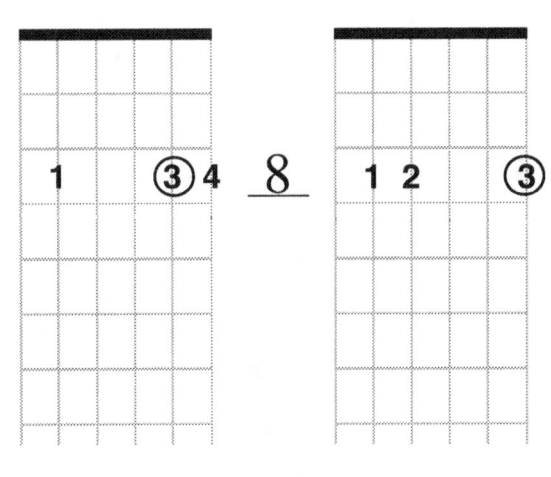

C-MA³   C-AM³

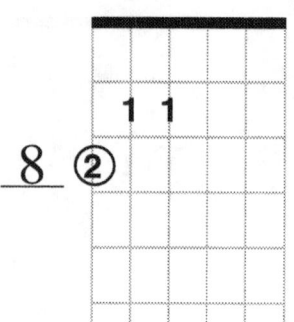
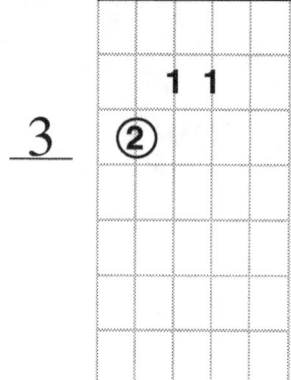
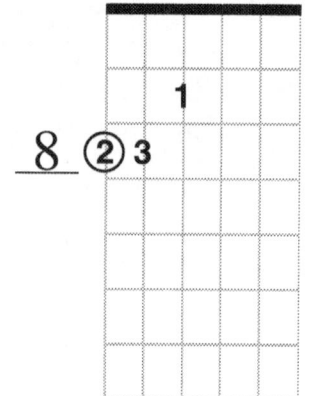
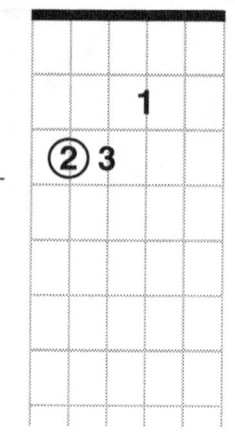

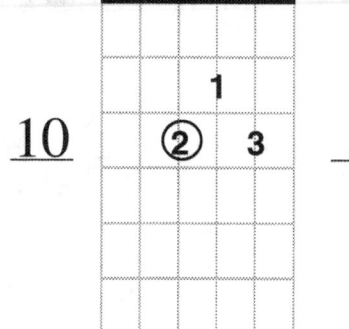
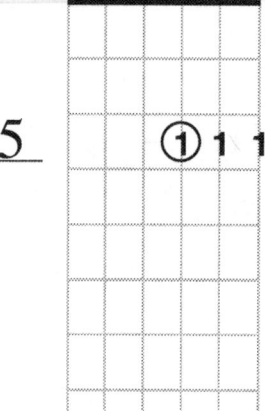
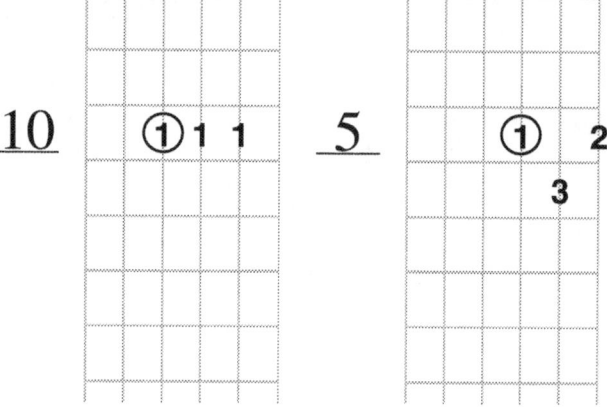

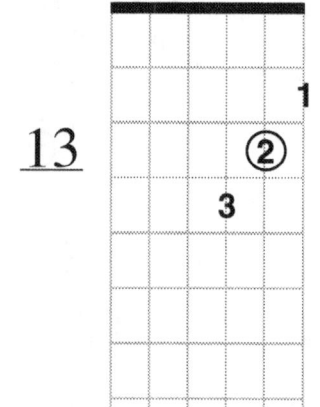
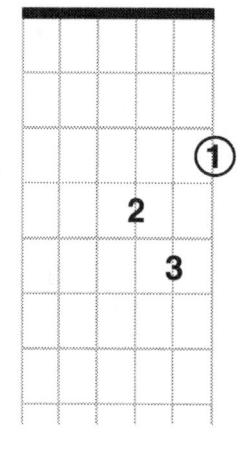
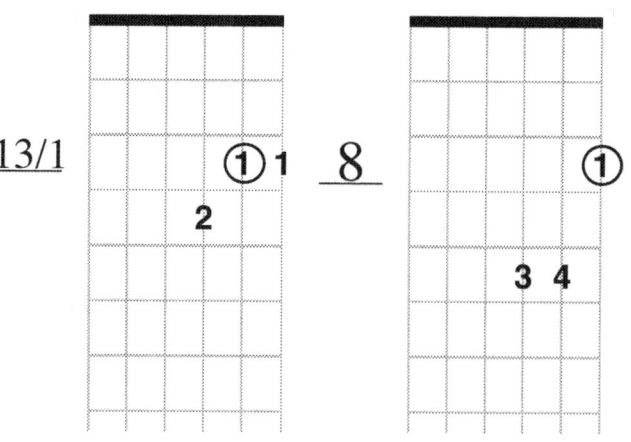

C-mA^3 C-Am^3

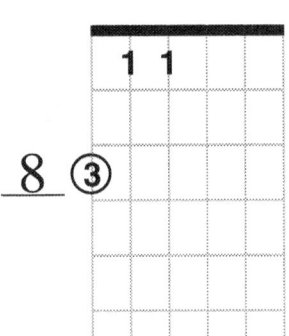 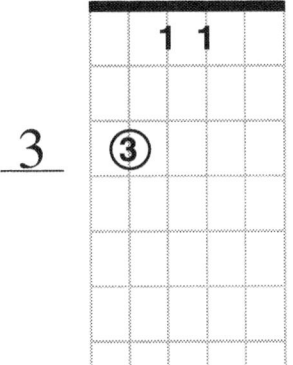 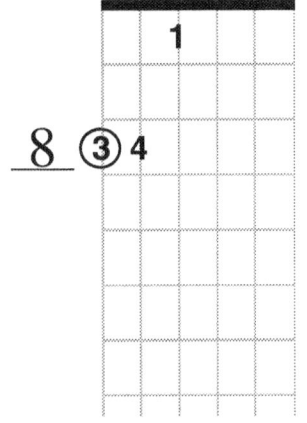 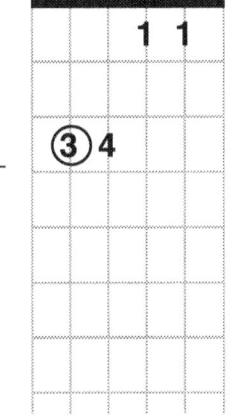

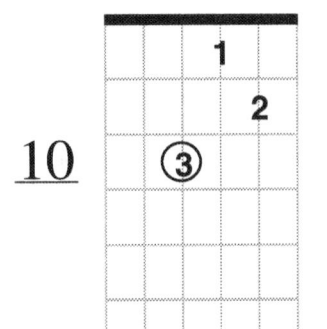 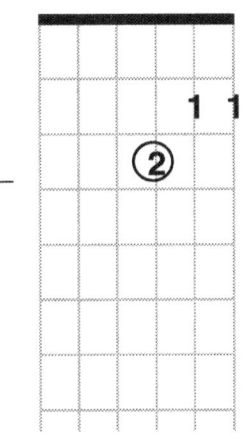 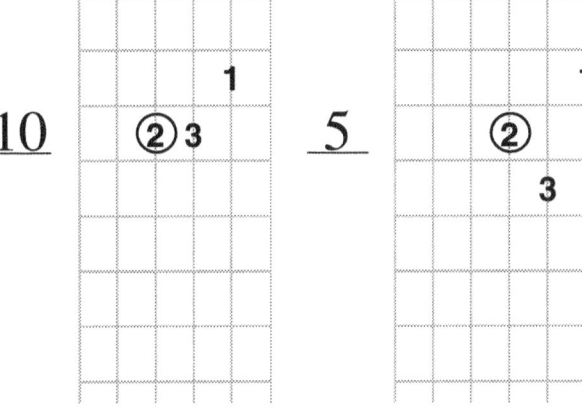

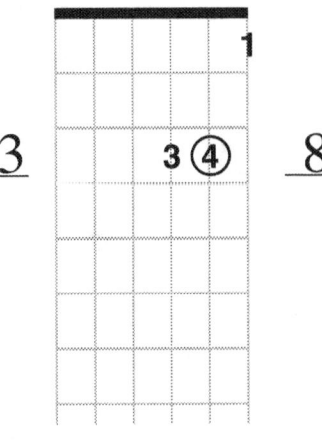 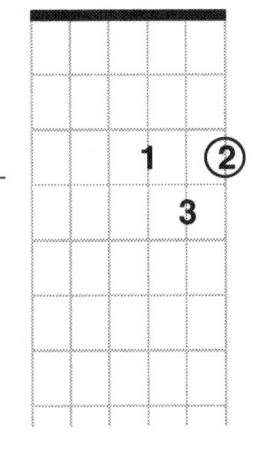 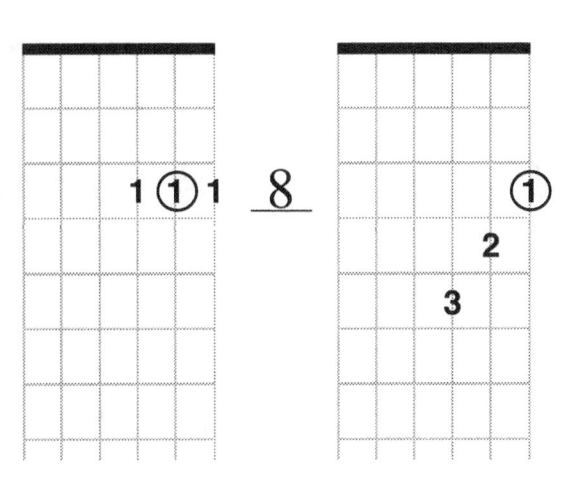

C-PPP⁴   C-DDP⁴

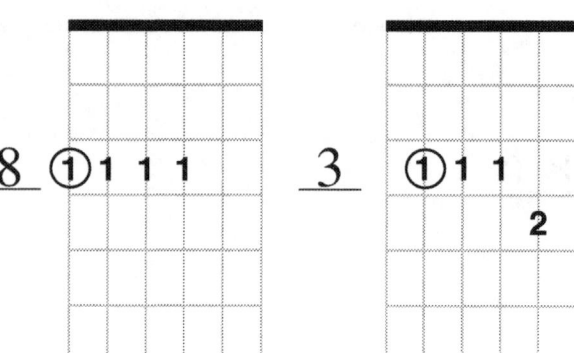
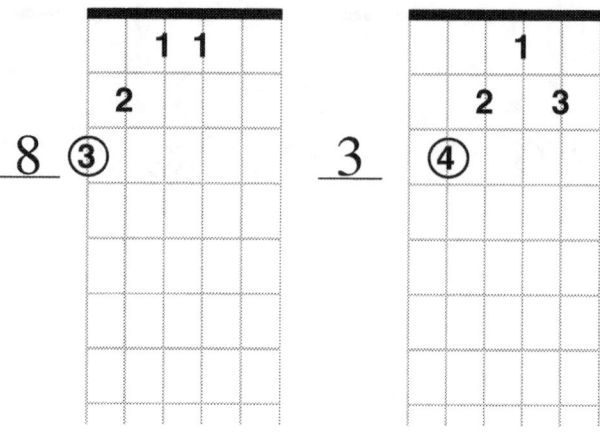
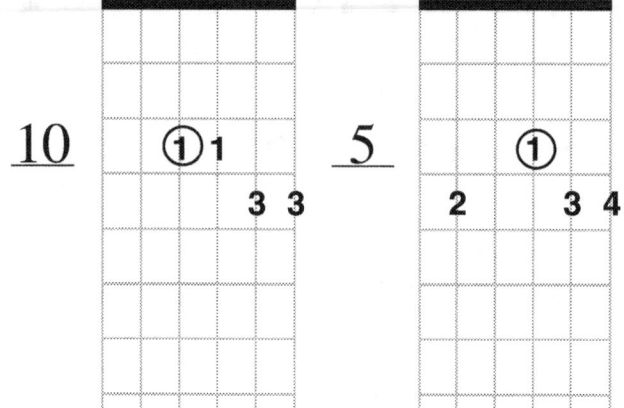
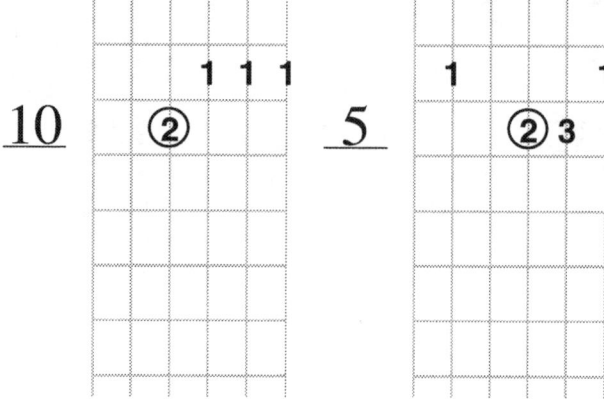
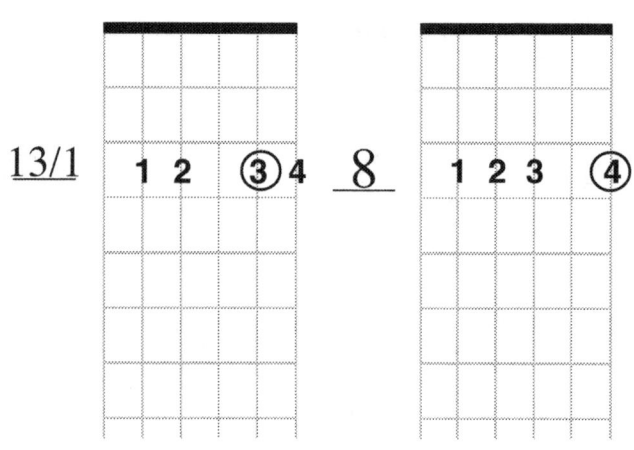
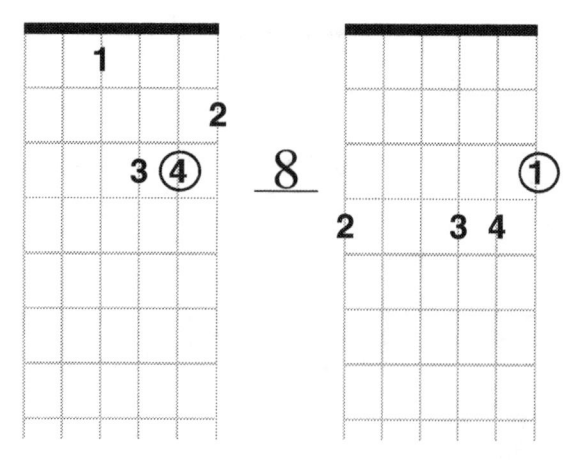

C-PDP^4 C-DPP^4

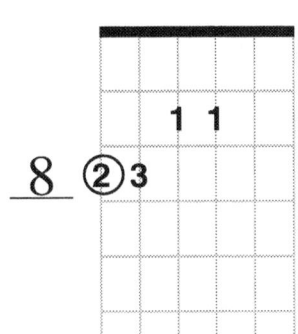
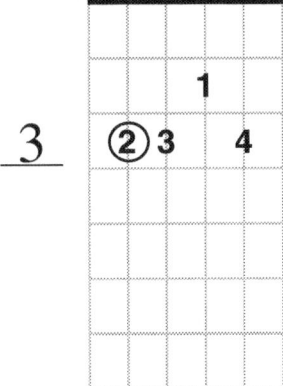
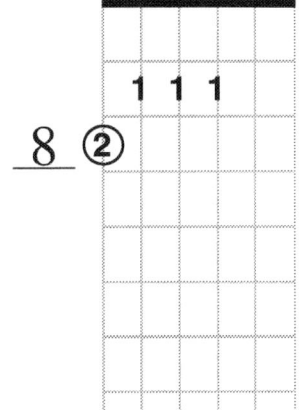
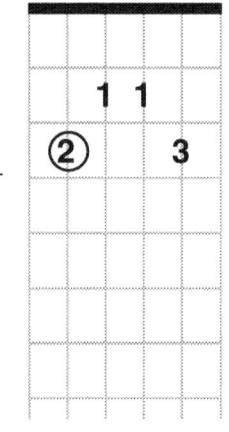
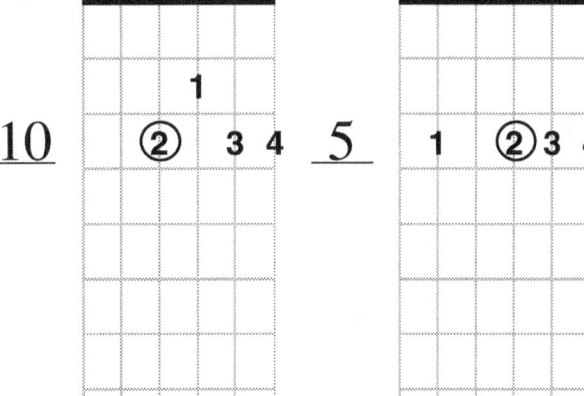
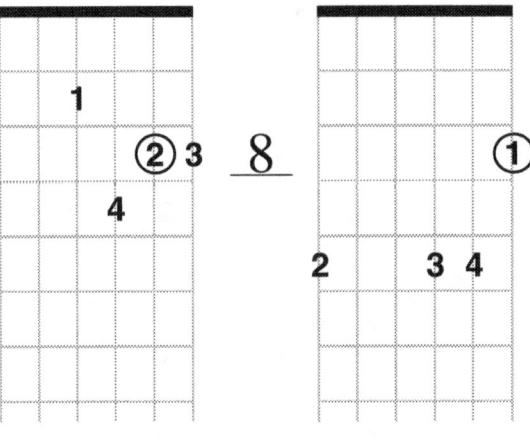
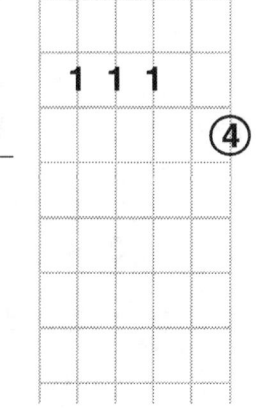

C-AAP⁴   C-PAP⁴

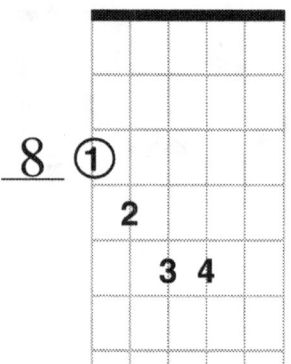
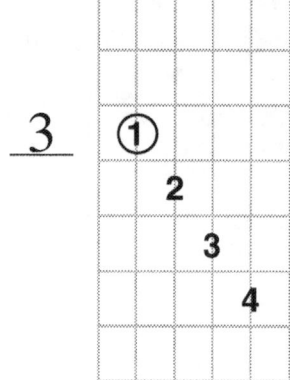
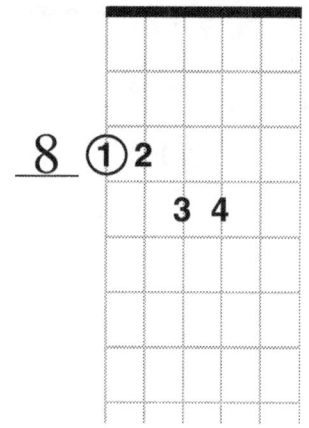
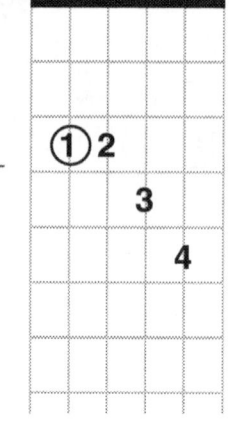
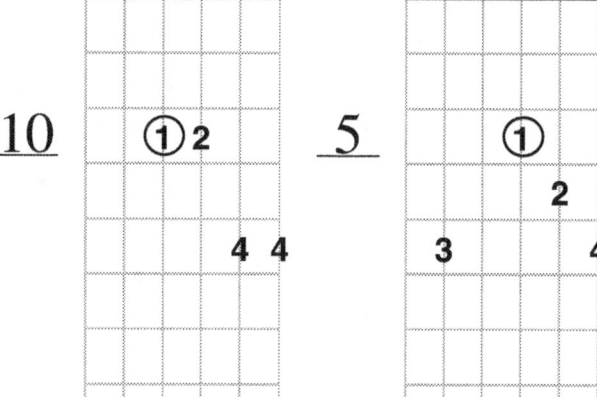
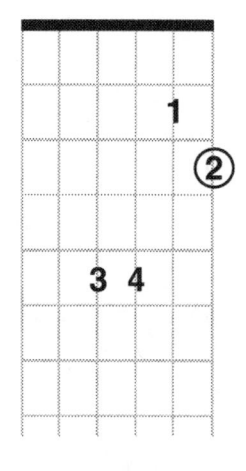
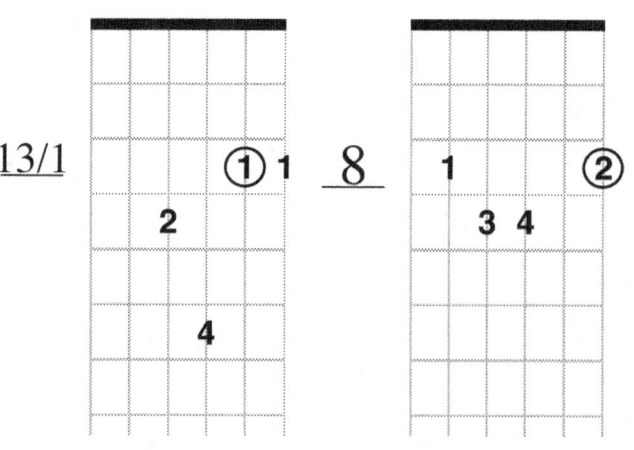

C-APP^4 C-DAP^4

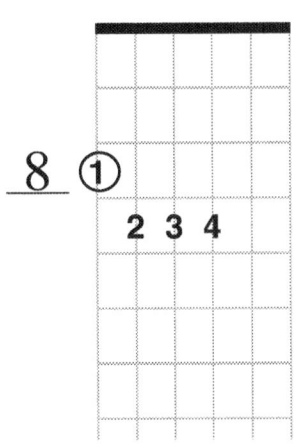
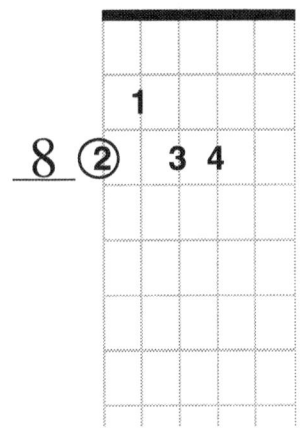
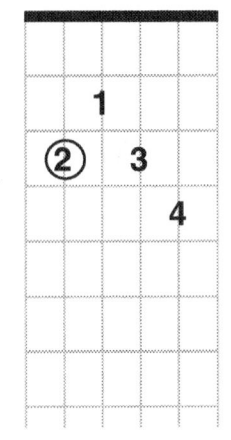
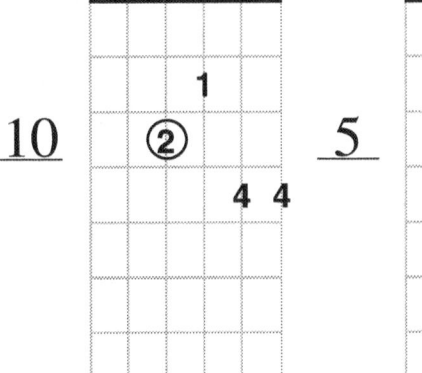
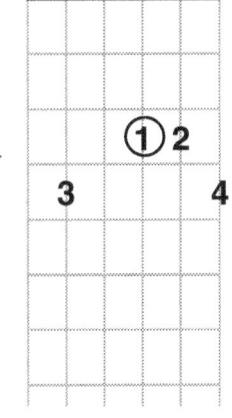
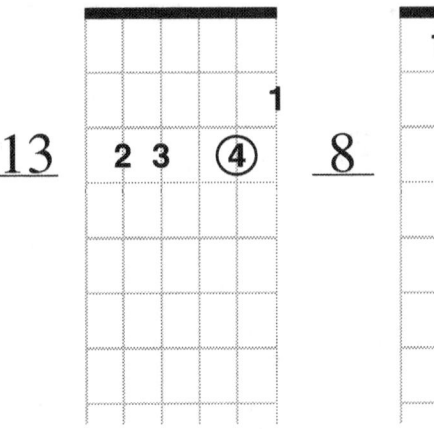

C-ADP^4 C-PP^5

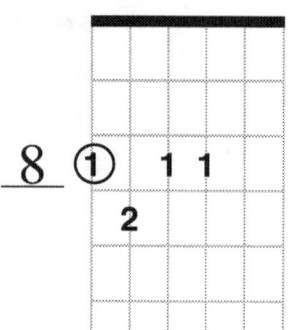 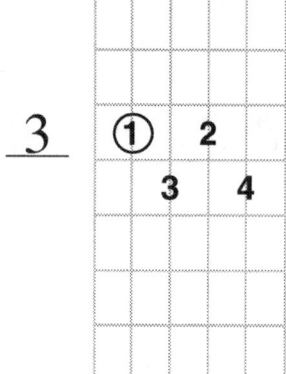 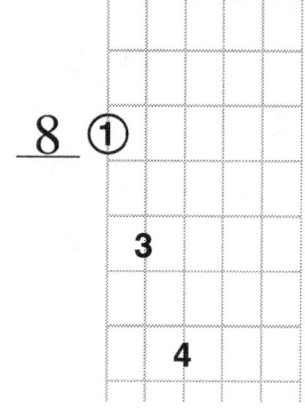 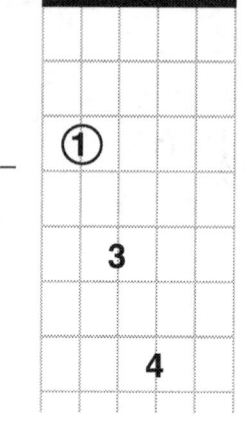

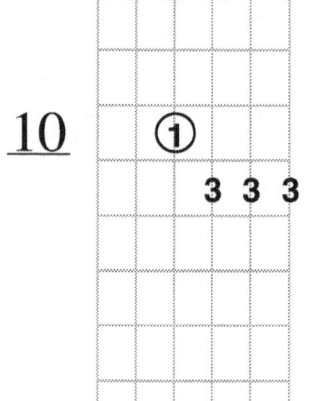 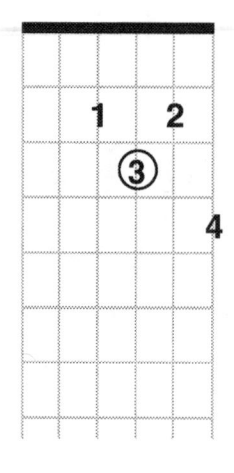 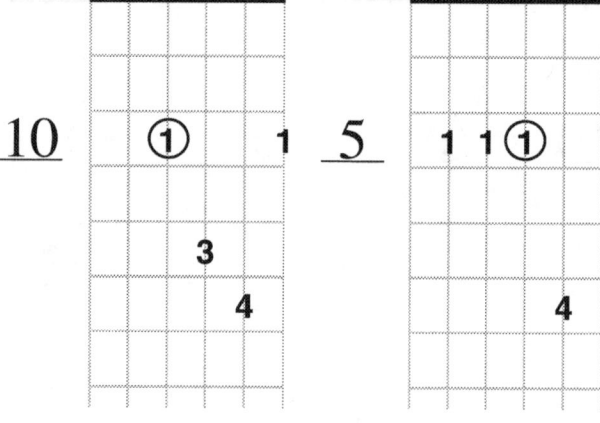

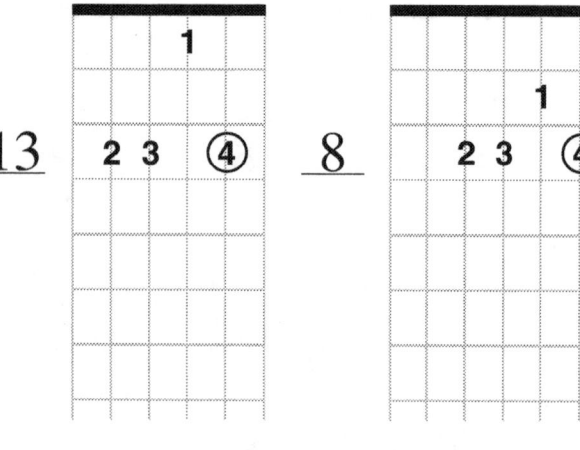 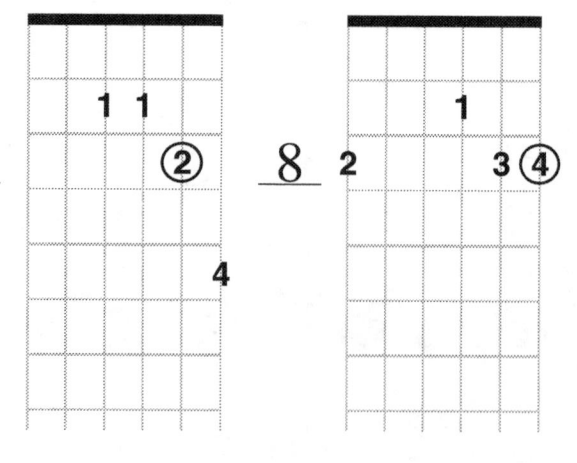

C-DD^5 C-PD^5

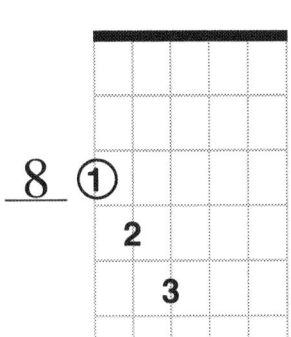
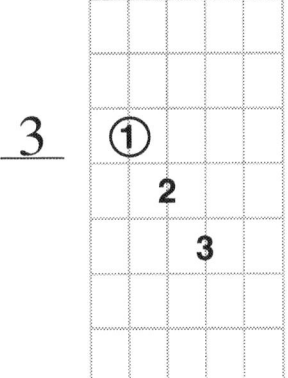
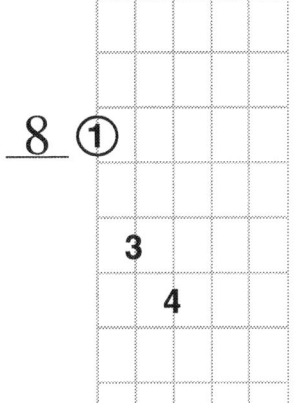
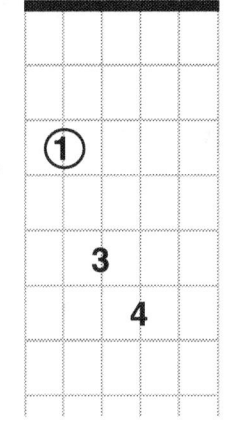

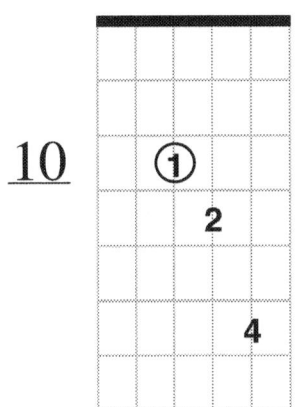
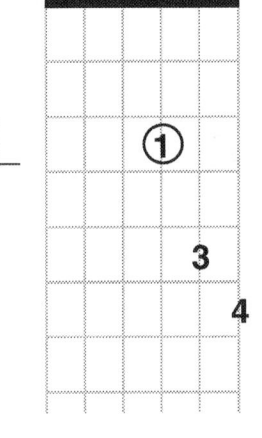
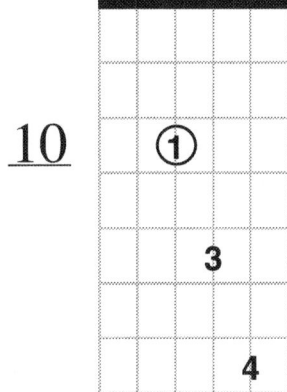
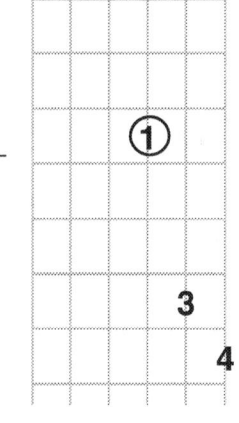

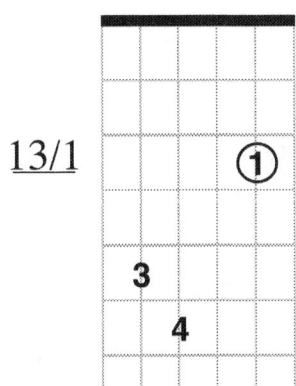
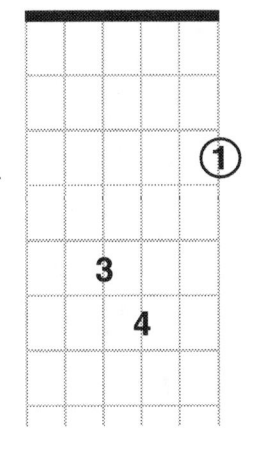
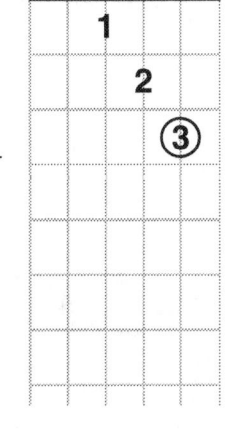
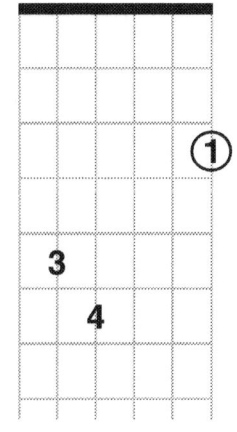

C-DP^5  C-AA^5

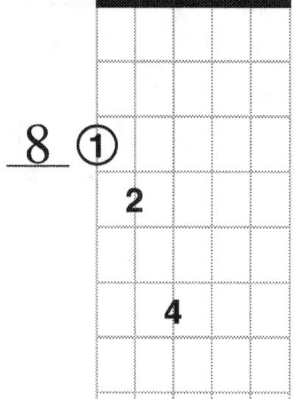 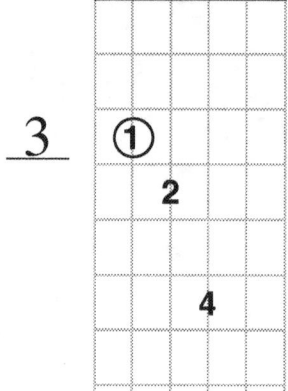 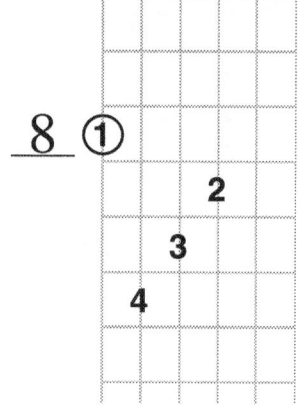 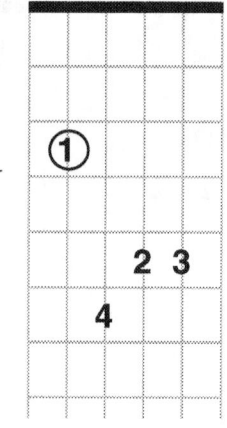

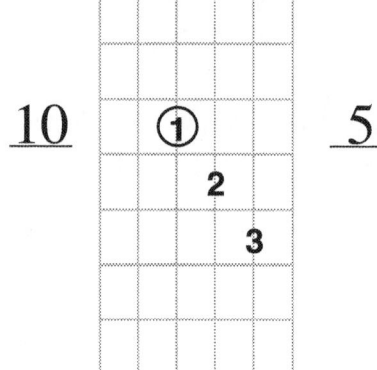 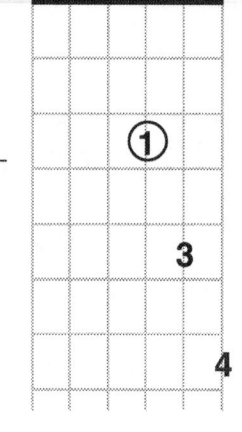 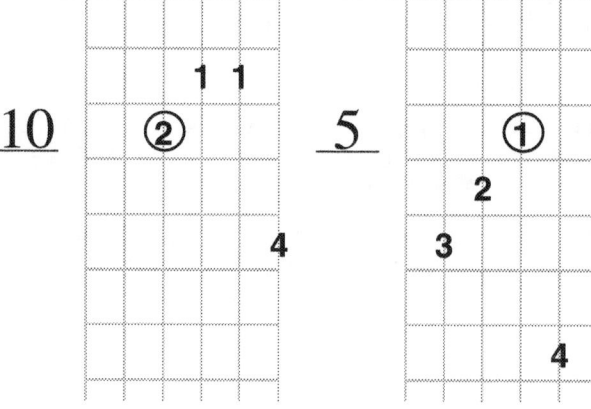

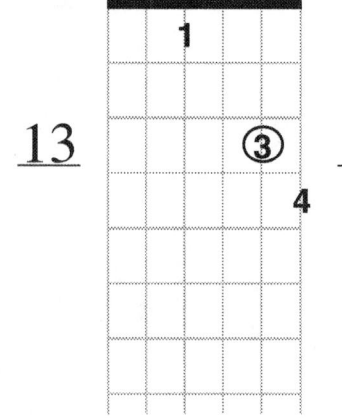 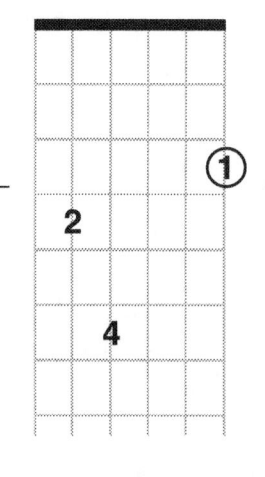 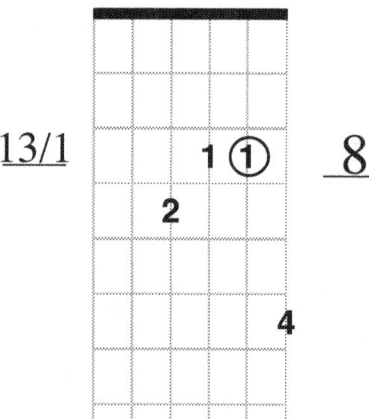 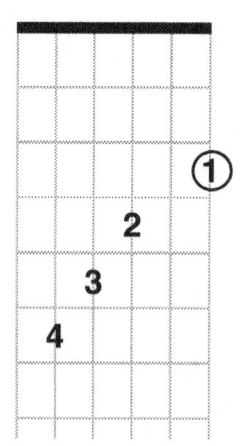

C-PA^5 C-AP^5

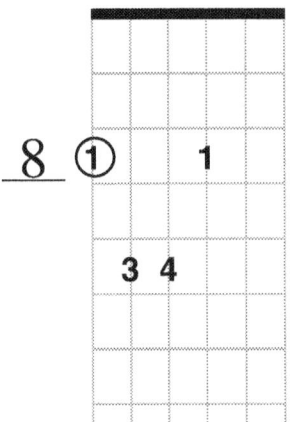
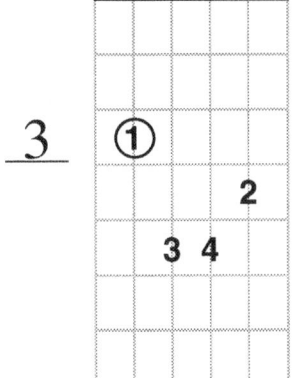
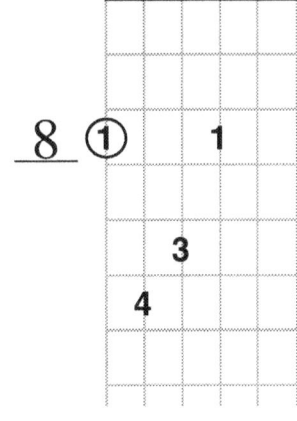
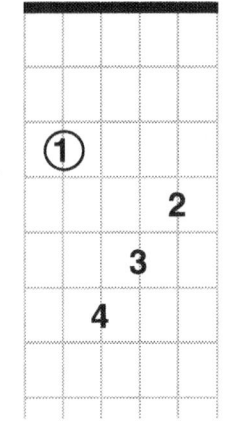

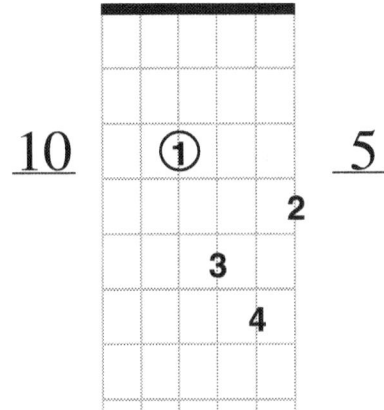
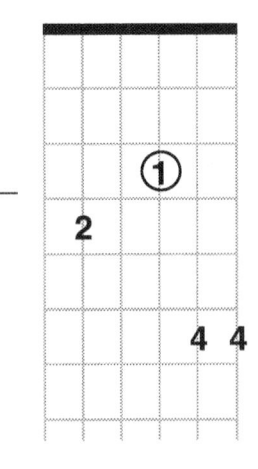
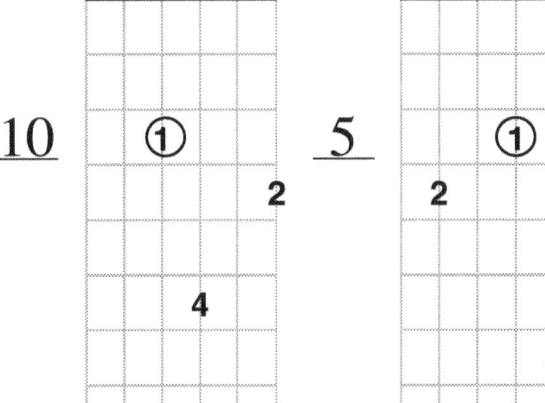

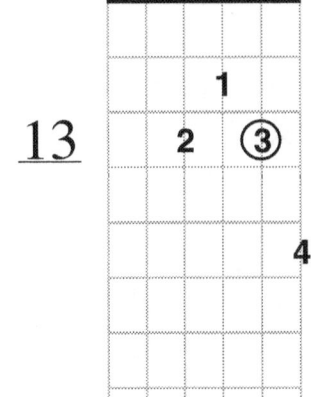
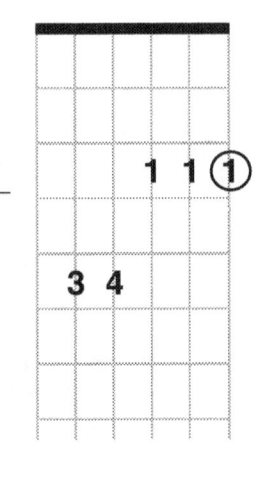
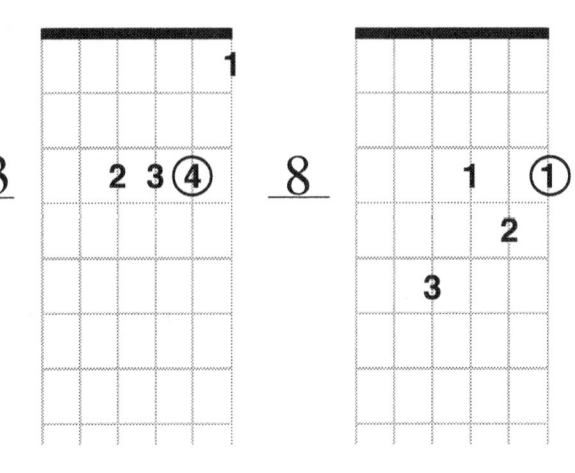

C-DA^5 C-AD^5

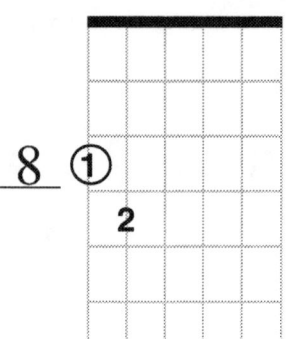 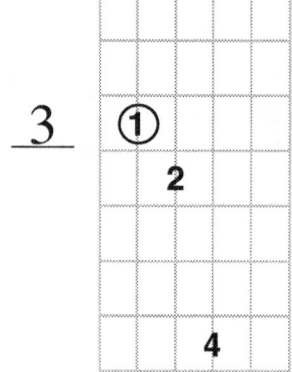 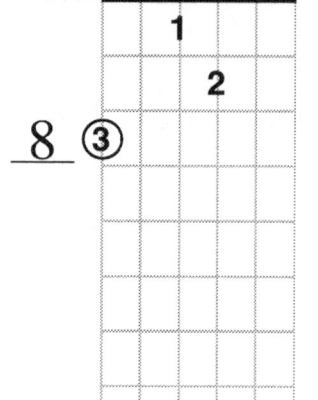 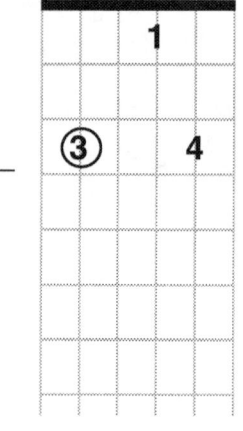

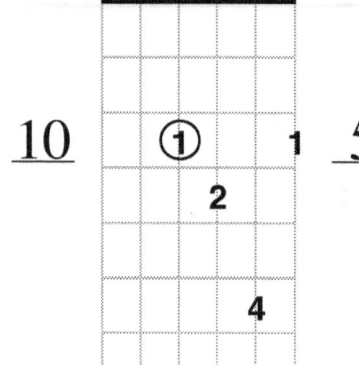 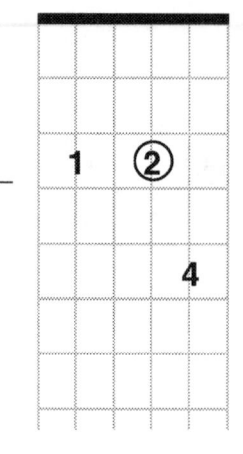 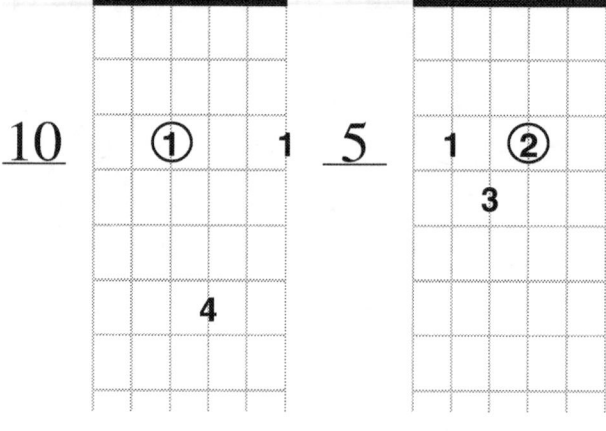

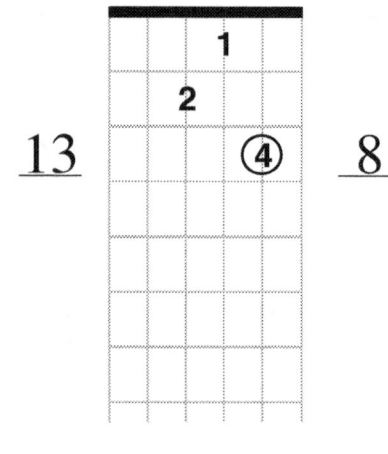 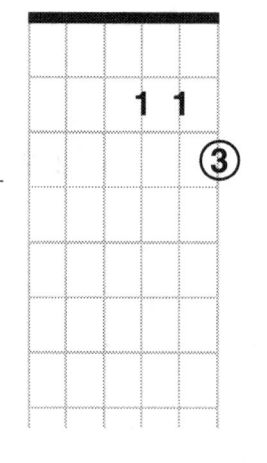 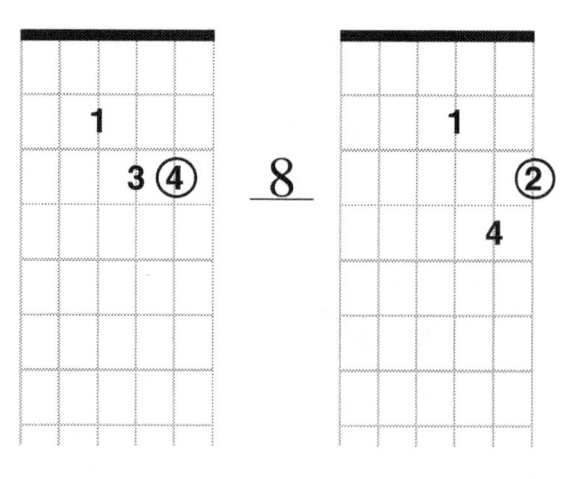

C-MM⁶   C-mm⁶

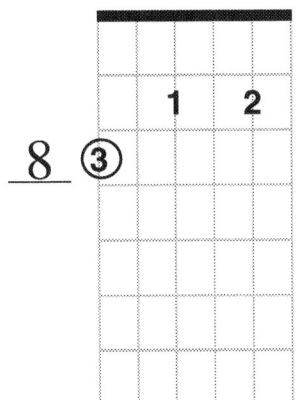
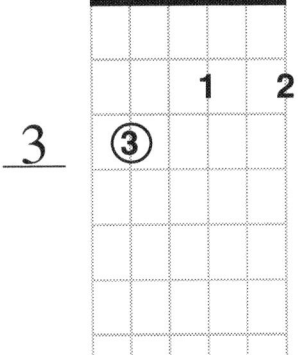
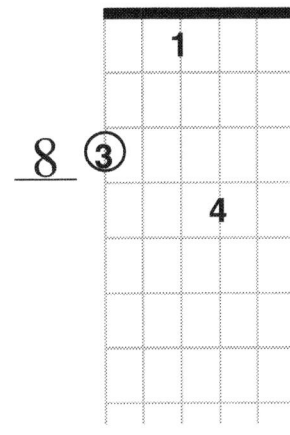
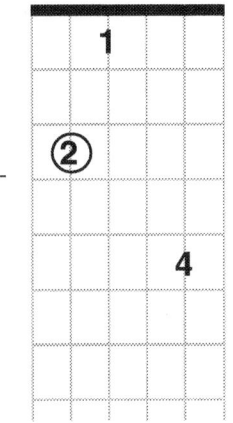
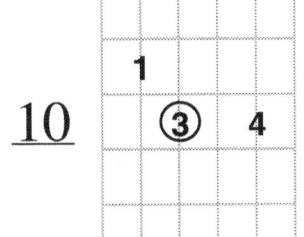
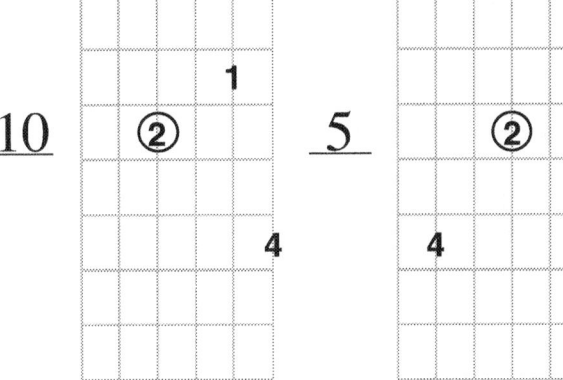
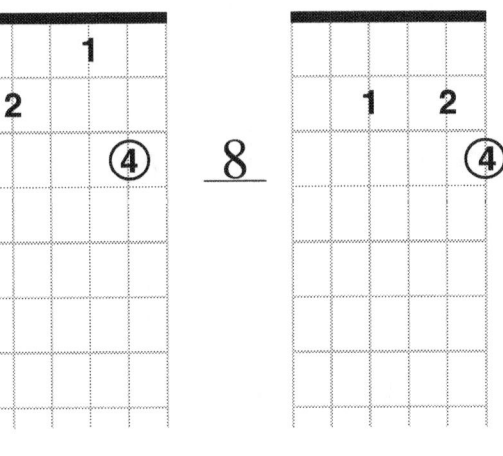
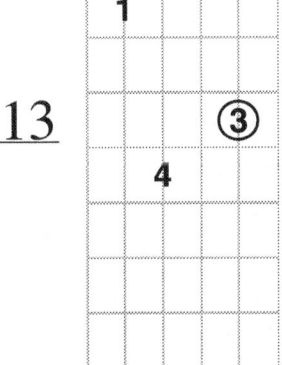

C-Mm^6　　　　　　　　C-mM^6

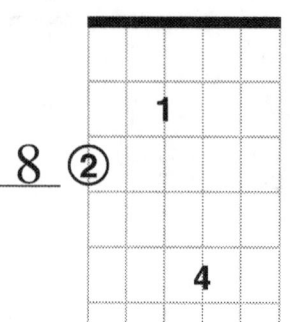 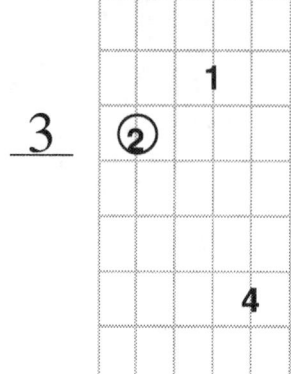 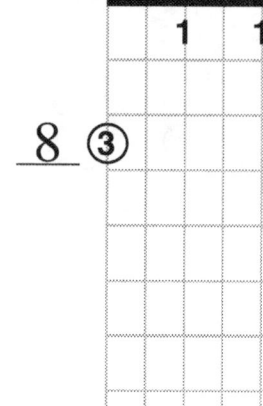 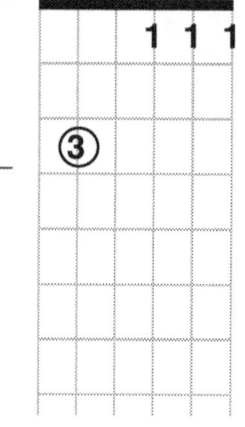

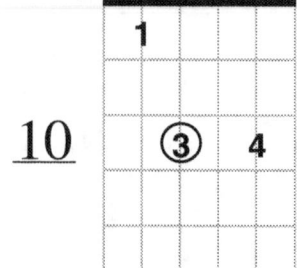 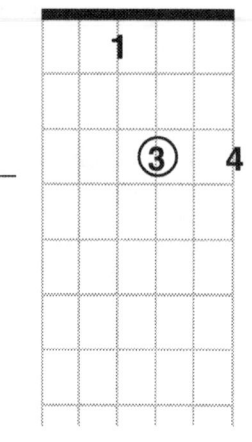 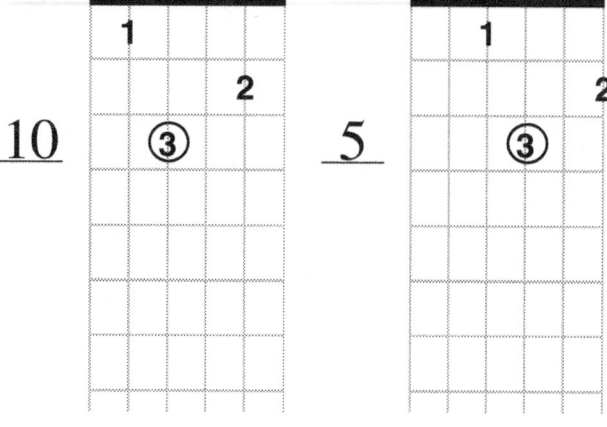

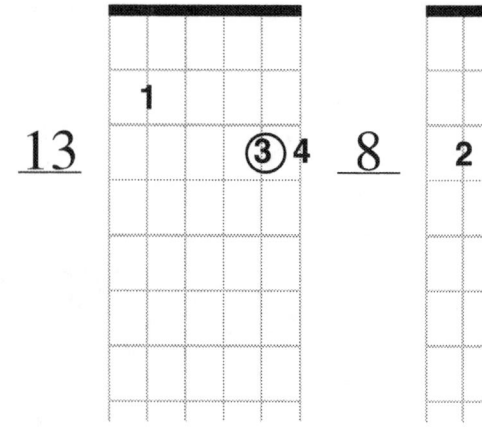 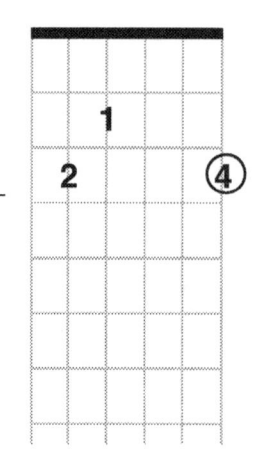 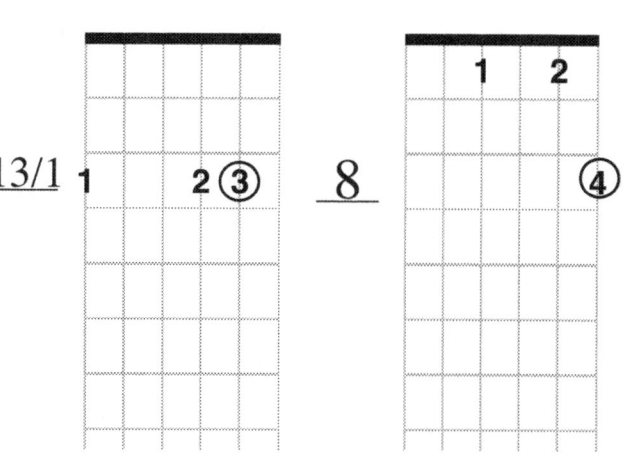

C-AA^6 C-MA^6

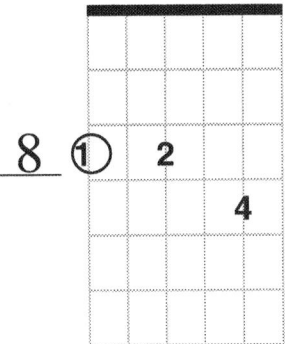 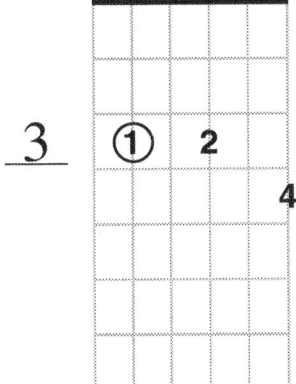   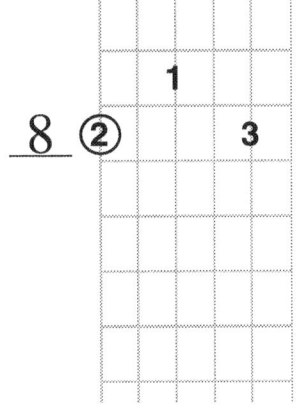 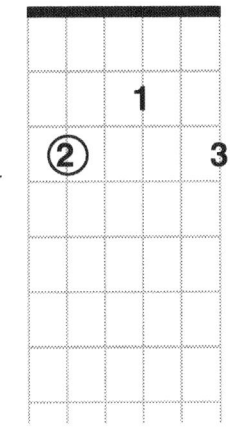

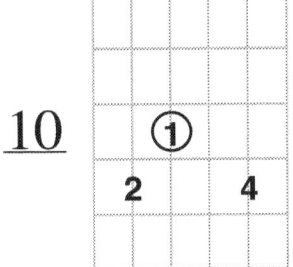   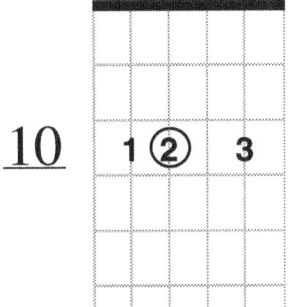 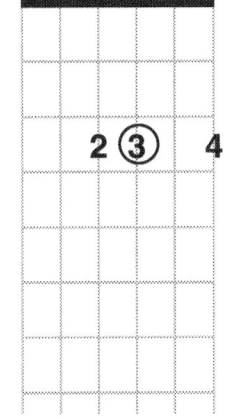

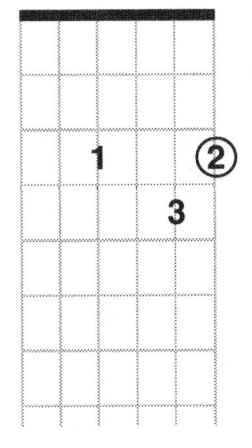   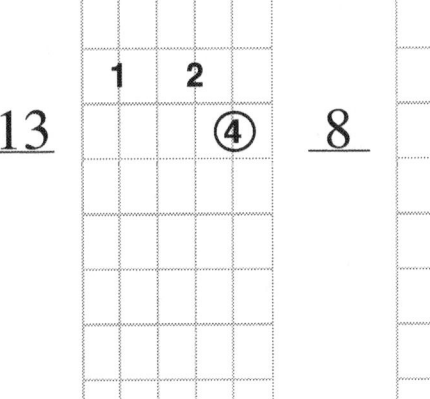

C-AM⁶   C-mA⁶

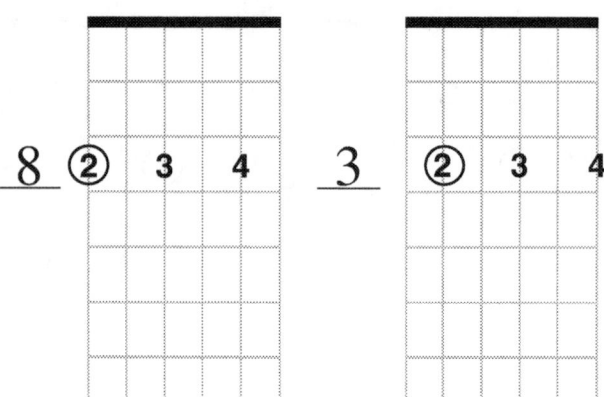
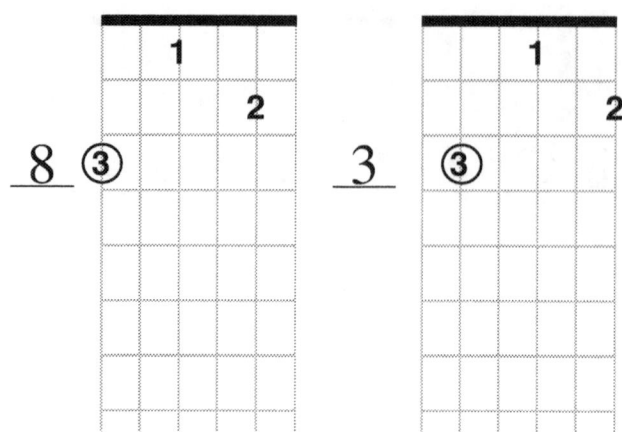
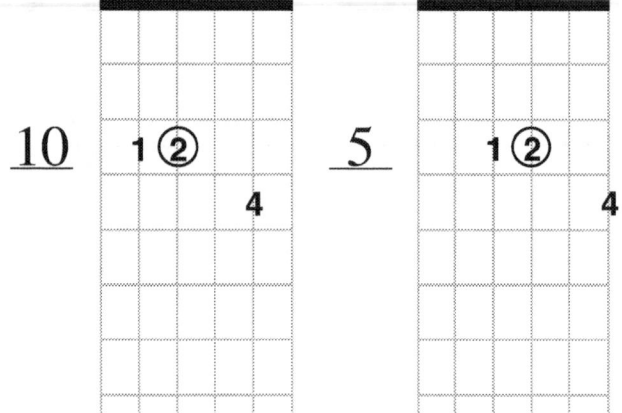
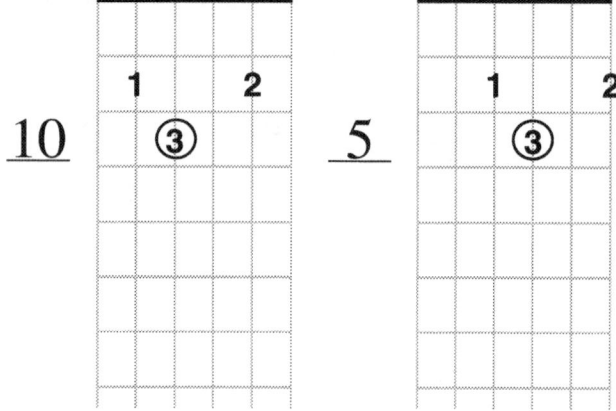
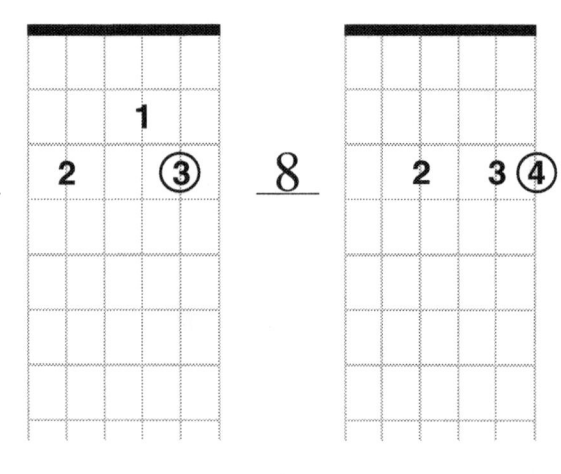
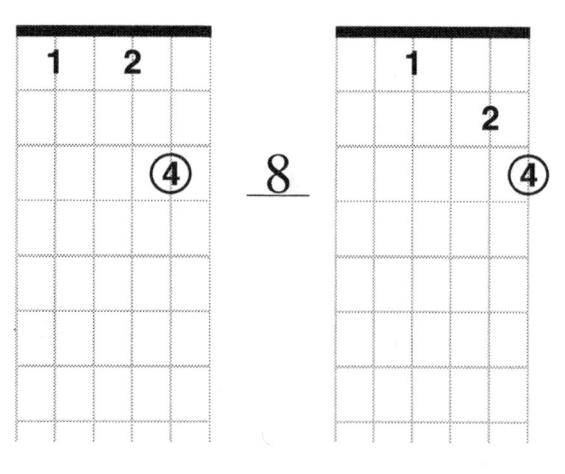

C-Am⁶ C-MM⁷

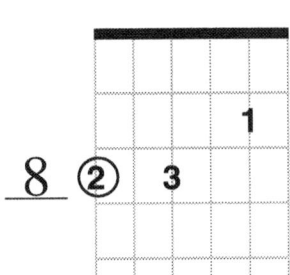 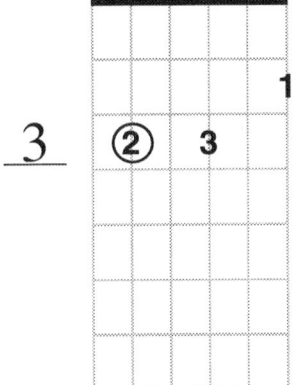 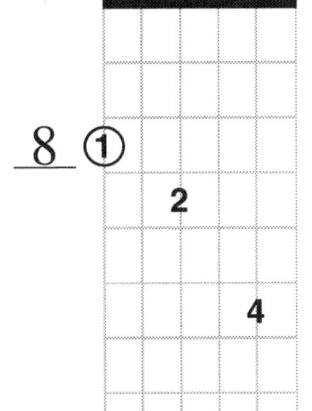 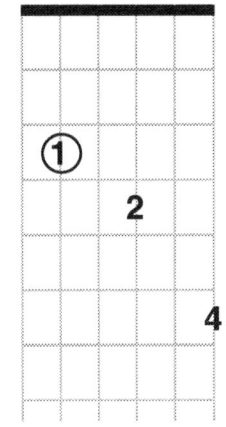

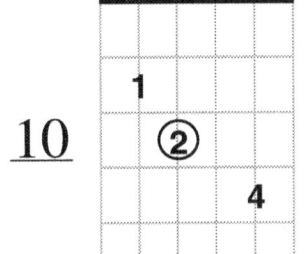 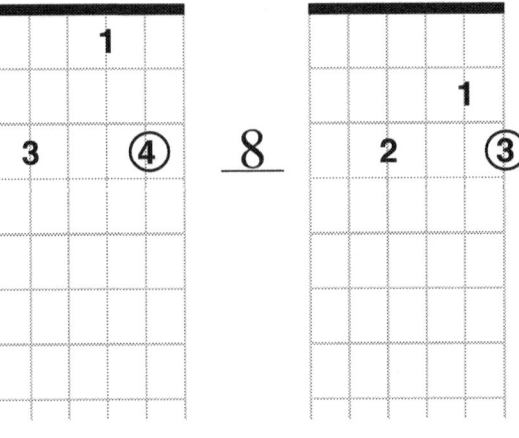 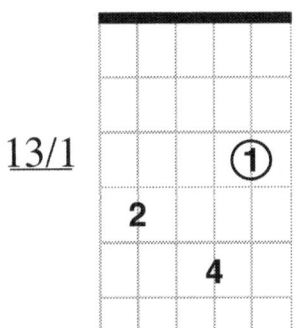 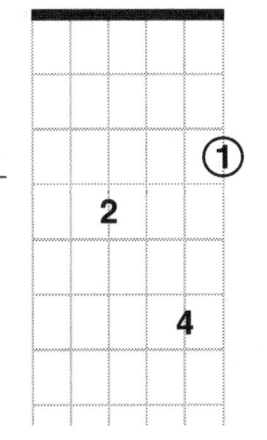

C-mm^7 C-Mm^7

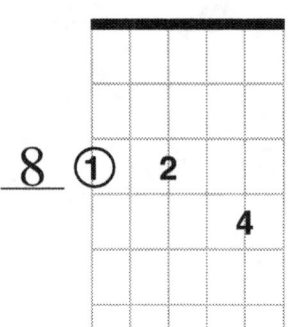
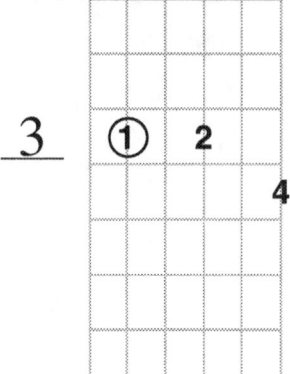
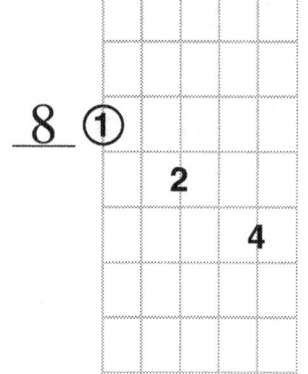
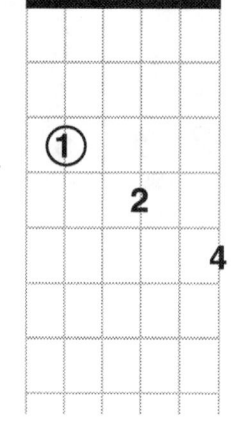

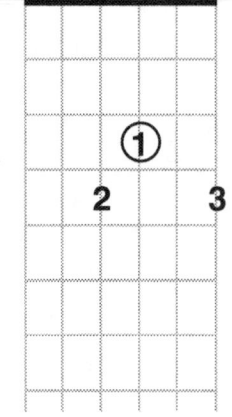
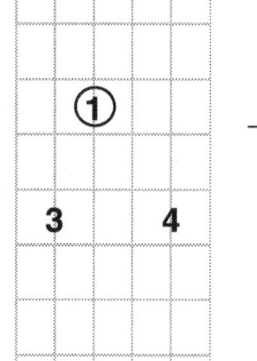
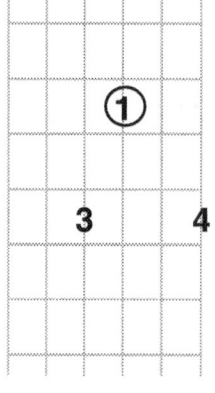

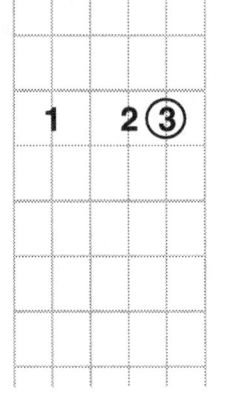
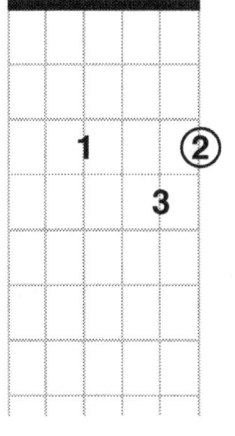
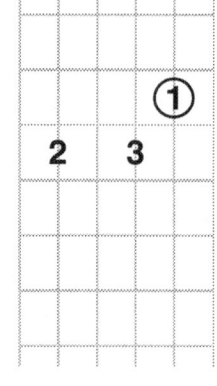
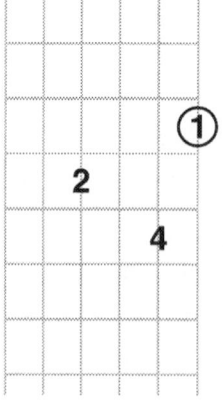

C-mM⁷   C-AA⁷

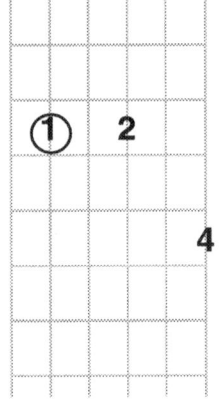 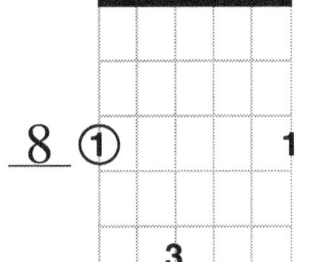 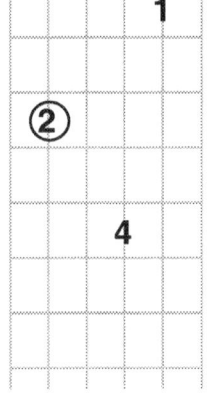

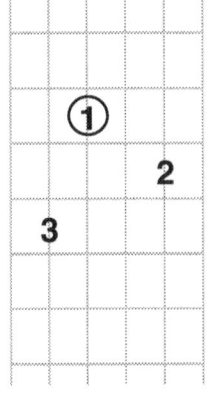 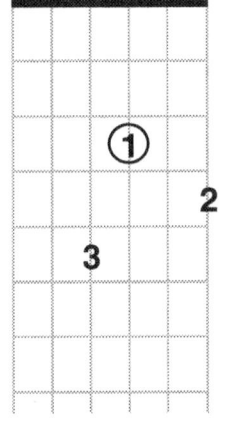 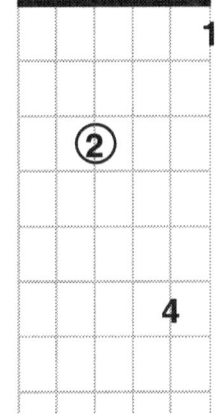 

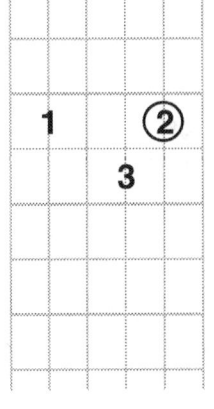 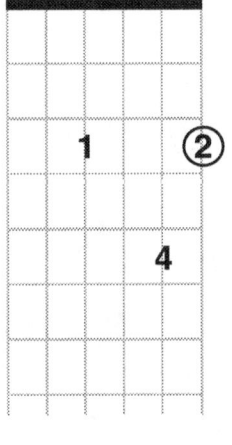 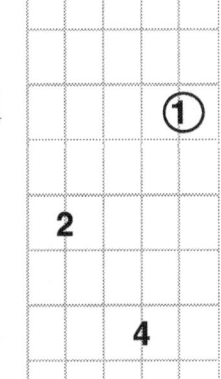 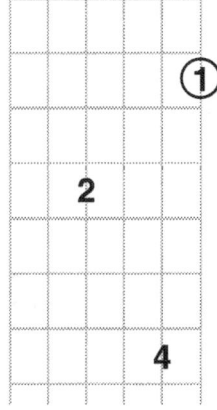

C-MA⁷   C-AM⁷

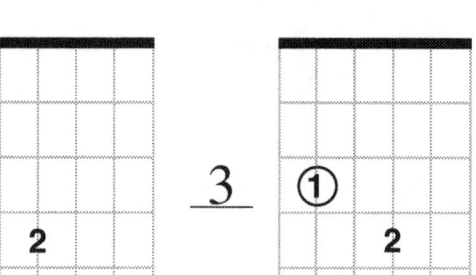
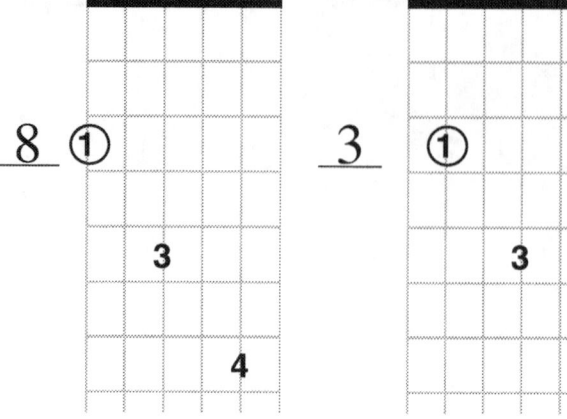
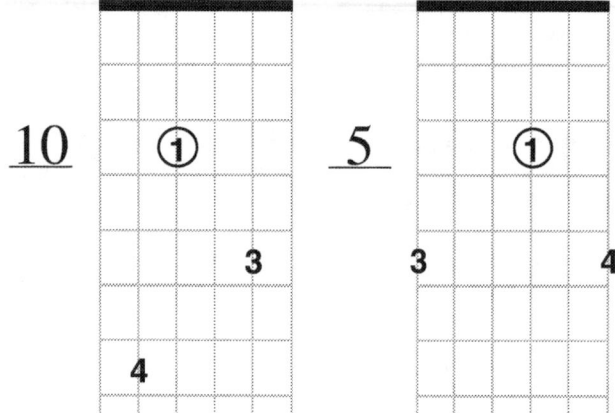
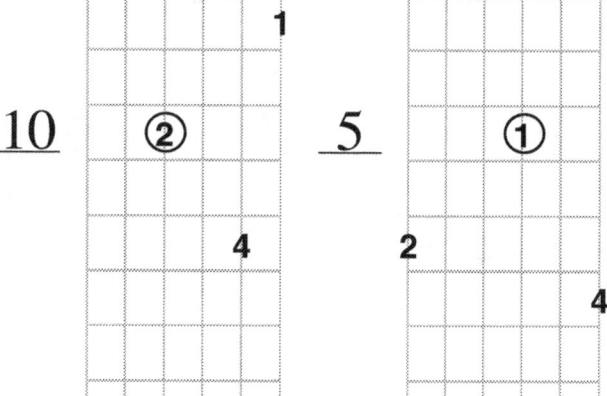
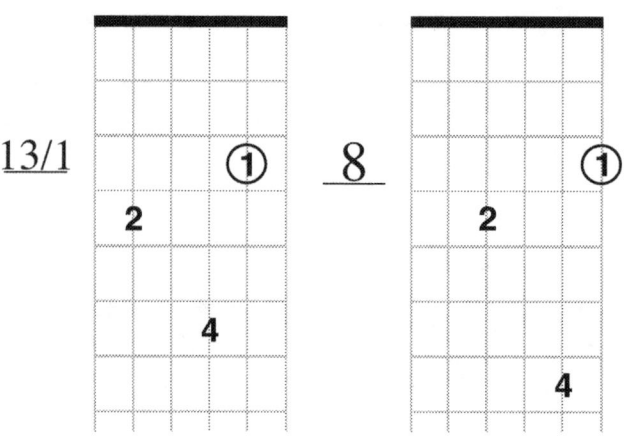
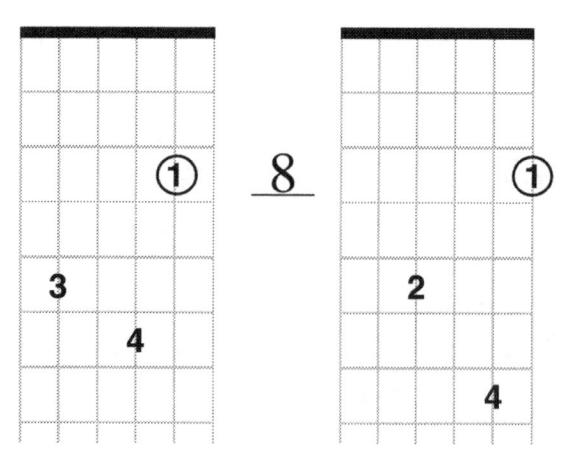

C-mA⁷   C-Am⁷

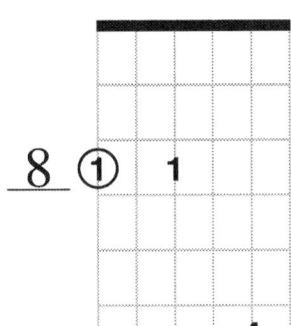
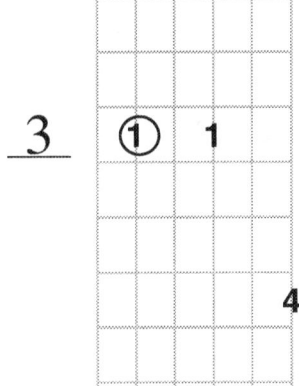
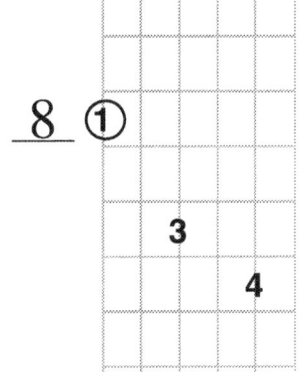
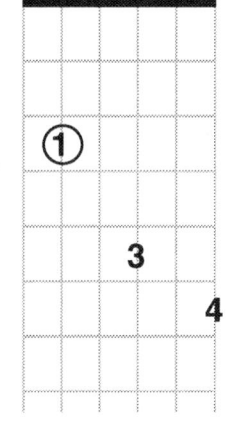

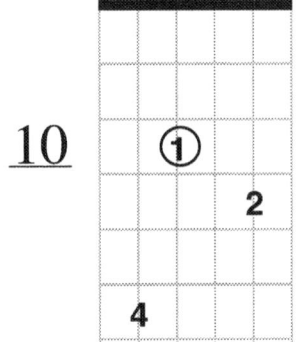
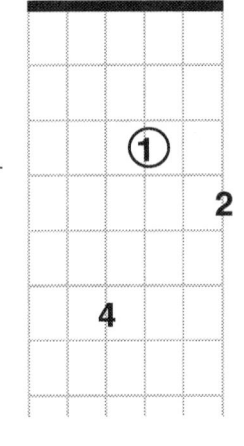
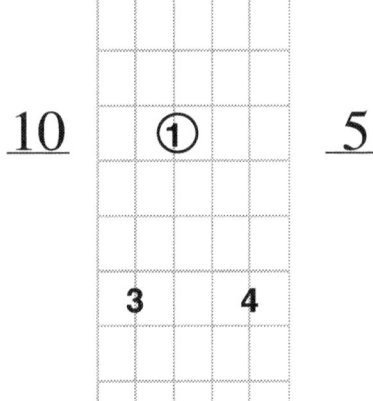
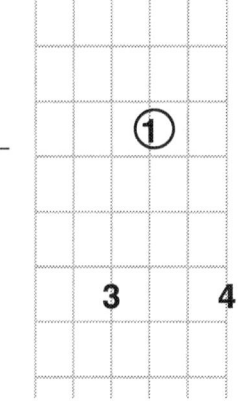

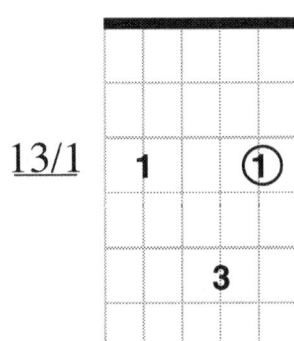
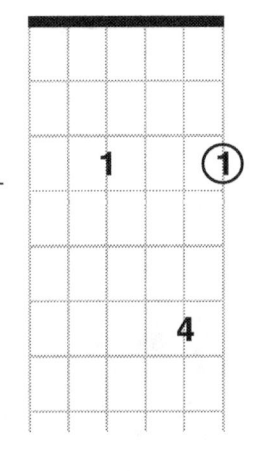
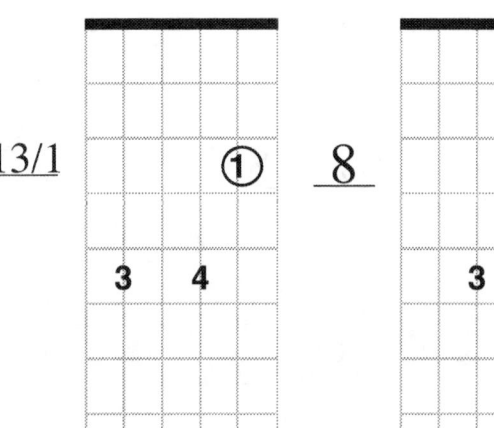

C-MM^2+   C-mm^2+

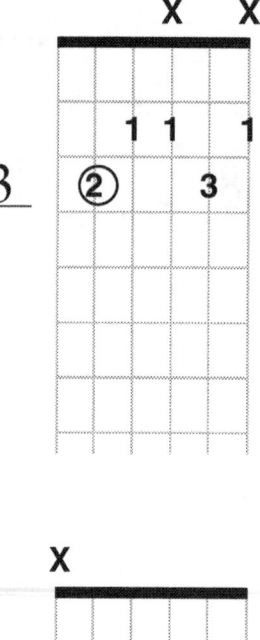
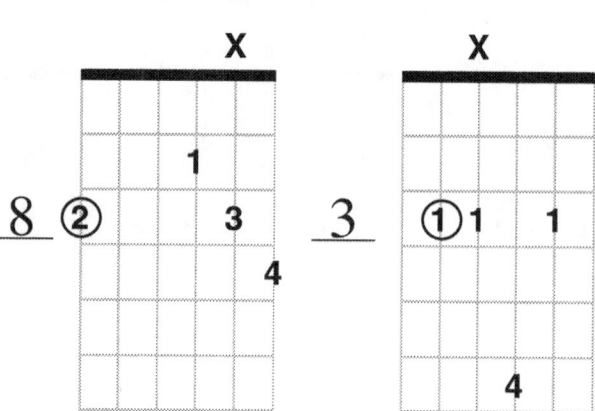
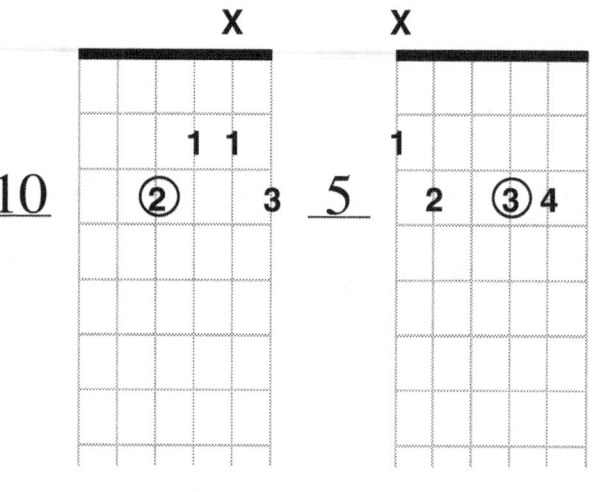
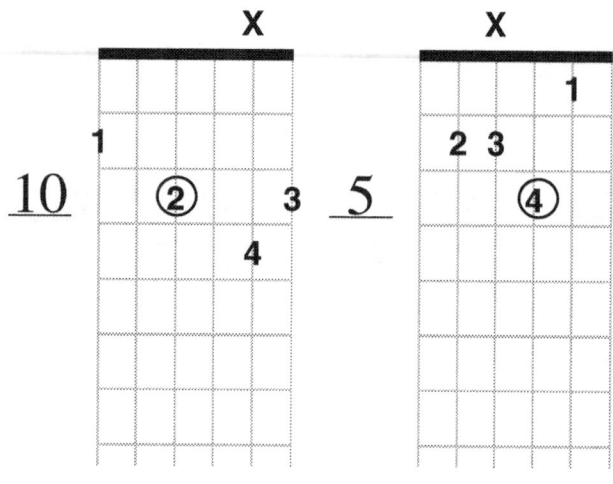
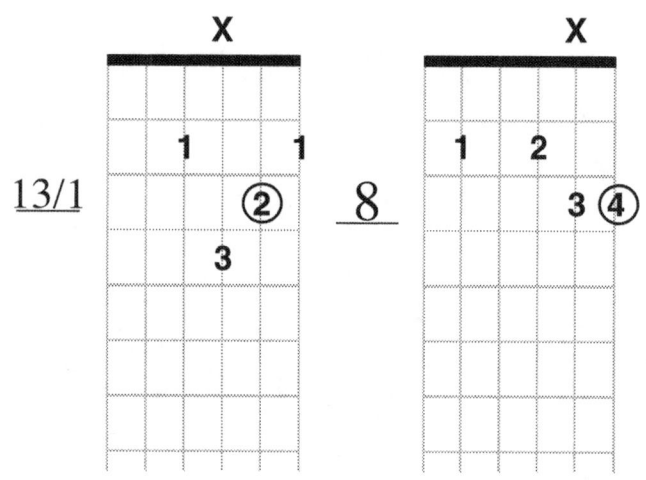
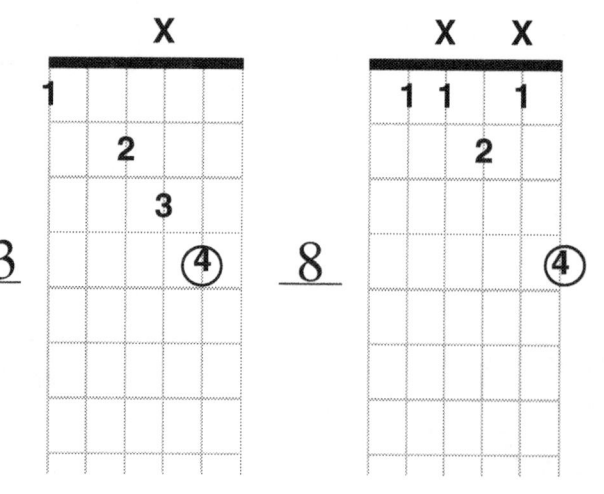

C-Mm^2+   C-mM^2+

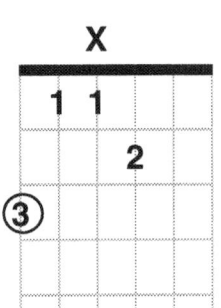
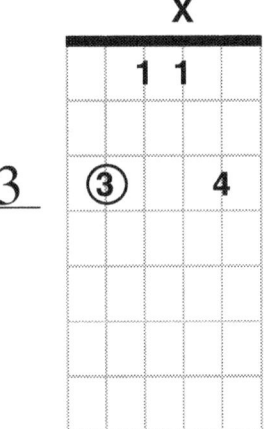
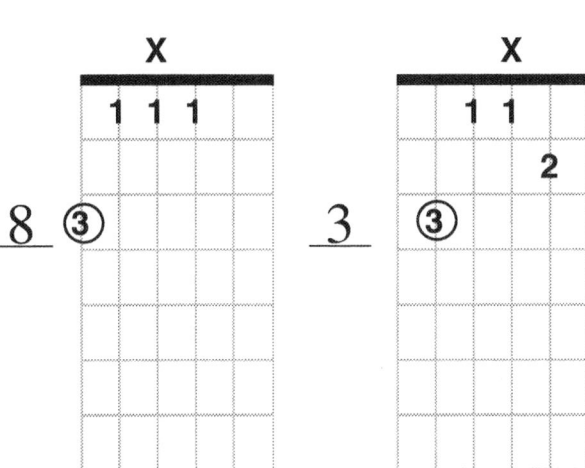
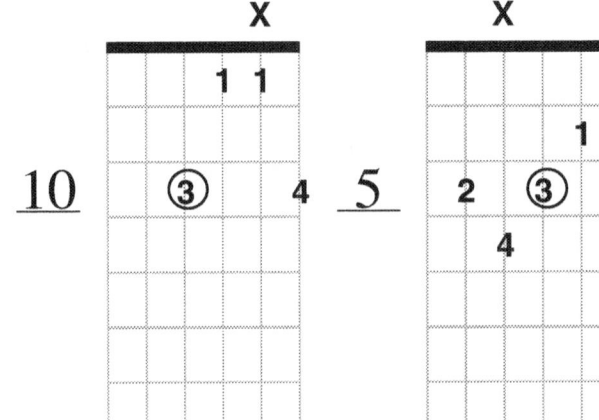
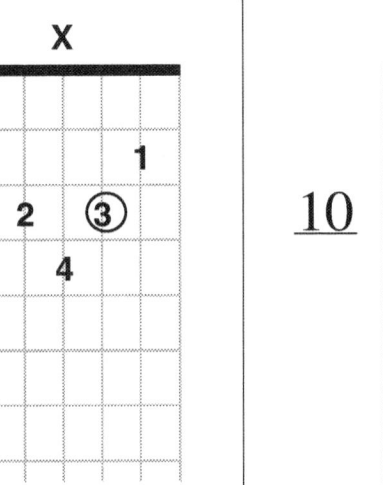
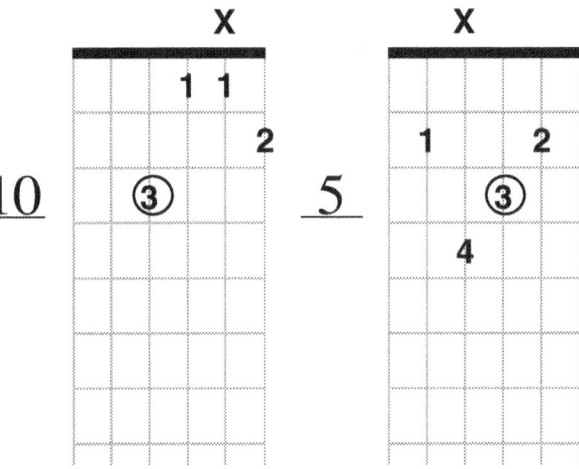
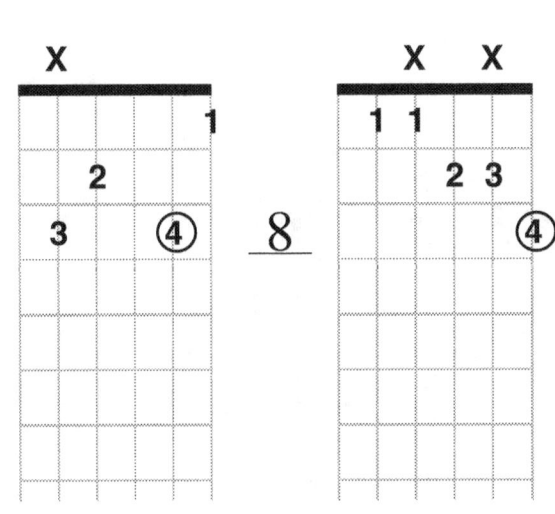
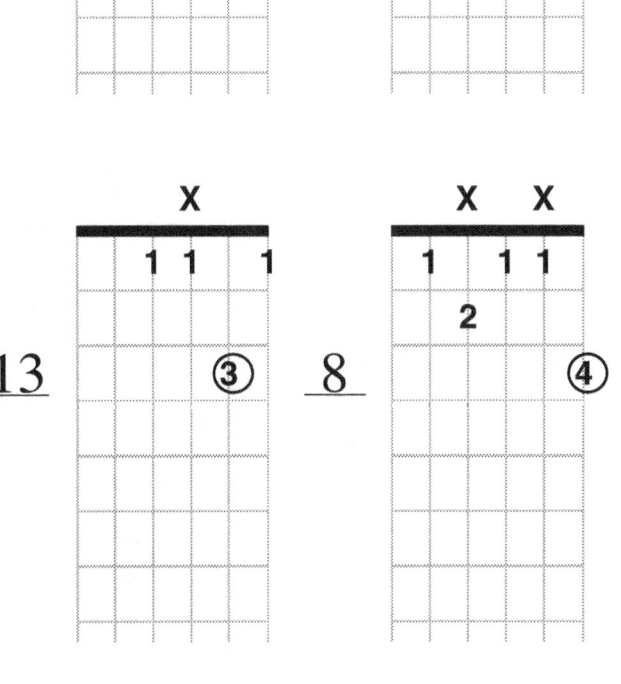

C-AA^2+   C-MA^2+

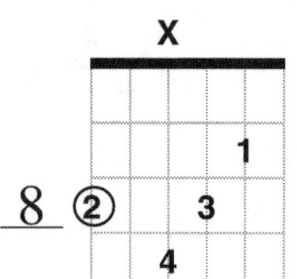
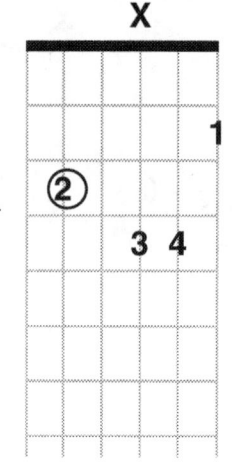
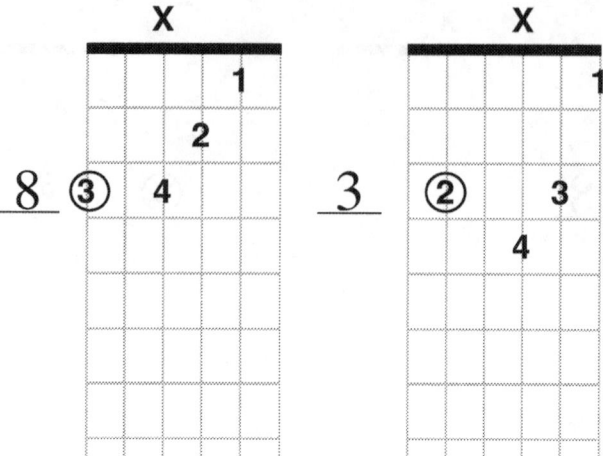
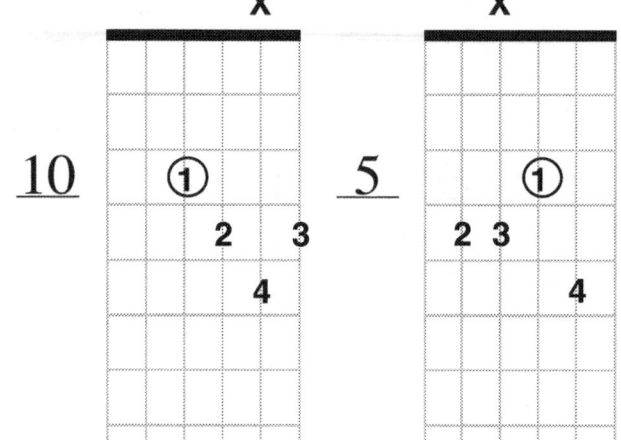
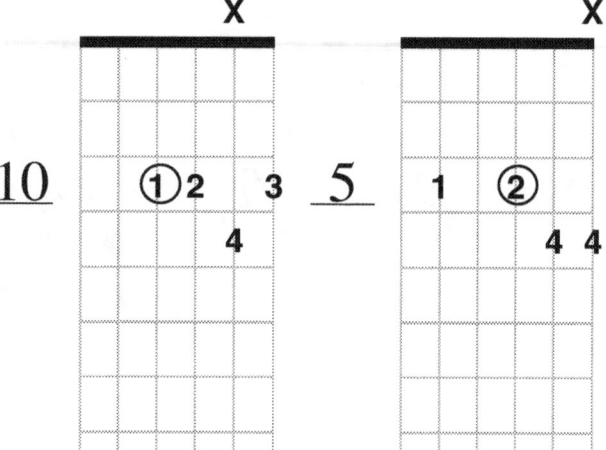
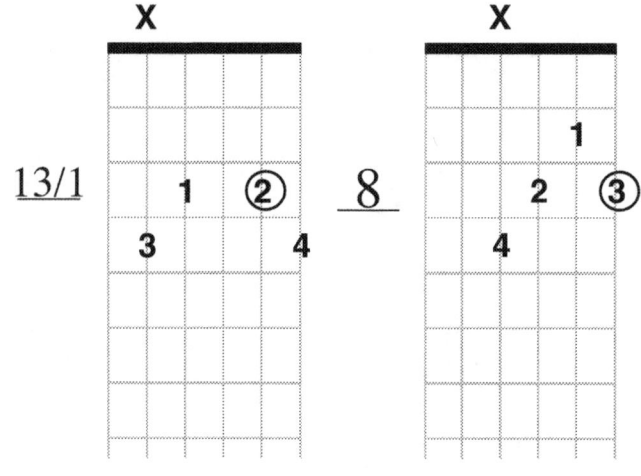
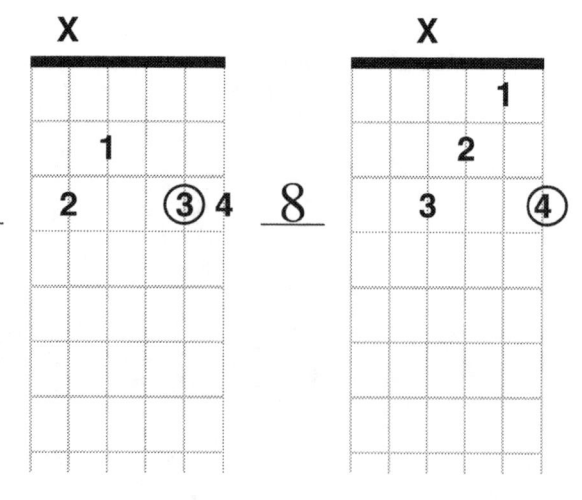

C-AM^2+   C-mA^2+

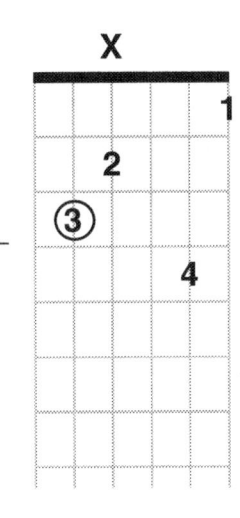
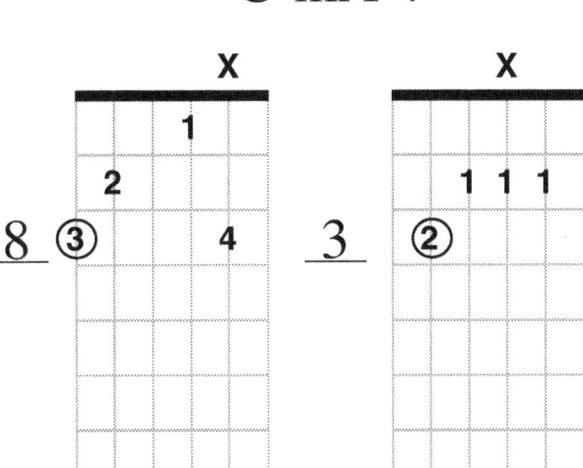
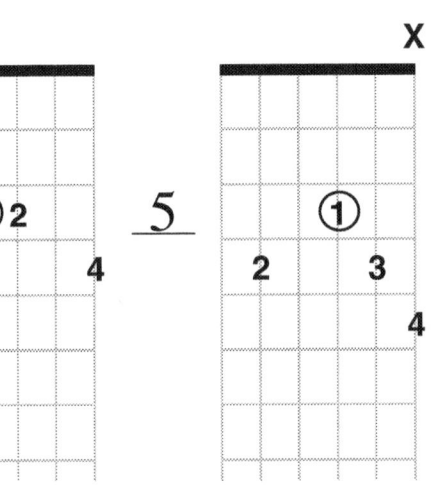
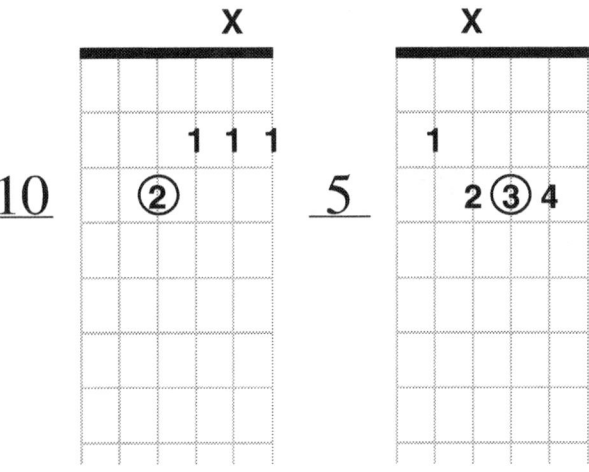
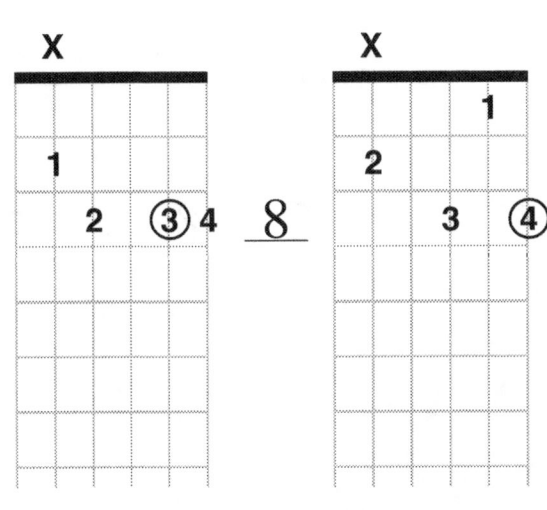
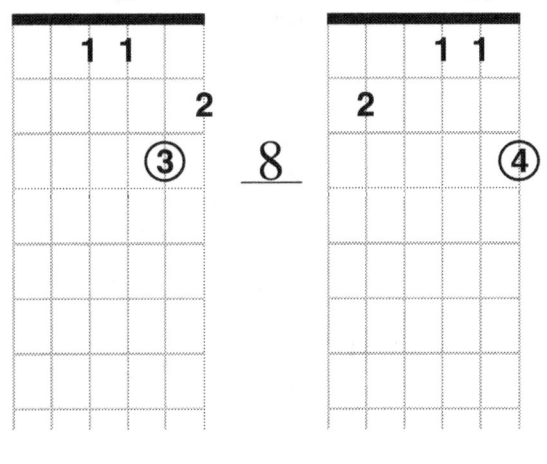

C-Am²+

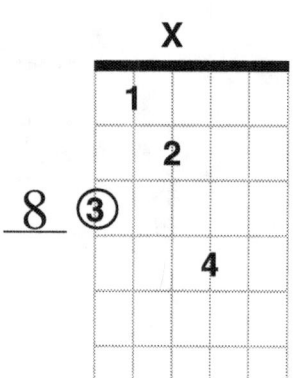
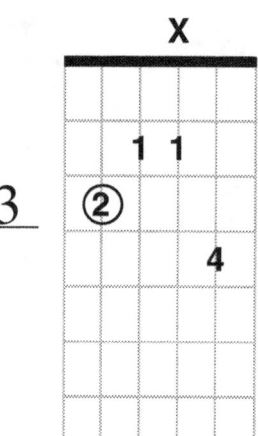
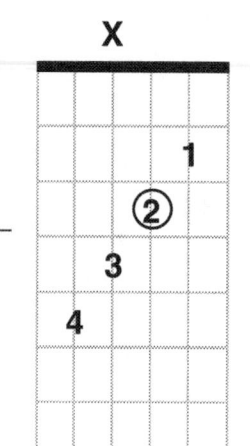
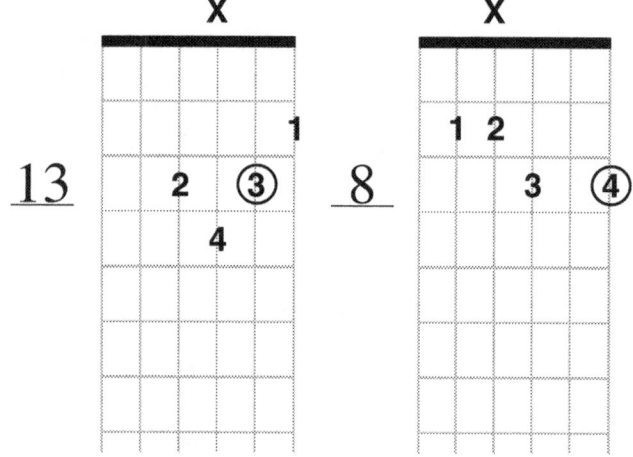

C-MM³+

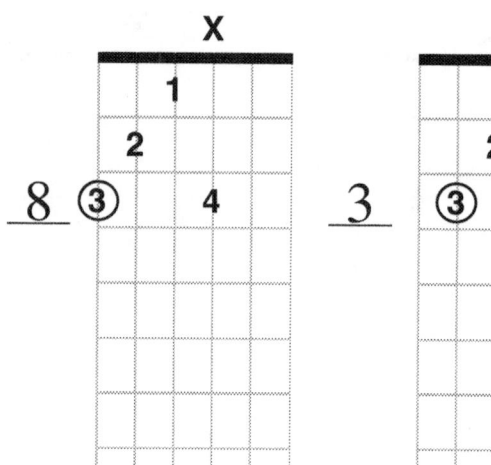
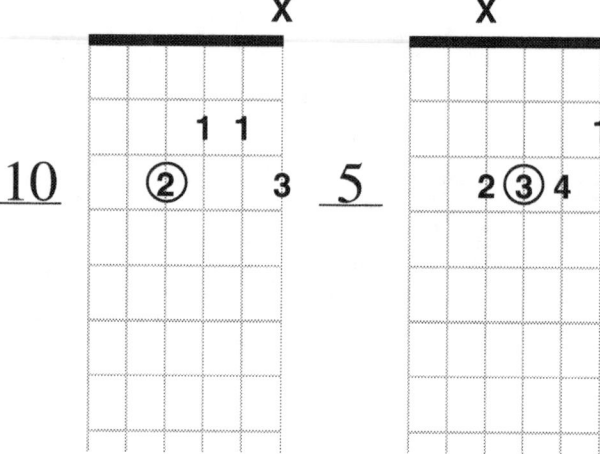
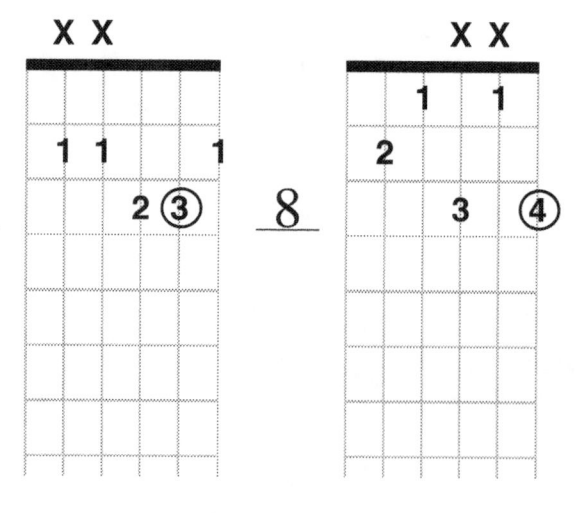

C-mm³+   C-Mm³+

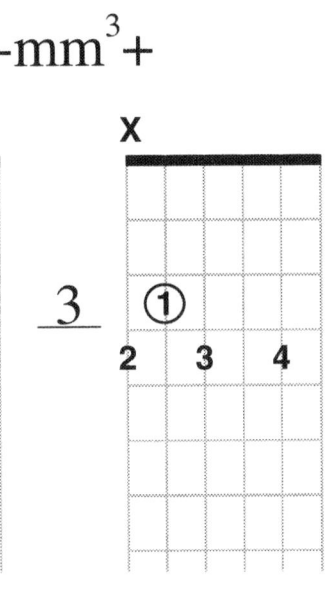
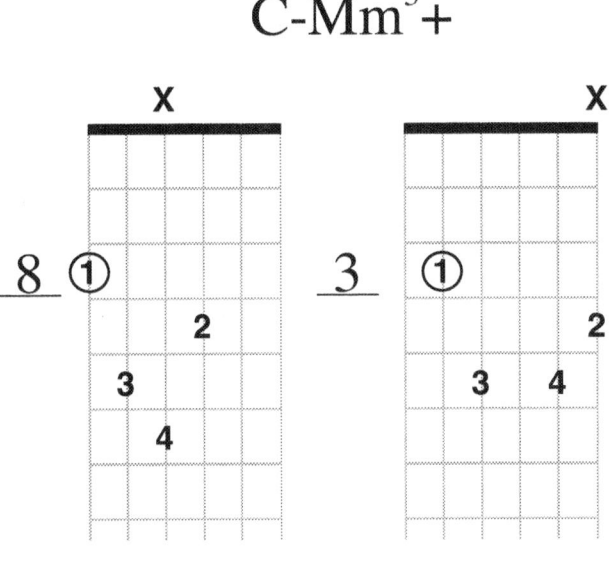

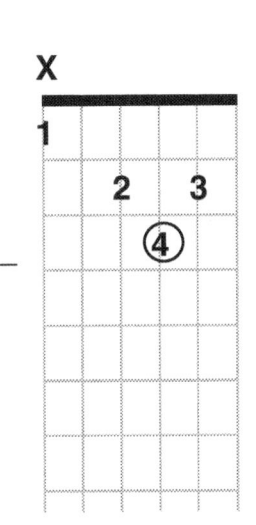
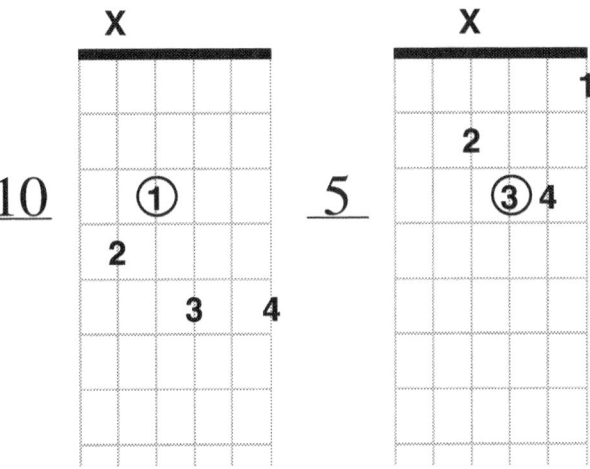
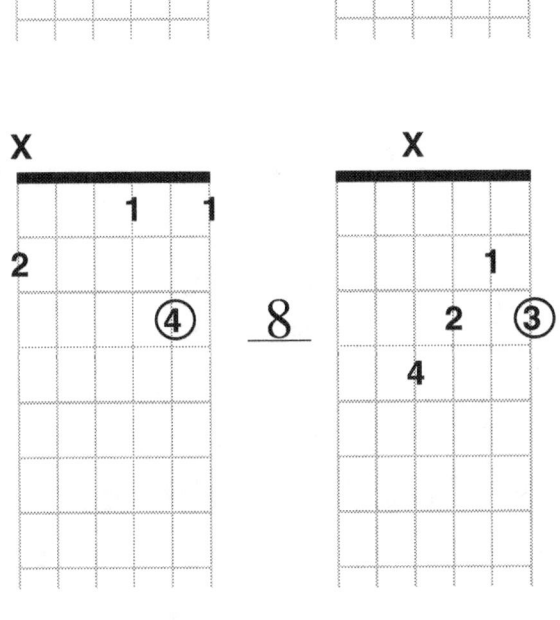
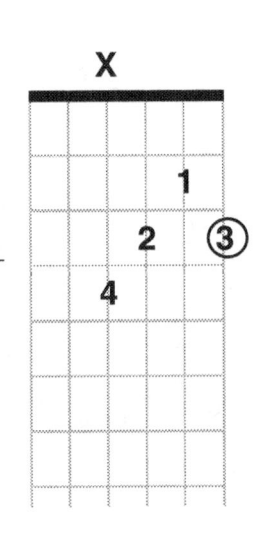
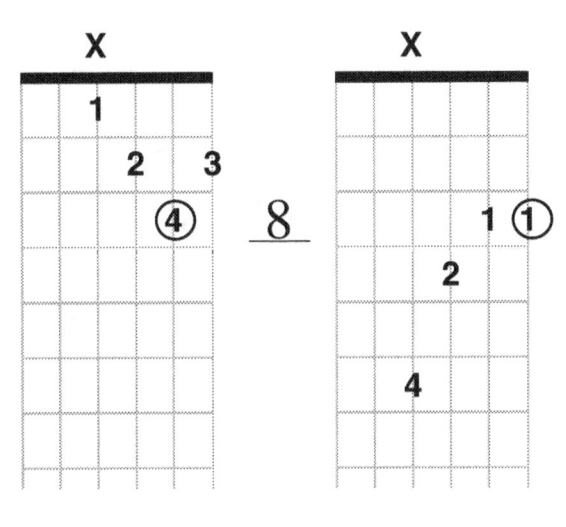

C-mM³+   C-AA³+

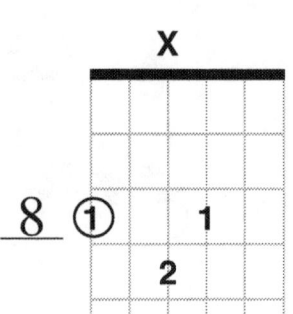
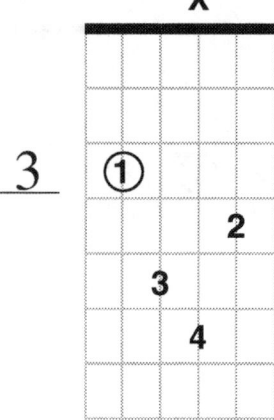
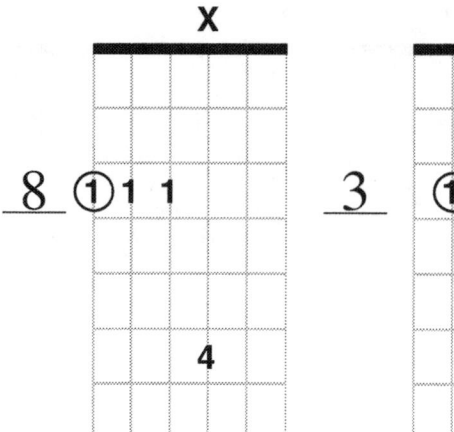
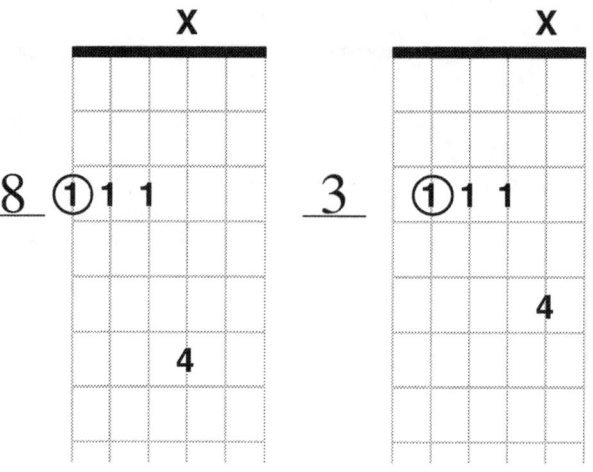
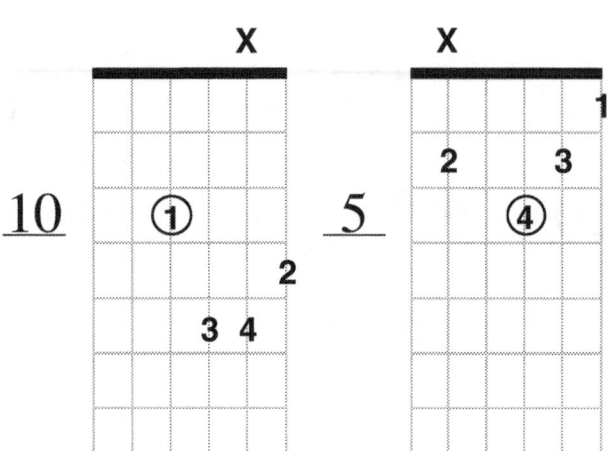
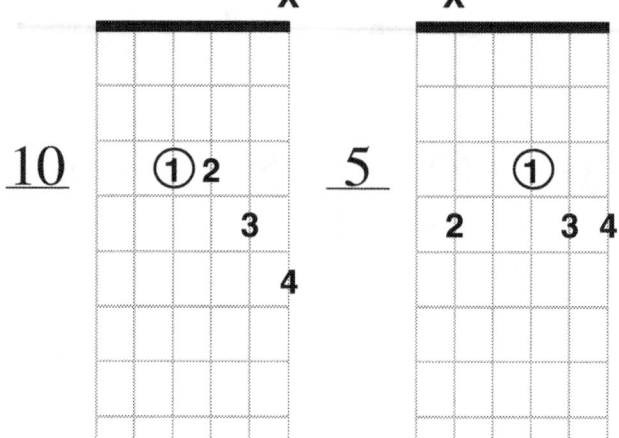
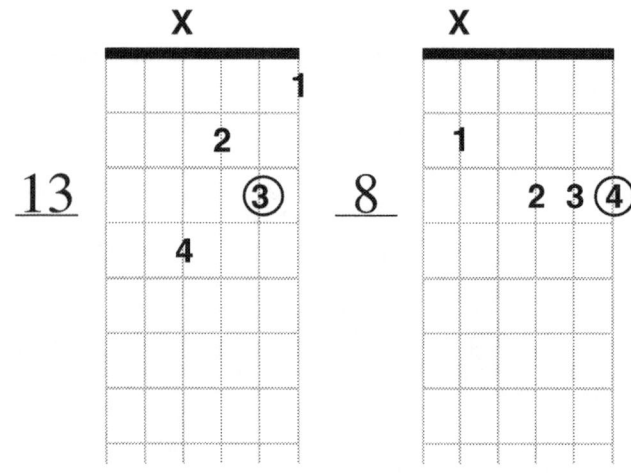
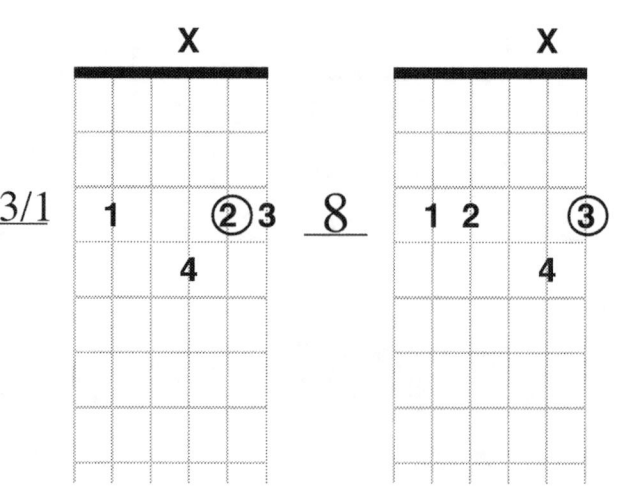

C-MA^3+

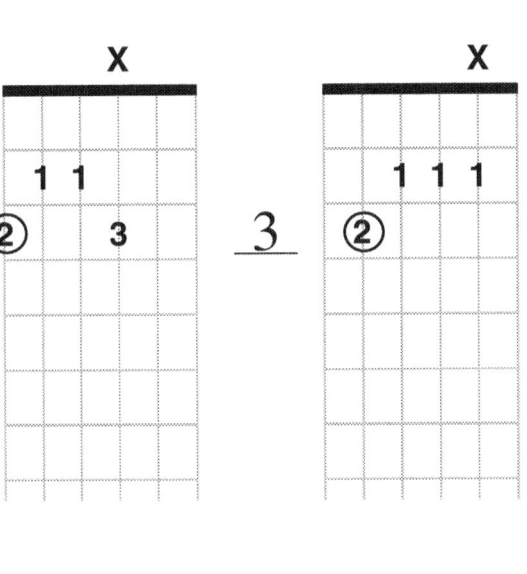
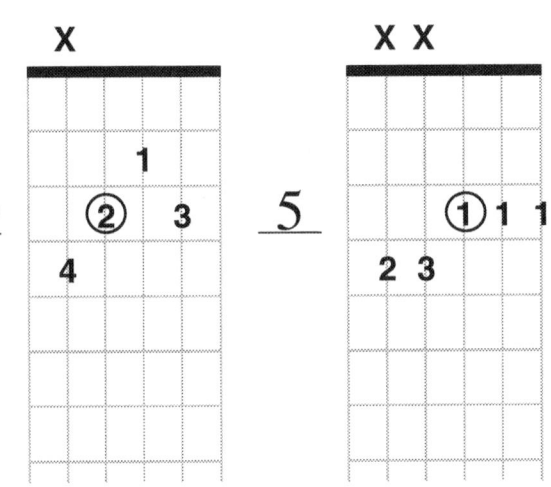
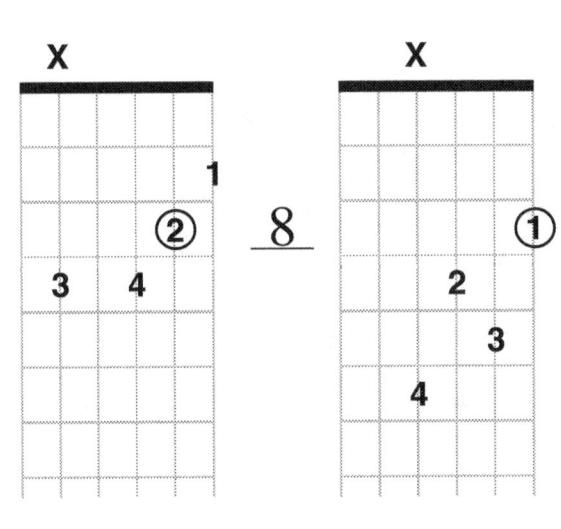

C-AM^3+

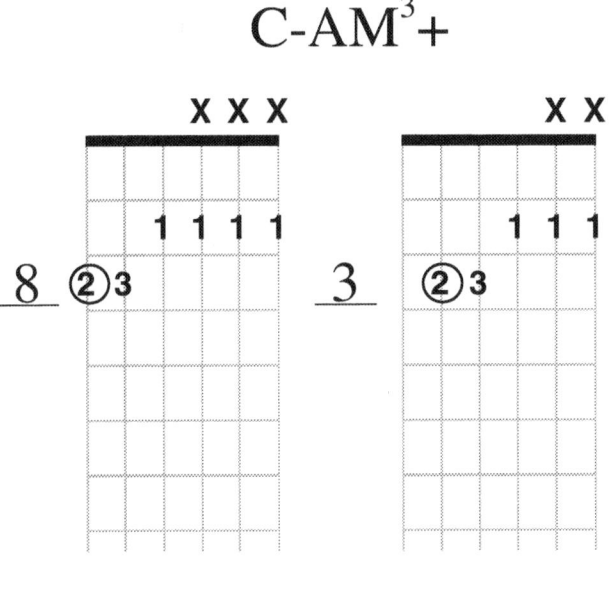
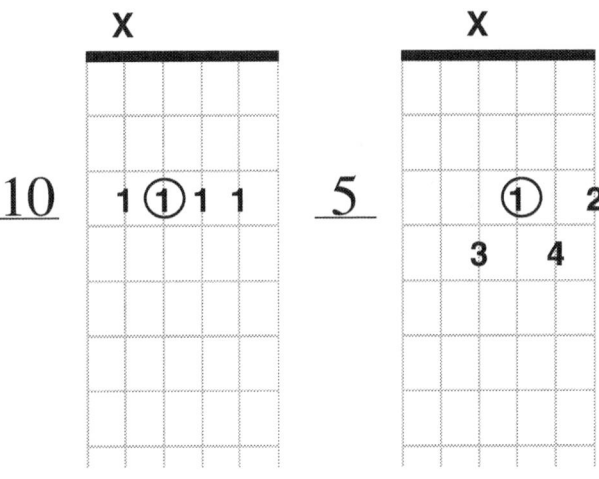
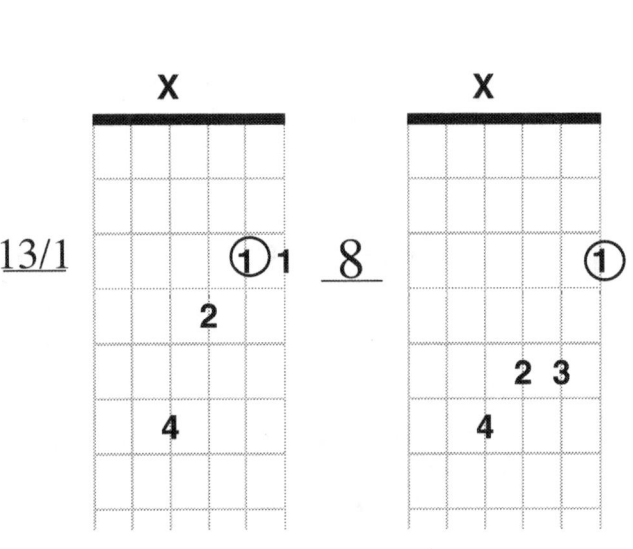

C-mA³+   C-Am³+

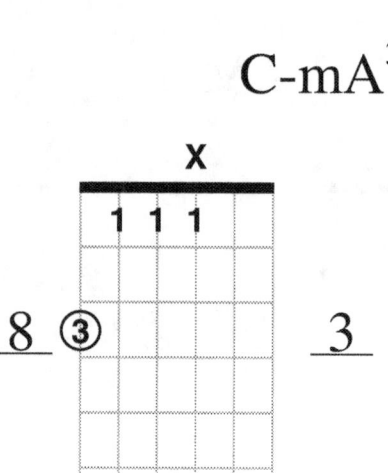 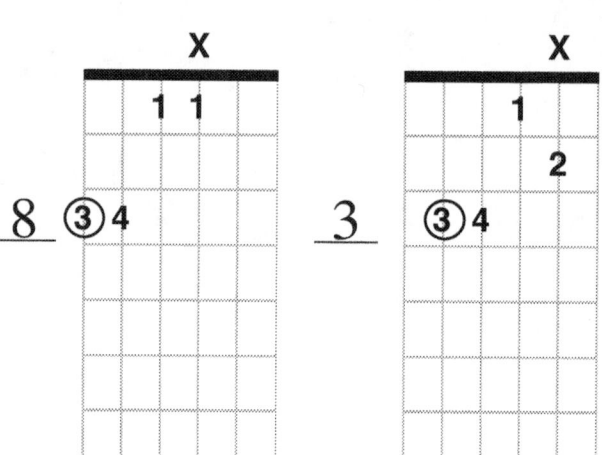

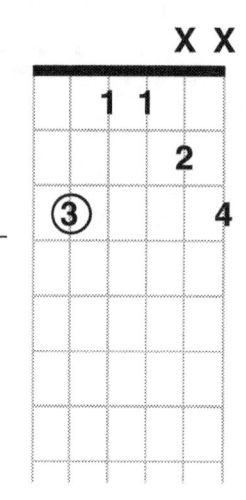 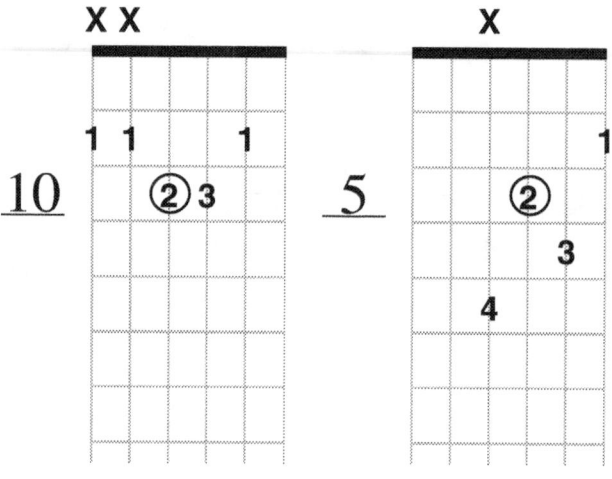

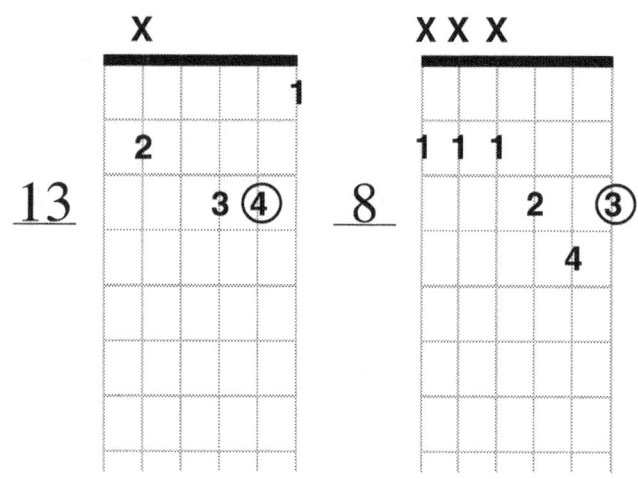 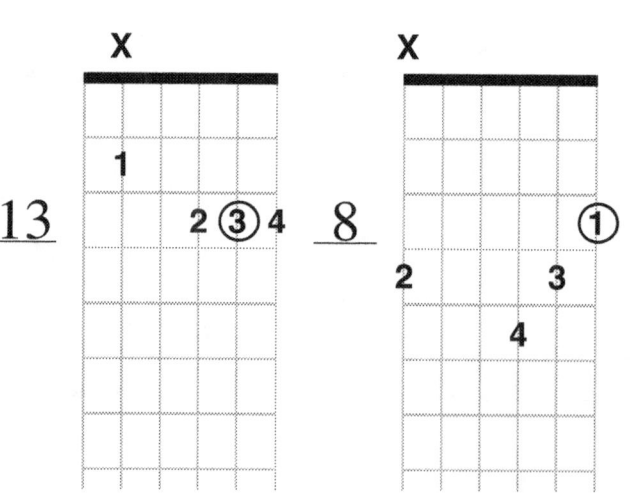

C-PPP^4+   C-DDP^4+

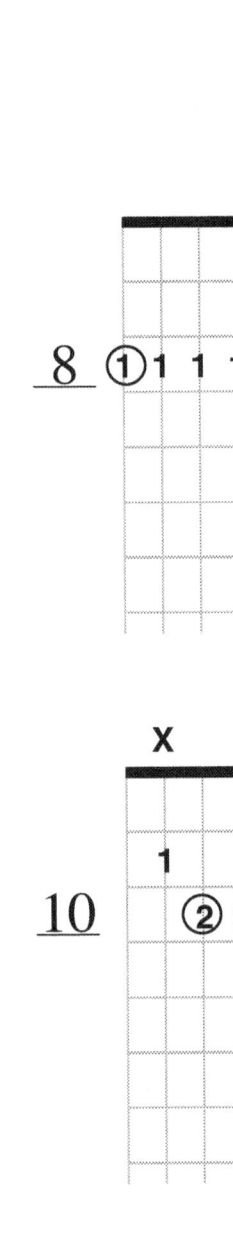
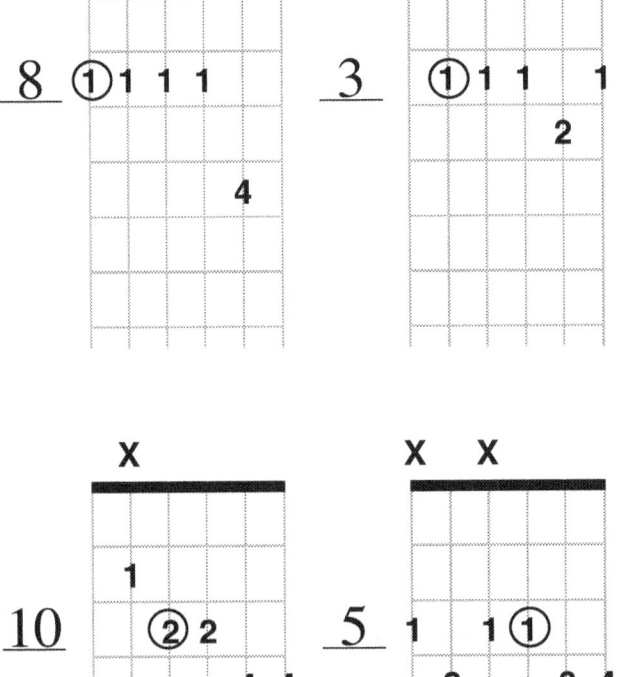
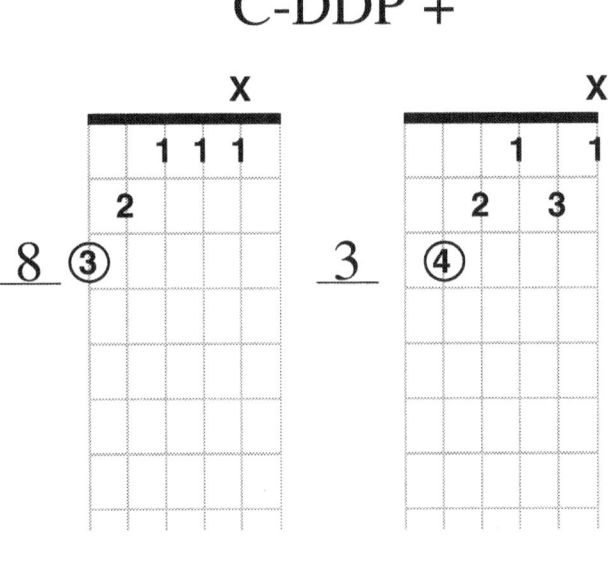
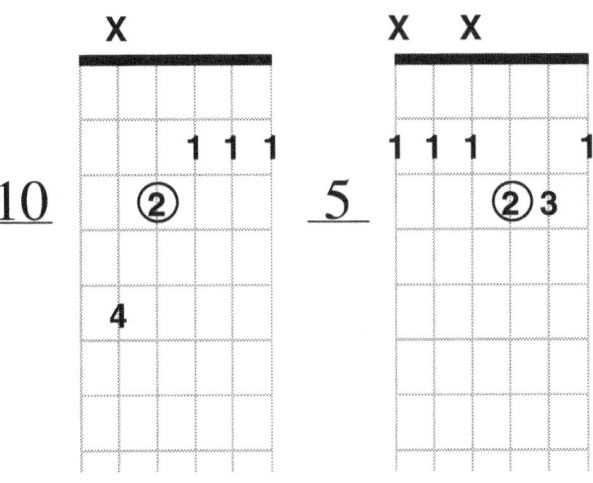
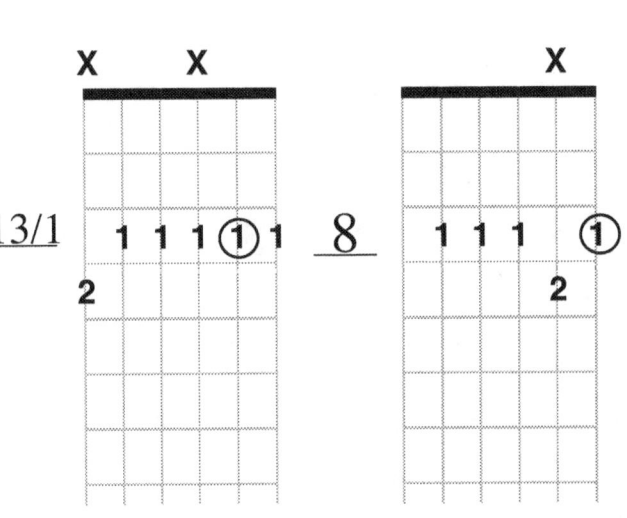
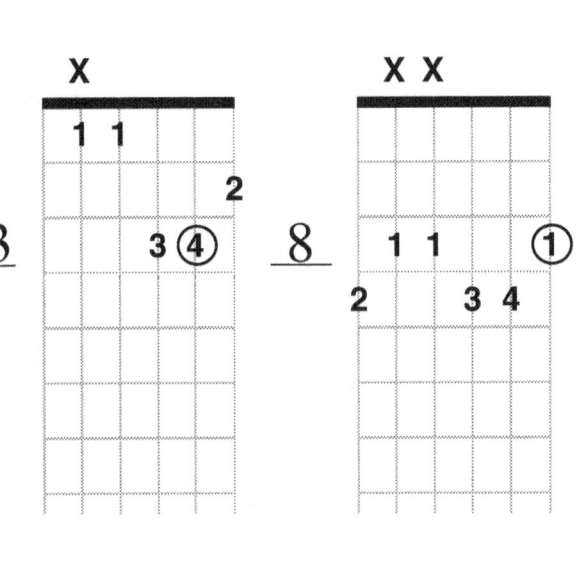

C-PDP^4+   C-DPP^4+

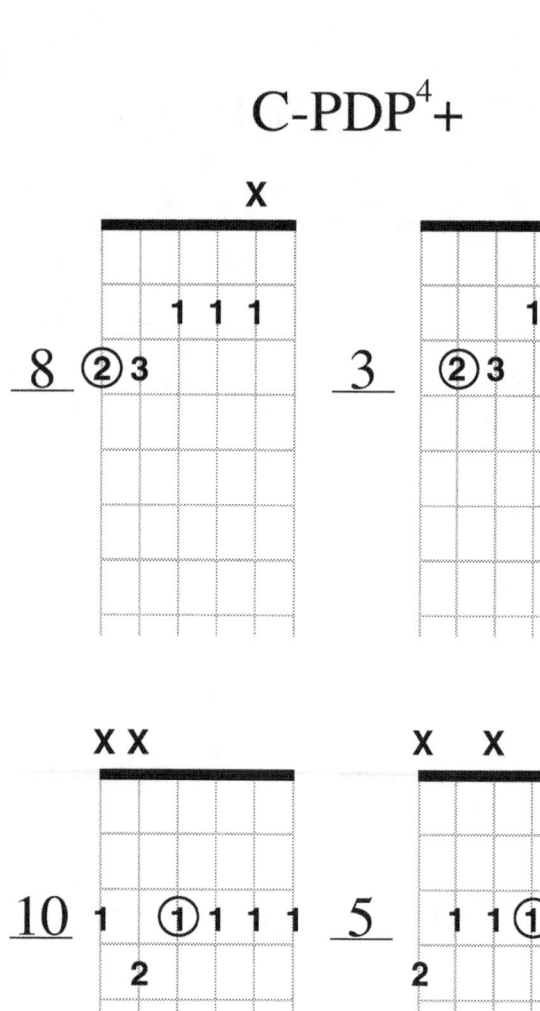
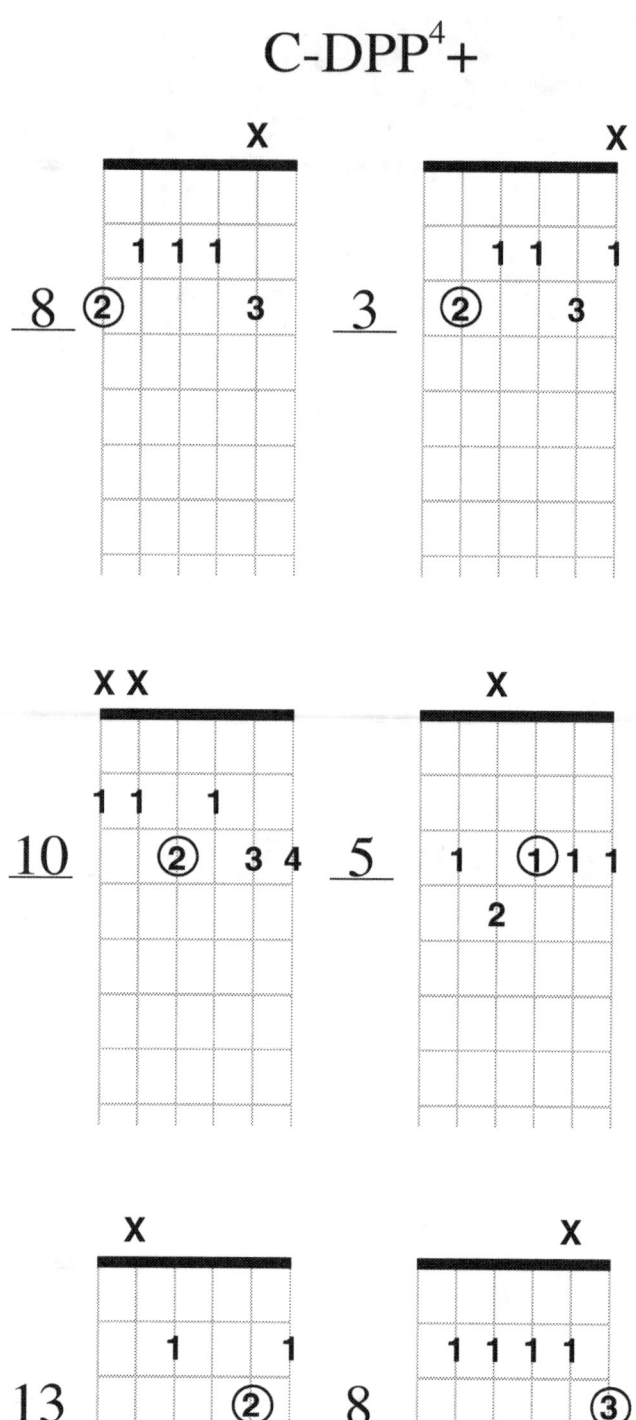
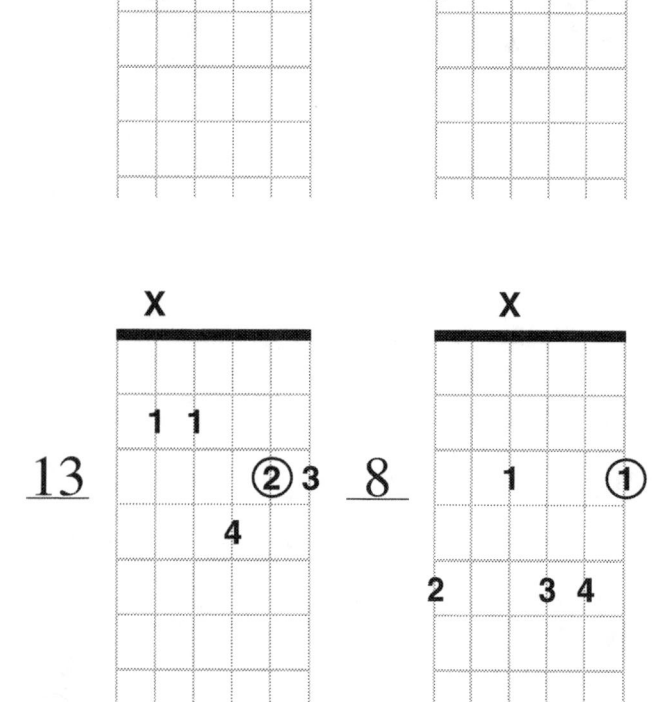
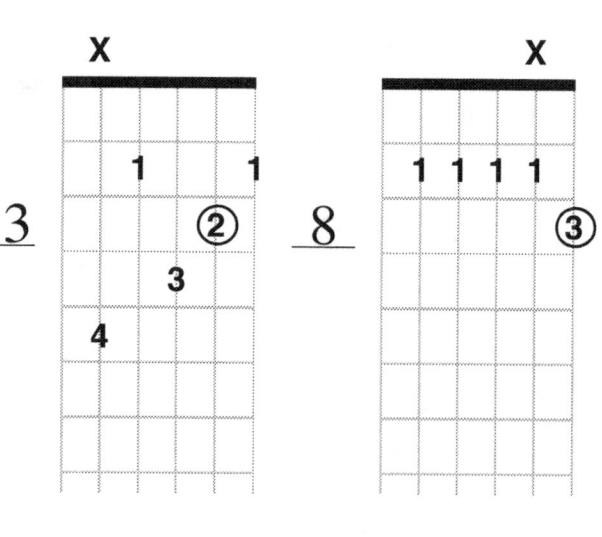

C-AAP^4+   C-PAP^4+

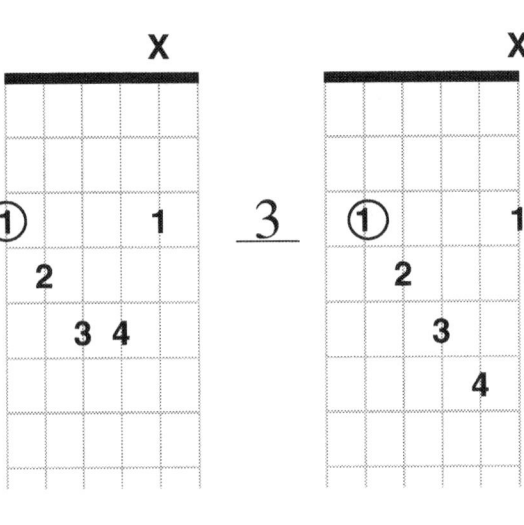
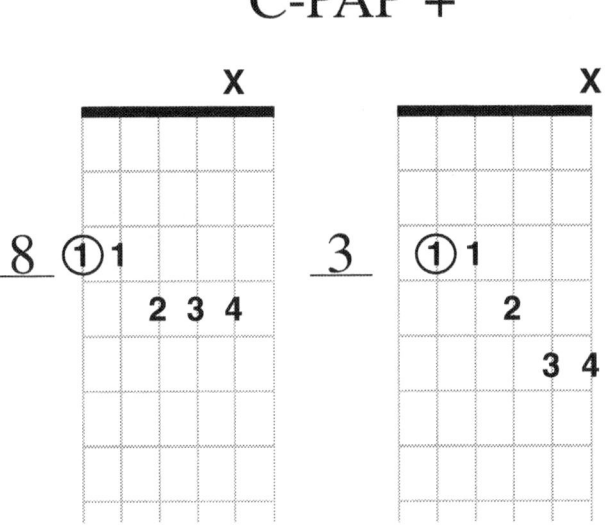
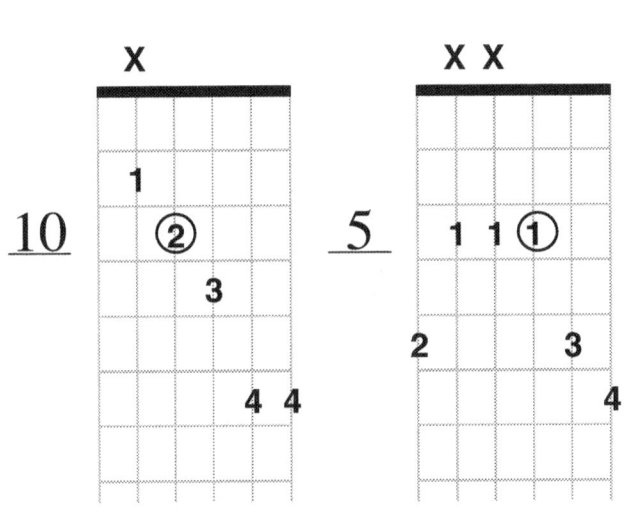
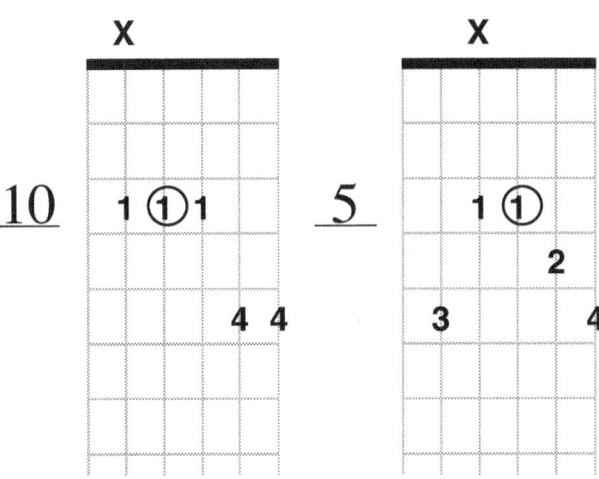
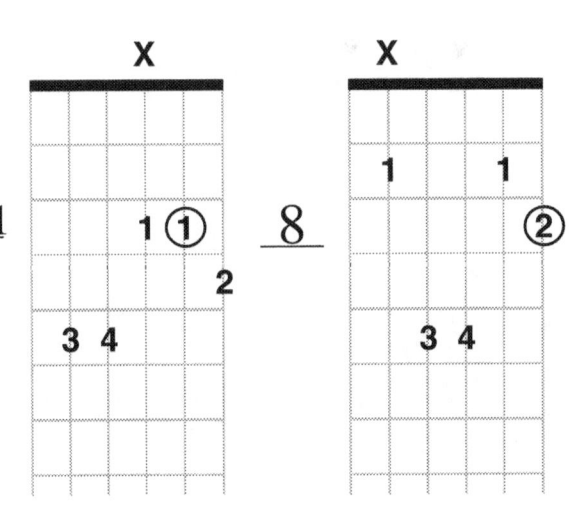
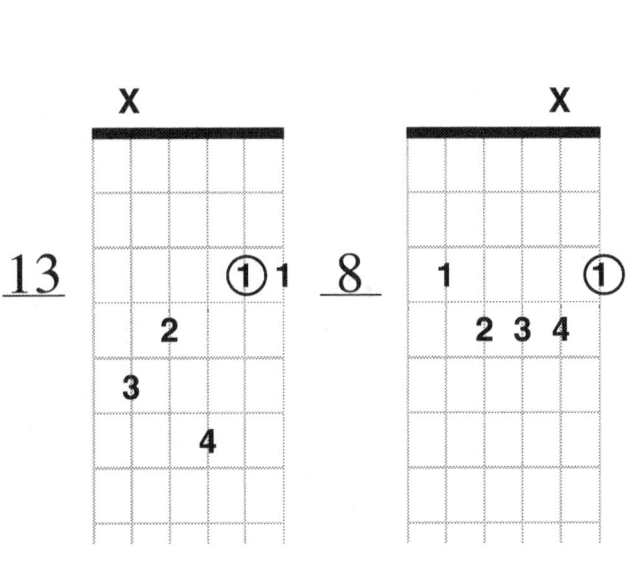

C-APP^4+   C-DAP^4+

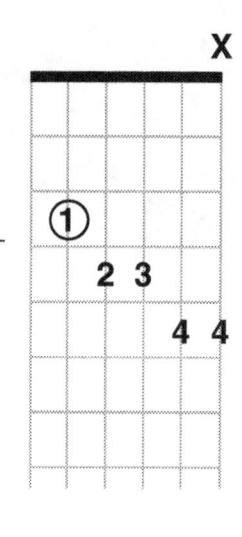
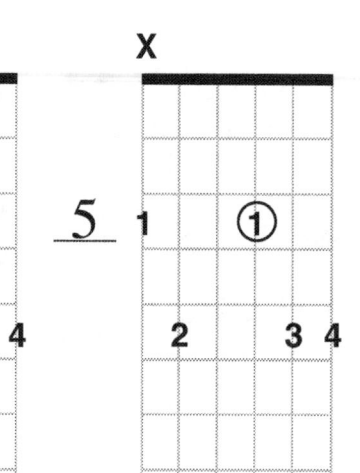
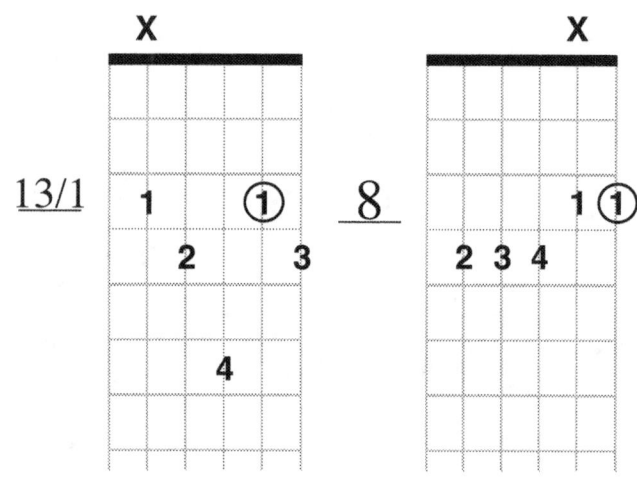

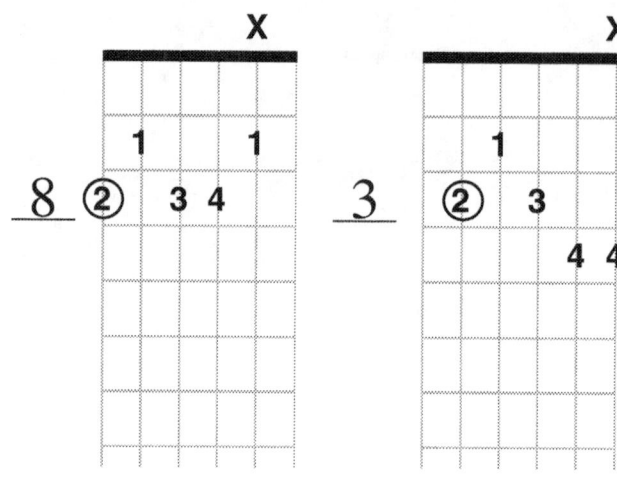
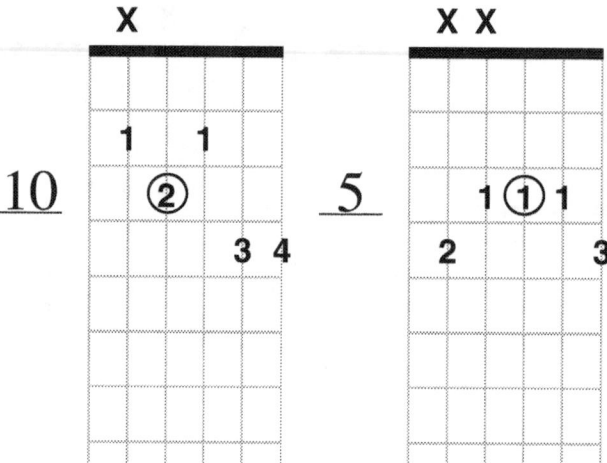
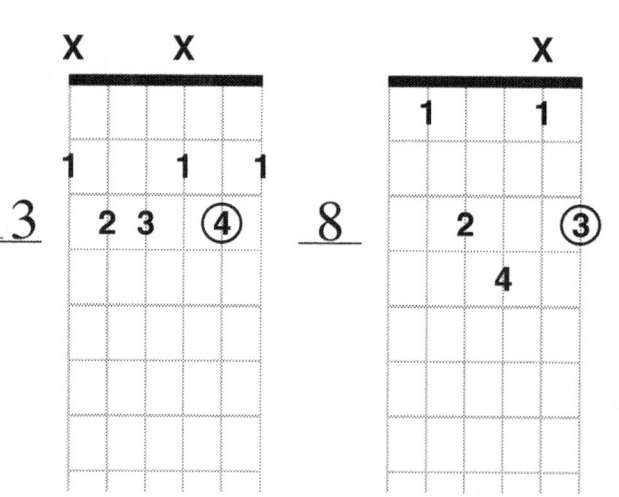

C-ADP^4+   C-PP^5+

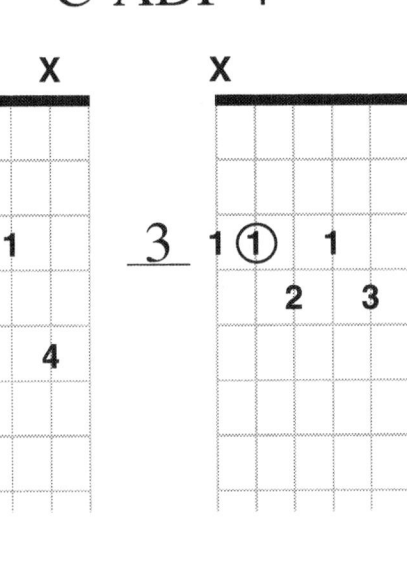
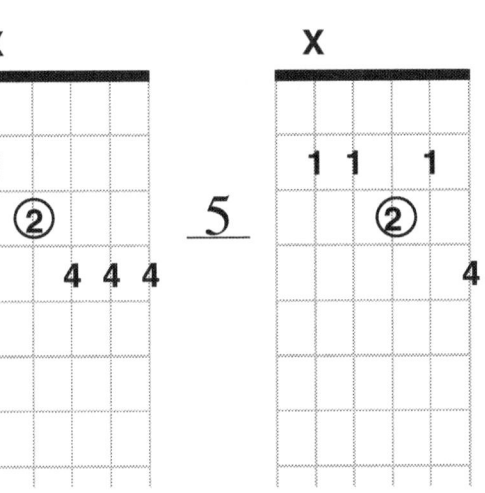
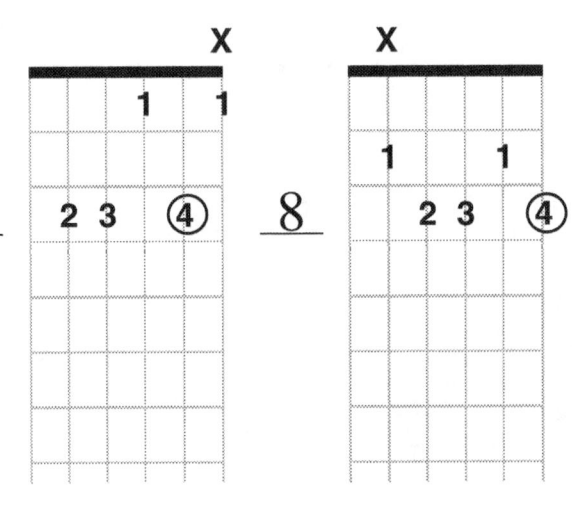
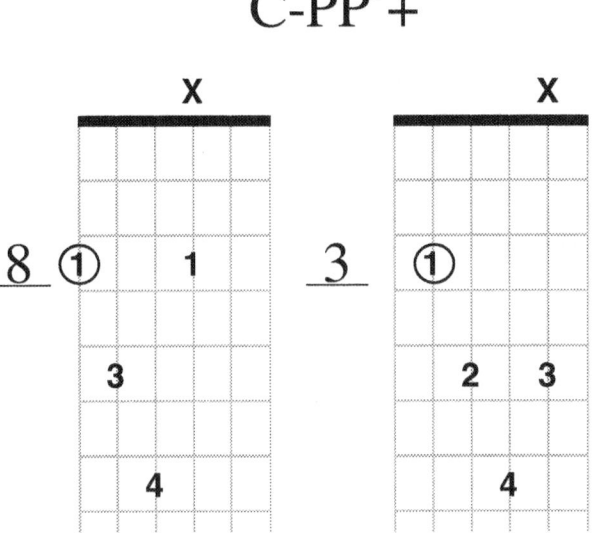
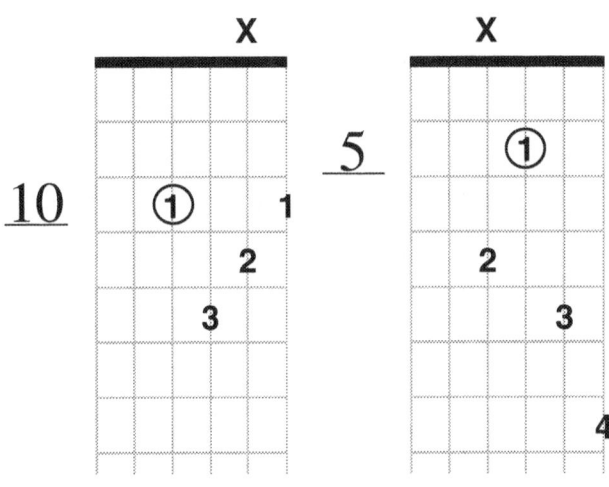
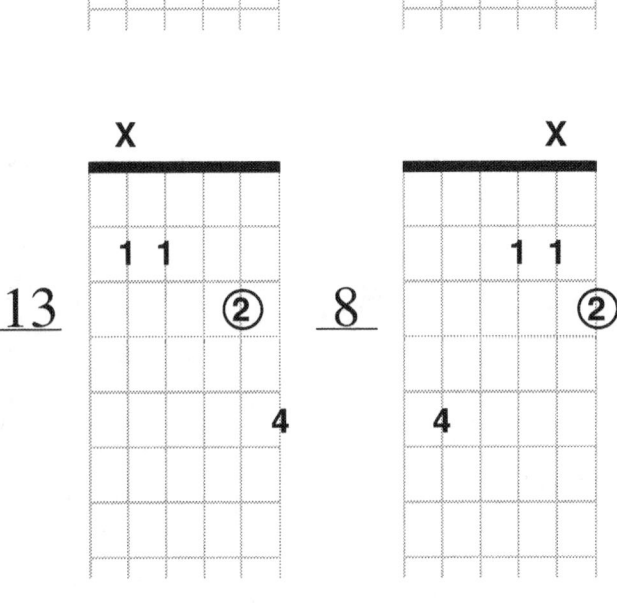

C-DD^5+   C-PD^5+

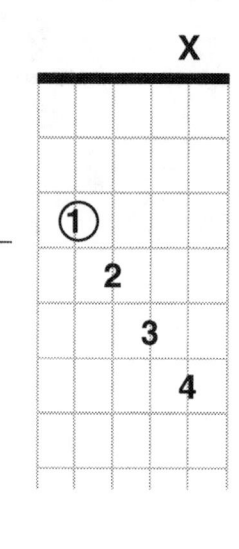
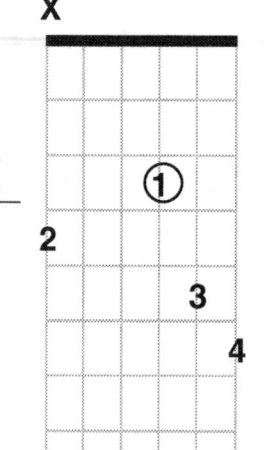
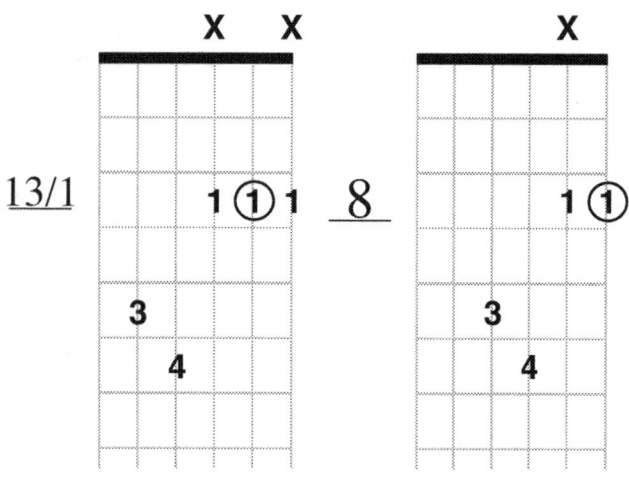
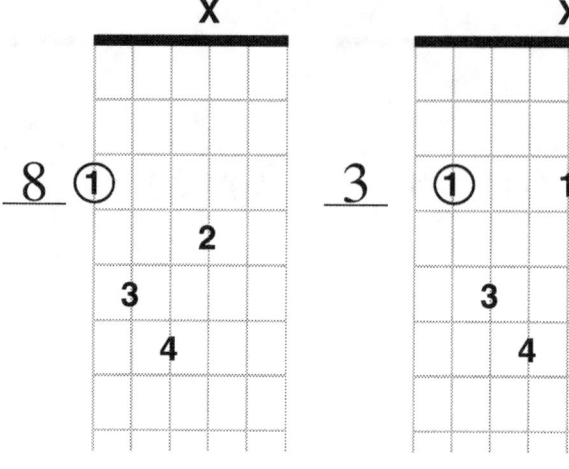
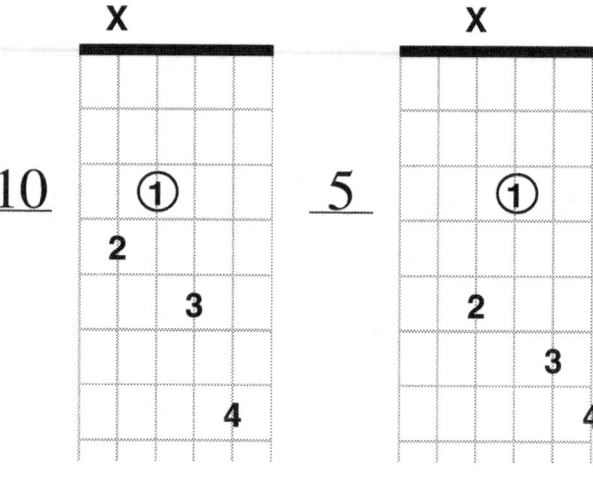
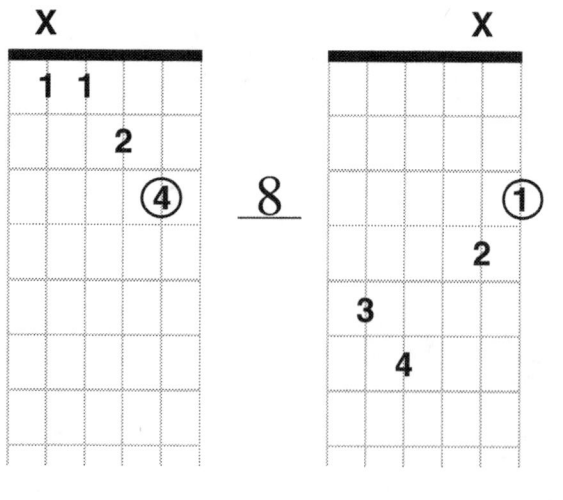

C-DP^5+   C-AA^5+

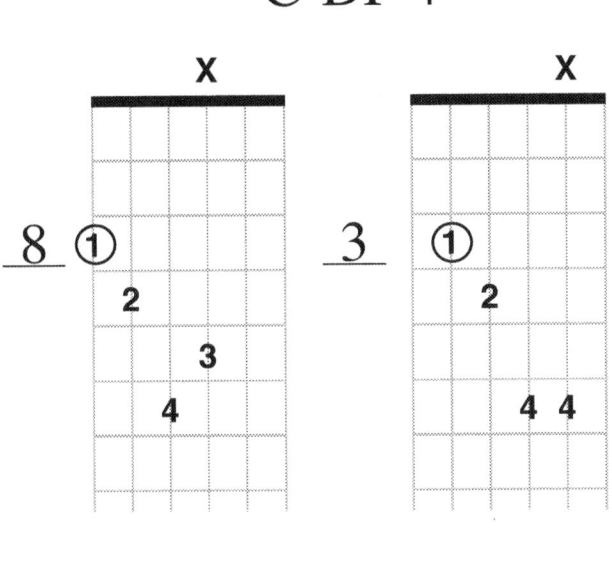

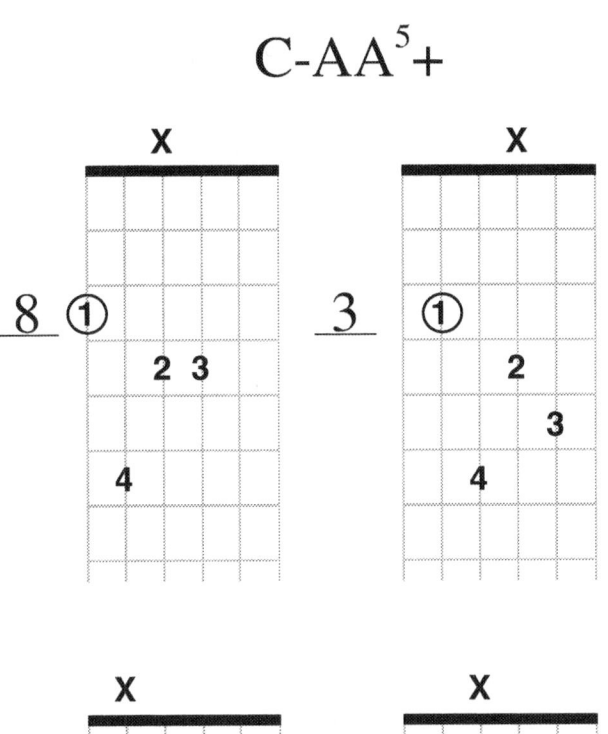

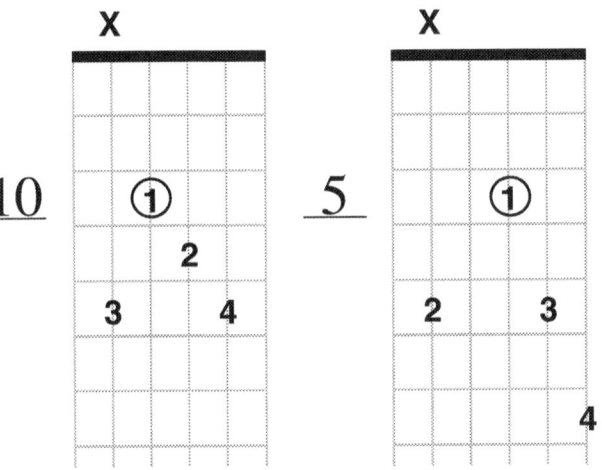

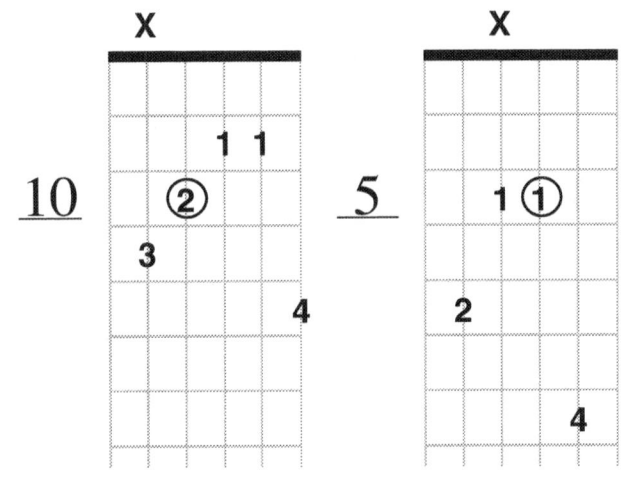

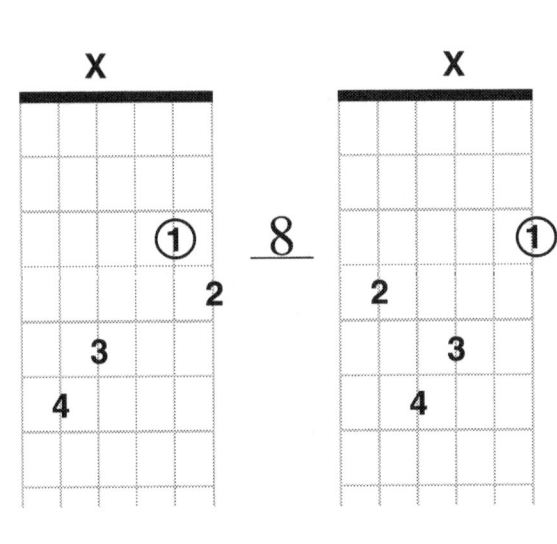

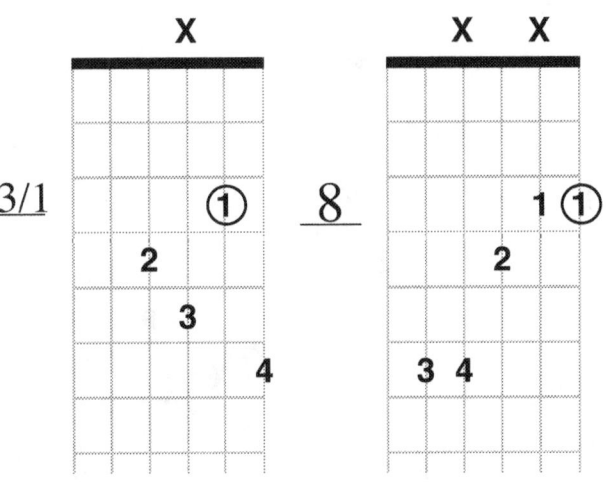

C-PA^5+   C-AP^5+

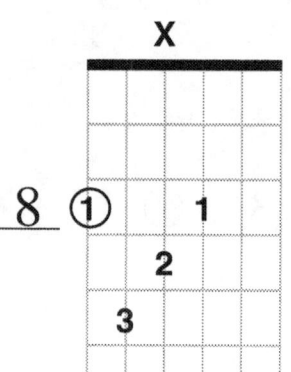
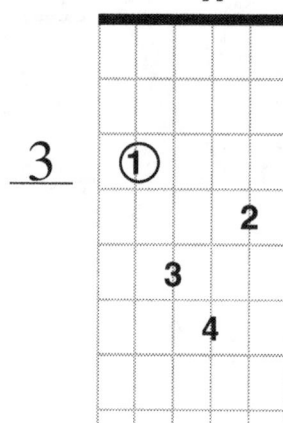
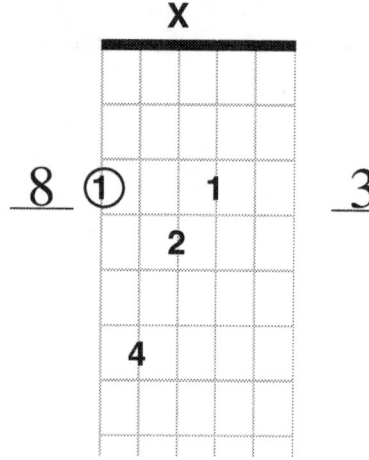
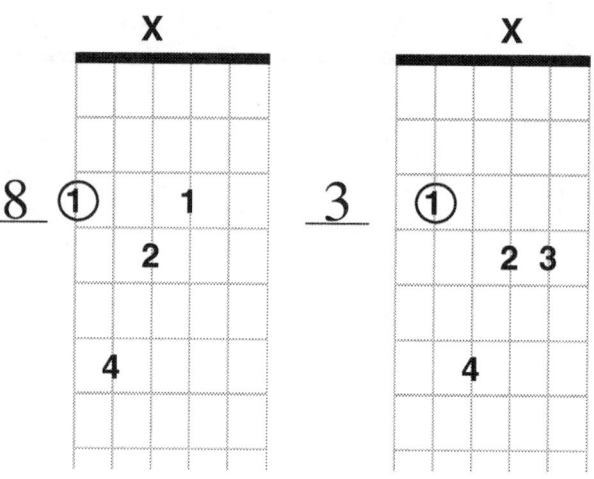
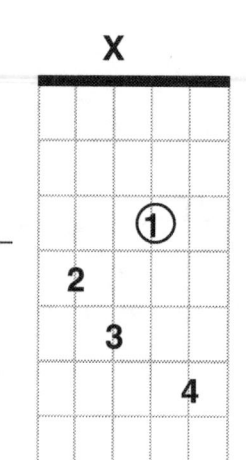
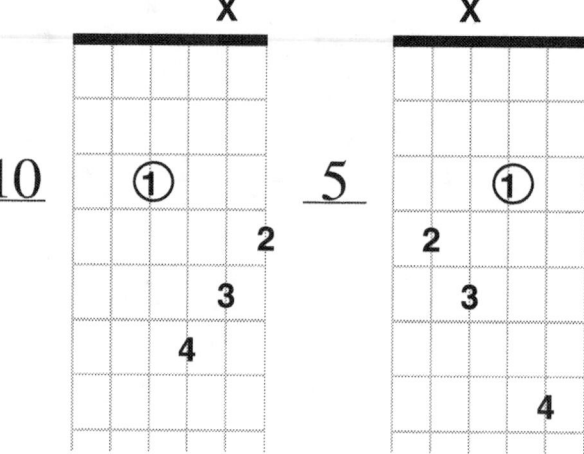
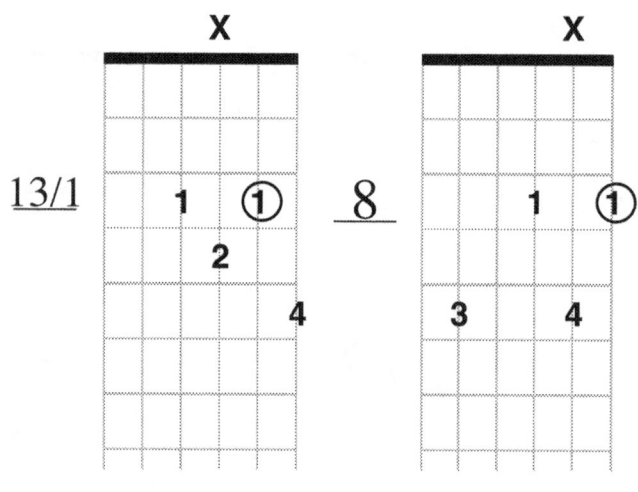
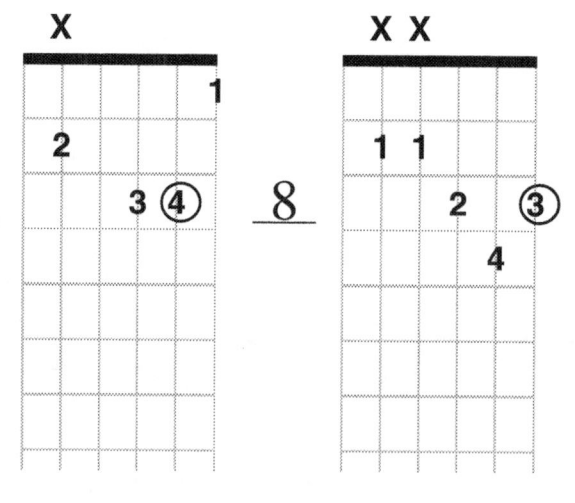

C-DA^5+   C-AD^5+

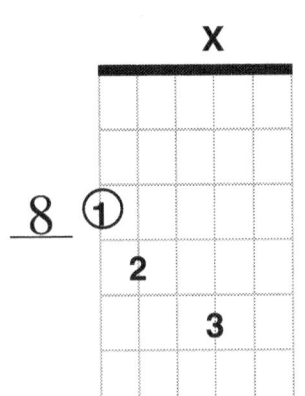
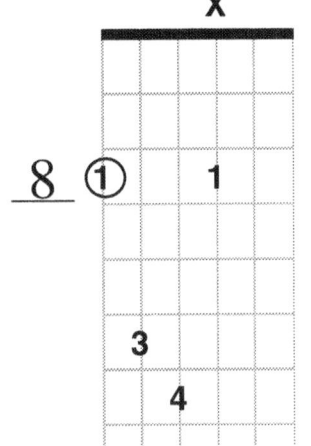
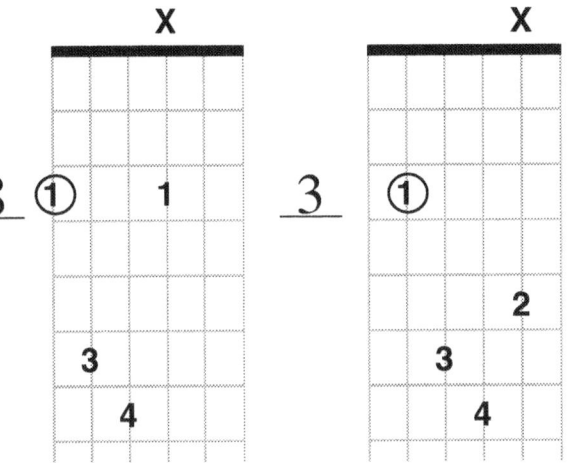
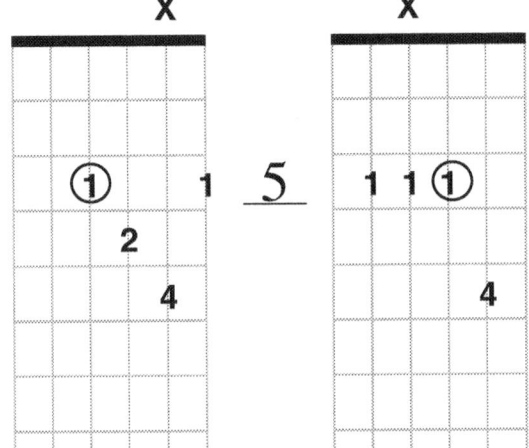
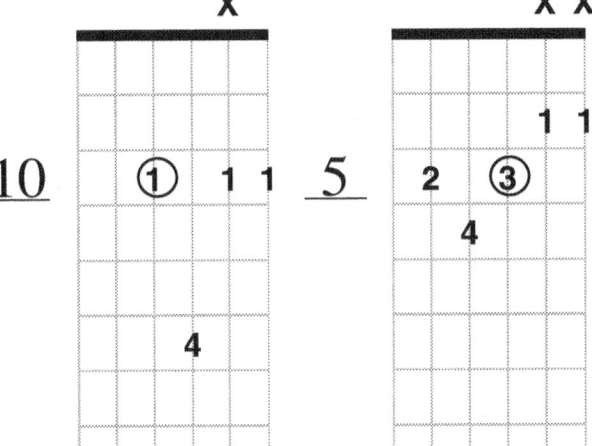
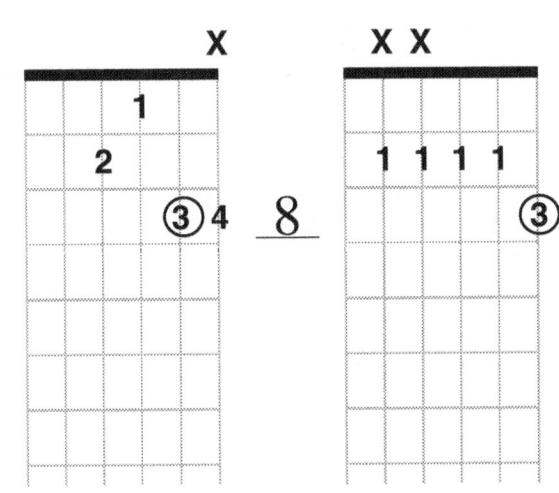
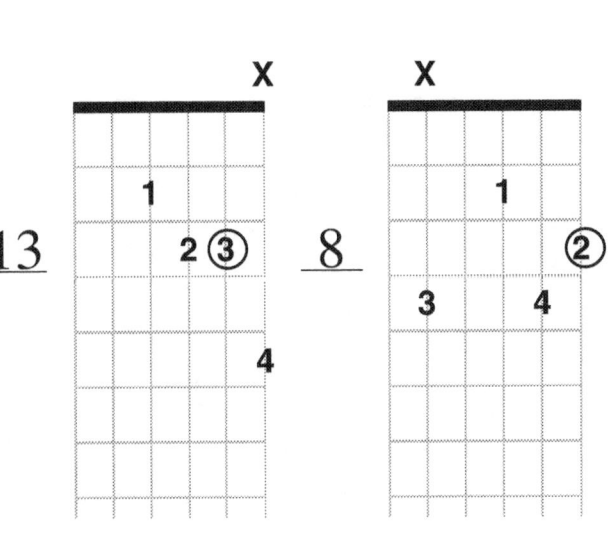

C-MM^6+   C-mm^6+

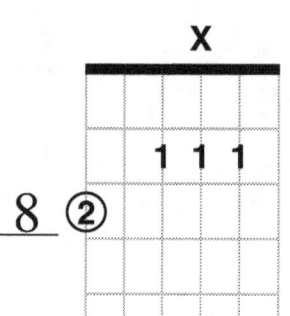
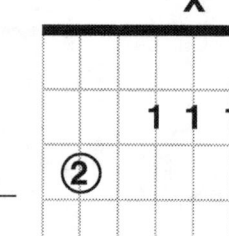
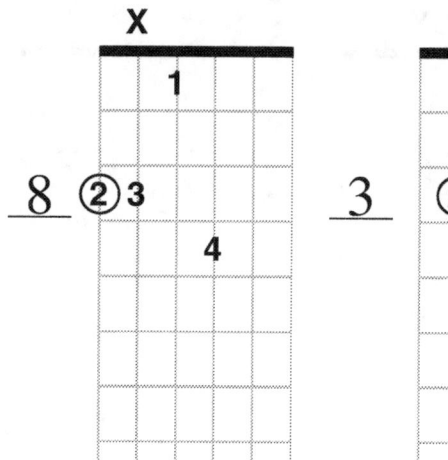
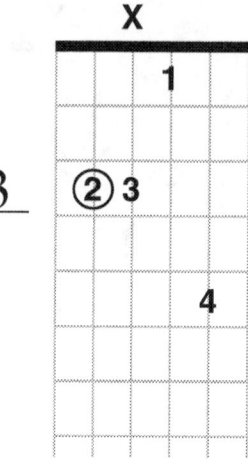
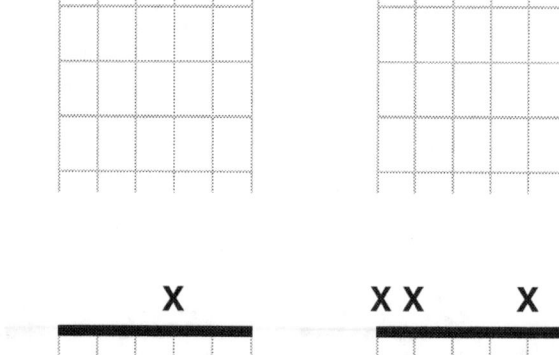
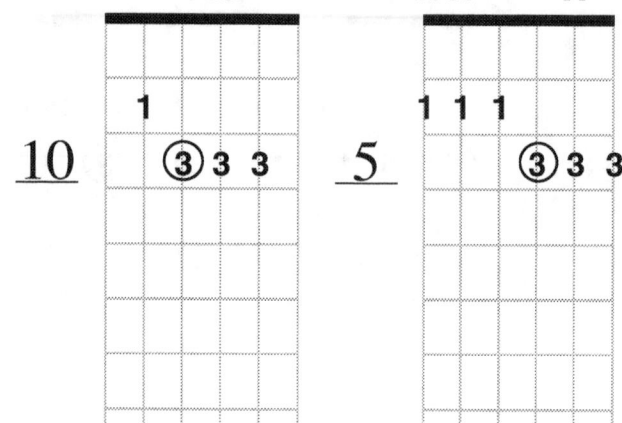
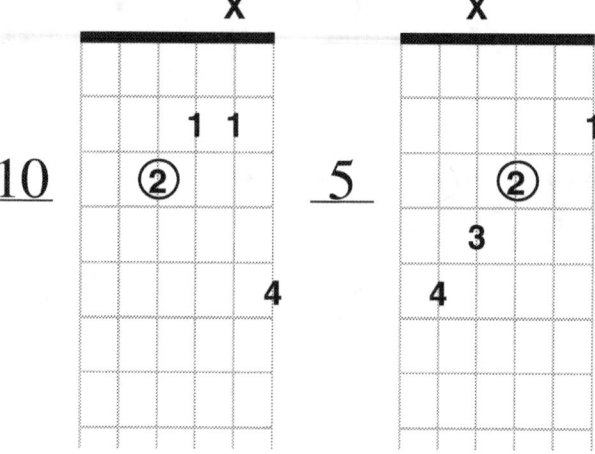
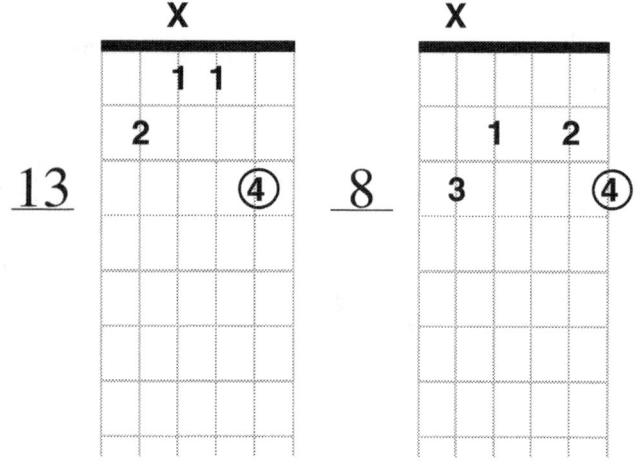
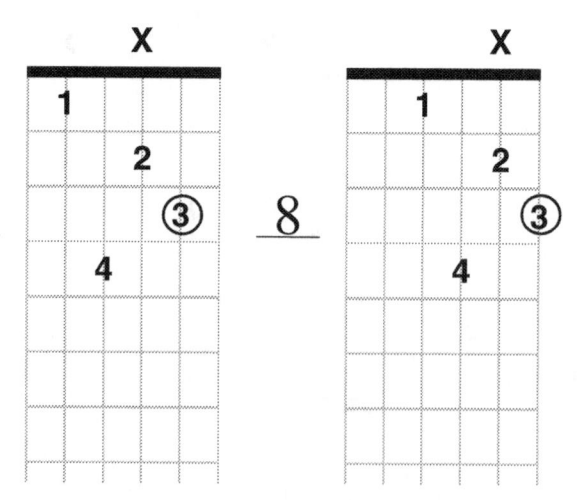

C-Mm⁶+

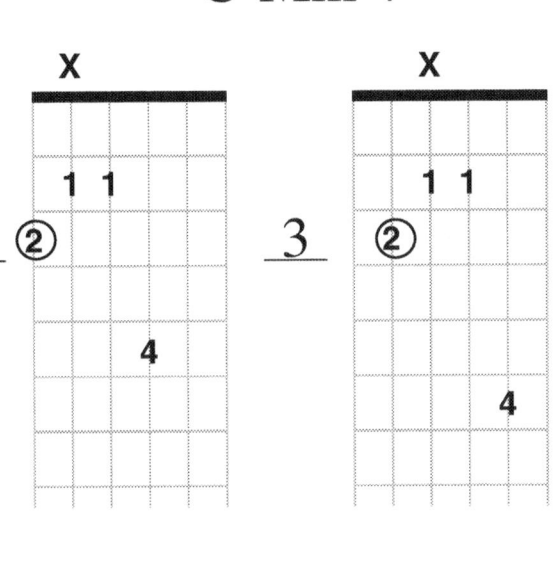
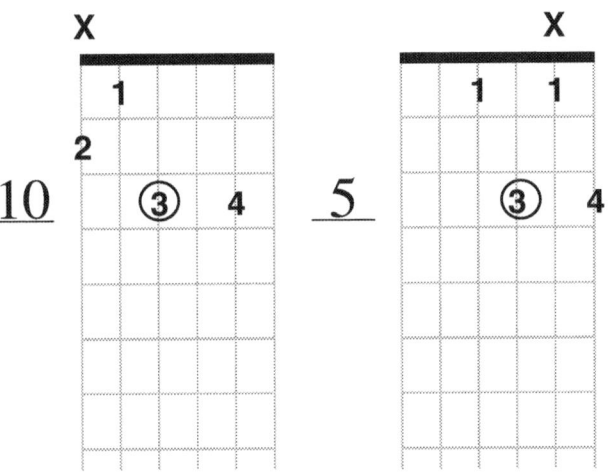
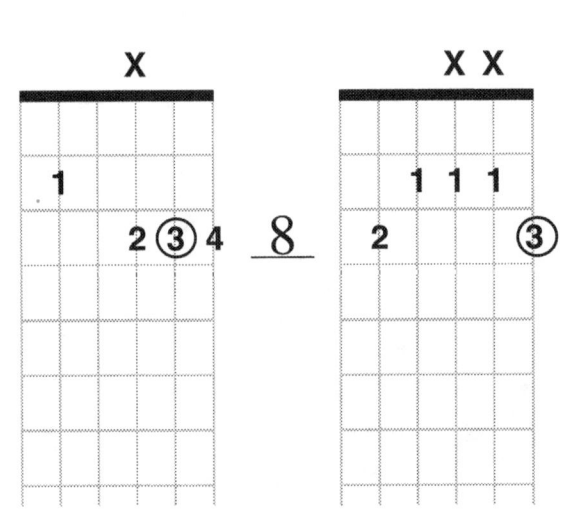

C-mM⁶+

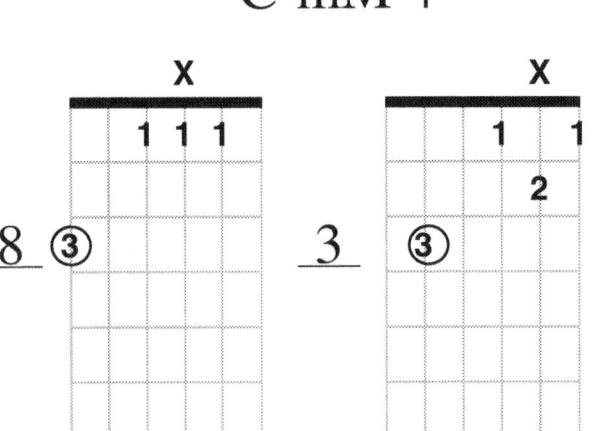
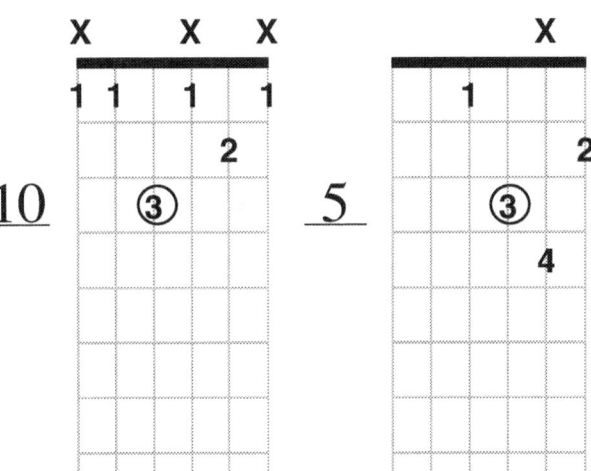
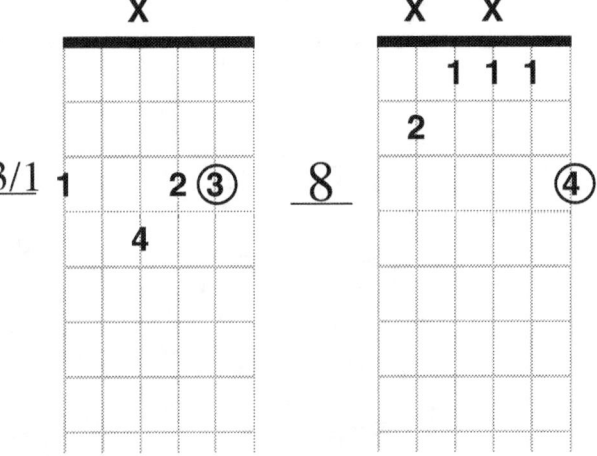

C-AA^6+   C-MA^6+

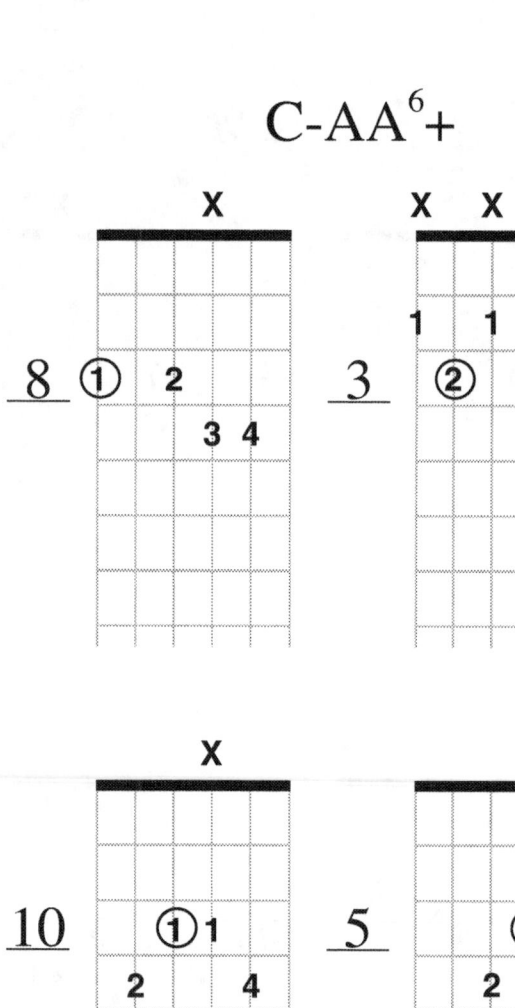
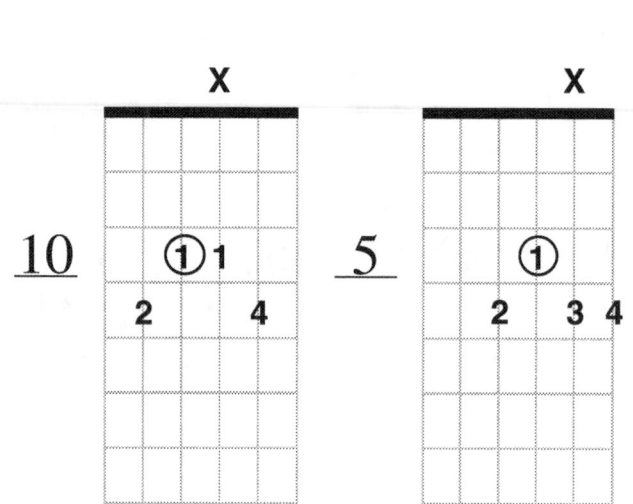
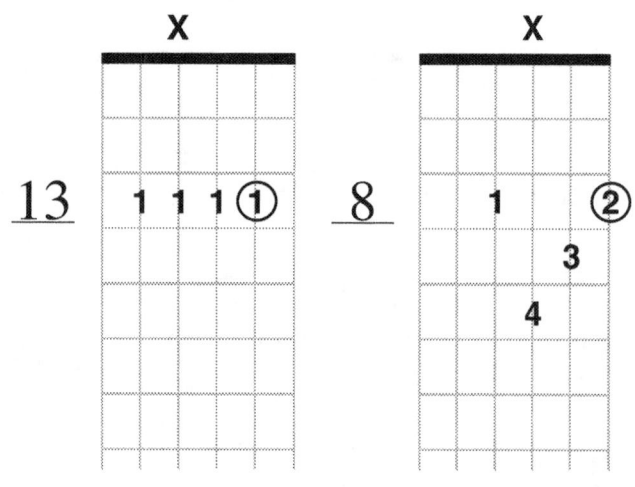
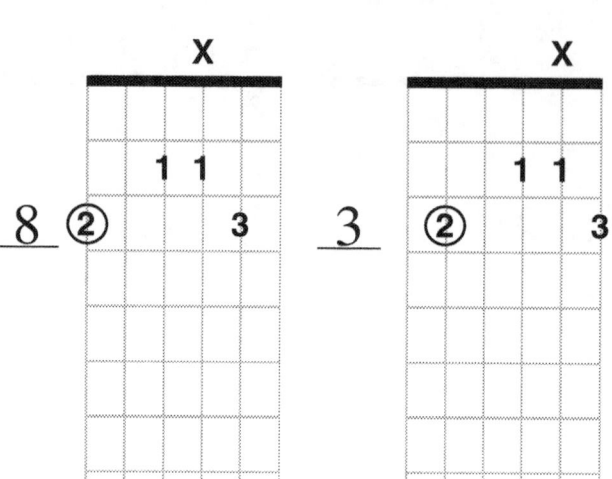
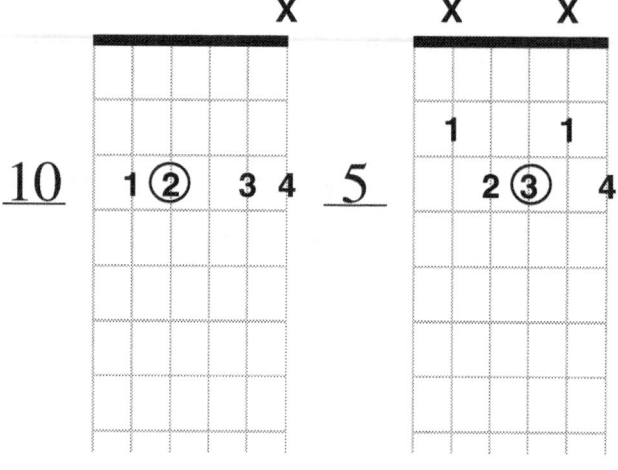
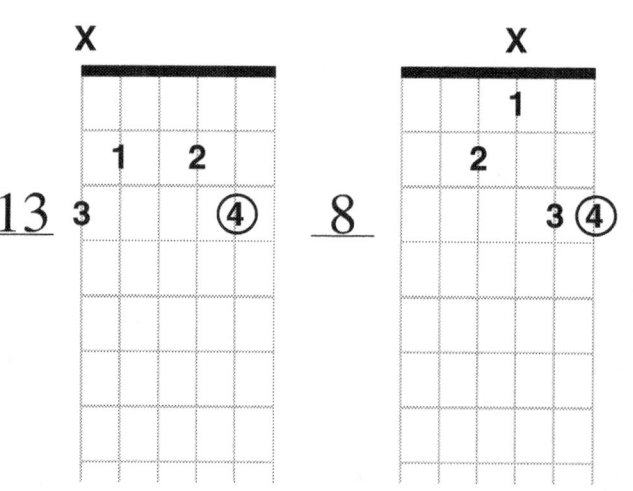

C-AM^6+   C-mA^6+

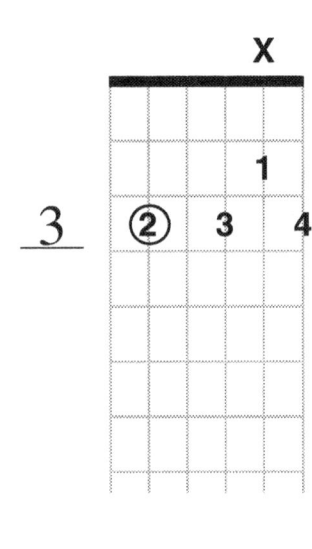
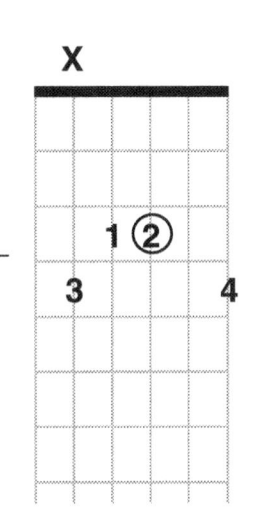
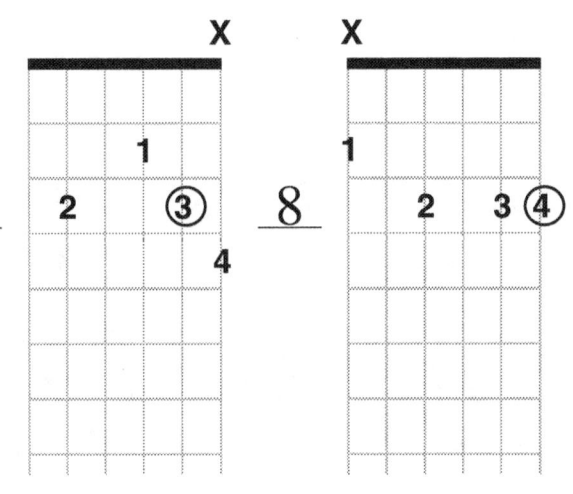
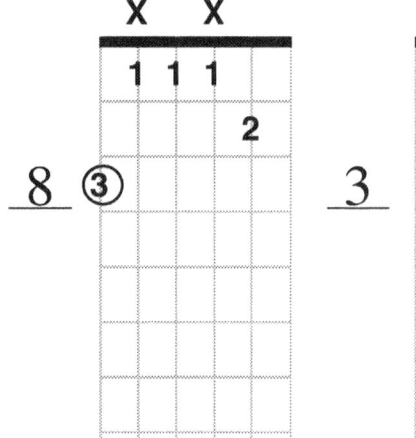
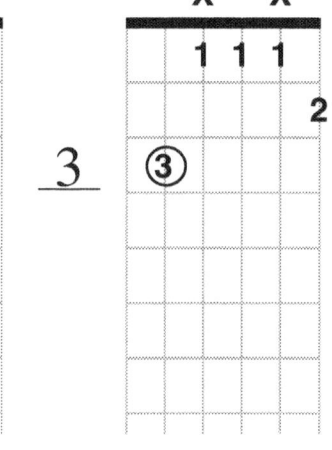
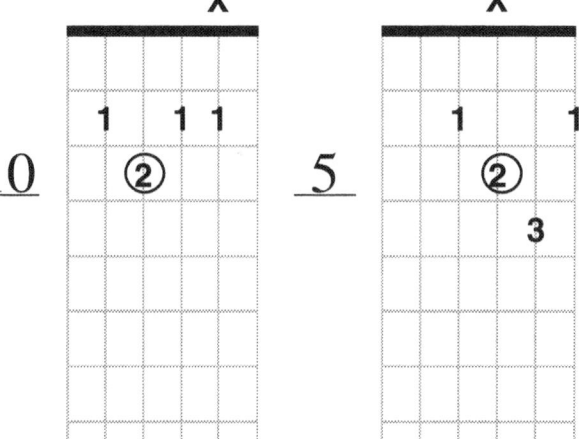
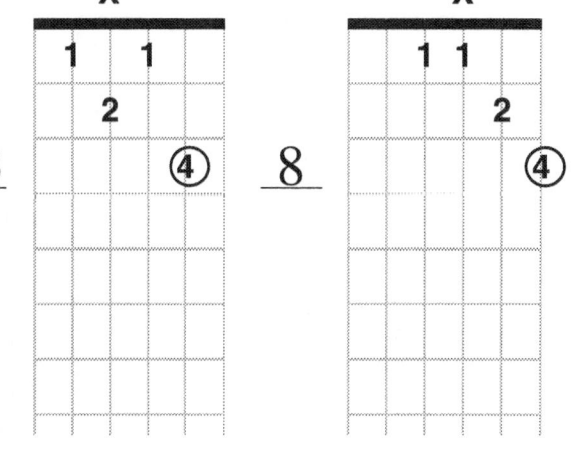

C-Am⁶+   C-MM⁷+

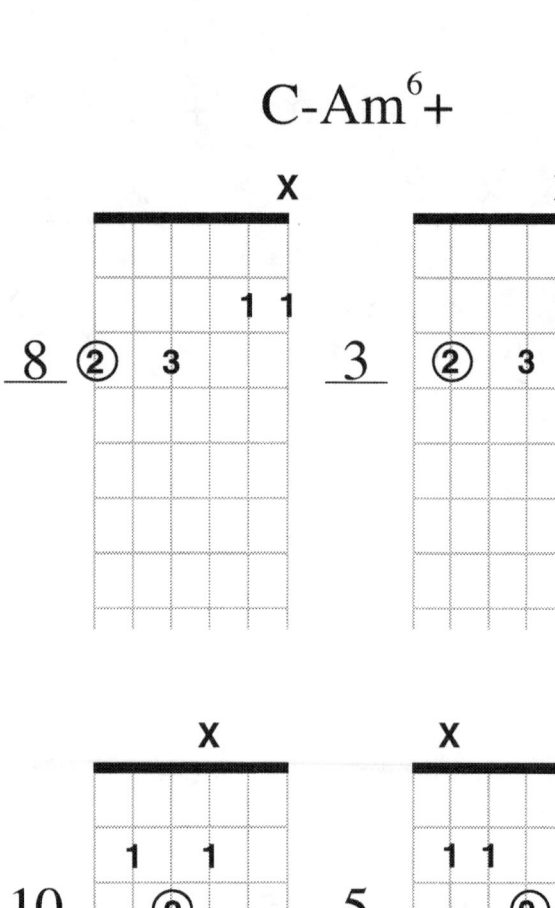
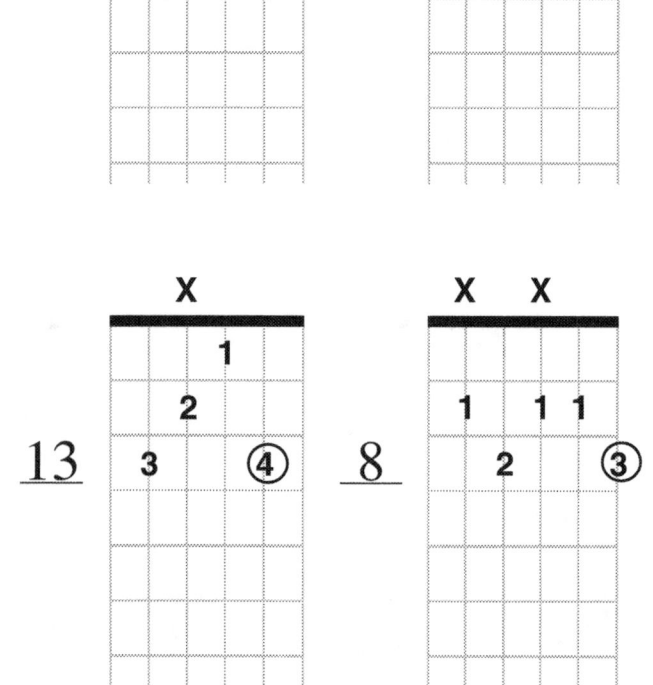
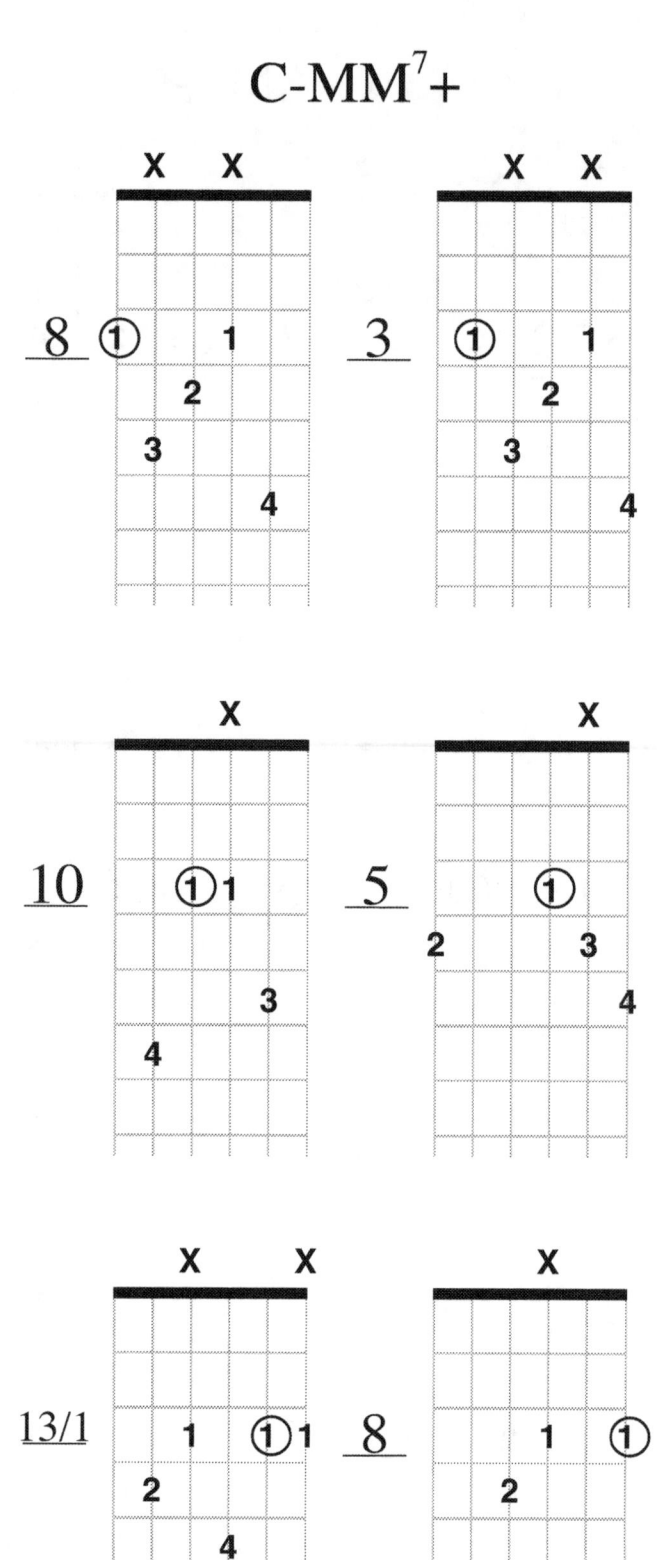

C-mm^7+   C-Mm^7+

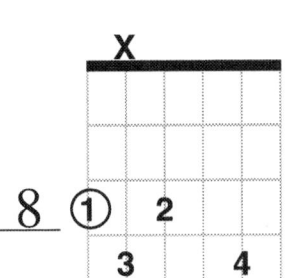
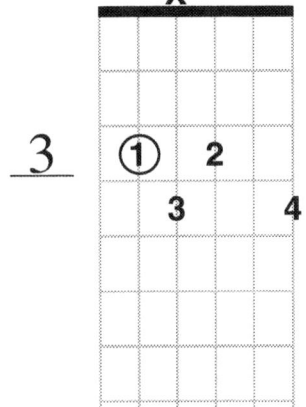
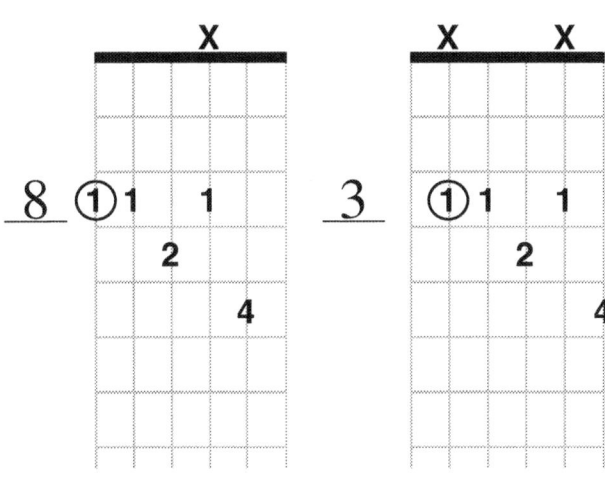
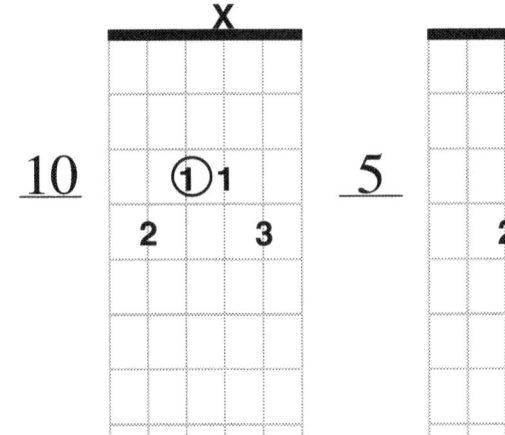
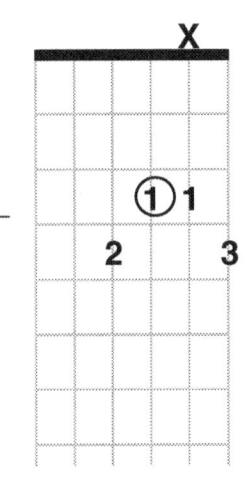
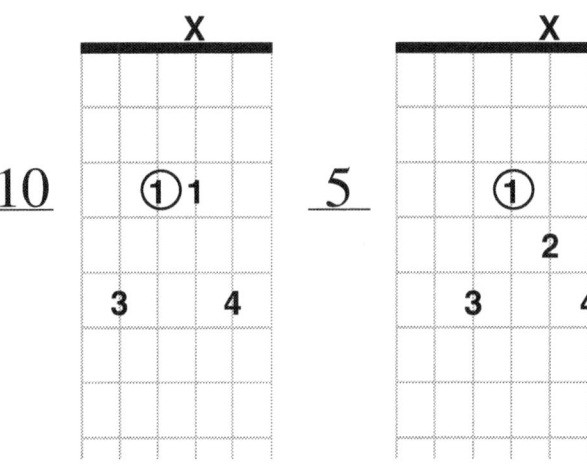
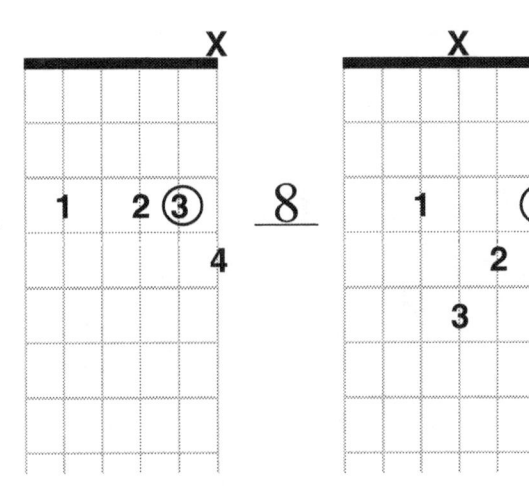
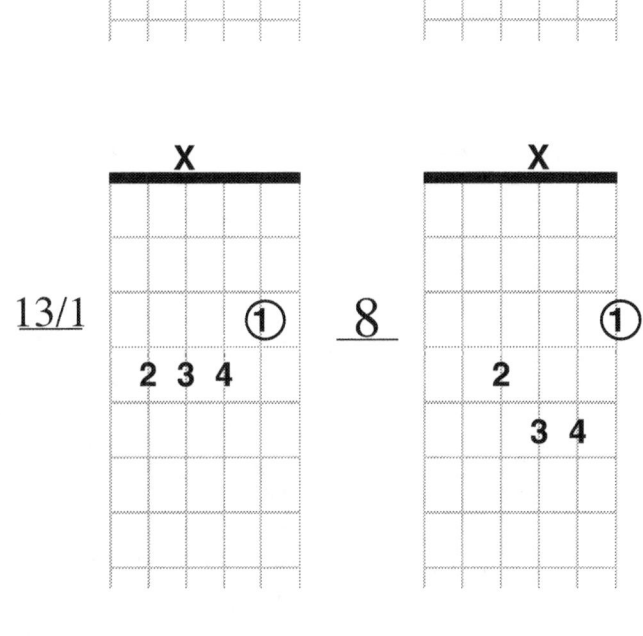

C-mM⁷+ | C-AA⁷+

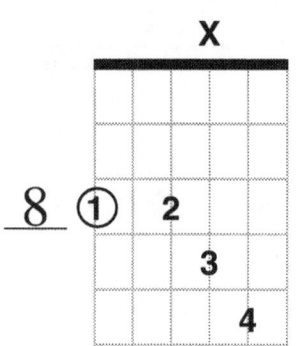 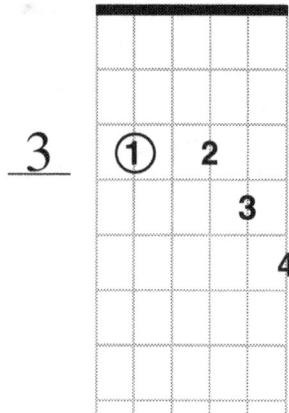 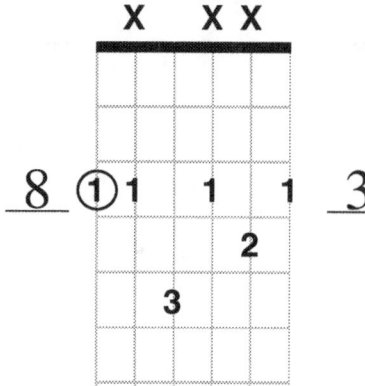 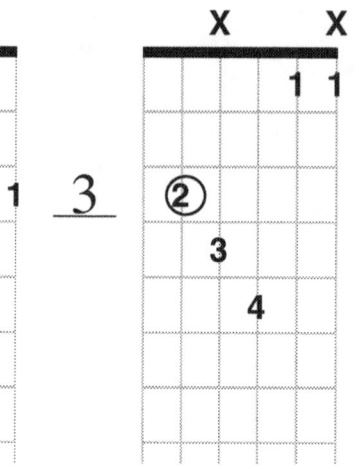

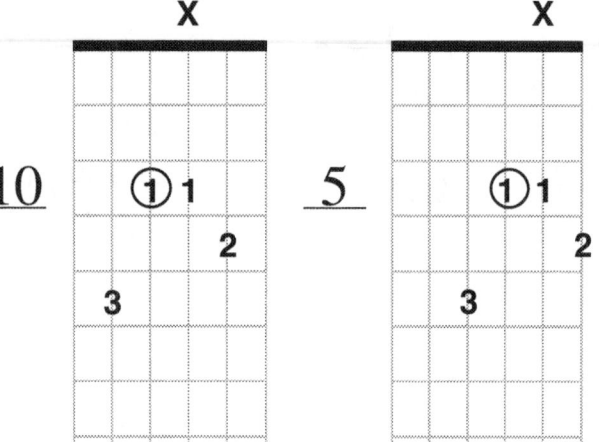 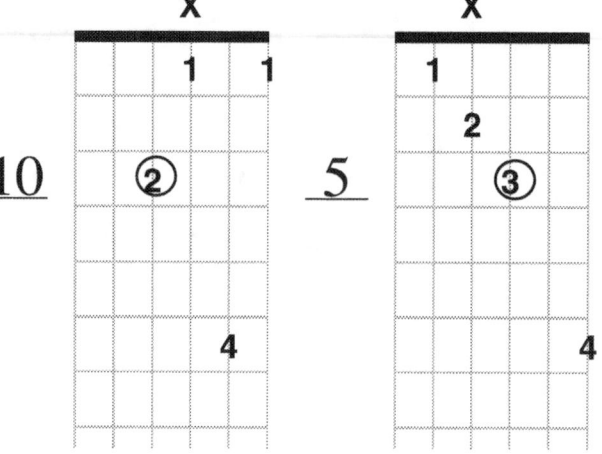

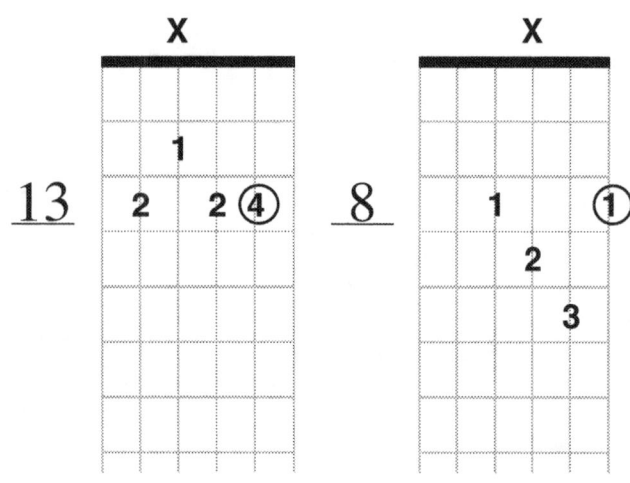 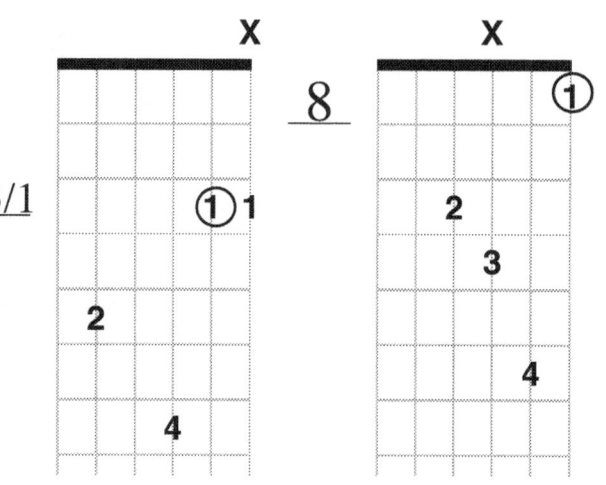

C-MA⁷+   C-AM⁷+

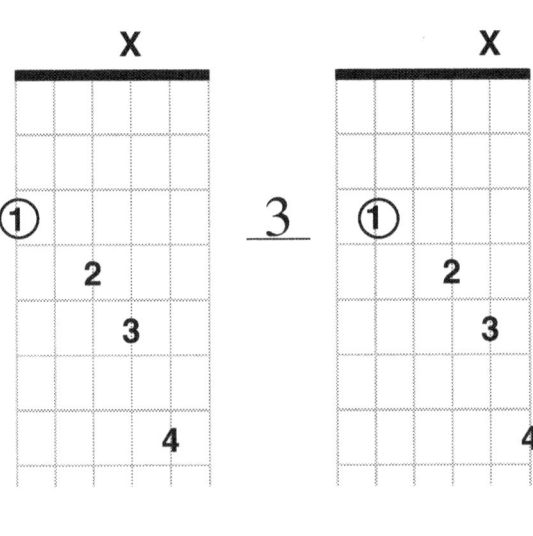
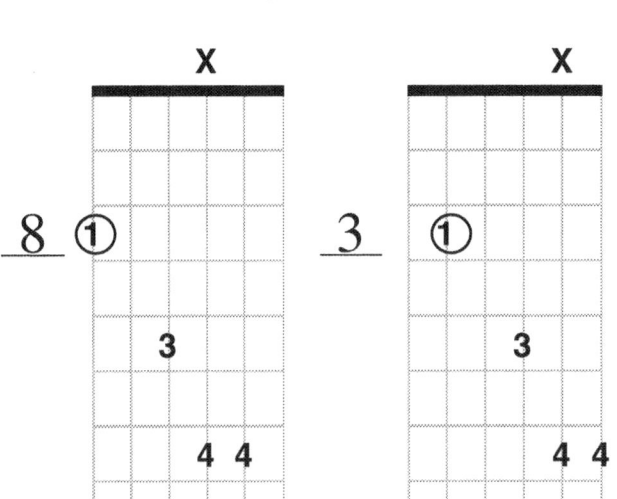
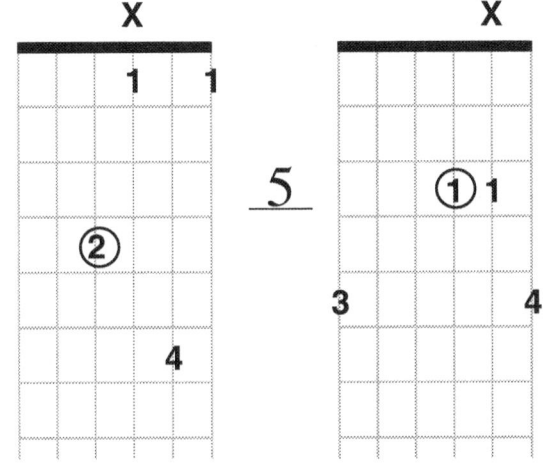
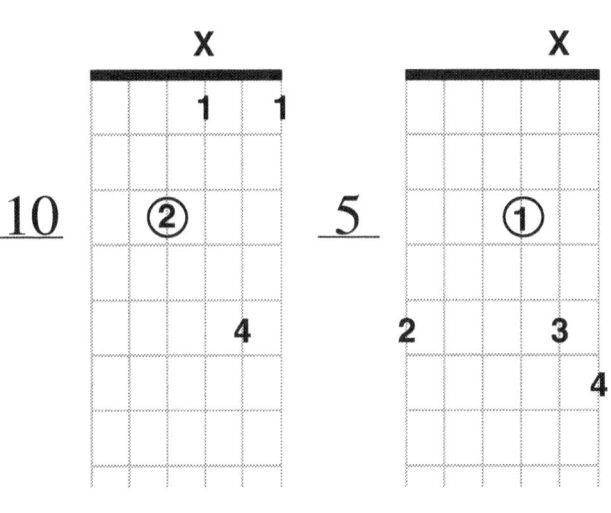
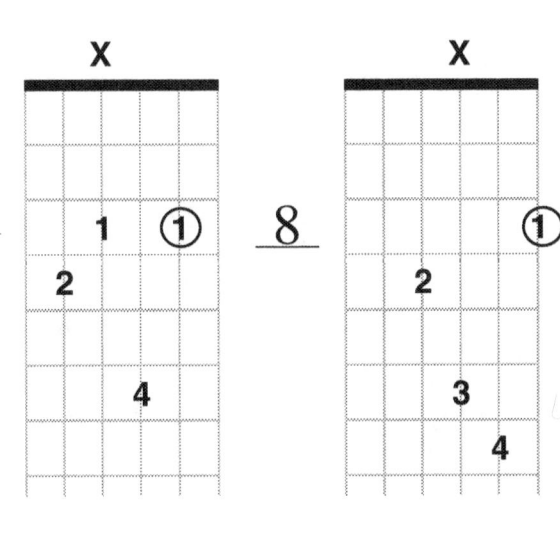
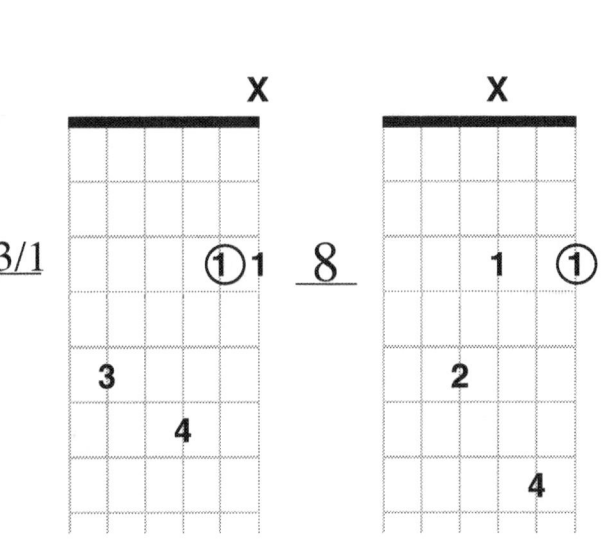

C-mA⁷+   C-Am⁷+

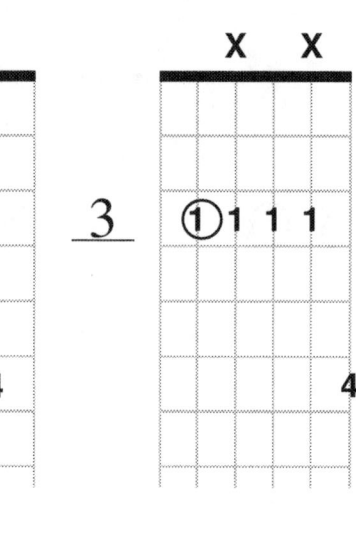
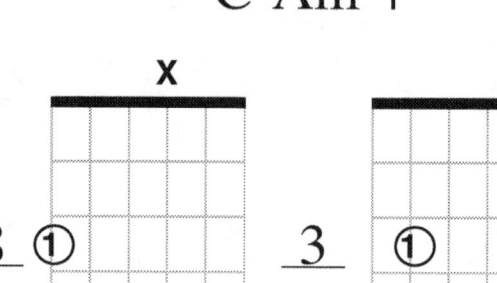
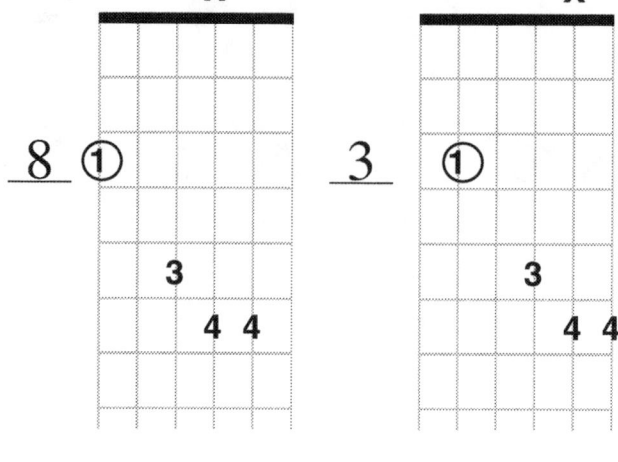
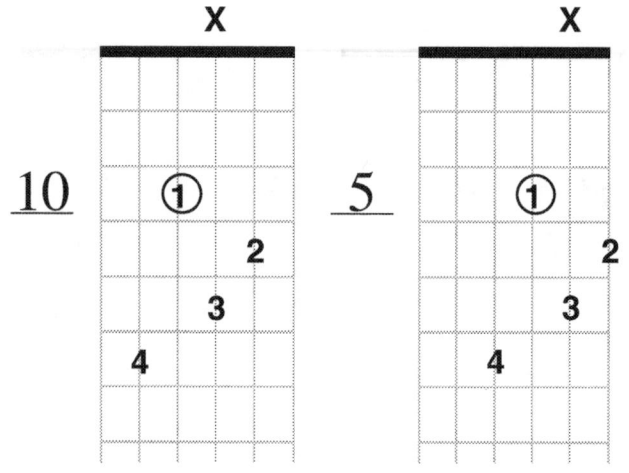
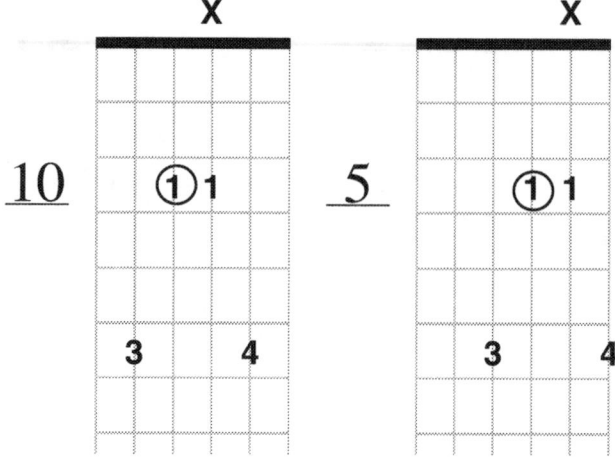
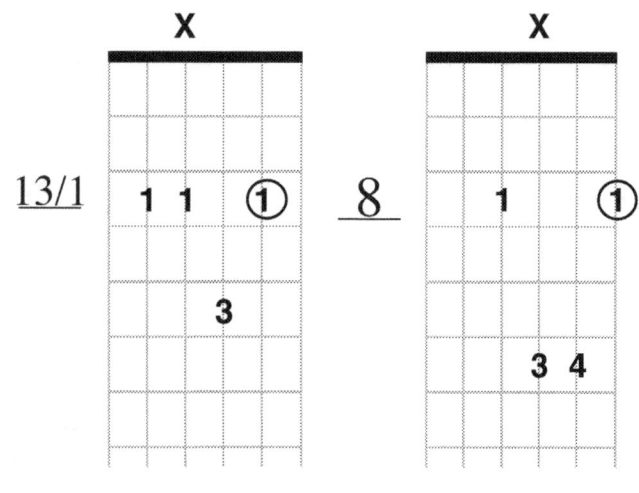
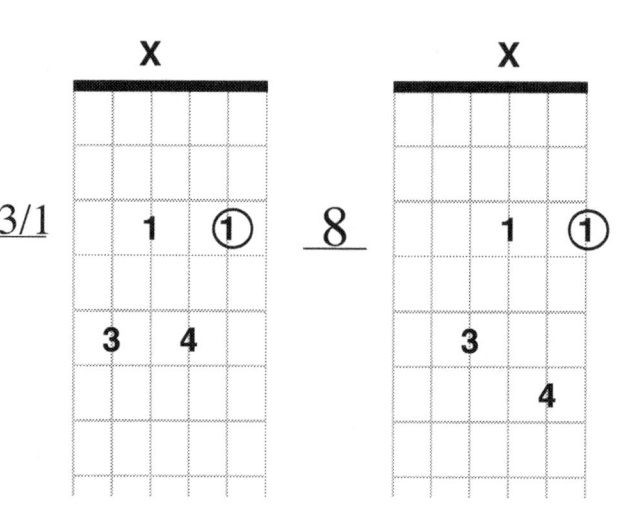

C-M² -m³   C-M² -M³

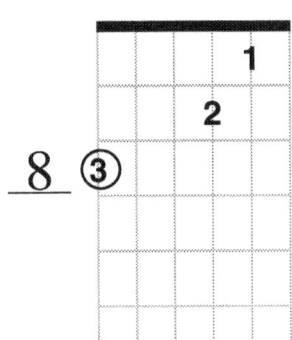
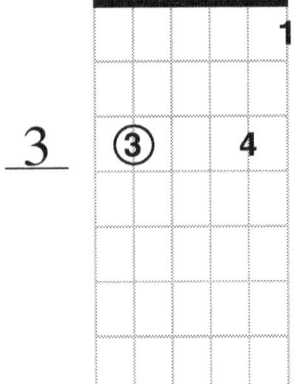
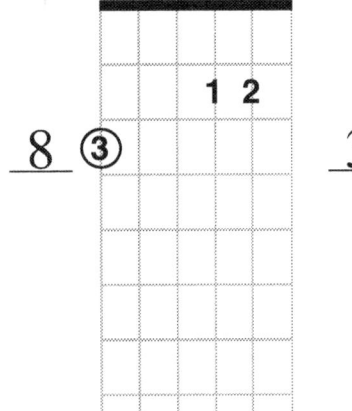
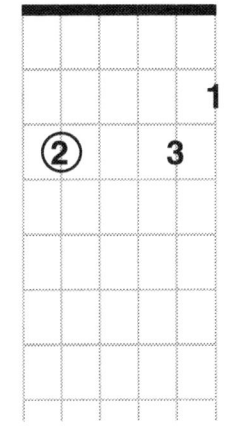

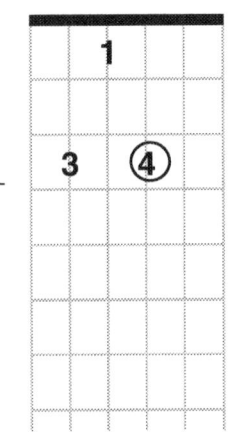
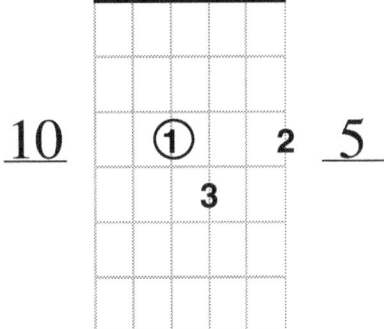
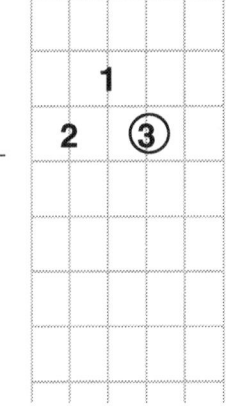

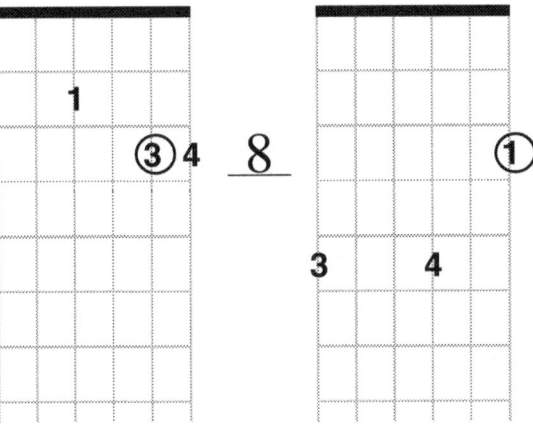
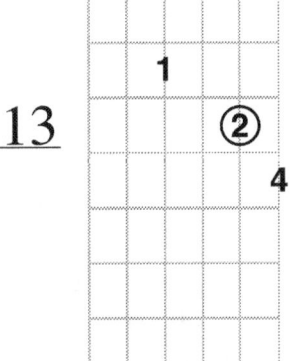
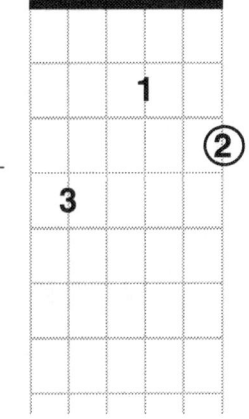

C-M²P⁴

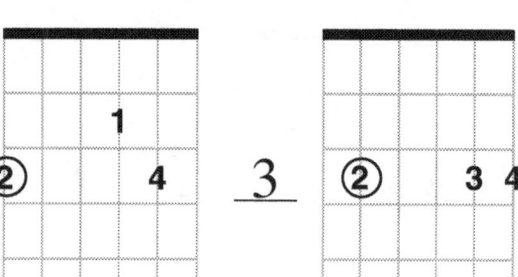
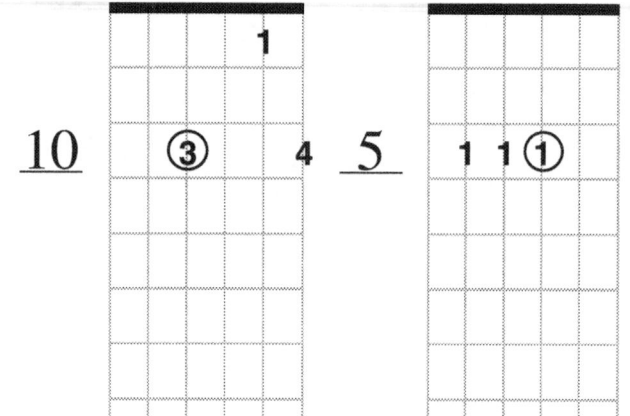
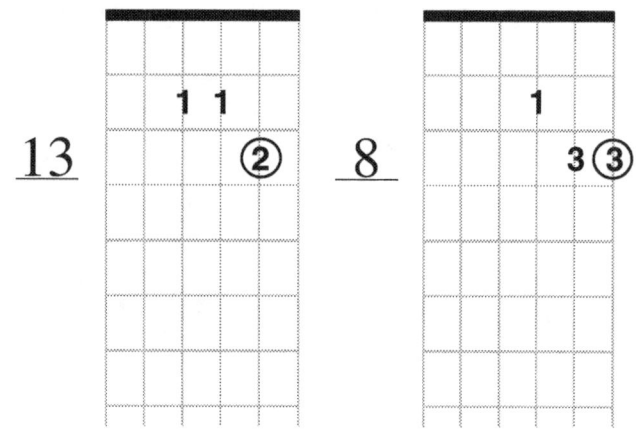

C-M²D⁵

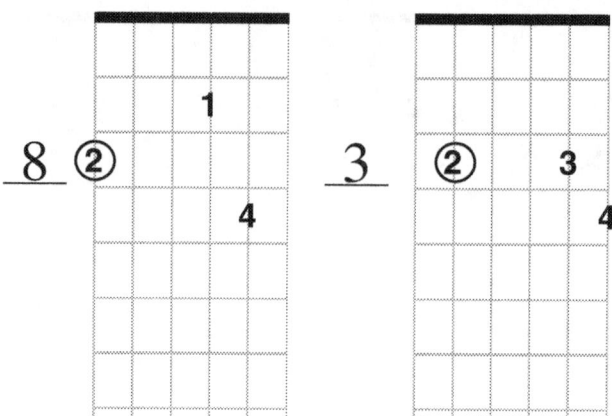
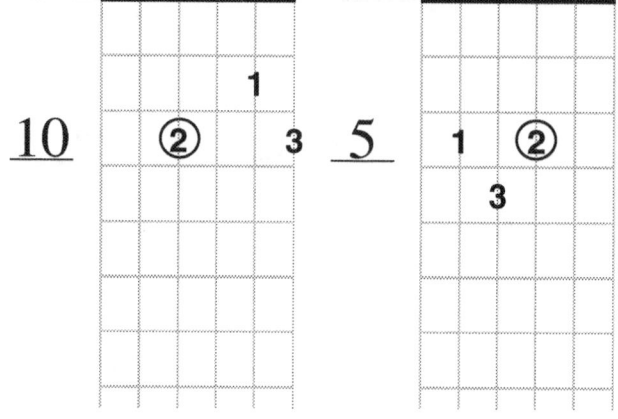
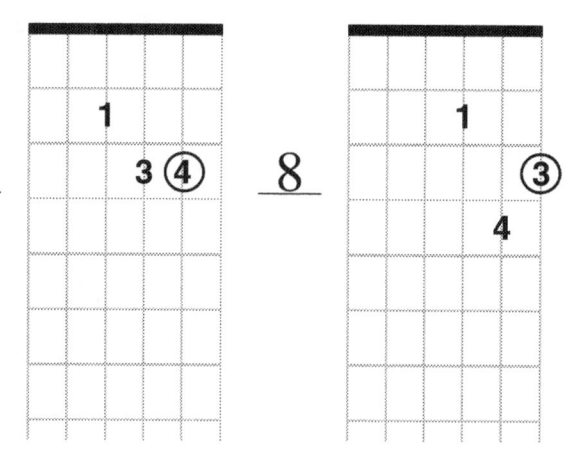

$C-M^2-P^5$ $\qquad$ $C-M^2-m^6$

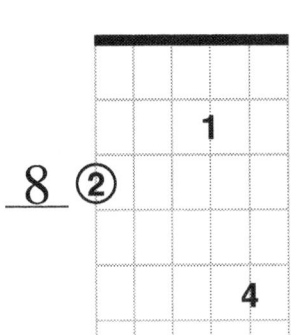
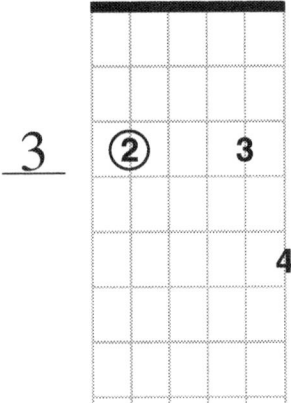
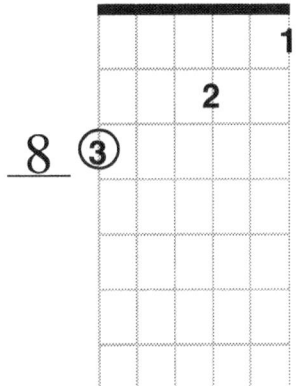
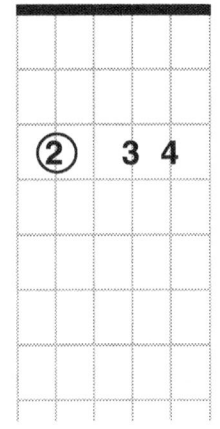
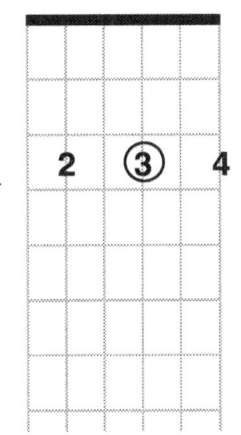
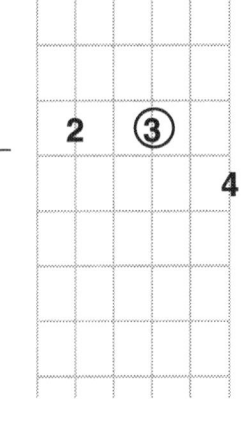
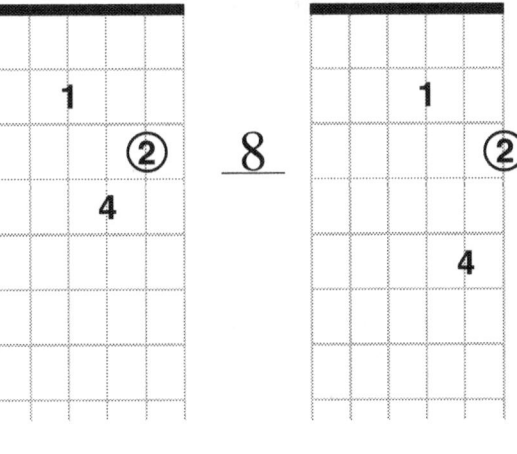
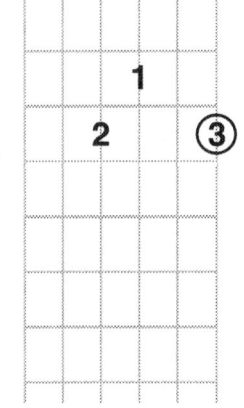

C-M²-M⁶   C-M²-m⁷

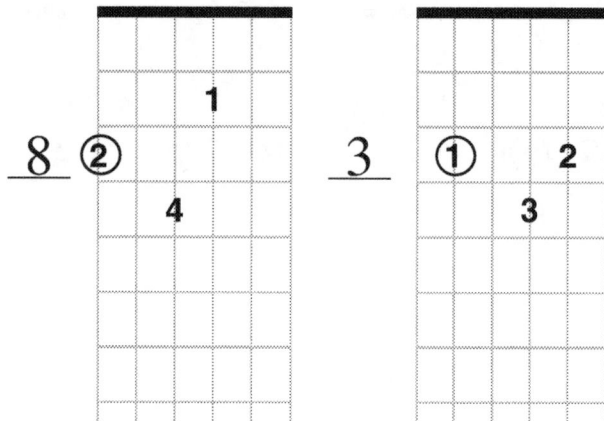
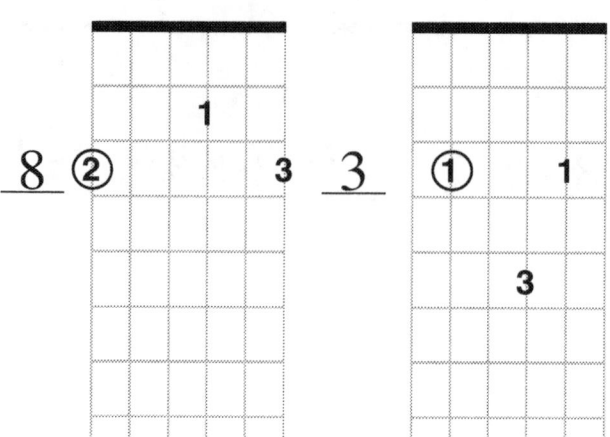
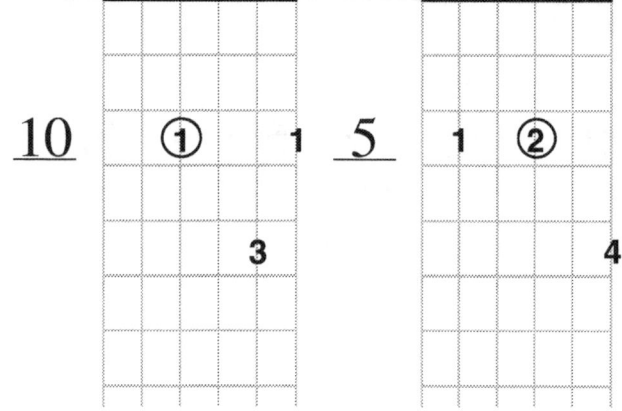
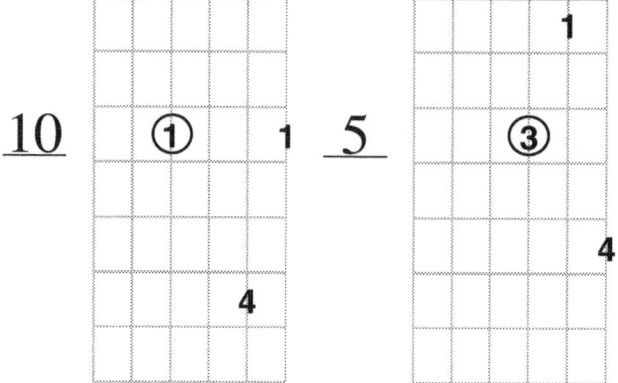
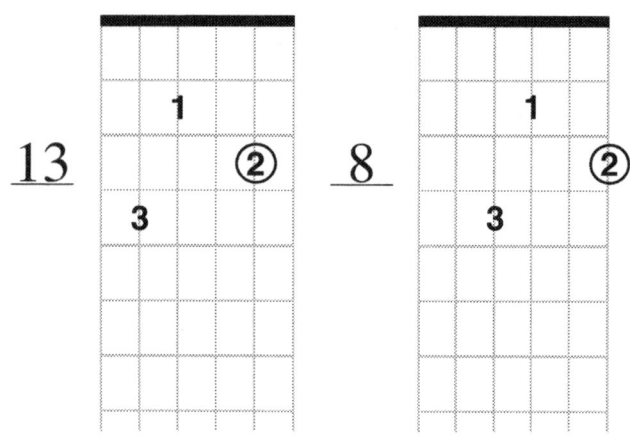
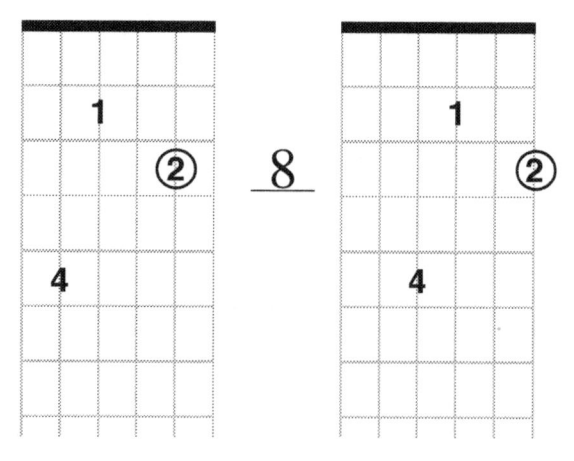

$C\text{-}M^2\text{-}M^7$ $C\text{-}m^2\text{-}m^3$

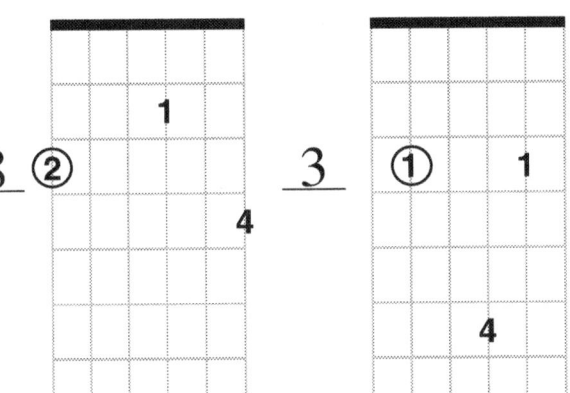
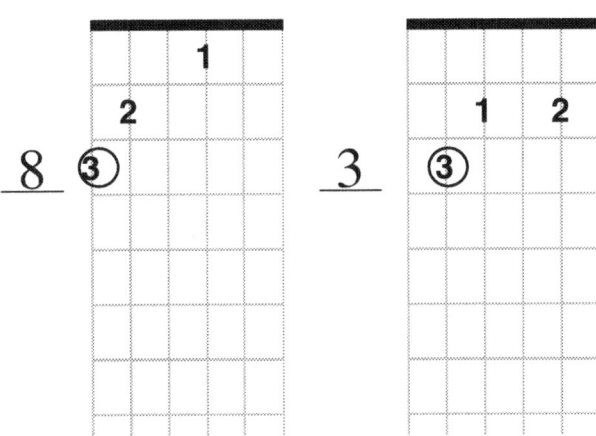
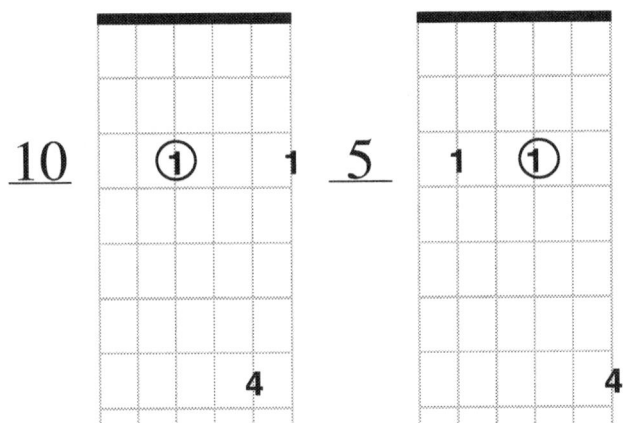
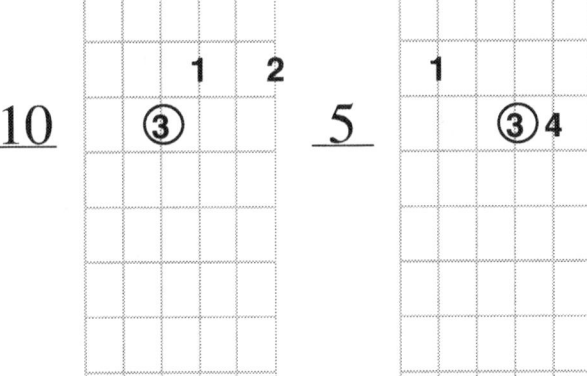
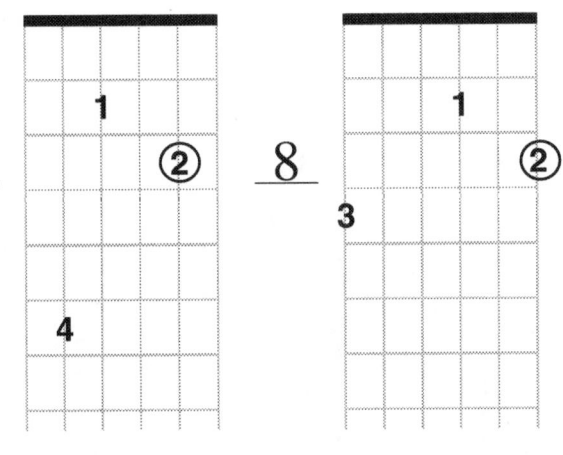
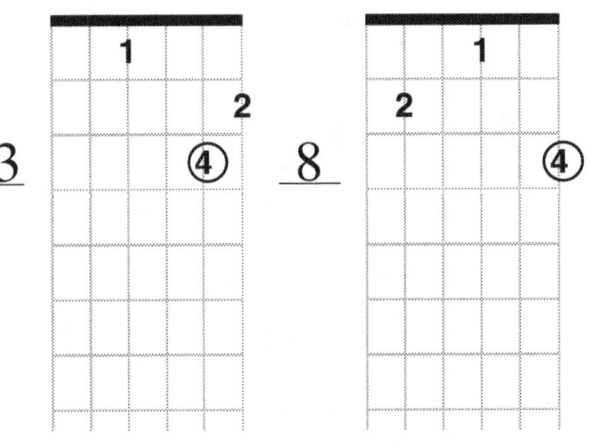

C-m²-M³   C-m²-P⁴

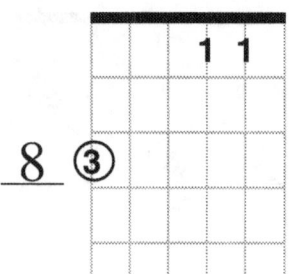 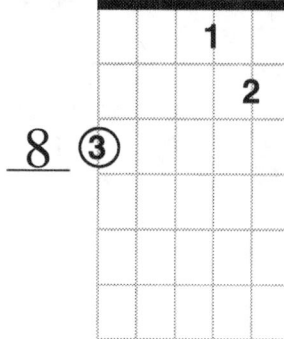
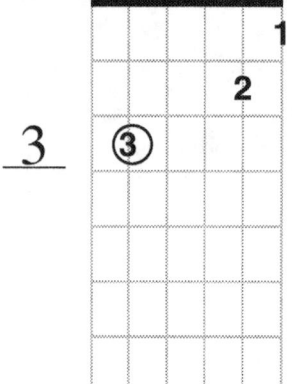 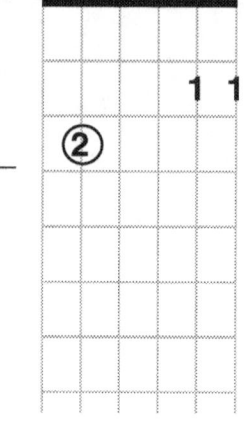
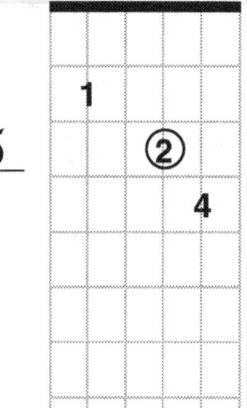 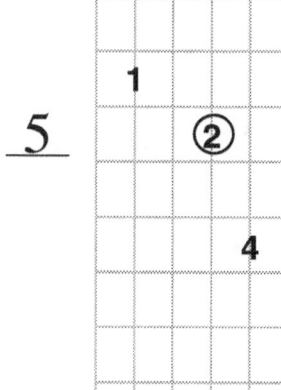
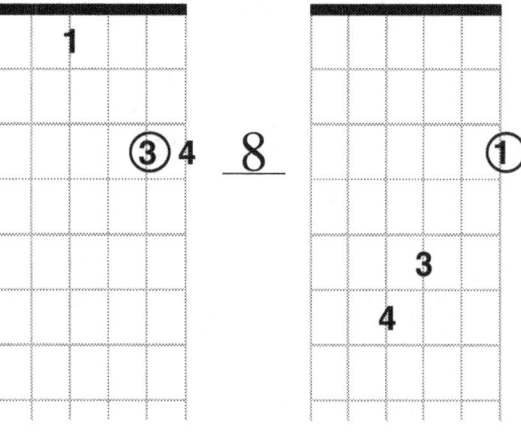 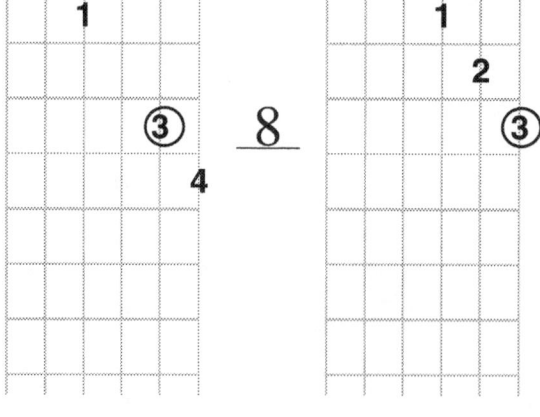

$C\text{-}m^2\text{-}D^5$ $C\text{-}m^2\text{-}P^5$

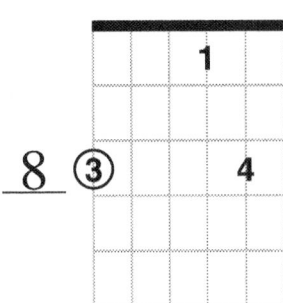
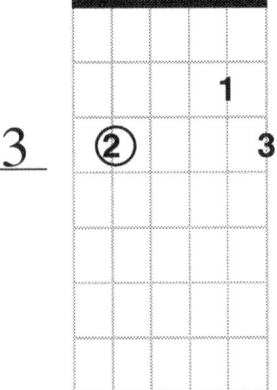
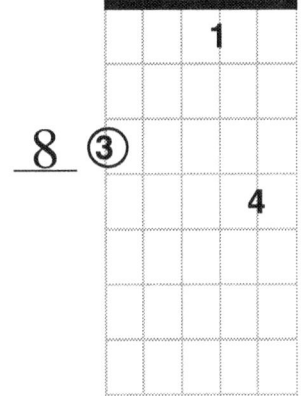
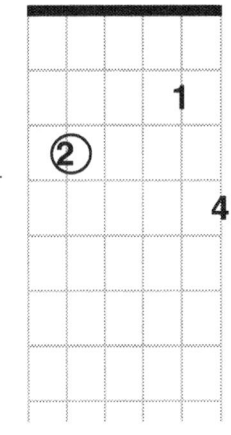
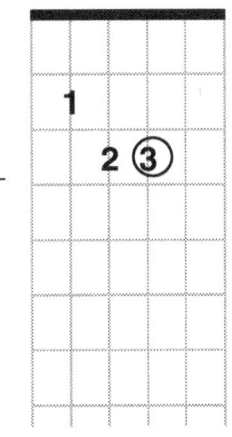
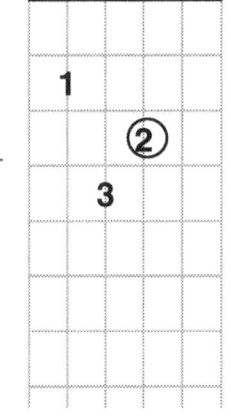
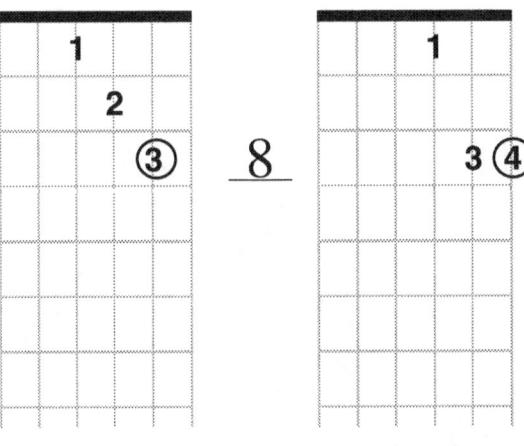
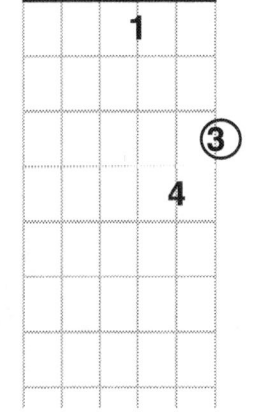

$C\text{-}m^2\text{-}m^6$ $C\text{-}m^2\text{-}M^6$

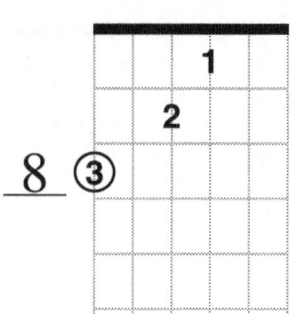
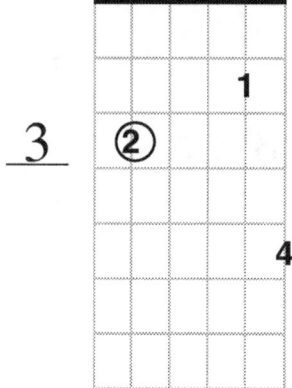
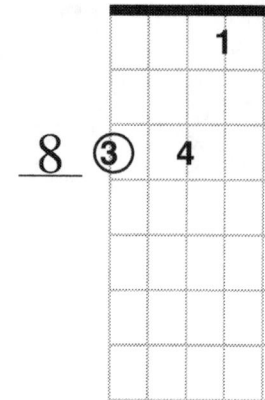
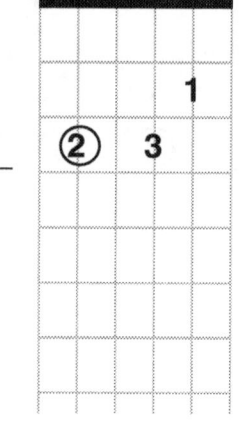
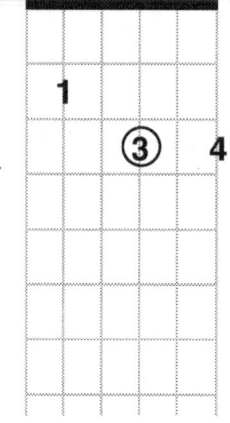
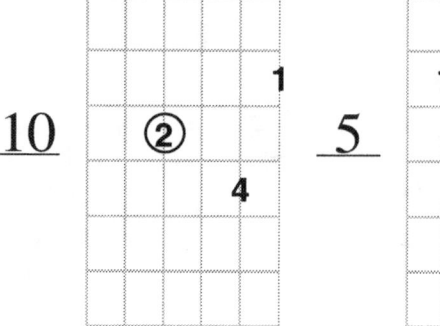
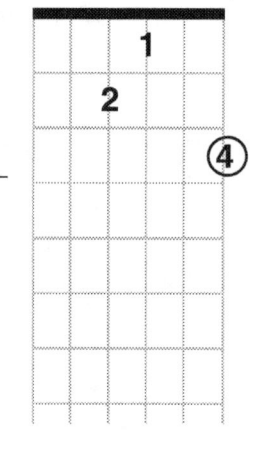
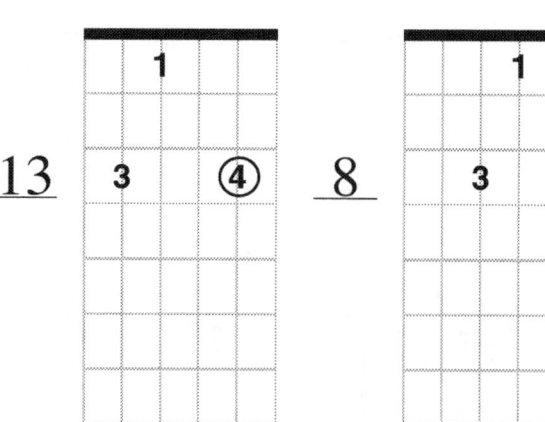

$C\text{-}m^2\text{-}m^7$ $C\text{-}m^2\text{-}M^7$

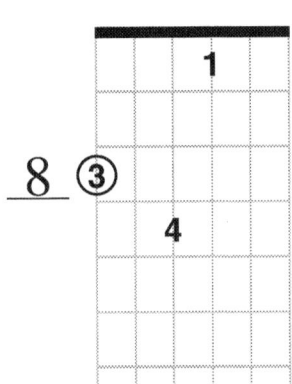
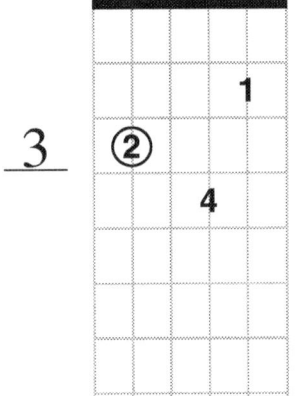
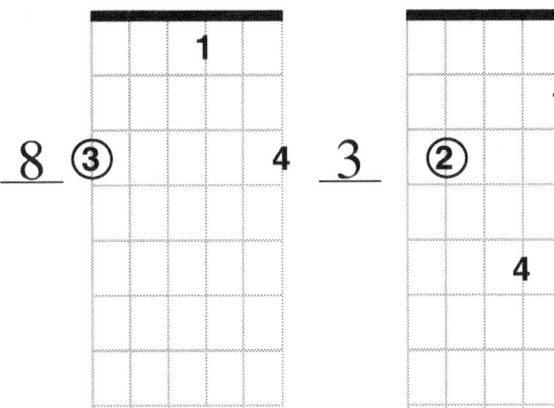
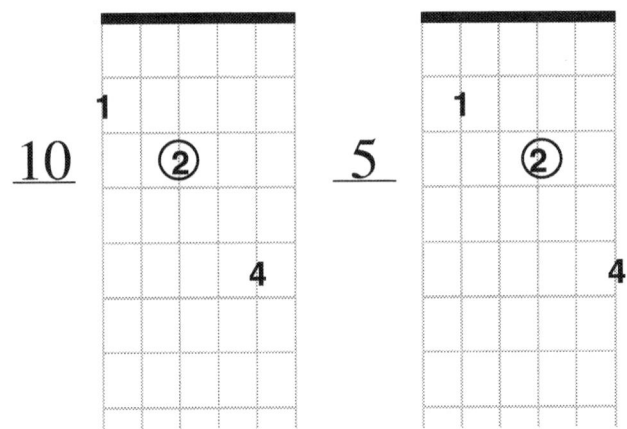
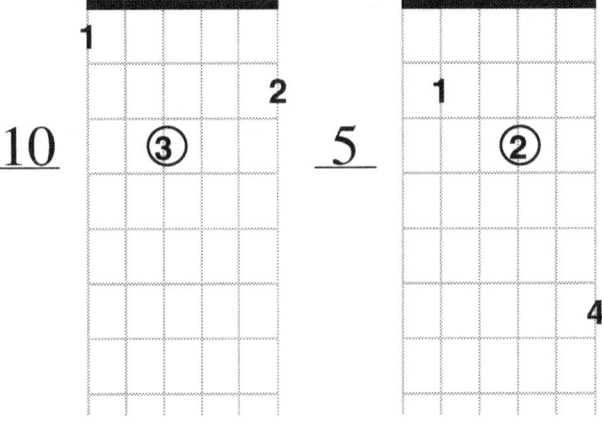
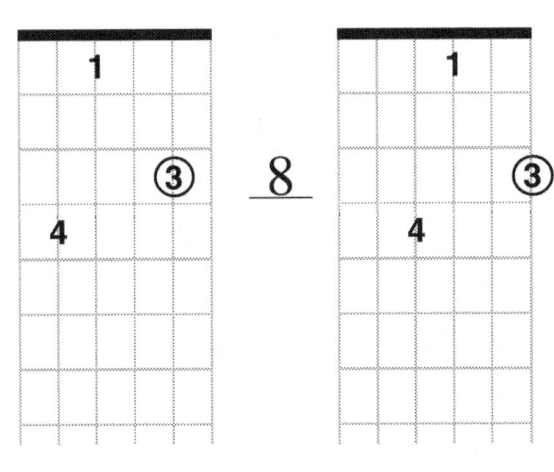
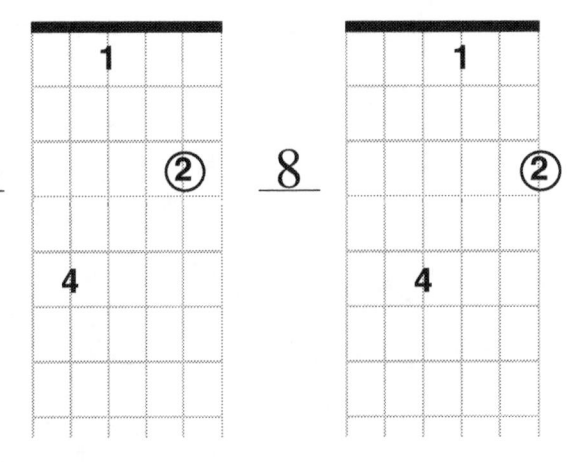

$C-M^3-m^2$ $C-M^3-M^2$

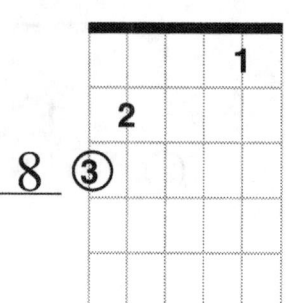 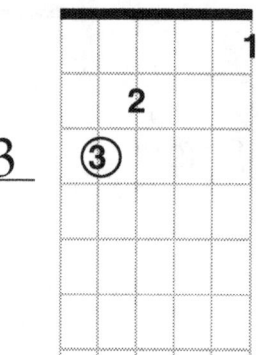 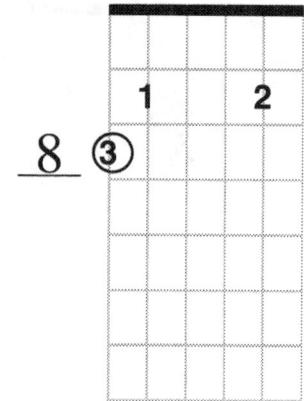 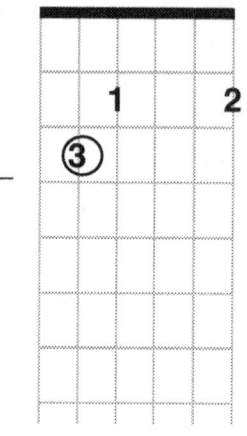

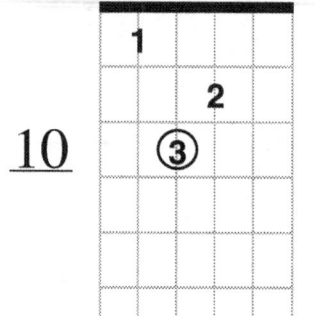 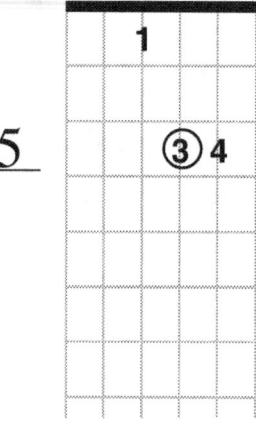 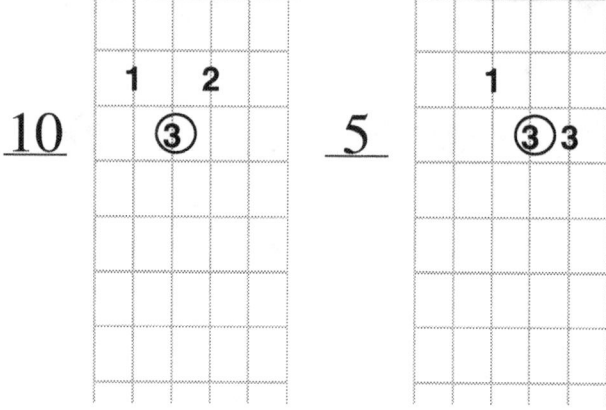

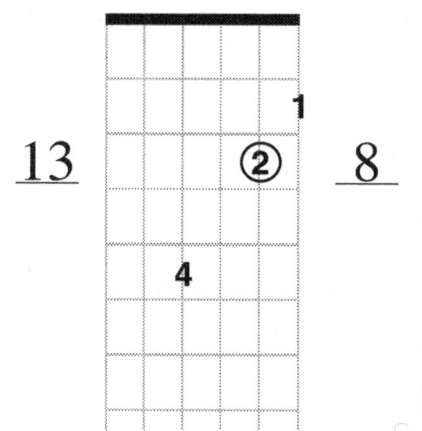 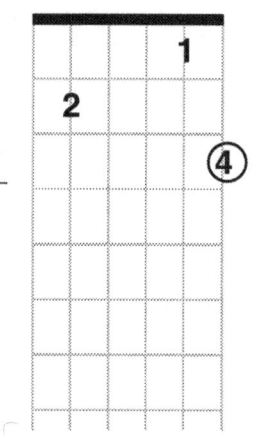 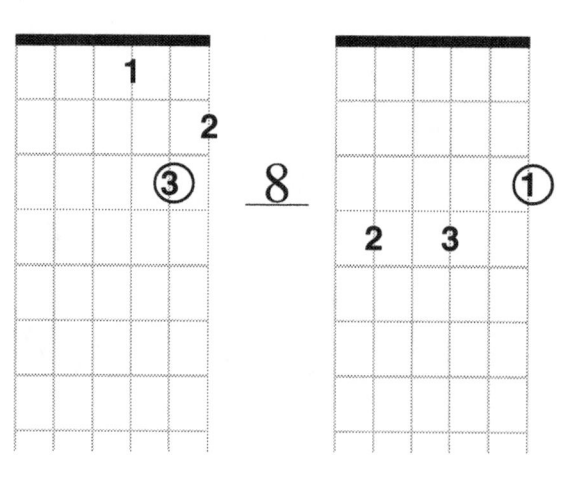

C-M³-P⁴   C-M³-D⁵

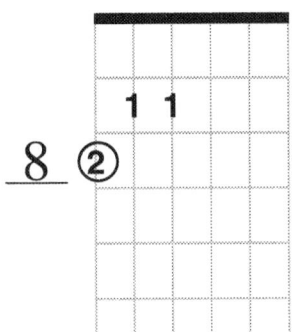 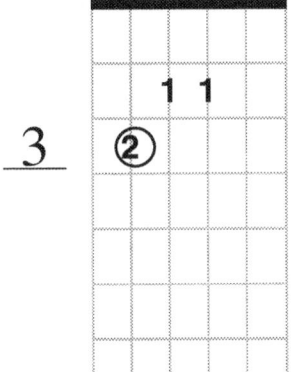 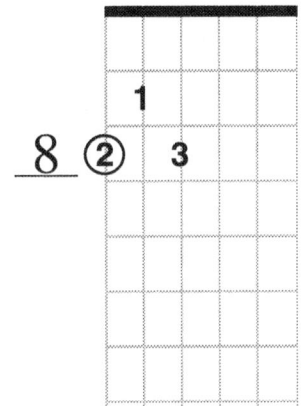 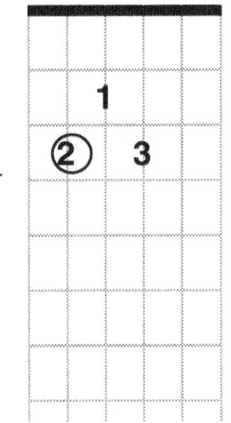

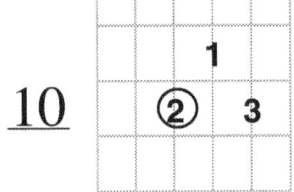 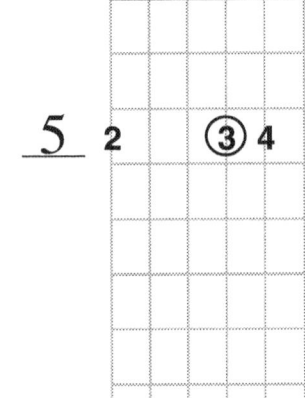 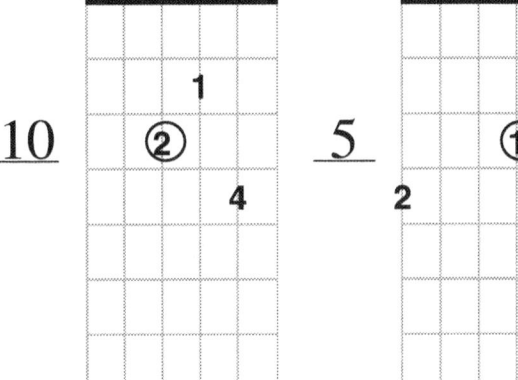

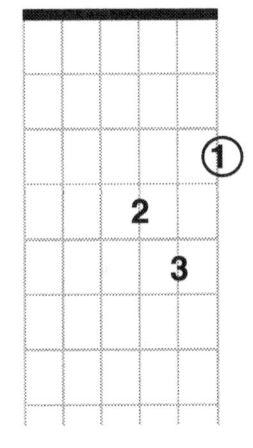 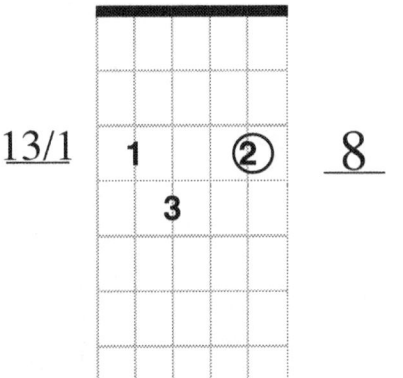 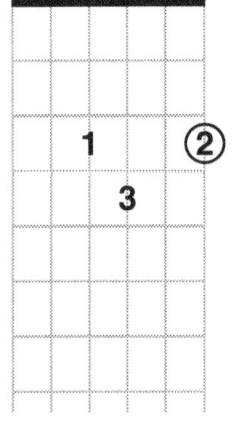

$C-M^3-P^5$ $C-M^3-m^6$

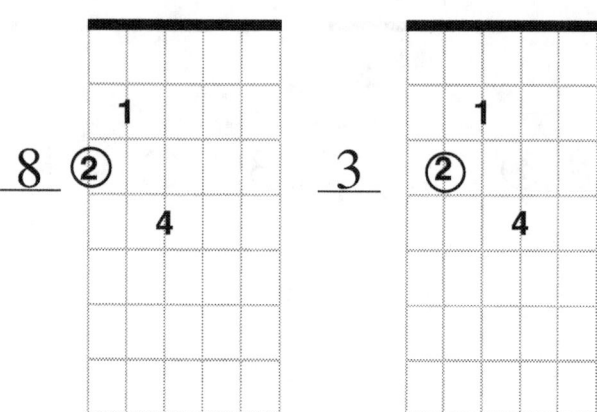
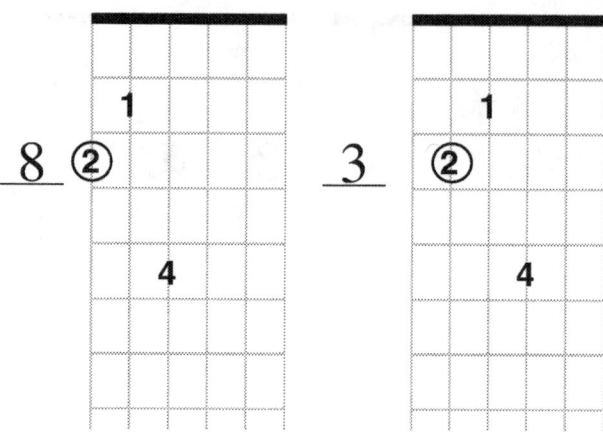
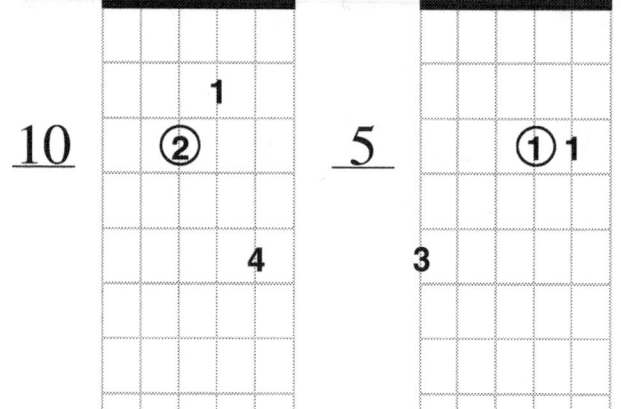
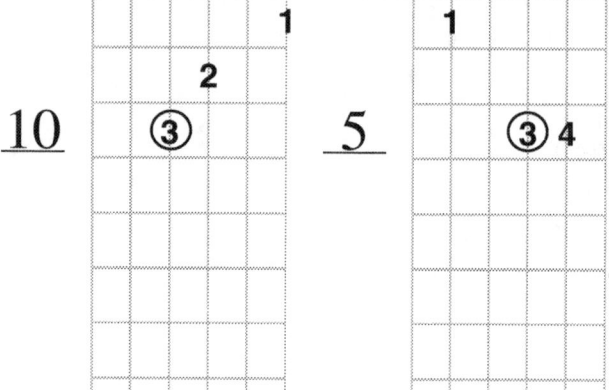
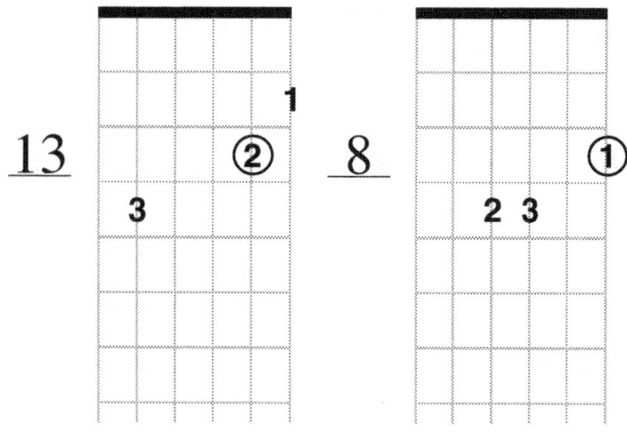
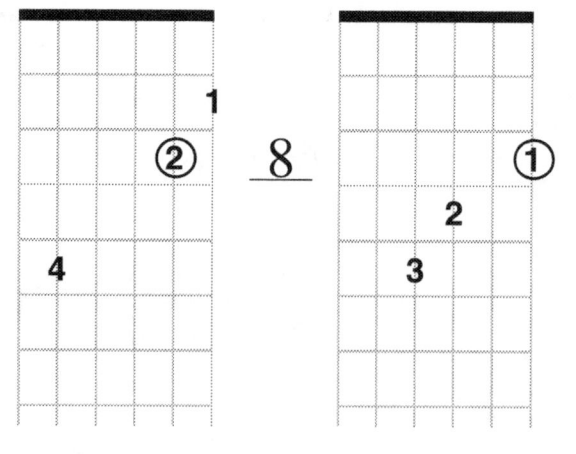

$C-M^3-M^6$ $C-M^3-m^7$

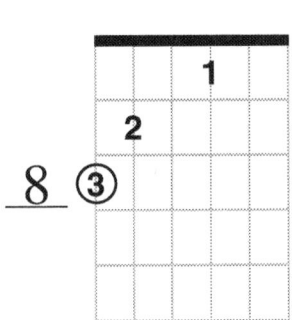
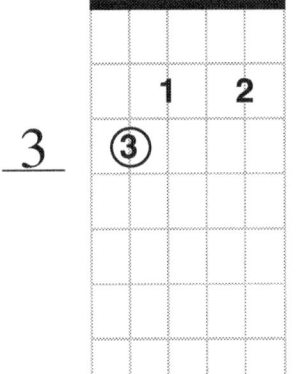
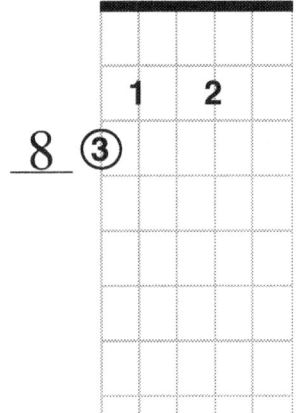
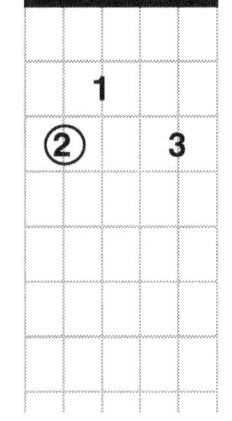
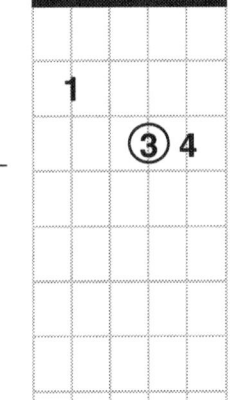
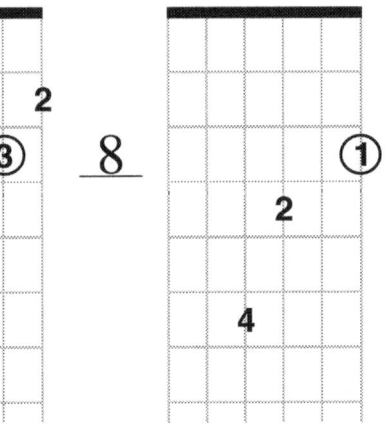
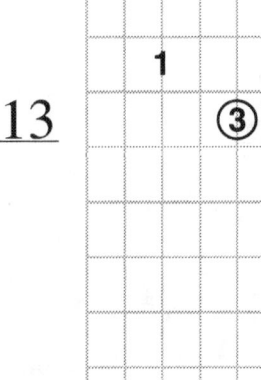
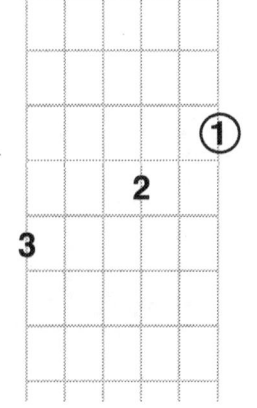

C-M³-M⁷   C-m³-m²

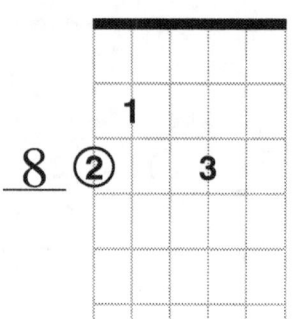
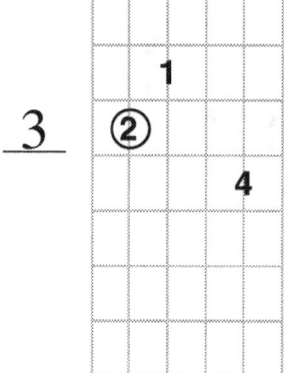
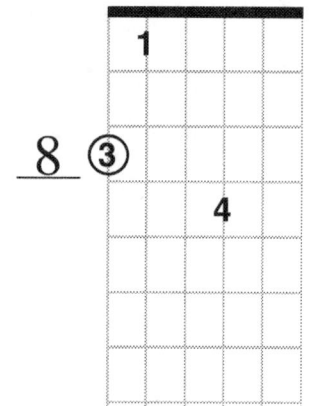
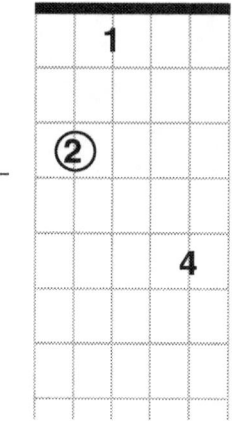
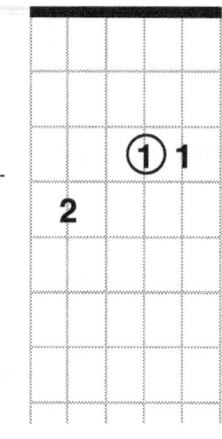
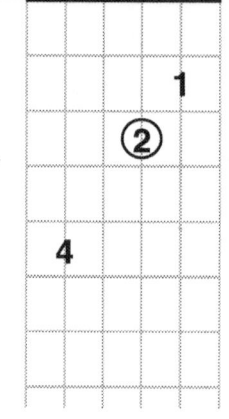
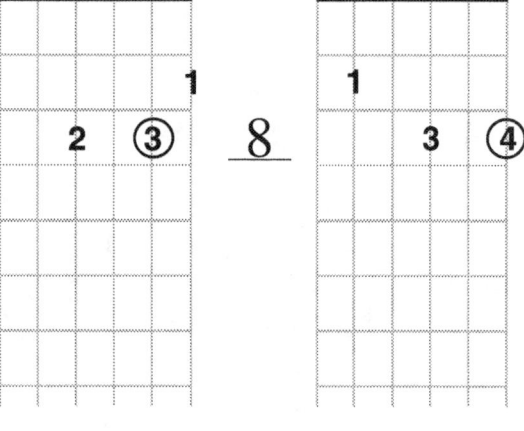
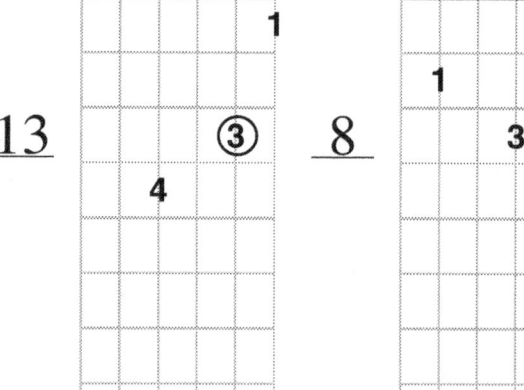

C-m³-M²   C-m³-P⁴

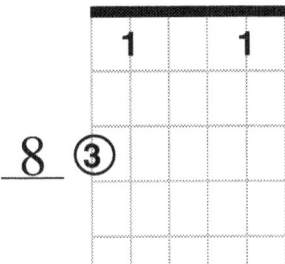
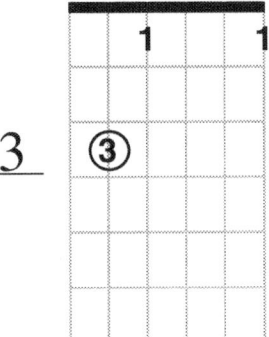
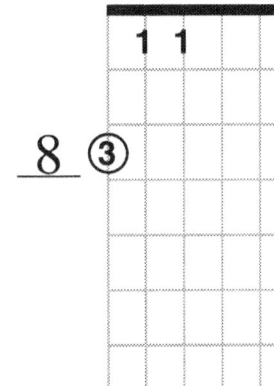
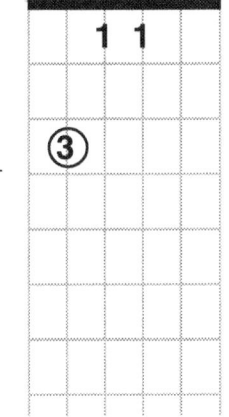
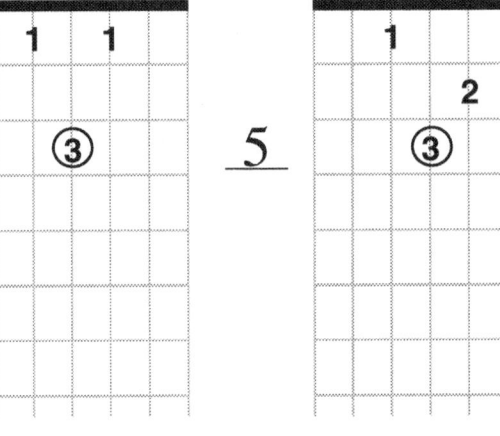

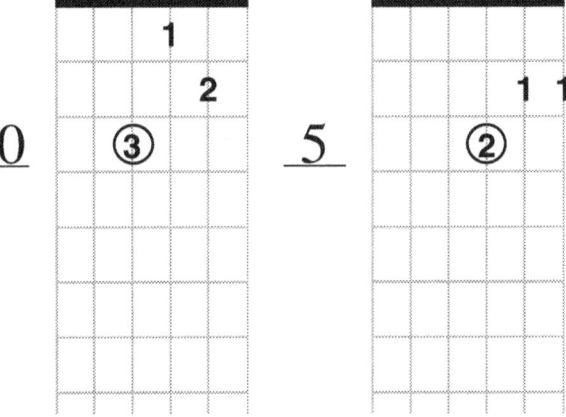
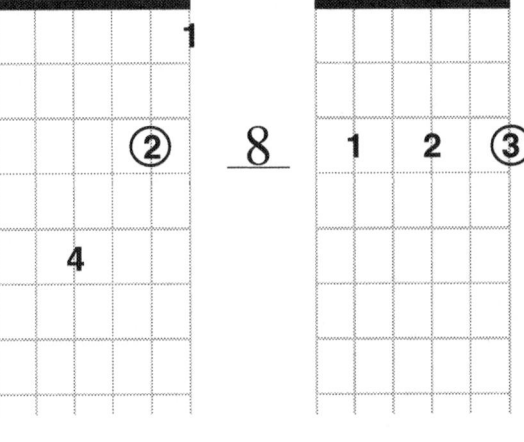
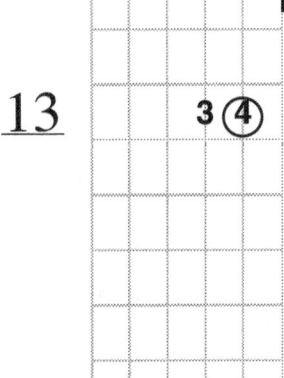
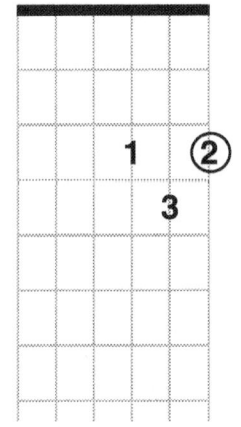

$C\text{-}m^3\text{-}D^5$ $C\text{-}m^3\text{-}P^5$

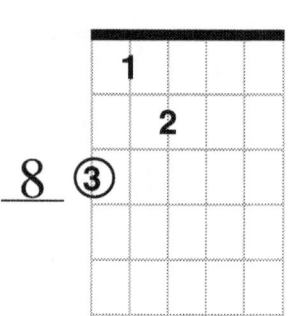
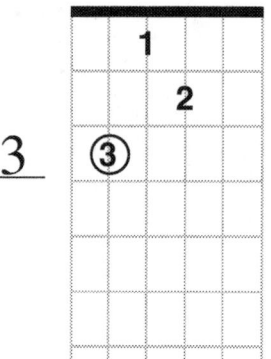
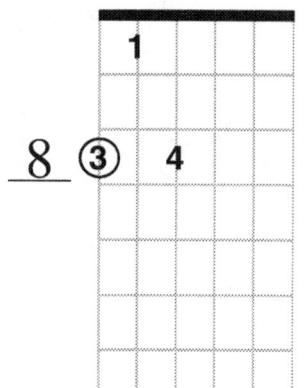
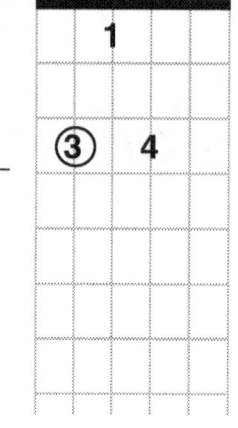

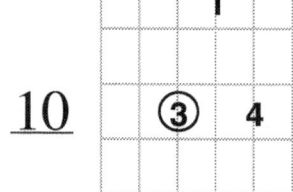
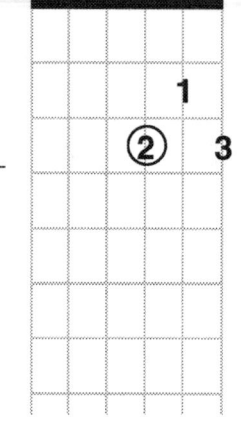
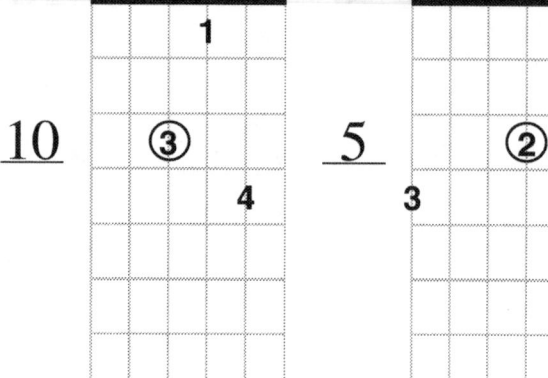

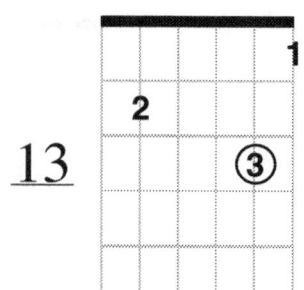
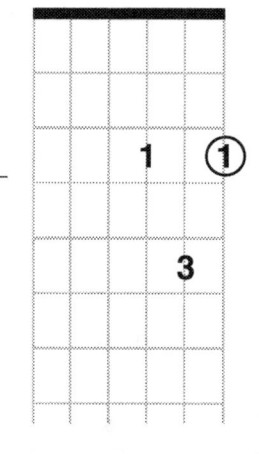
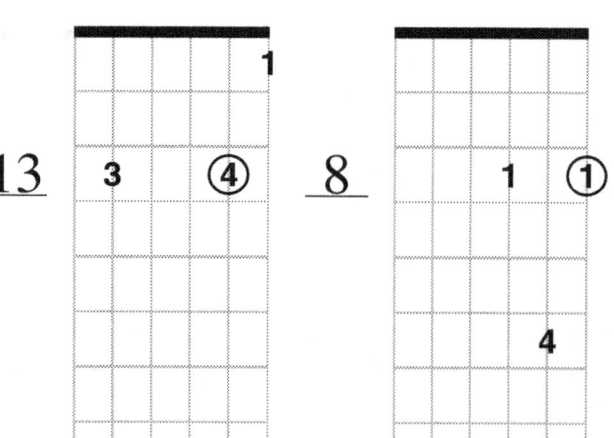

C-m³-m⁶   C-m³-M⁶

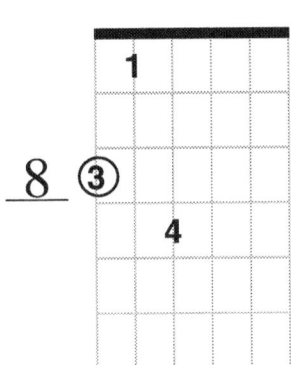 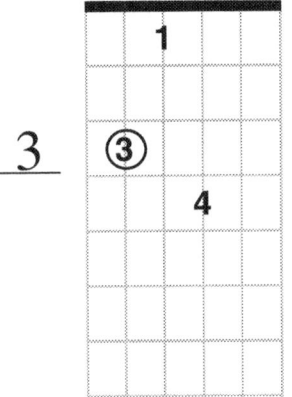 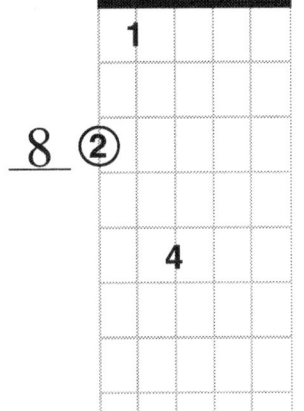 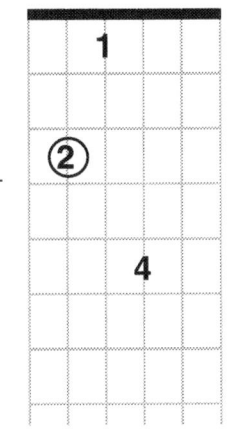

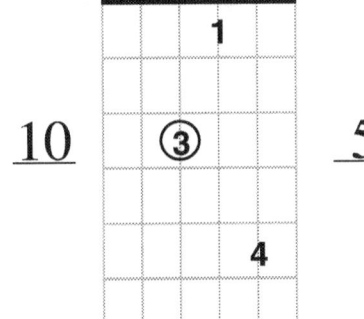 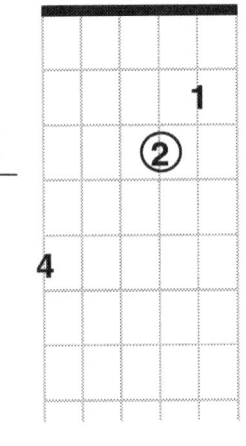 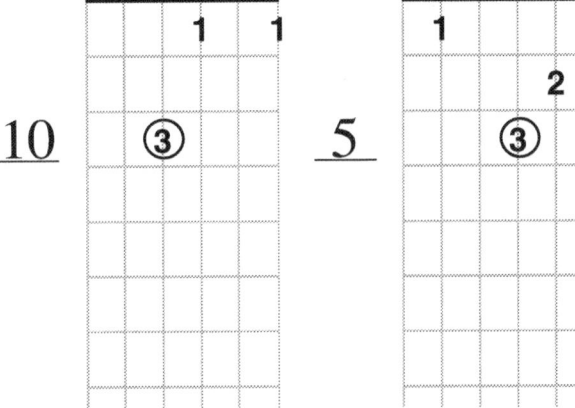

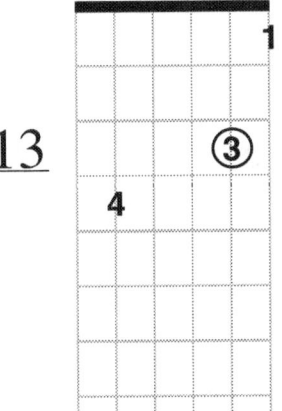 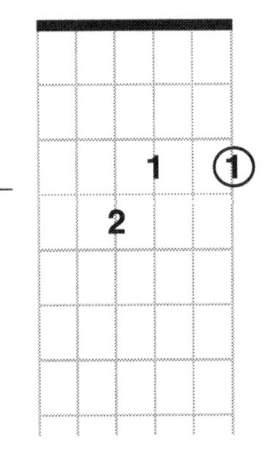 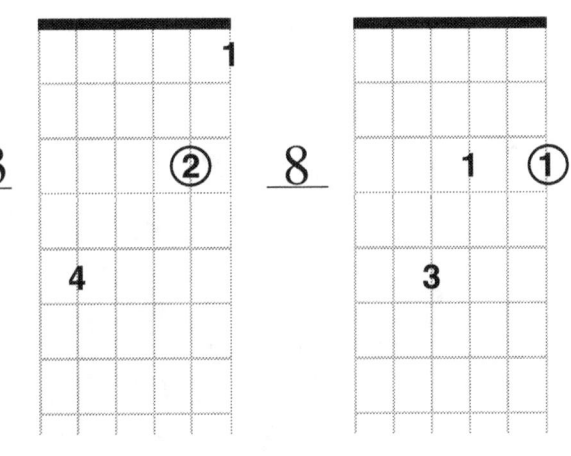

C-m³-m⁷ C-m³-M⁷

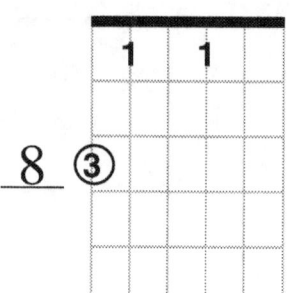
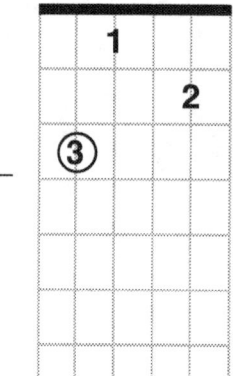
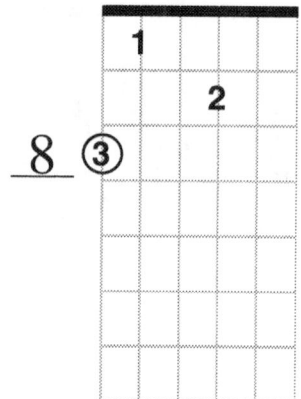
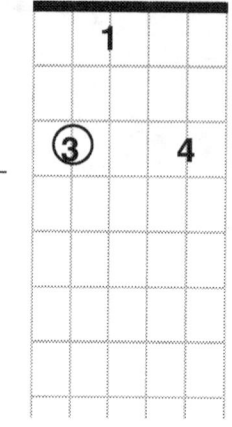
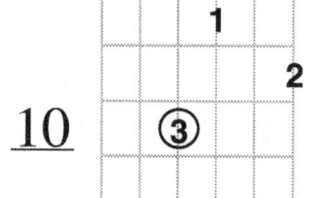
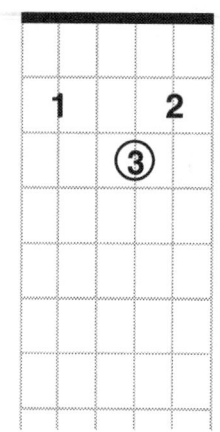
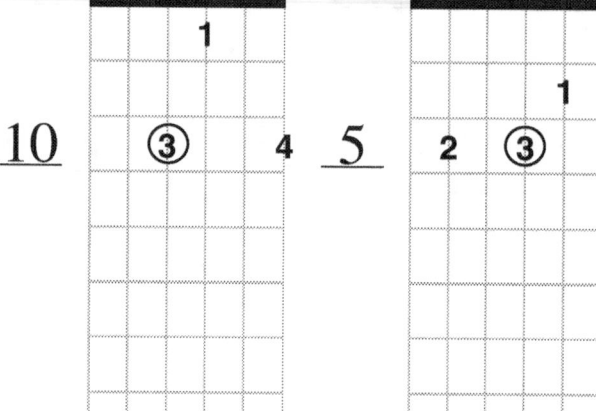
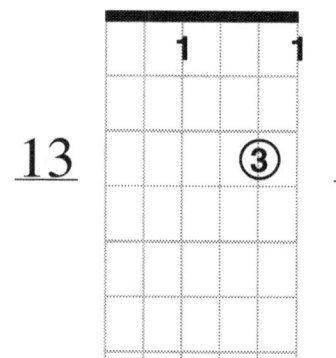
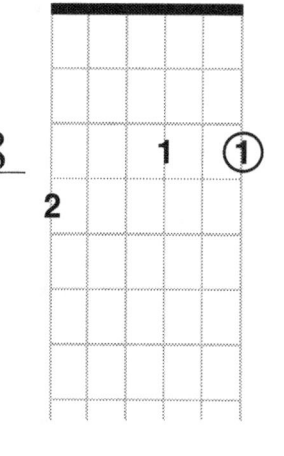
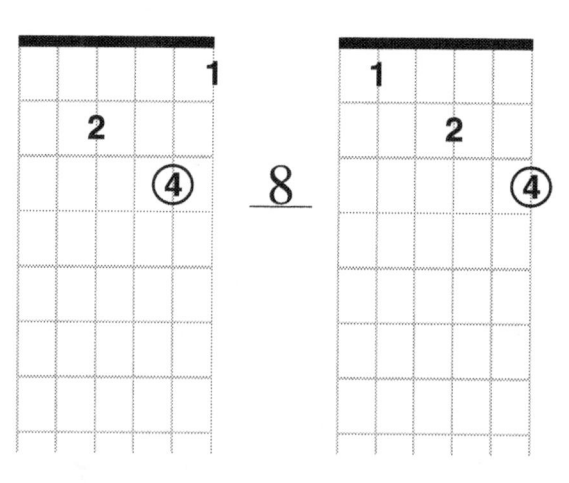

C-P⁴-m²   C-P⁴-M²

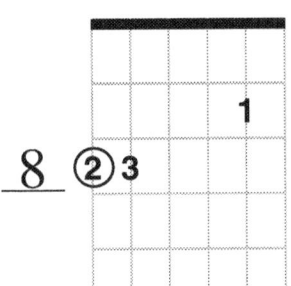
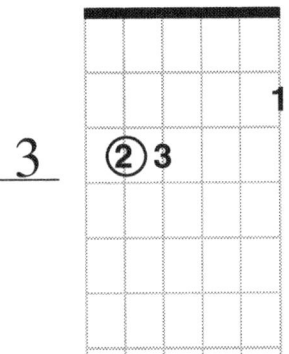
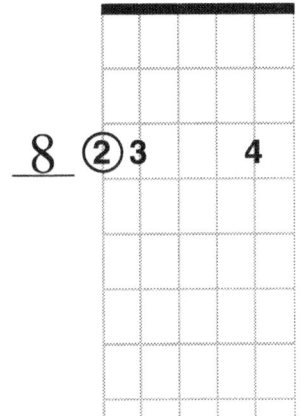
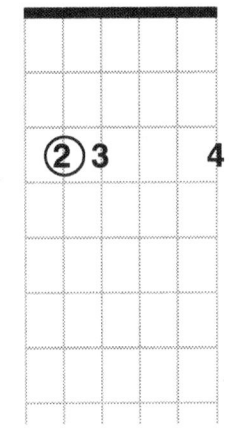

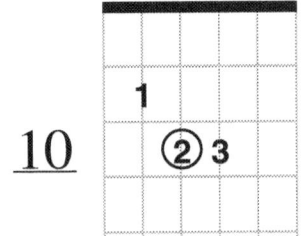
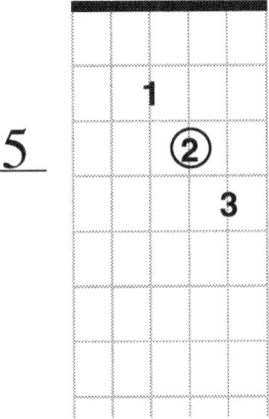
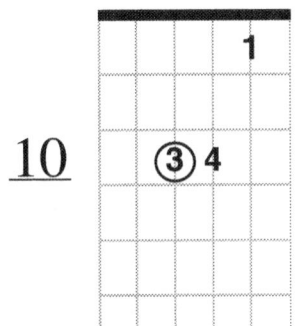
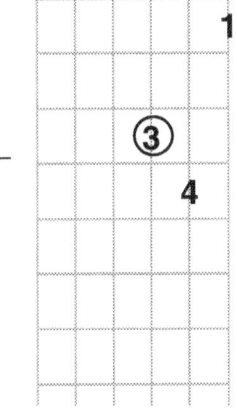

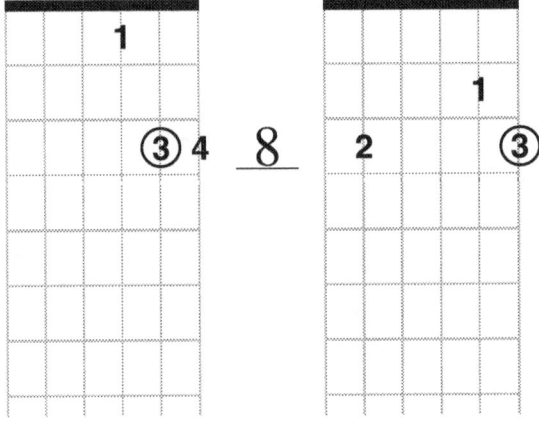
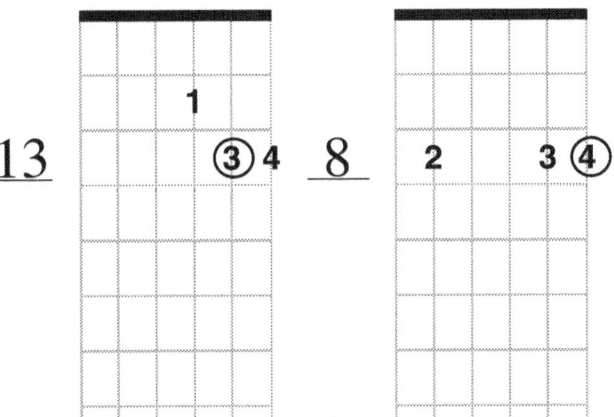

$C\text{-}P^4\text{-}m^3$ | $C\text{-}P^4\text{-}M^3$

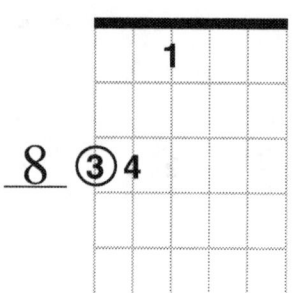
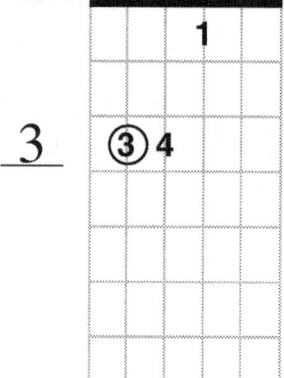
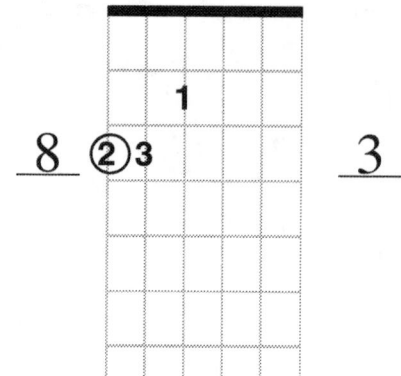
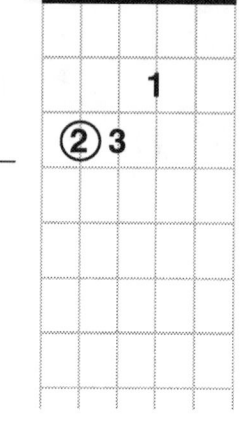

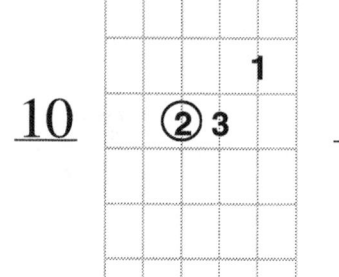
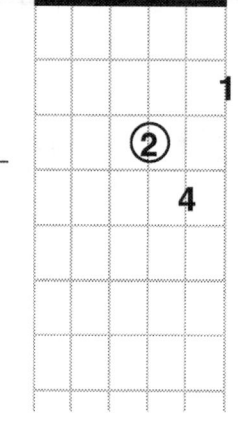
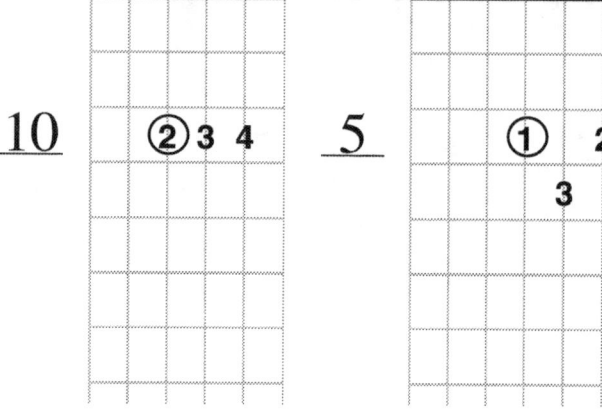

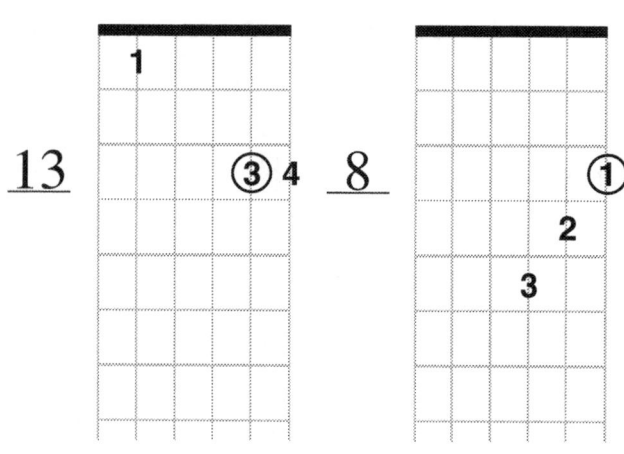
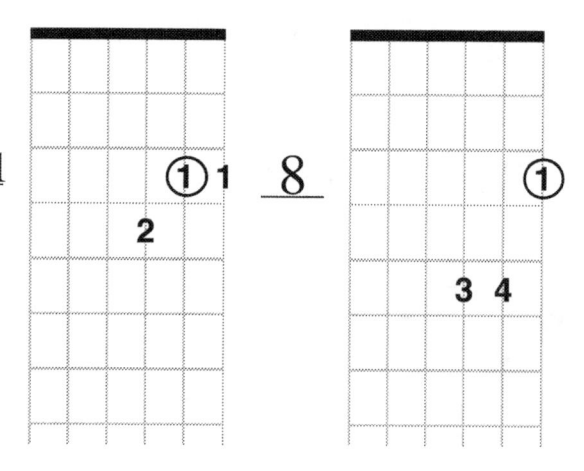

$C-P^4-D^5$ $C-P^4-P^5$

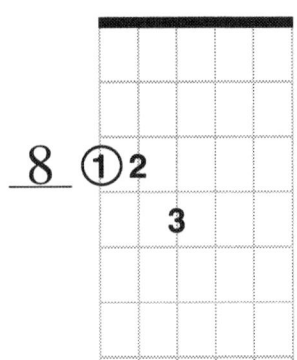 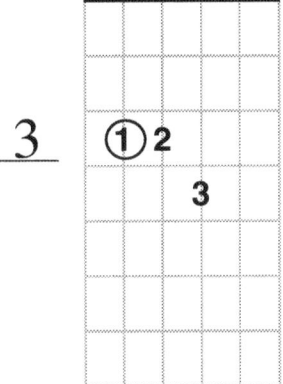   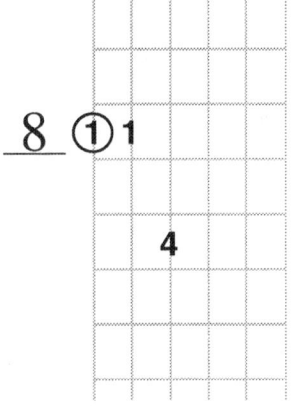 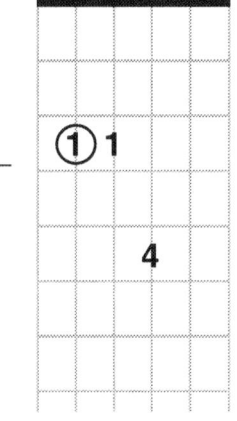

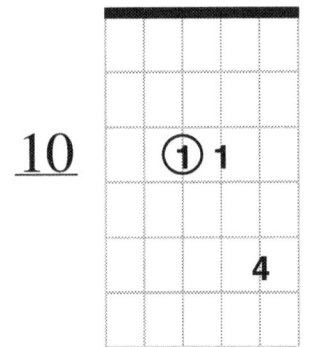 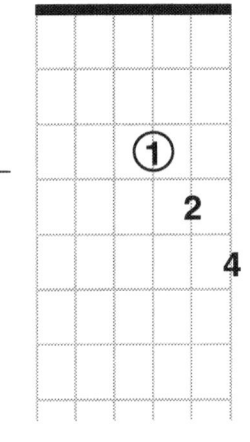   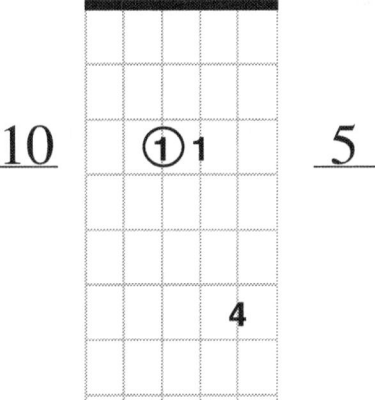 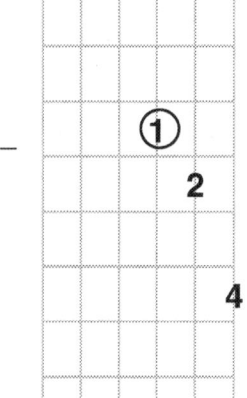

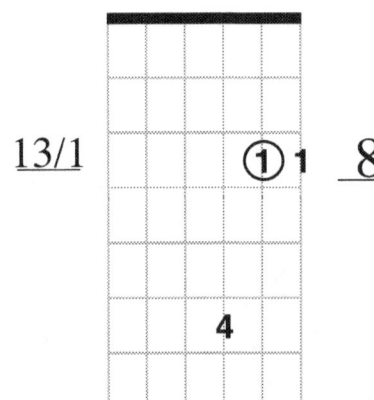 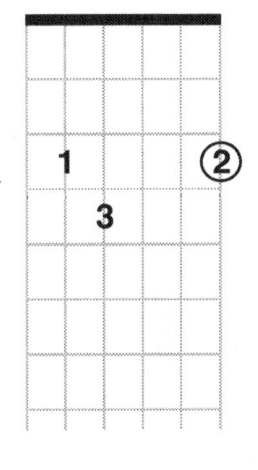   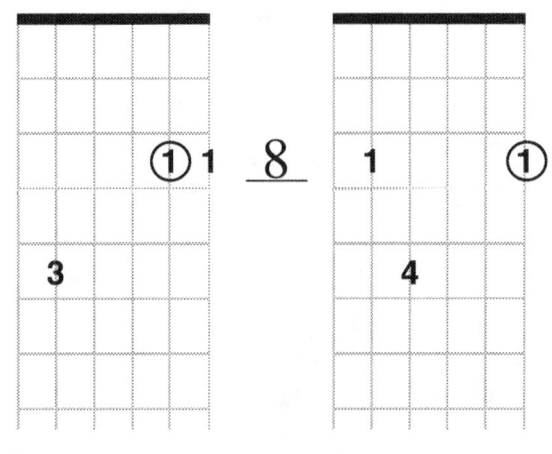

C-P⁴-m⁶   C-P⁴-M⁶

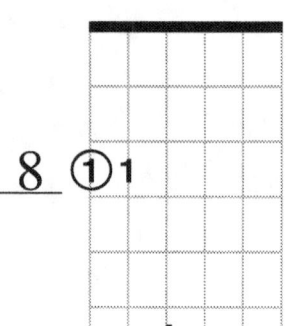 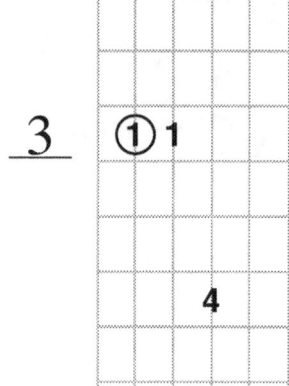 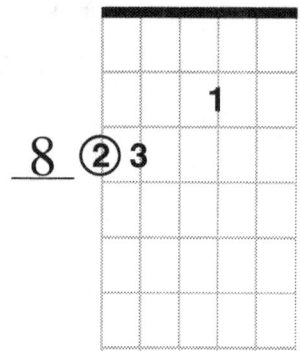 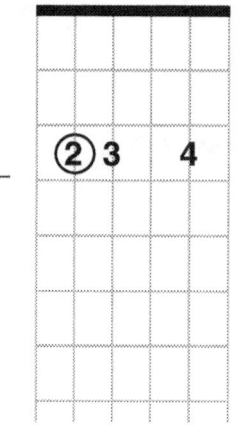

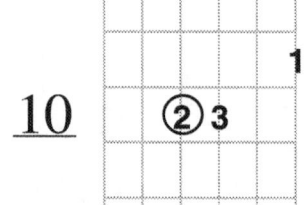 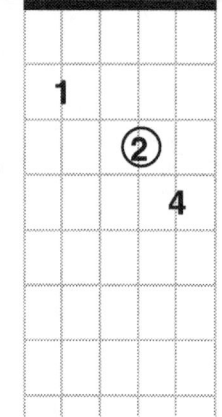 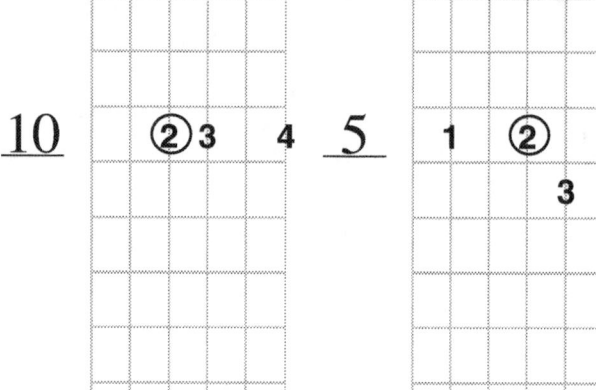

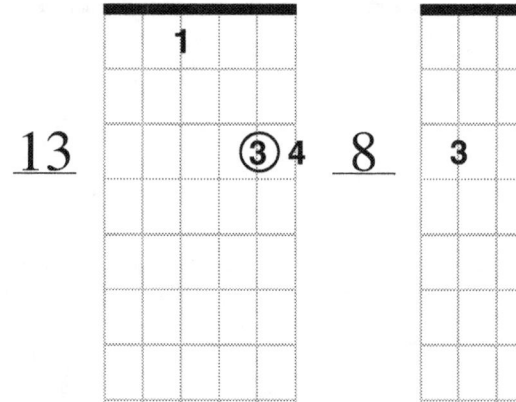 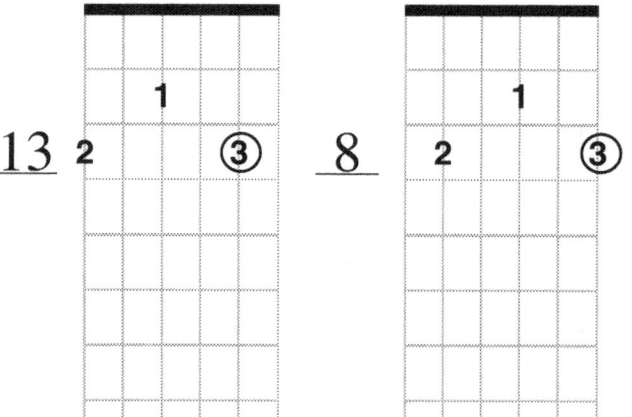

C-P^4-m^7 | C-P^4-M^7

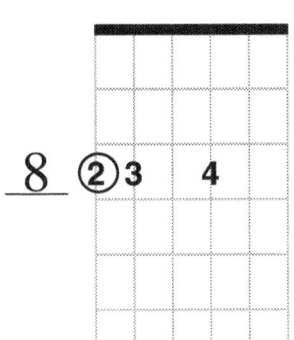 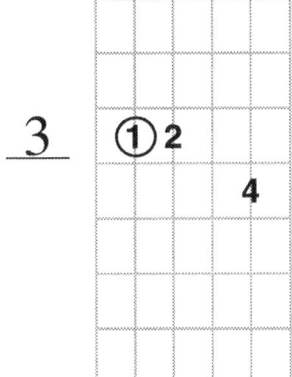 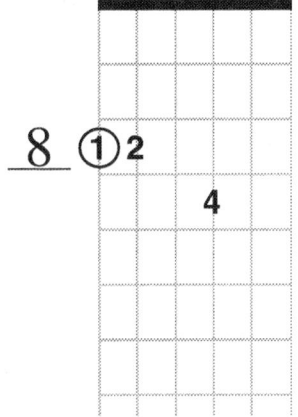 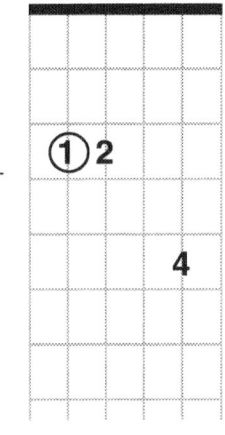

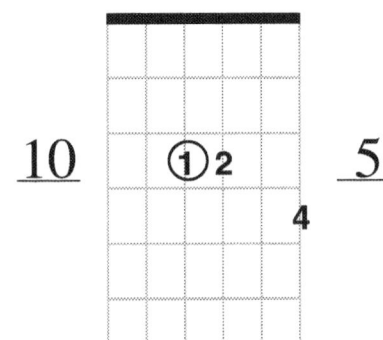 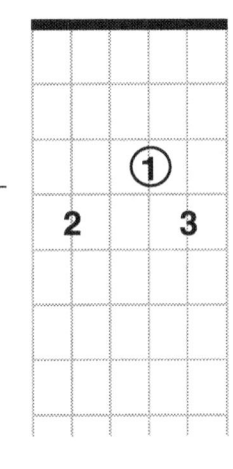 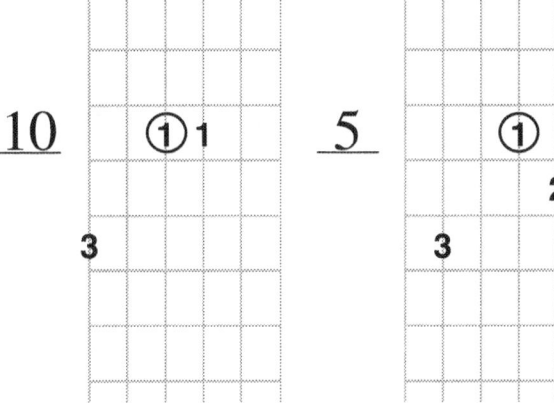

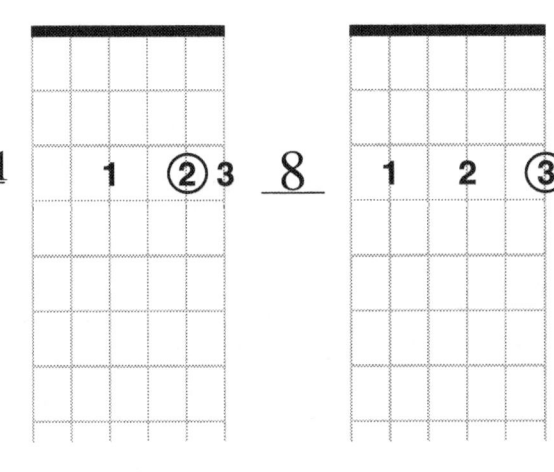 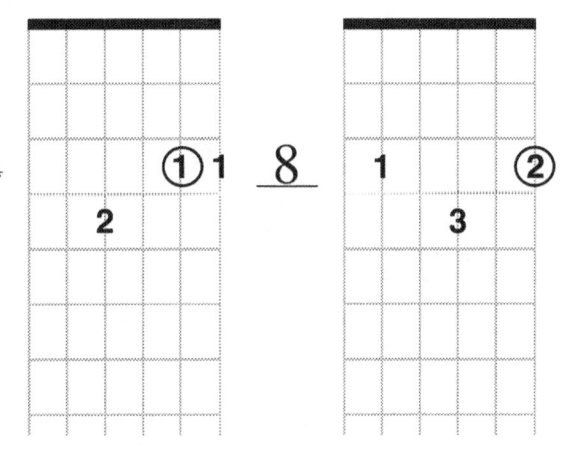

C-P⁵-m²   C-P⁵-M²

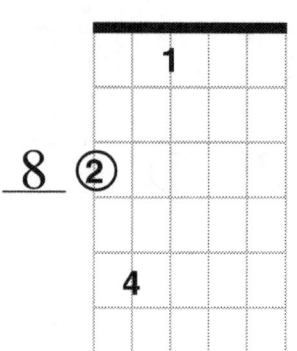
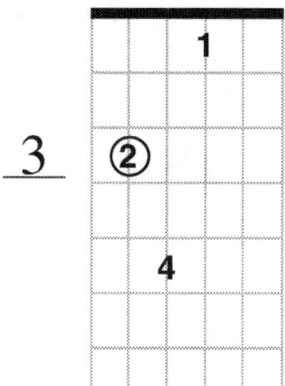
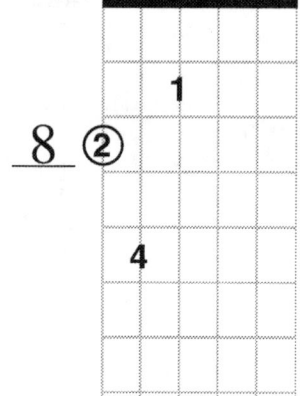
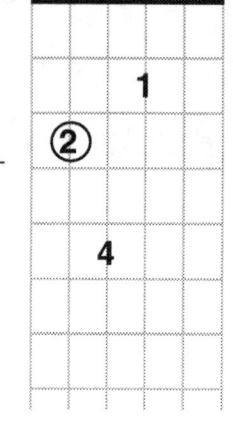

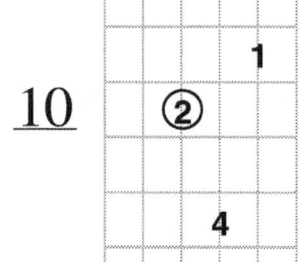
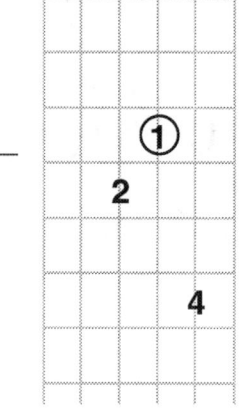
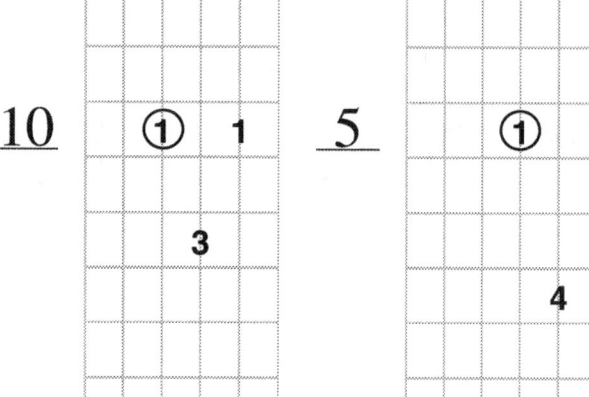

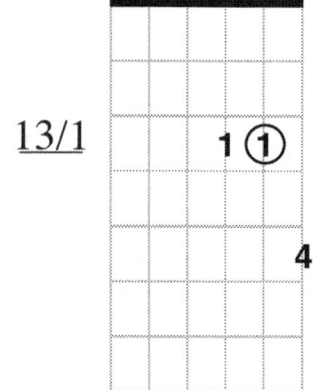
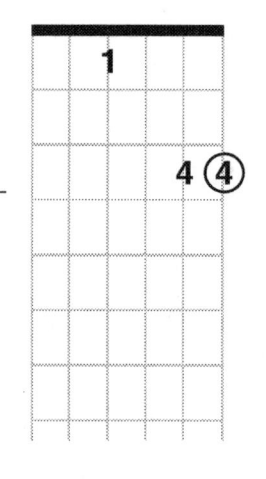
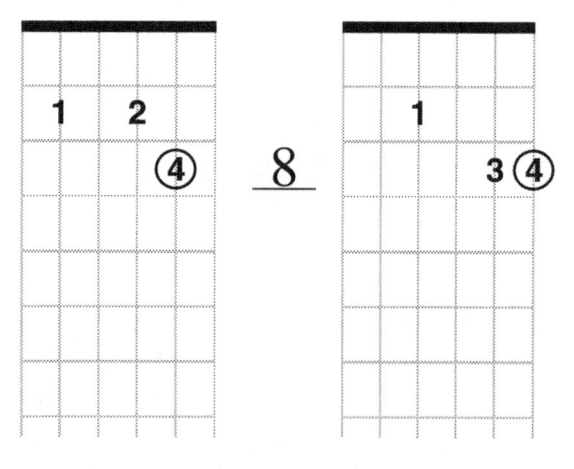

$C-P^5-m^3$ $C-P^5-M^3$

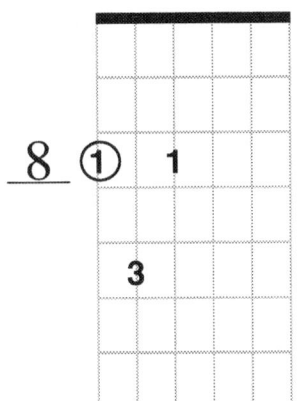
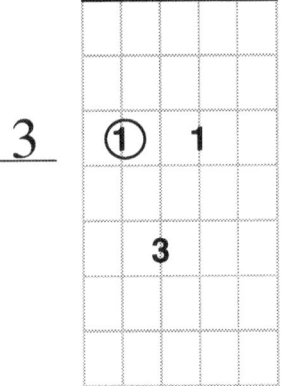
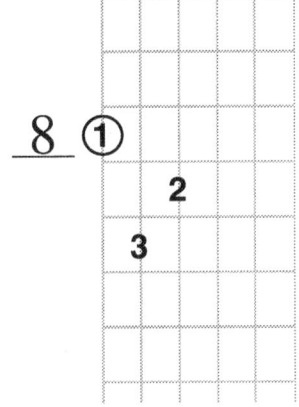
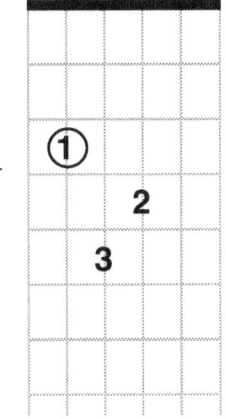

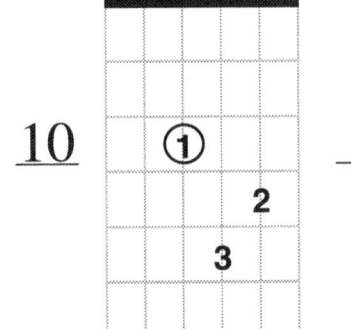
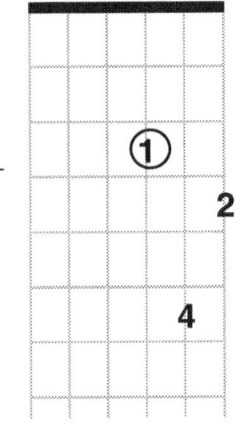
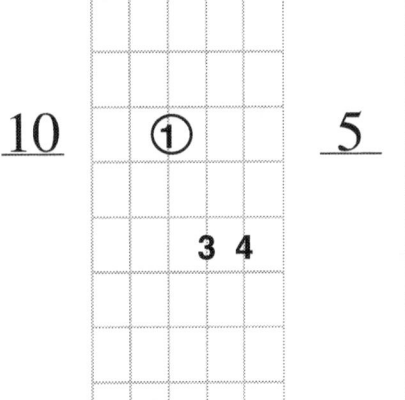
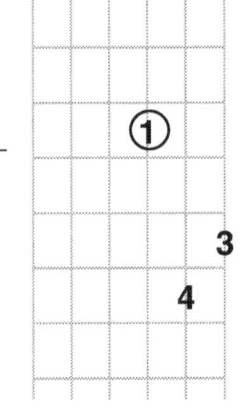

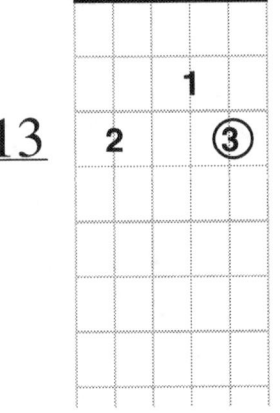
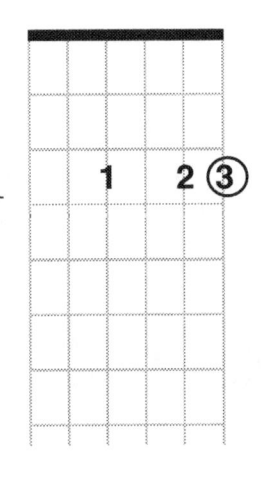
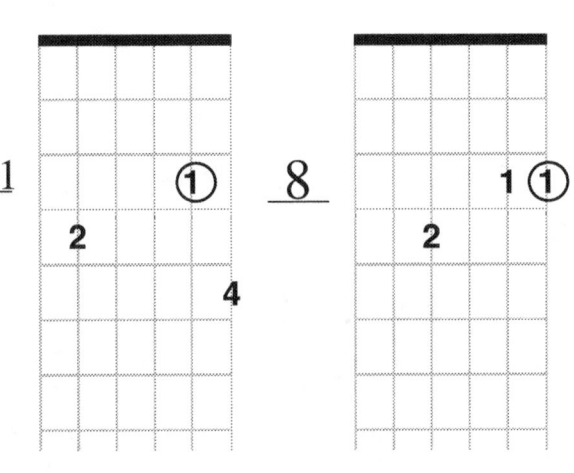

$C\text{-}P^5\text{-}P^4$ $C\text{-}P^5\text{-}m^6$

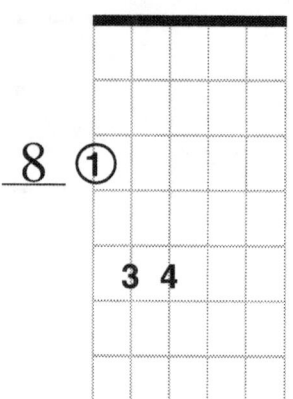
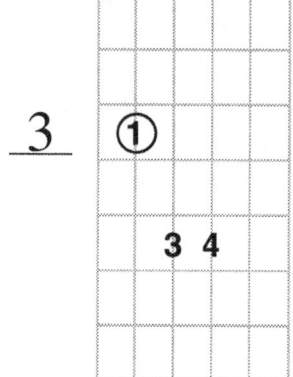
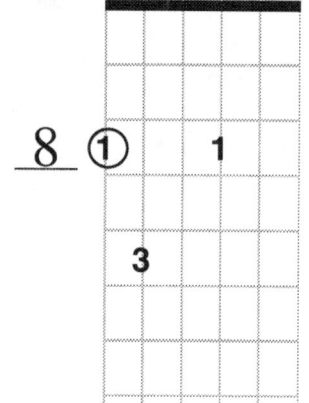
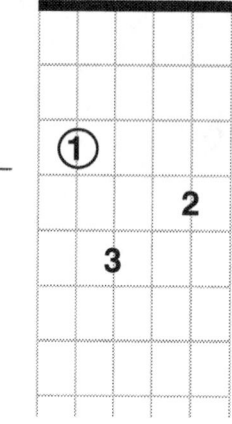
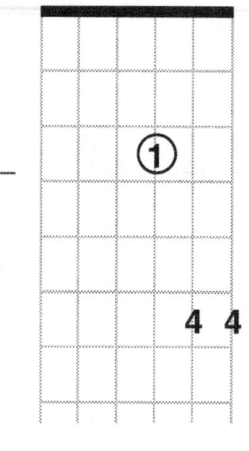
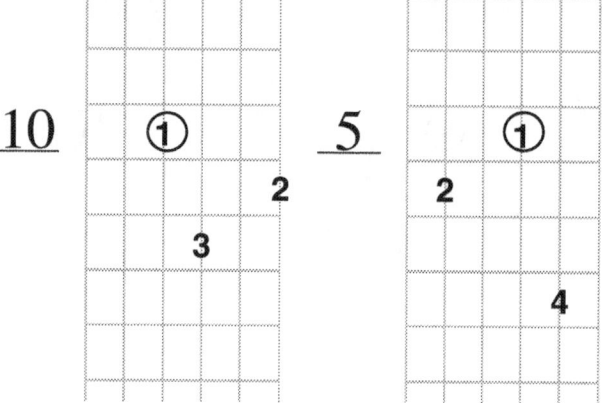
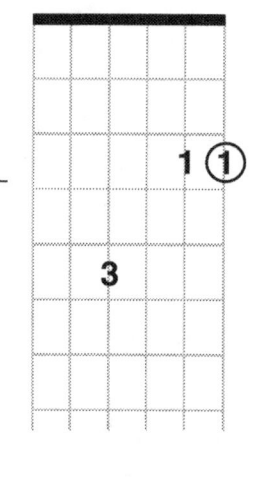
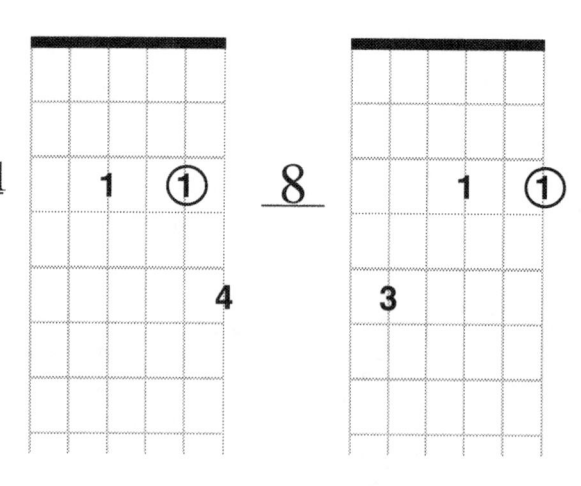

C-P^5-M^6 C-P^5-m^7

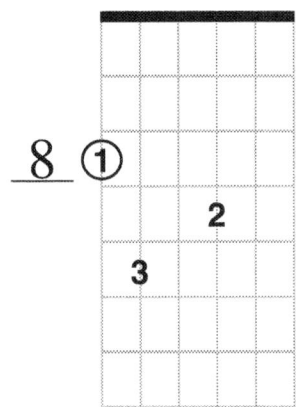
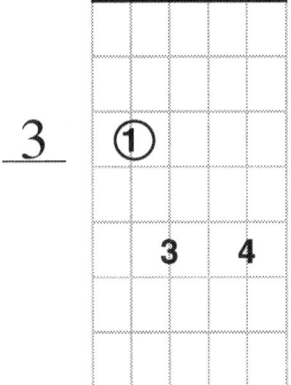
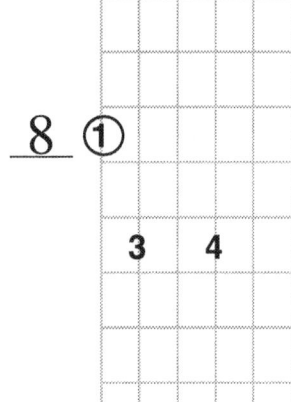
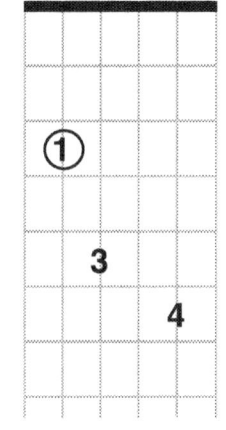

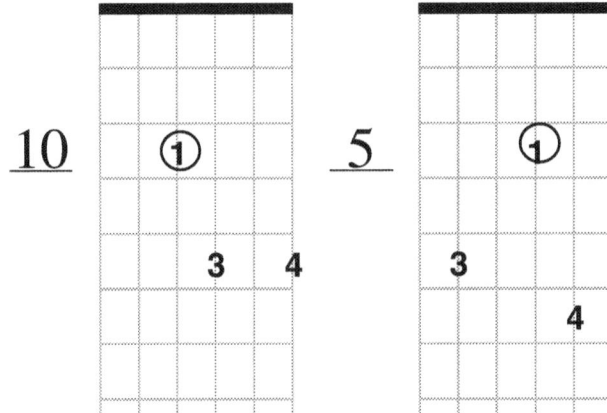
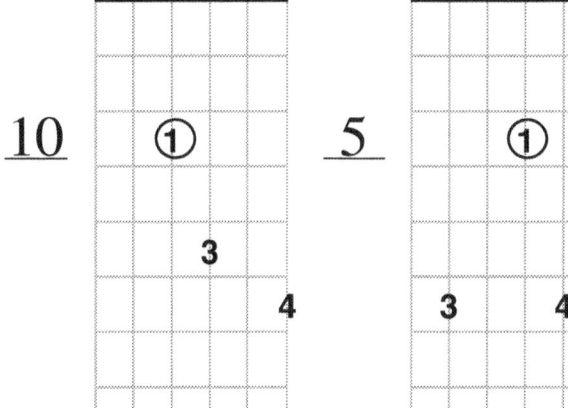

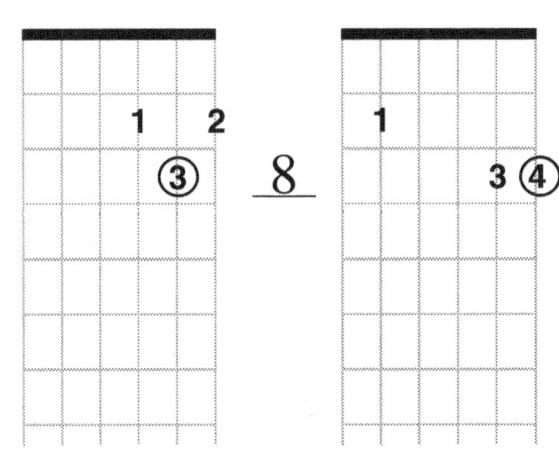
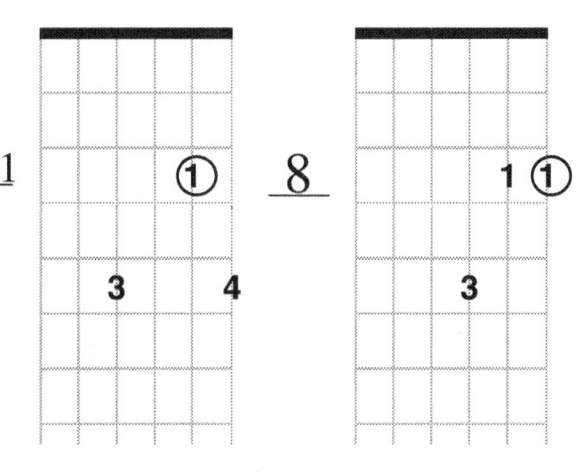

C-P^5-M^7 C-D^5-m^2

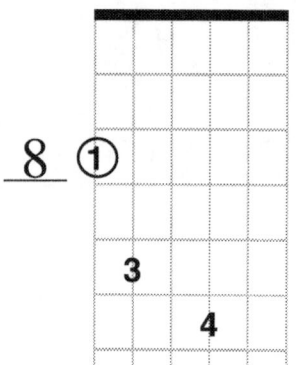
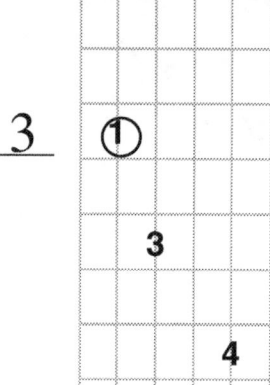
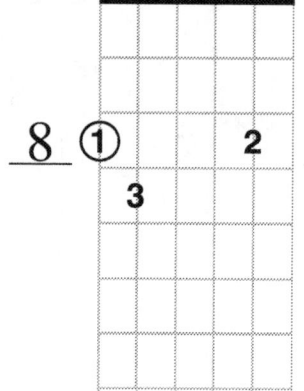
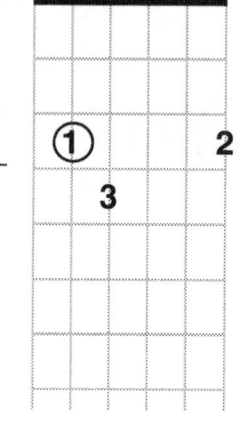

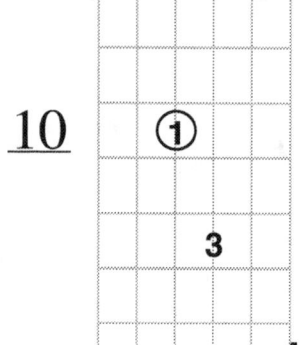
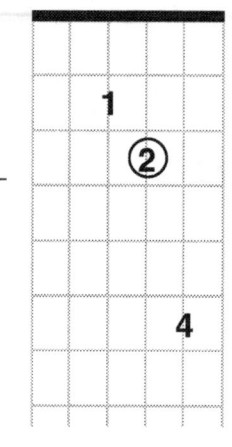
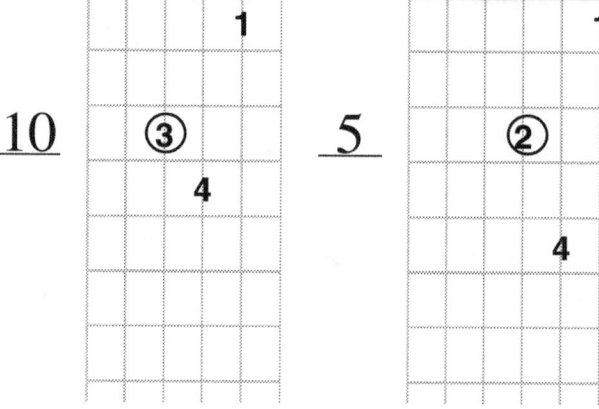

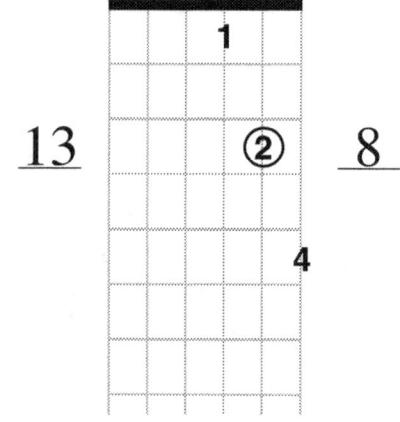
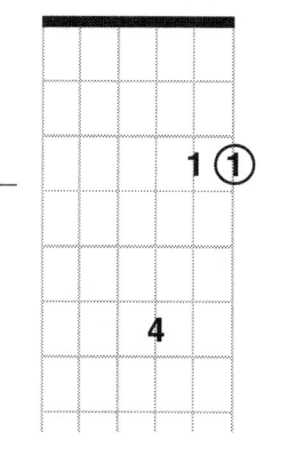
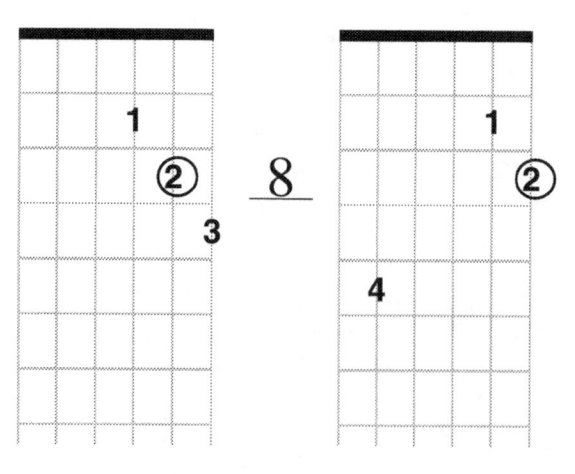

C-D^5-M^2 C-D^5-m^3

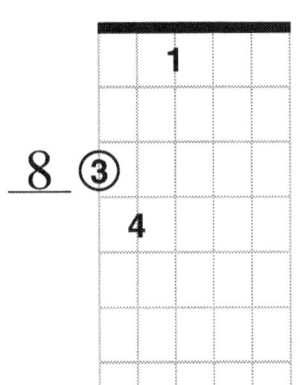
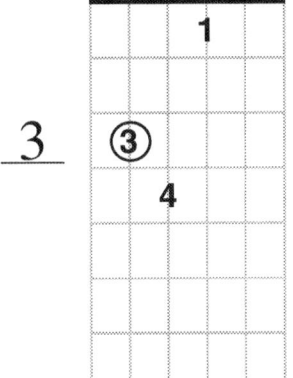
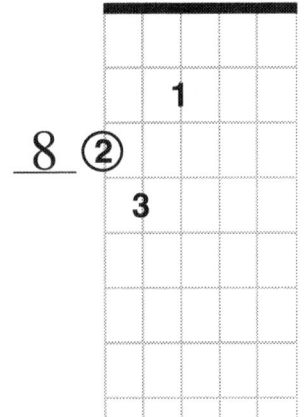
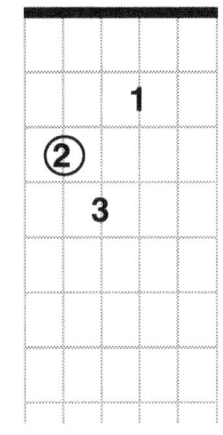
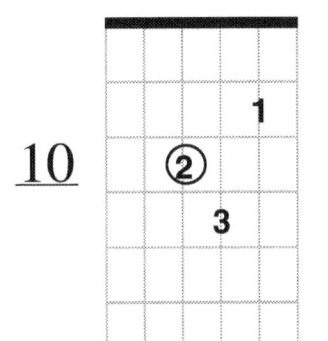
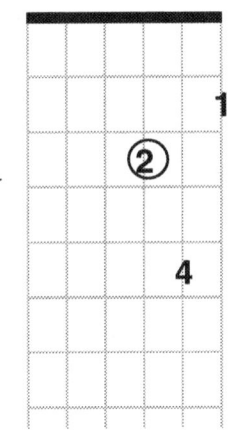
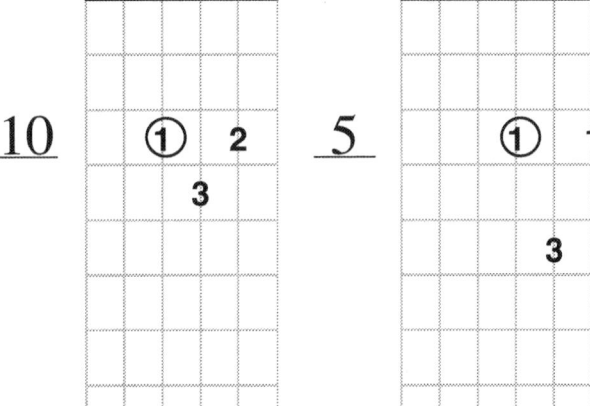
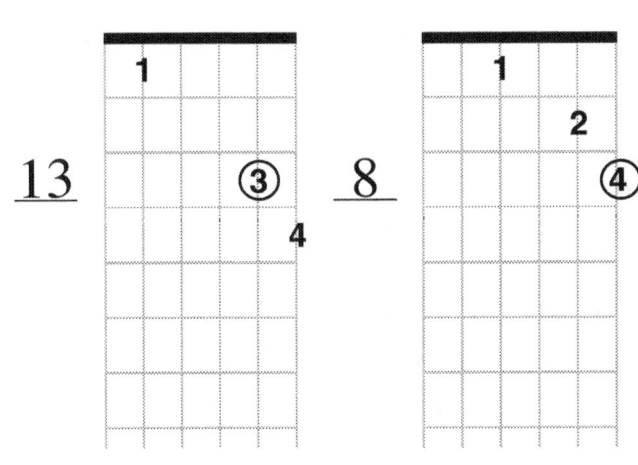
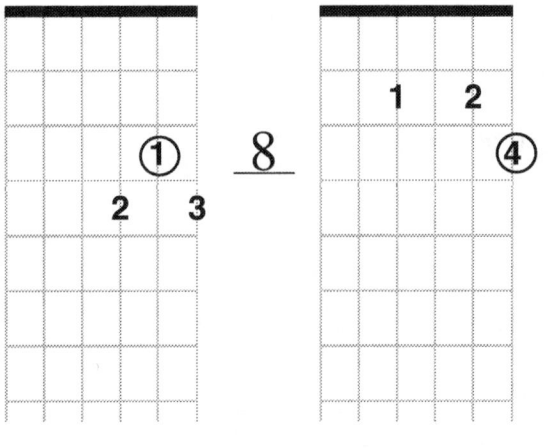

C-D⁵-M³   C-D⁵-P⁴

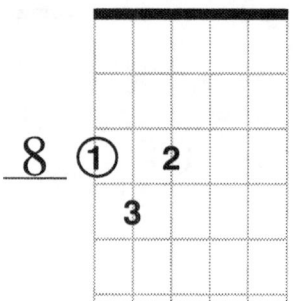
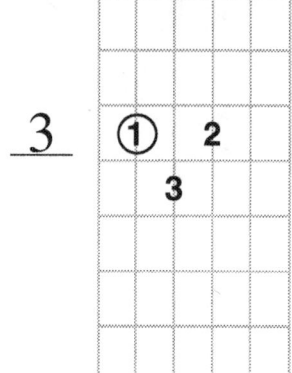
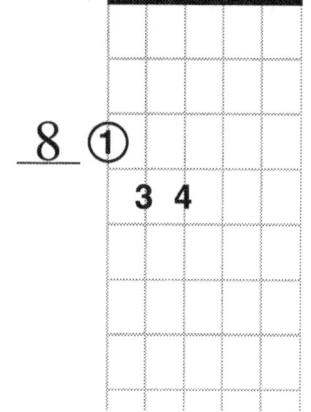
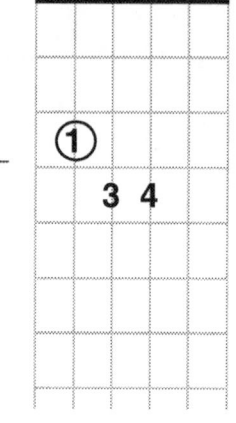
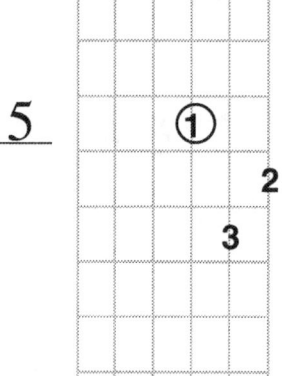
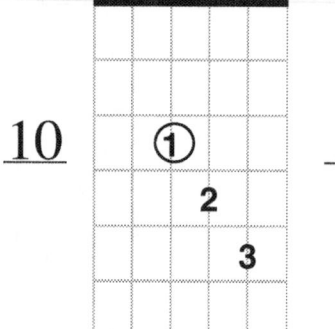
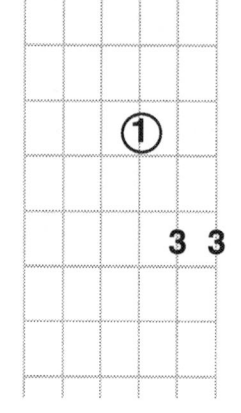
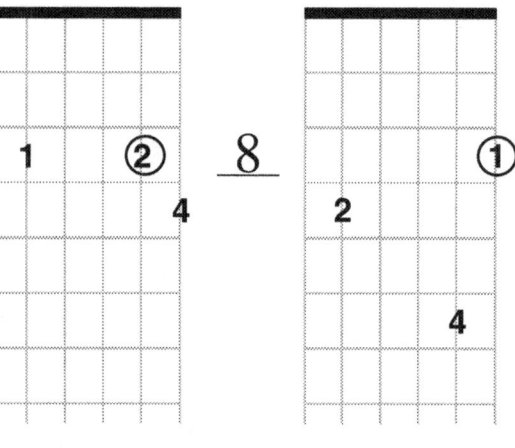
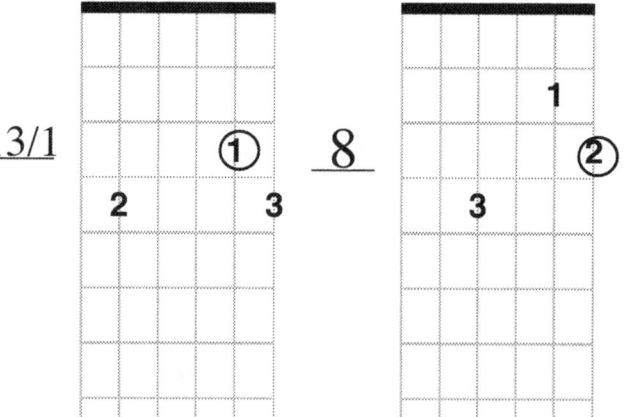

C-D^5-m^6 C-D^5-M^6

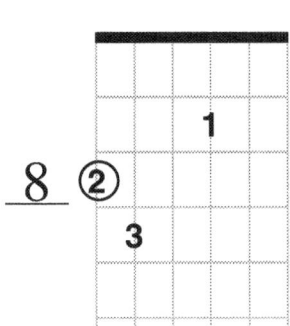 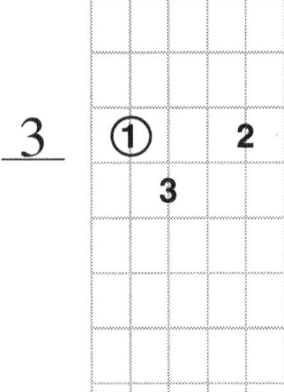 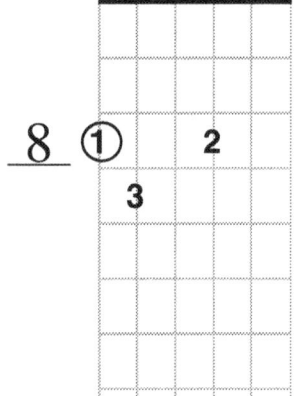 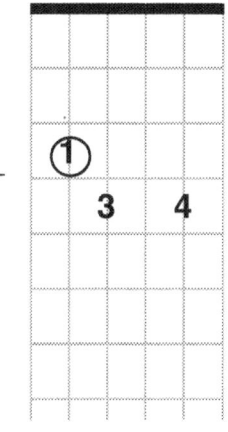

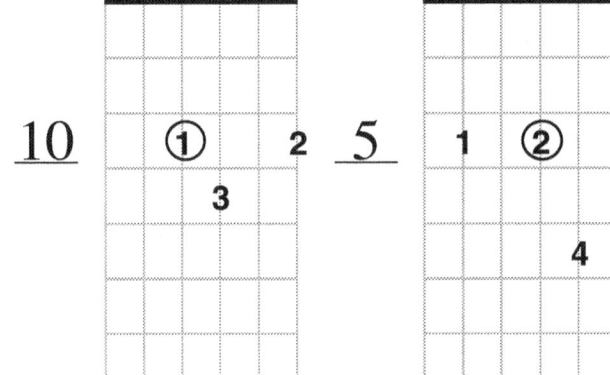 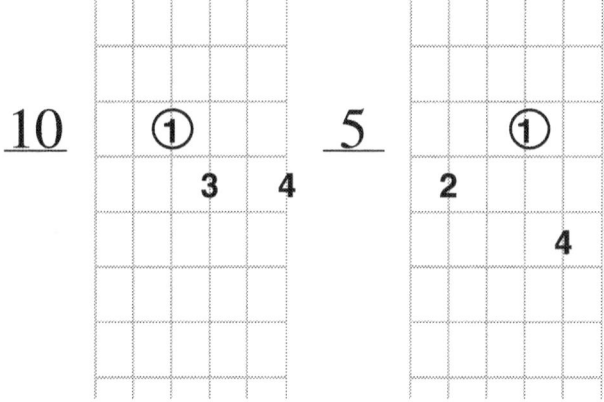

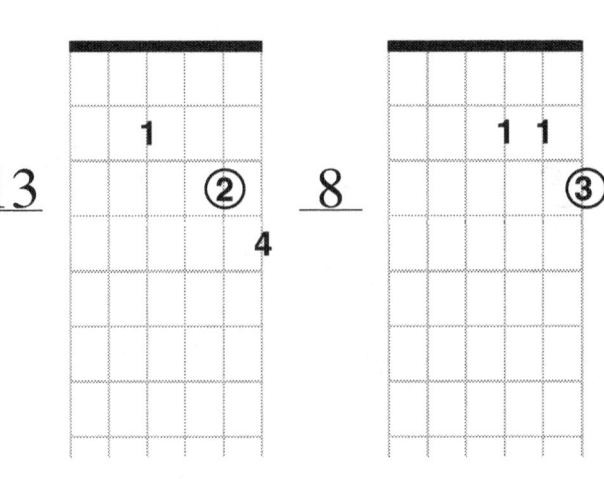 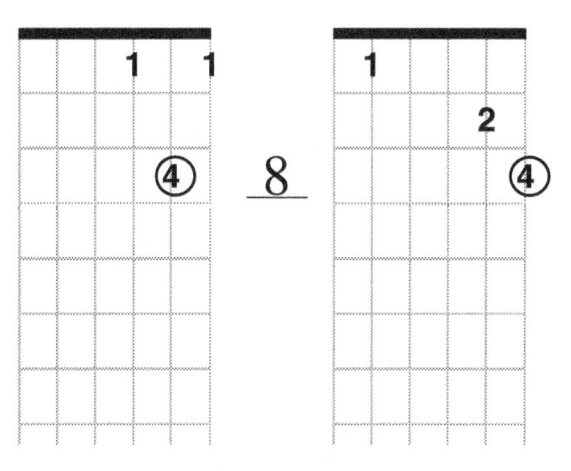

C-D^5-m^7 C-D^5-M^7

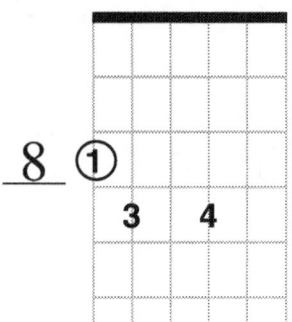
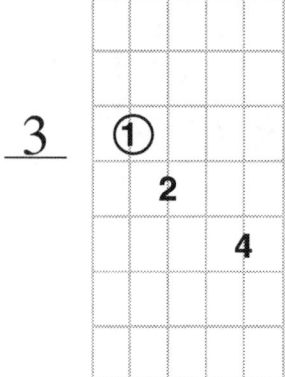
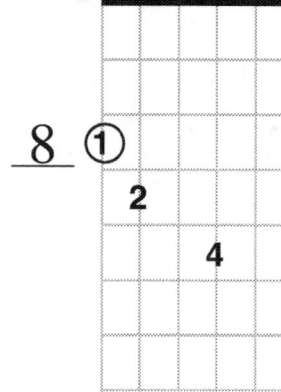
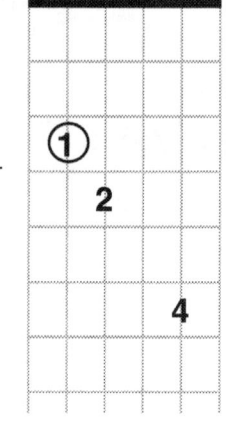

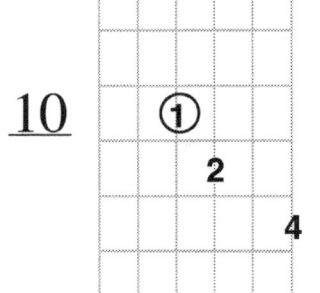
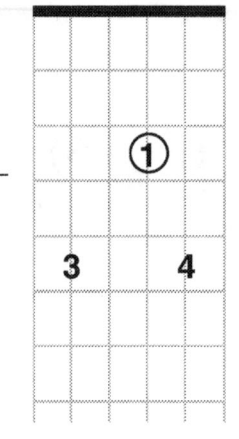
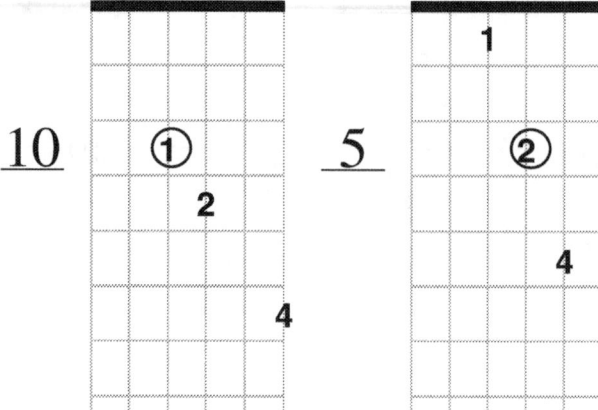

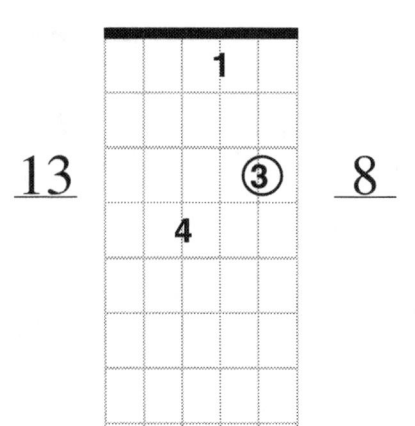
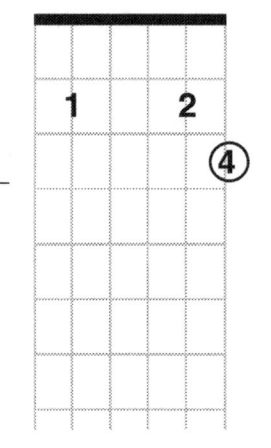
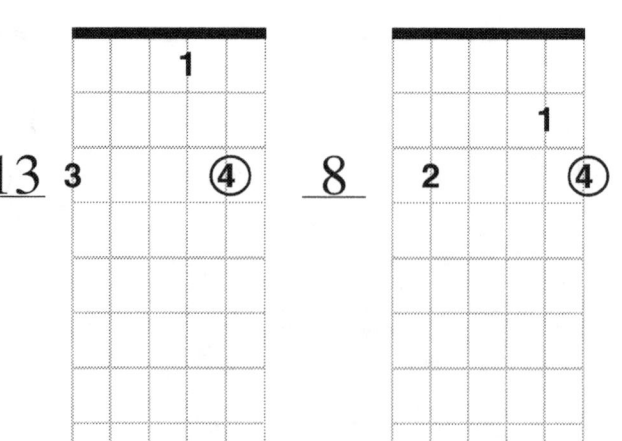

C-M⁶-m²   C-M⁶-M²

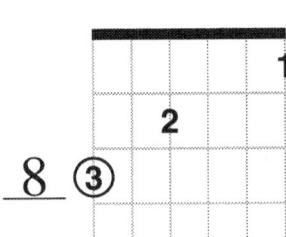
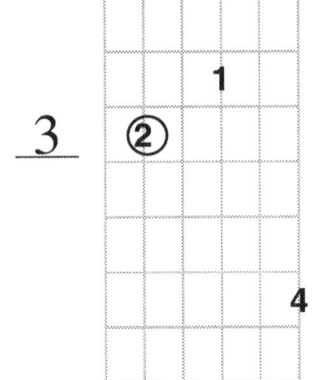
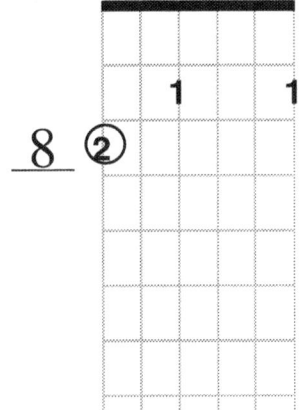
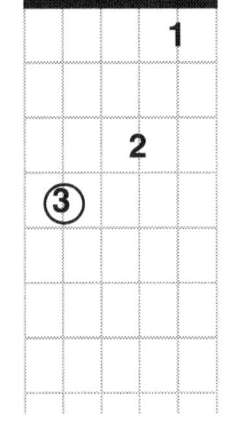

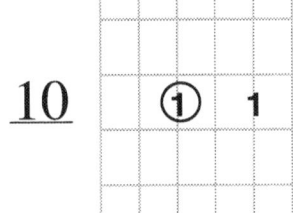
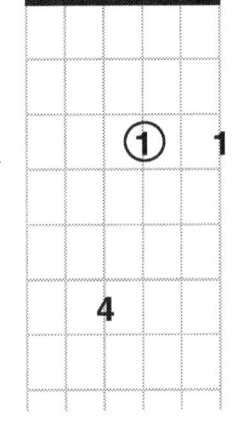
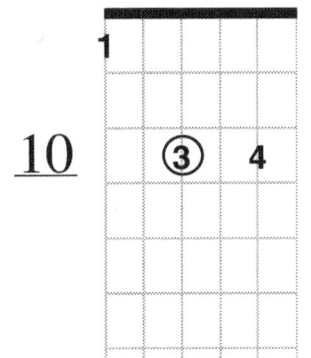
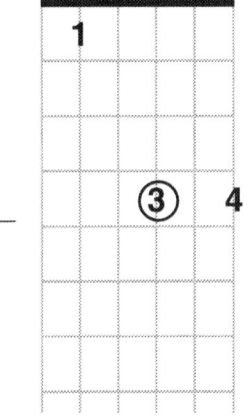

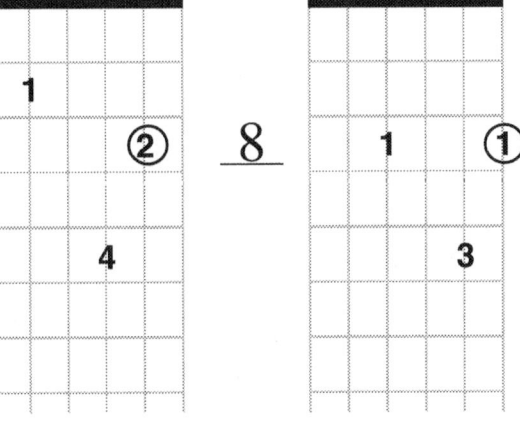
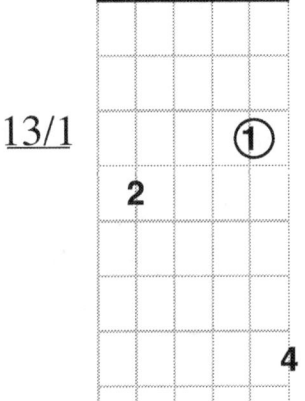
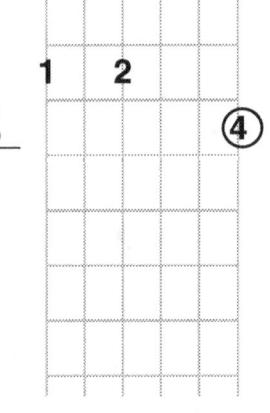

C-M⁶-m³   C-M⁶-M³

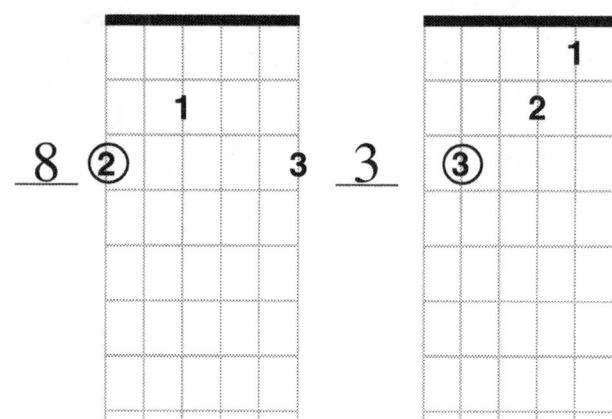
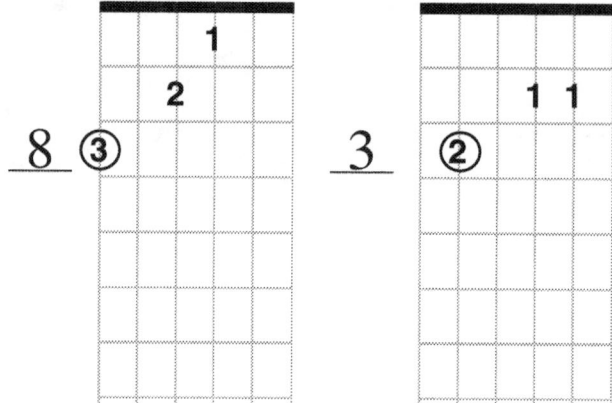
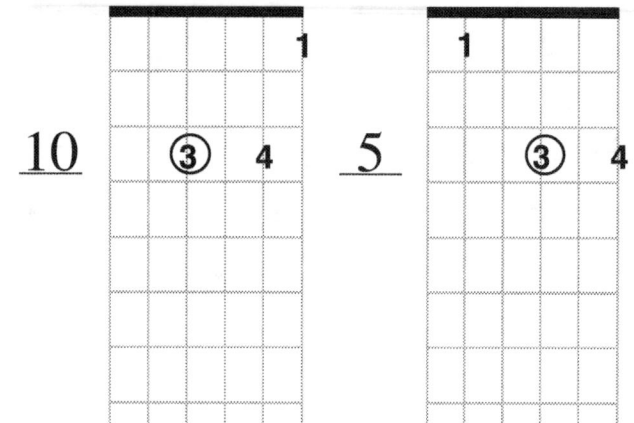
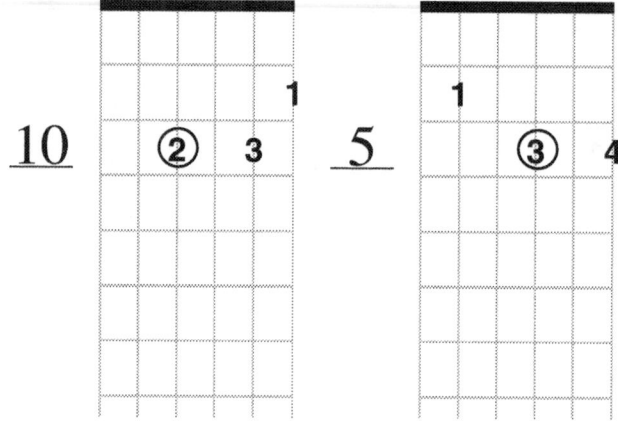
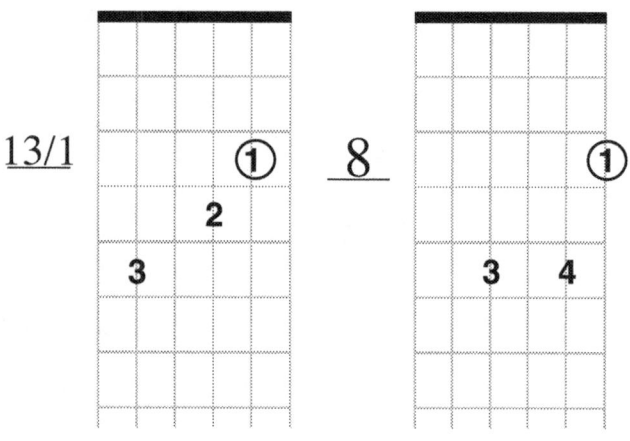
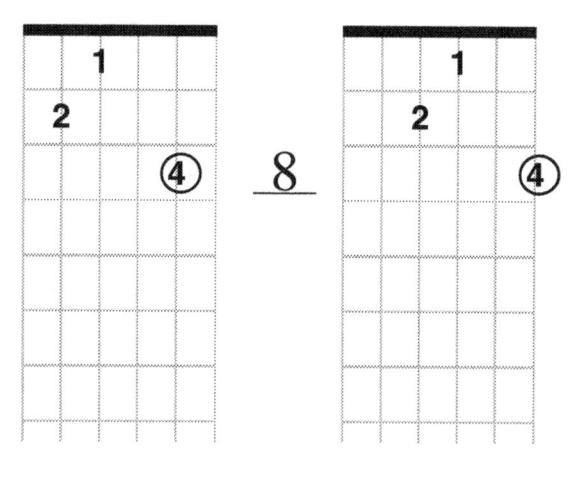

C-M⁶-P⁴   C-M⁶-D⁵

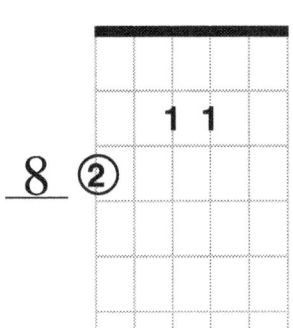
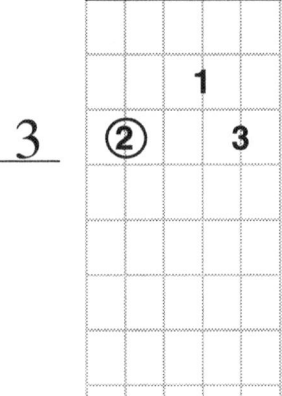
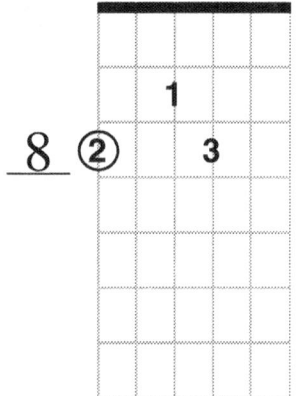
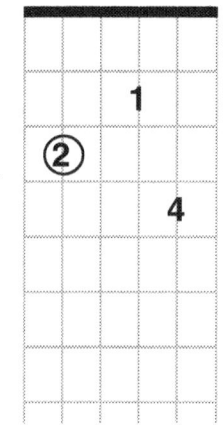

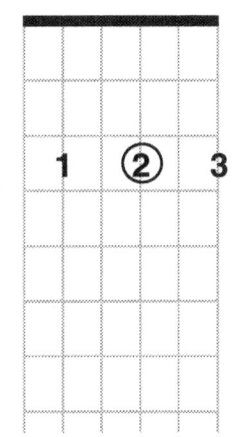
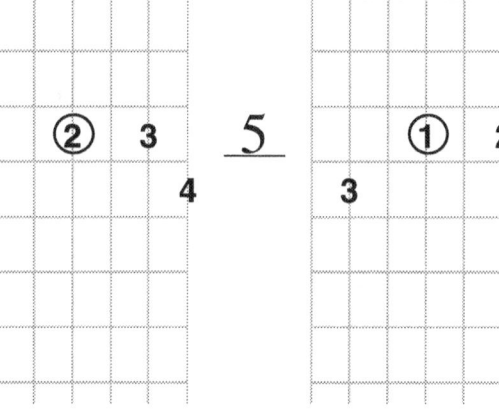

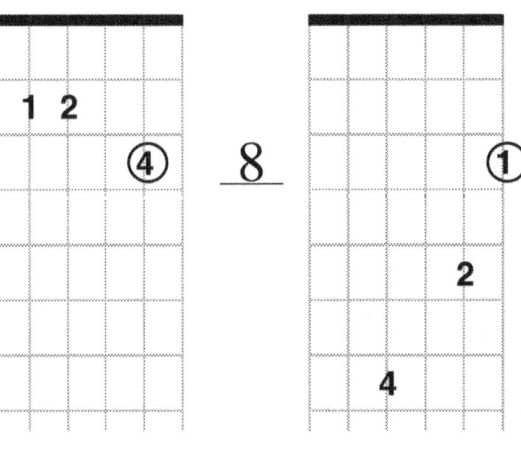
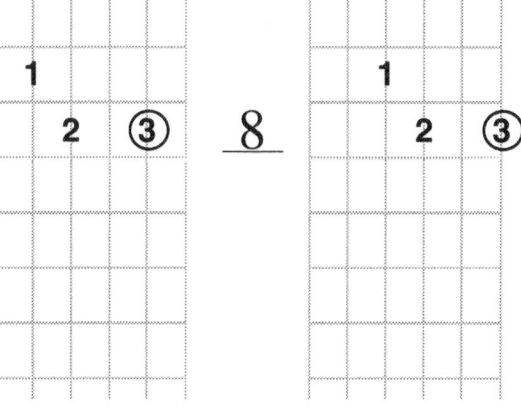

C-M⁶-P⁵   C-M⁶-m⁷

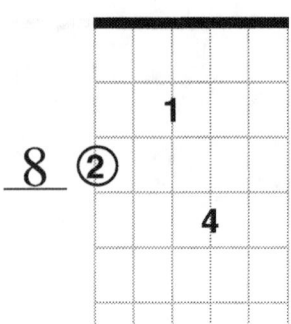
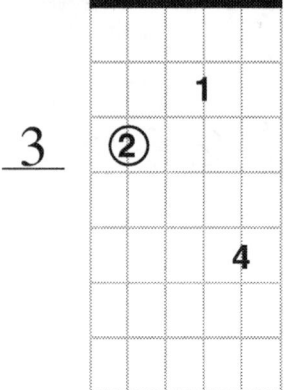
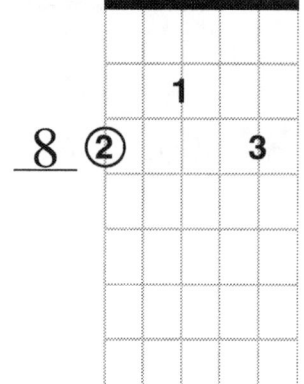
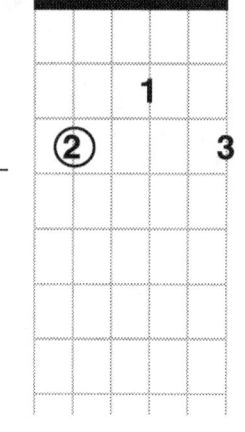
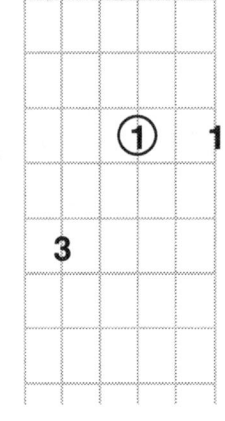
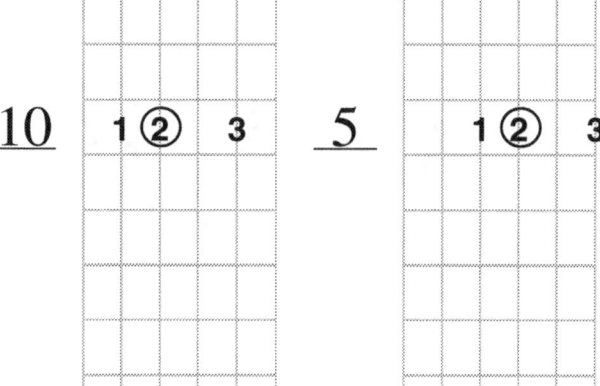
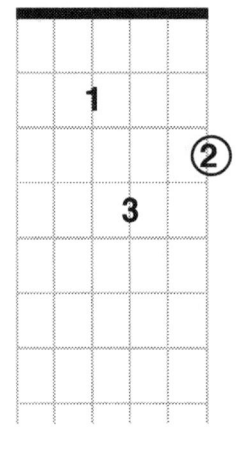
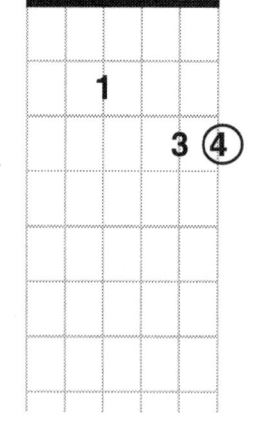

C-M⁶-M⁷   C-m⁶-m²

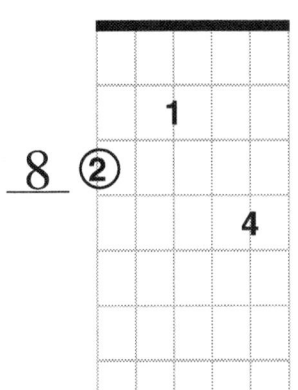
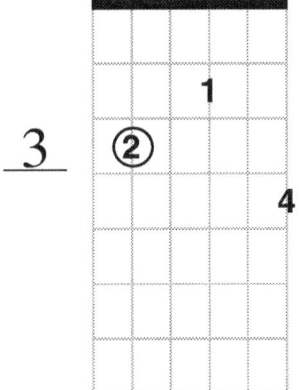
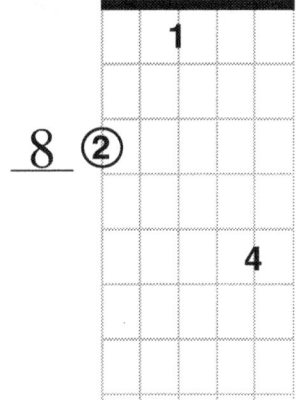
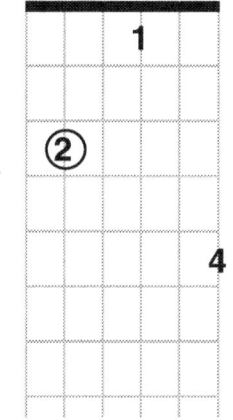
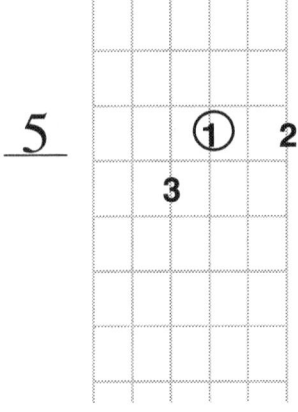
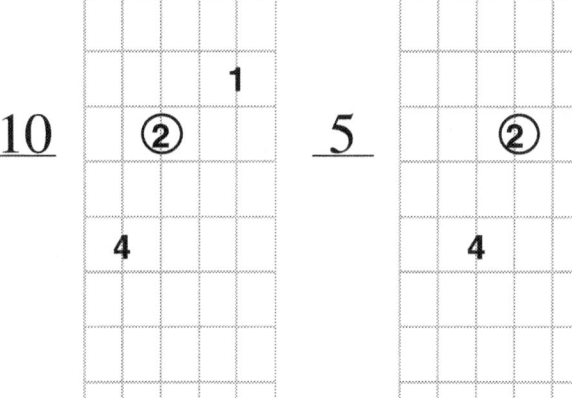
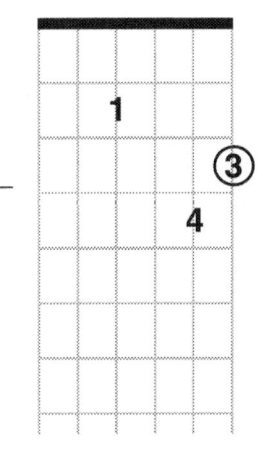
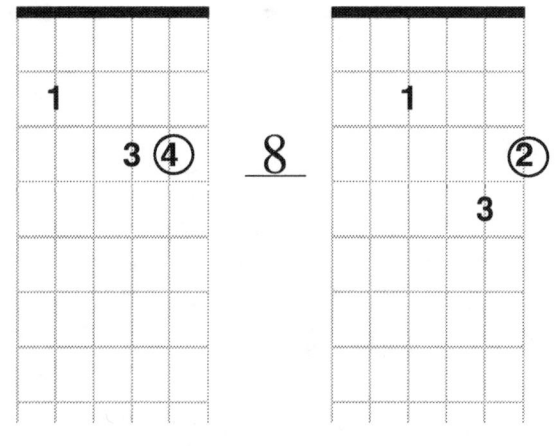

$C\text{-}m^6\text{-}M^2$ $C\text{-}m^6\text{-}m^3$

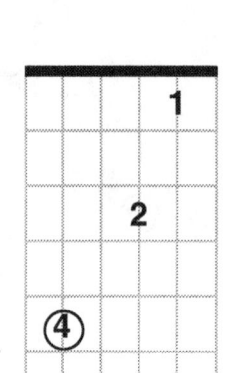
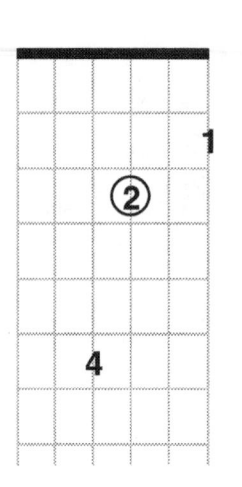
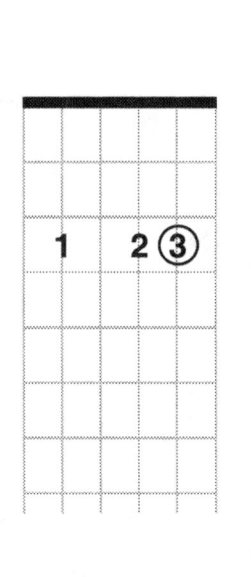
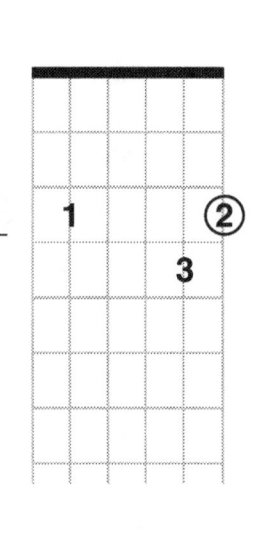
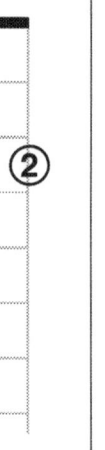
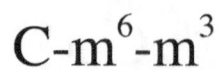
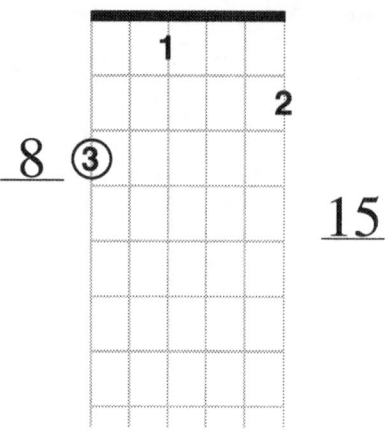
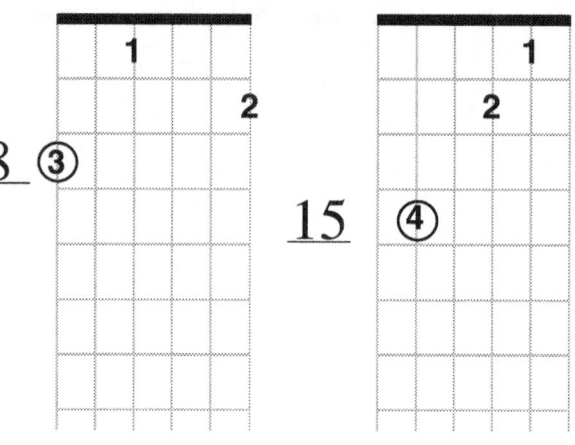
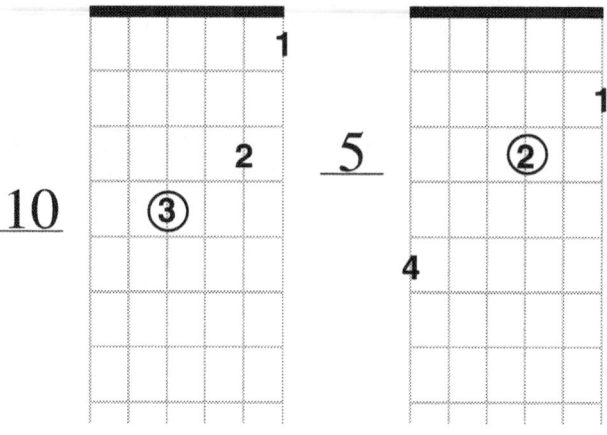
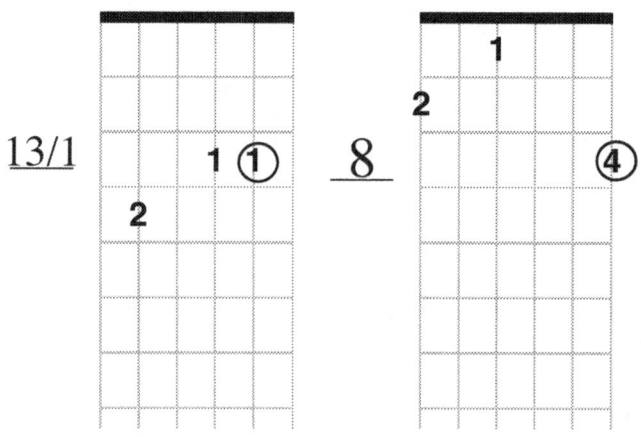

$C\text{-}m^6\text{-}M^3$ $C\text{-}m^6\text{-}P^4$

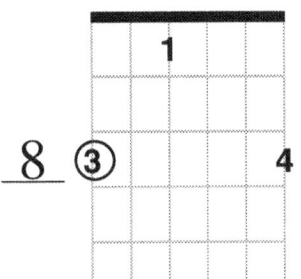
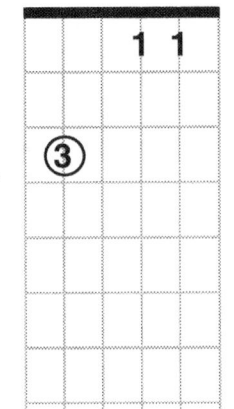
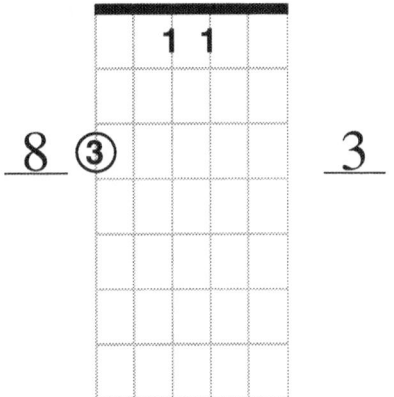
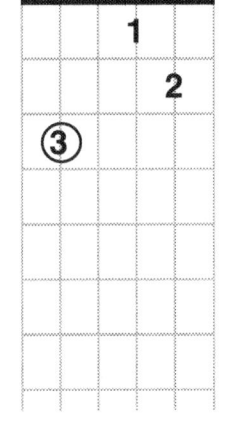

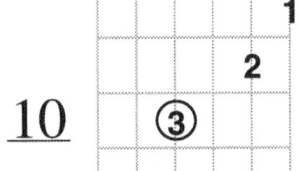
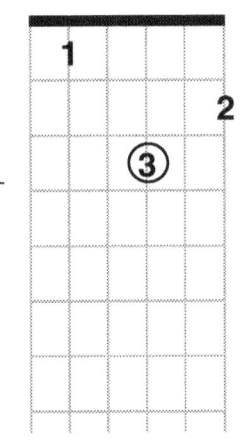
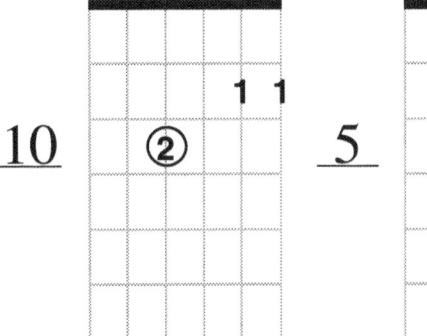
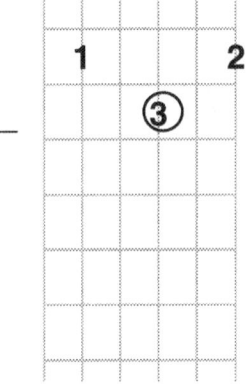

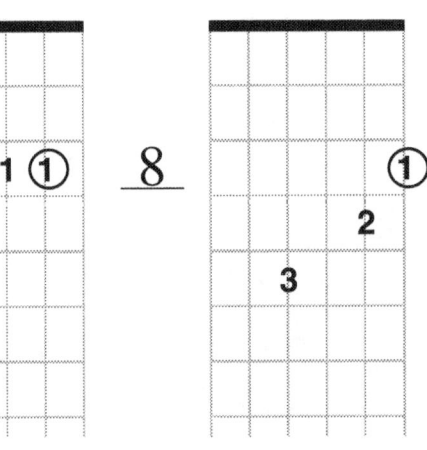
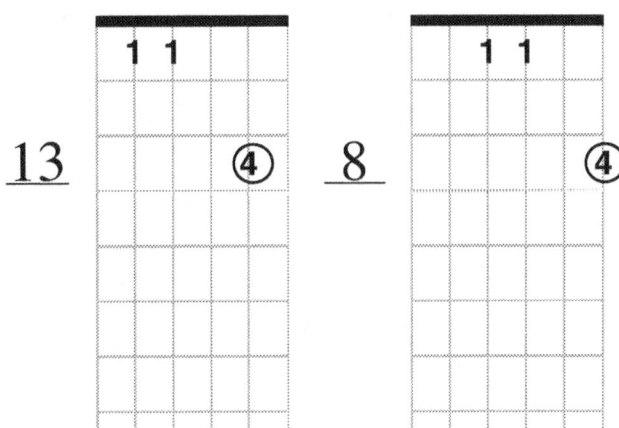

C-m⁶-D⁵   C-m⁶-P⁵

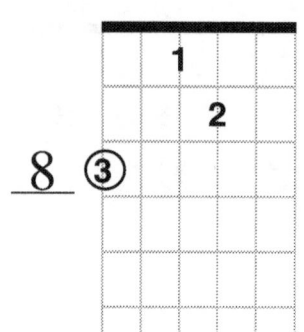 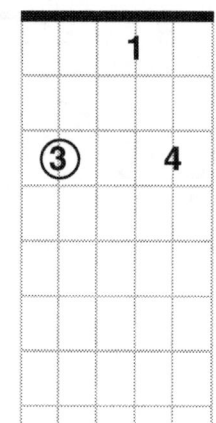 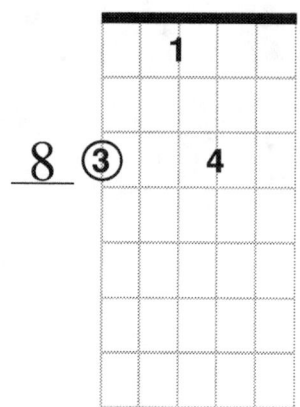 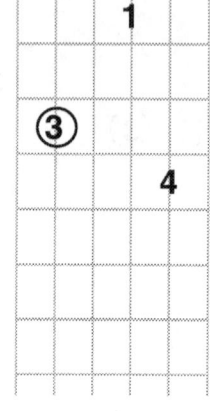

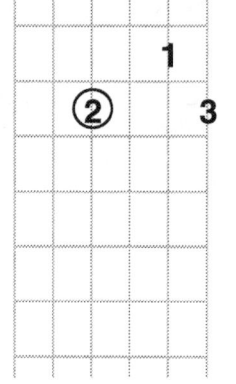 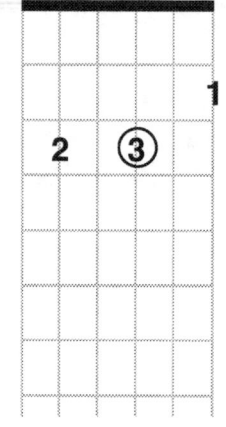 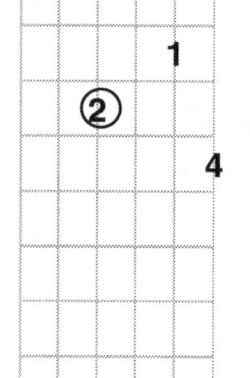 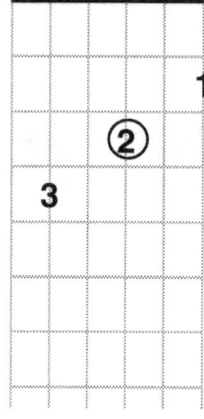

 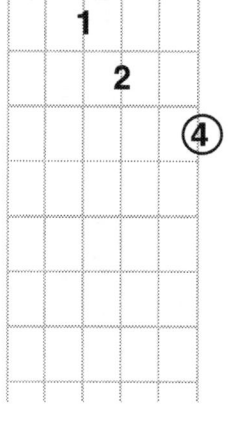 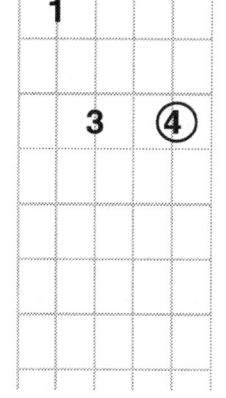 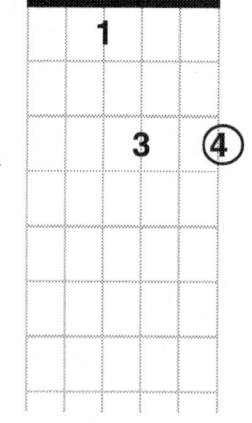

C-m^6-m^7 C-m^6-M^7

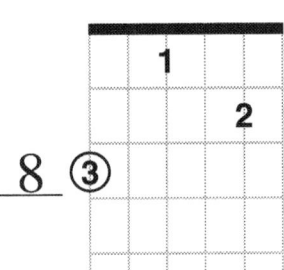
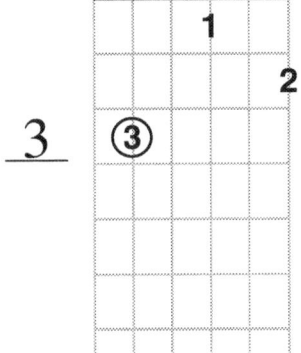
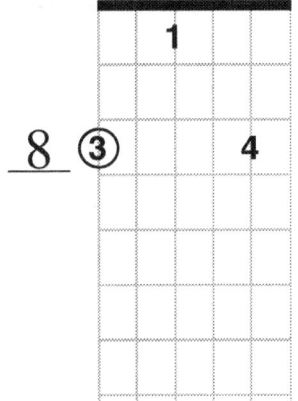
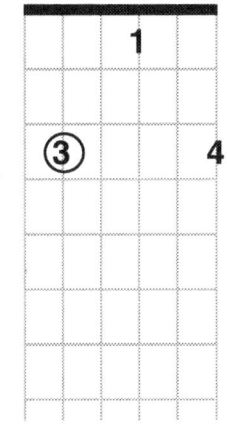
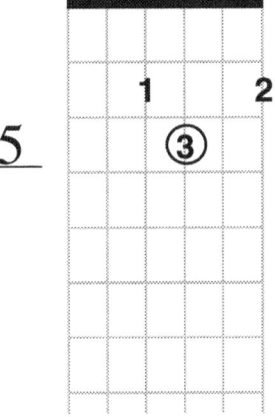
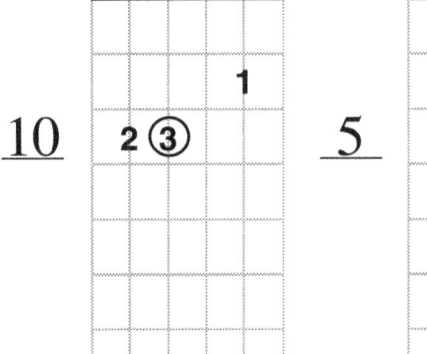
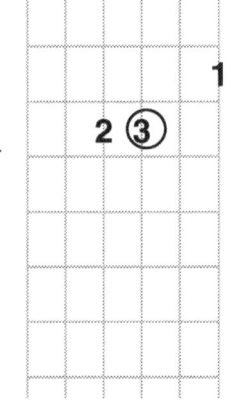
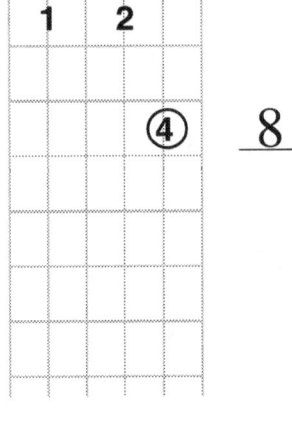
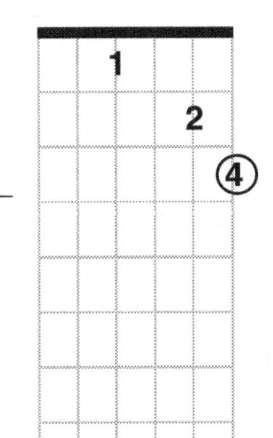
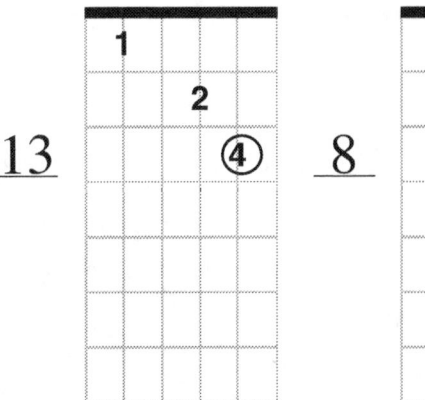

C-M⁷-m²   C-M⁷-M²

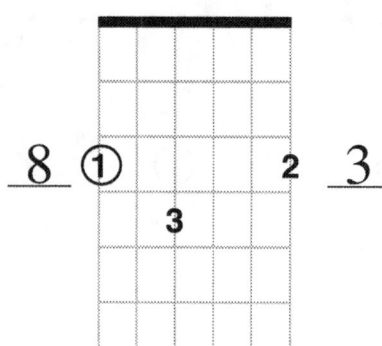
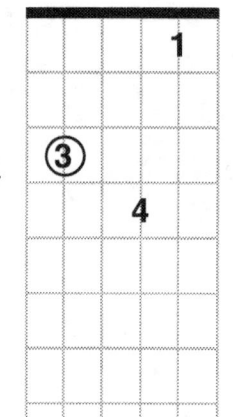
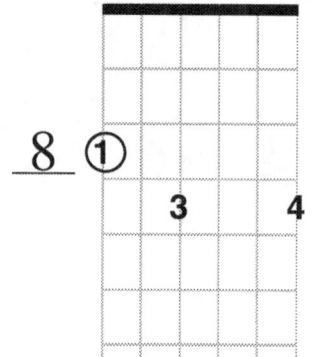
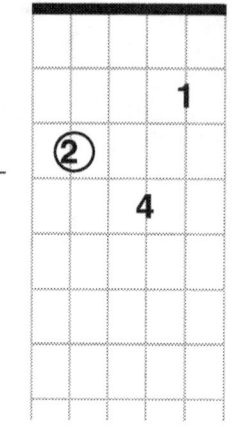

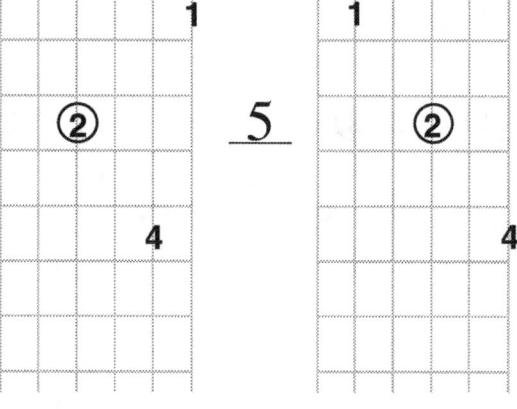
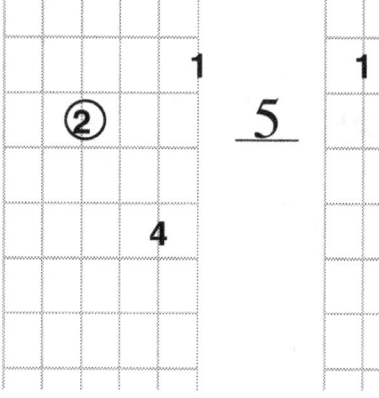
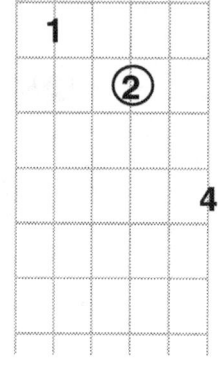

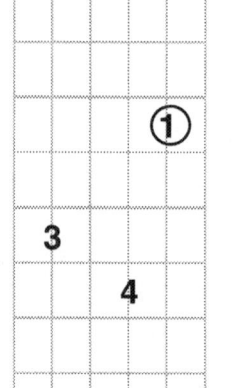
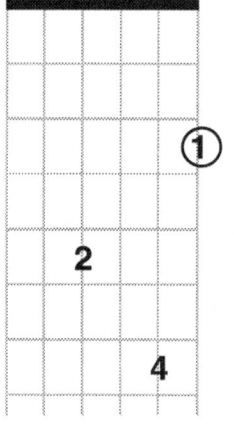
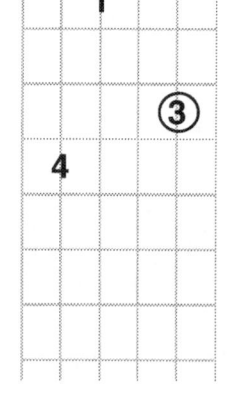
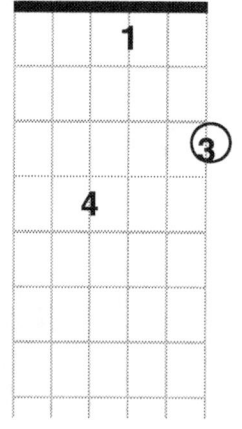

$C\text{-}M^7\text{-}m^3$ | $C\text{-}M^7\text{-}M^3$

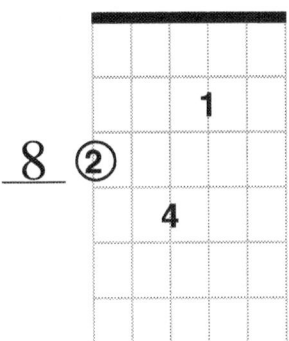
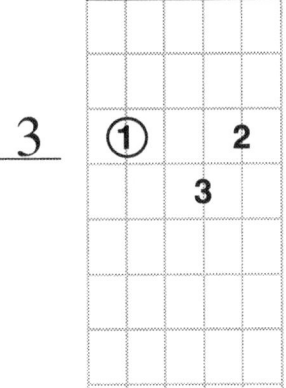
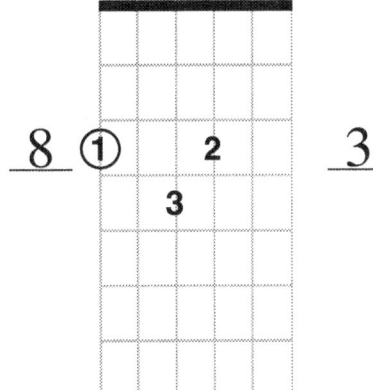
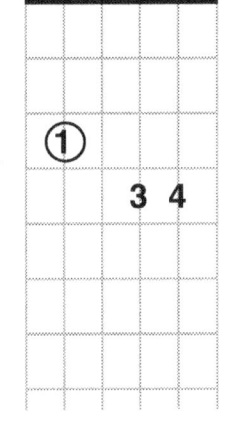
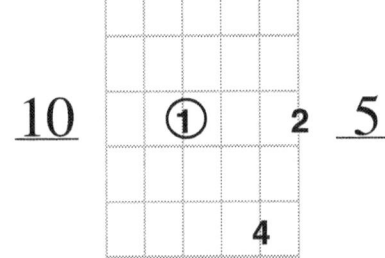
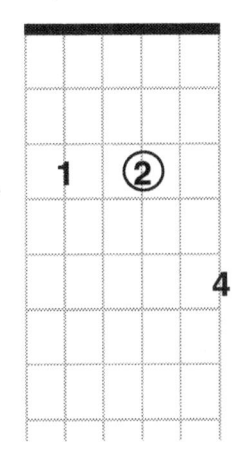
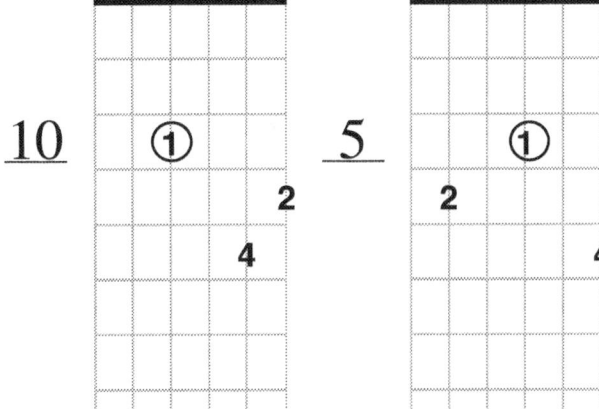
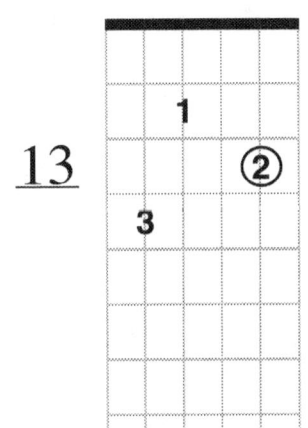
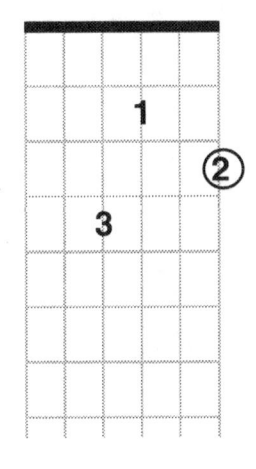
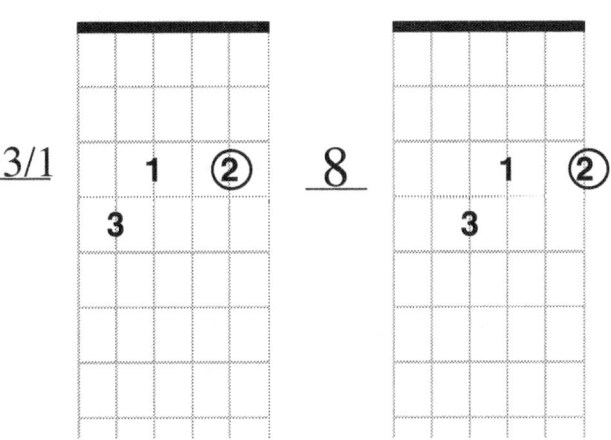

C-M⁷-P⁴   C-M⁷-D⁵

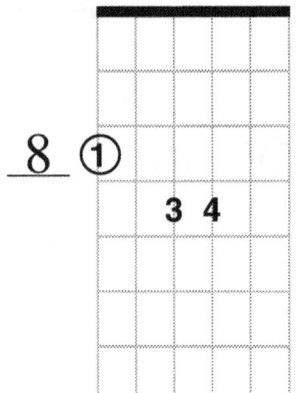
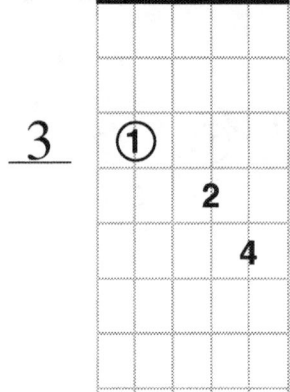
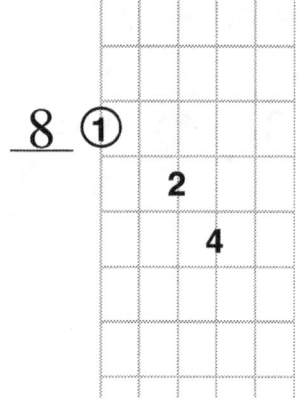
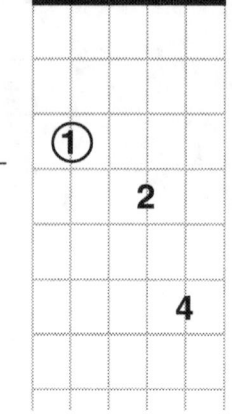
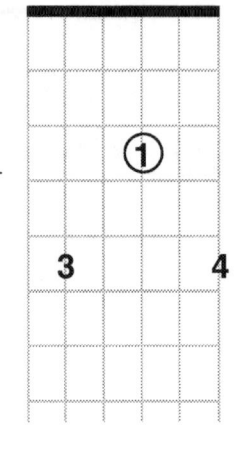
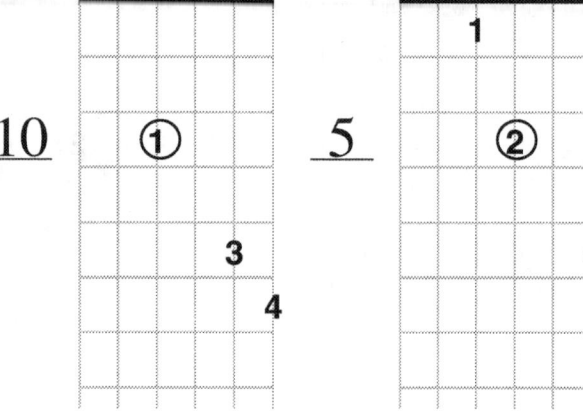
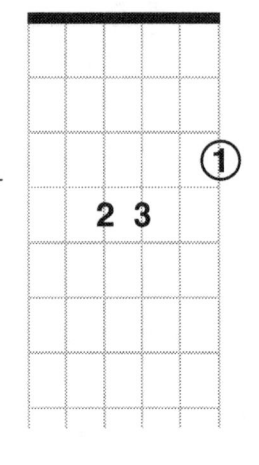
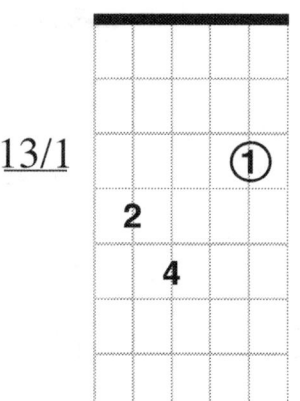
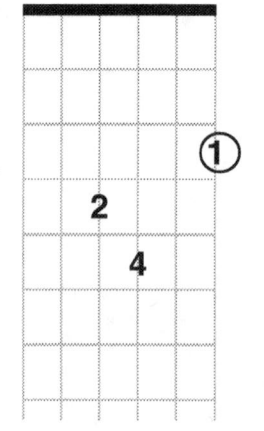

C-M⁷-P⁵   C-M⁷-m⁶

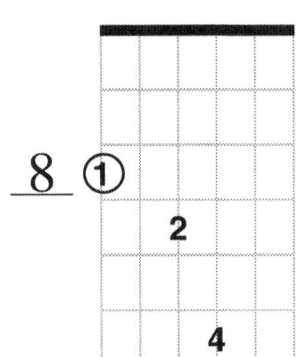 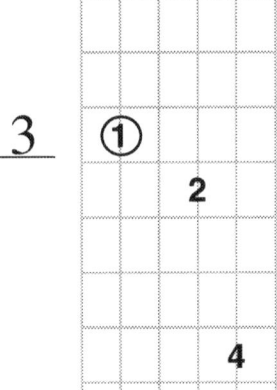 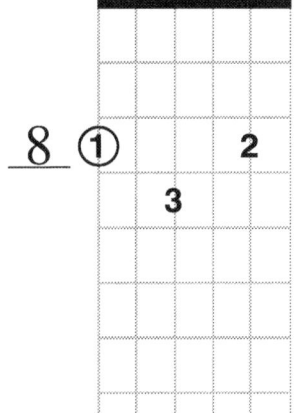 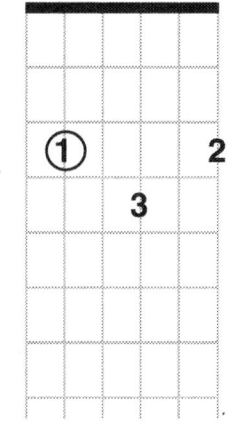

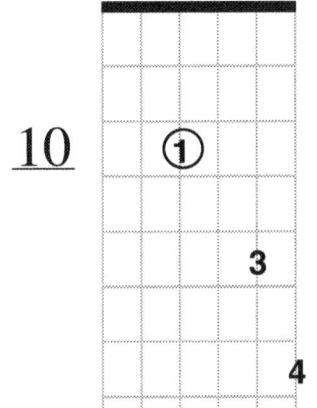 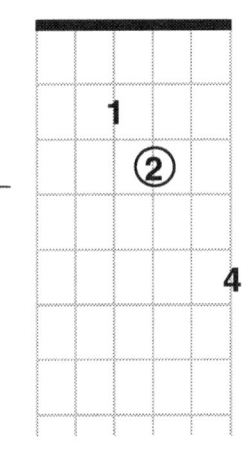 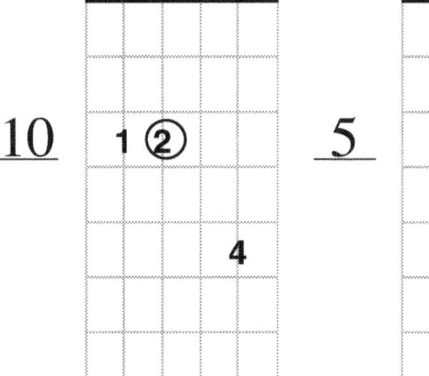

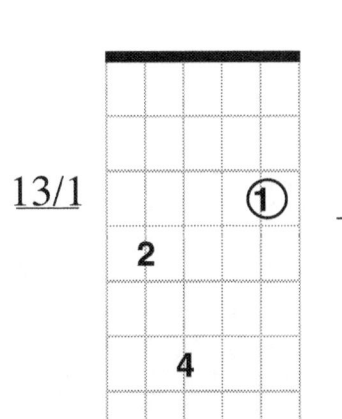 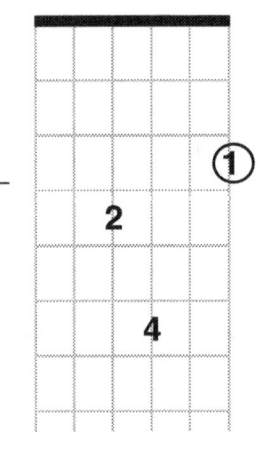 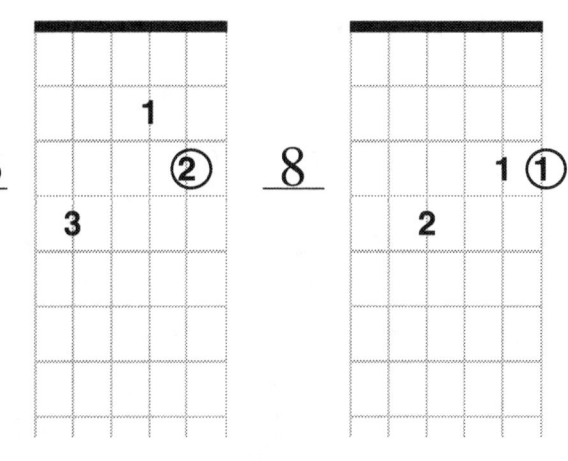

C-M⁷-M⁶   C-m⁷-m²

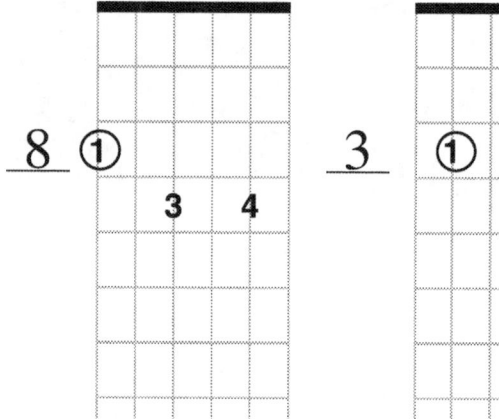
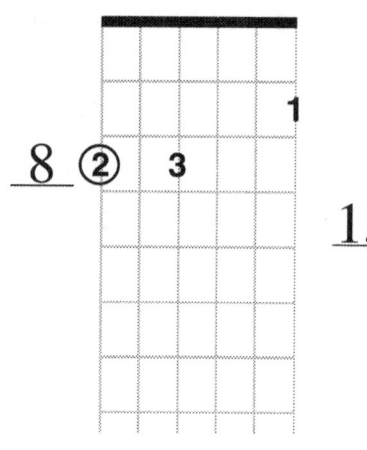
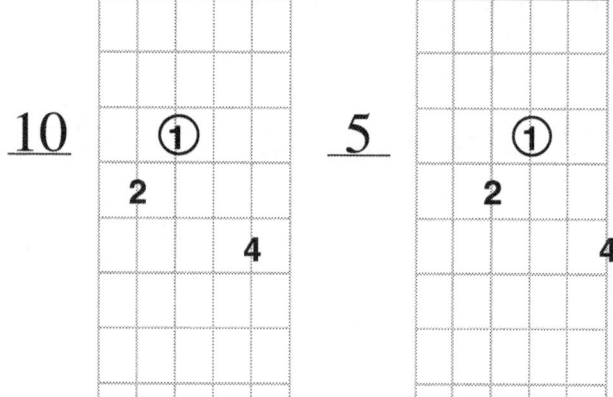
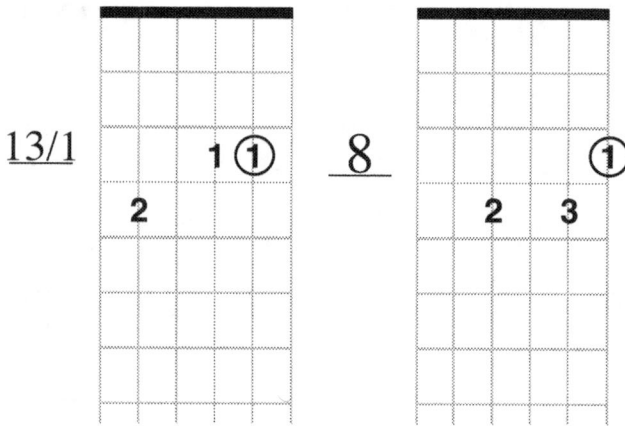
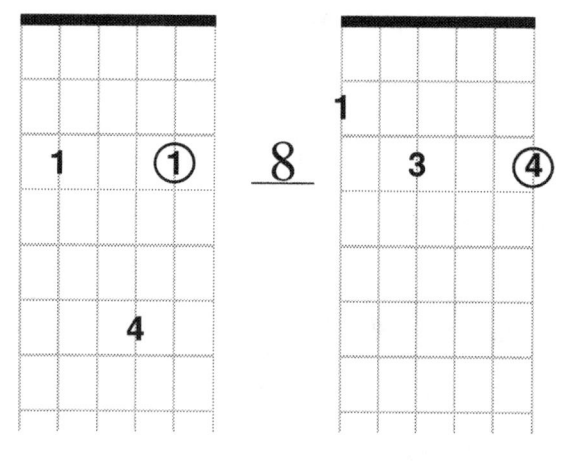

C-m⁷-M²   C-m⁷-m³

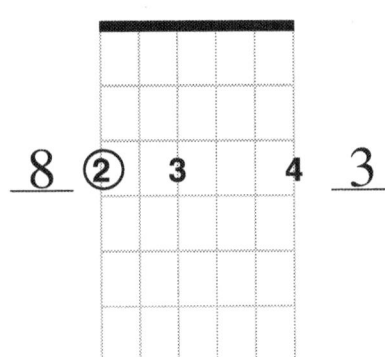
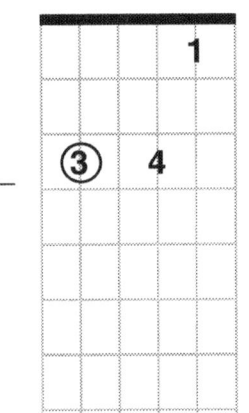
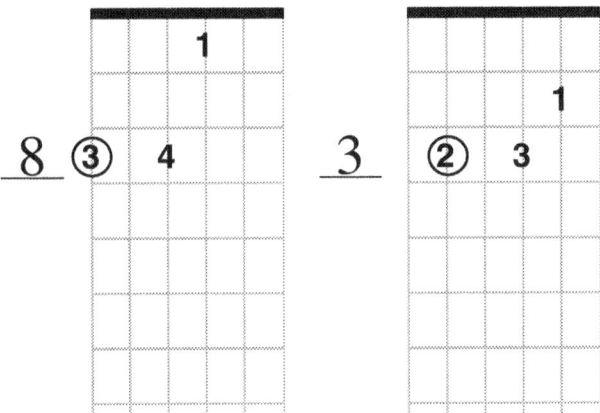
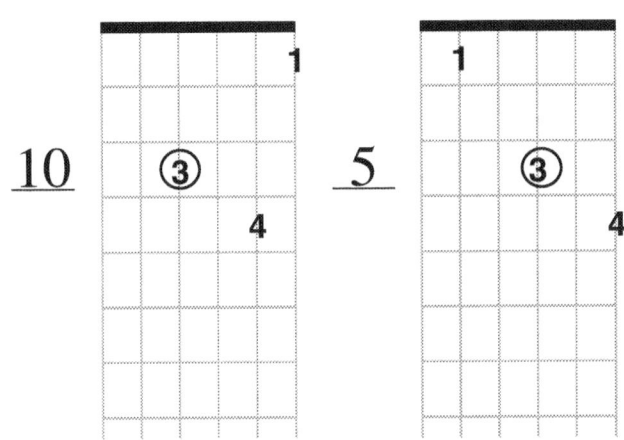
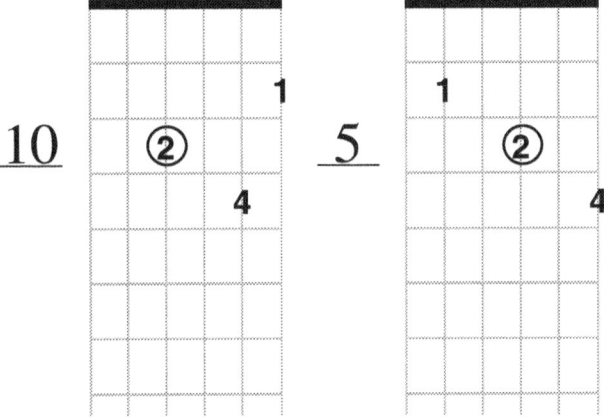
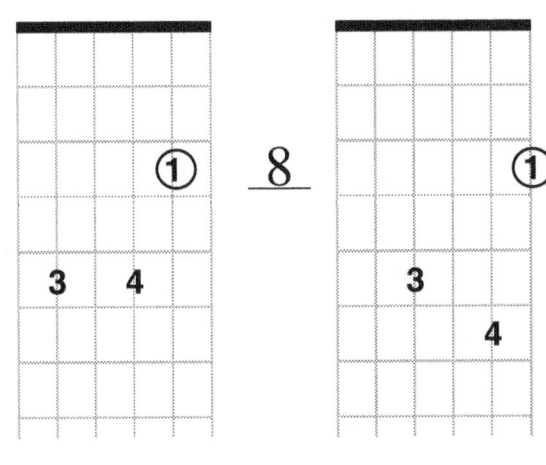
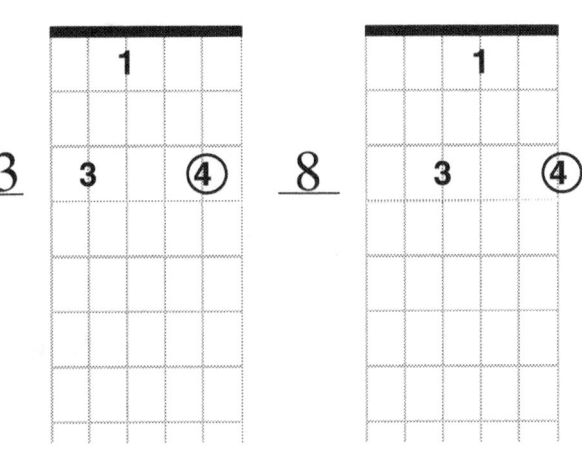

C-m⁷-M³   C-m⁷-P⁴

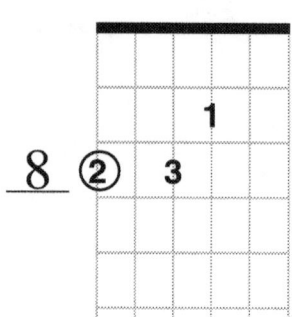
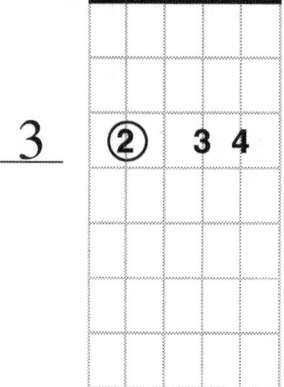
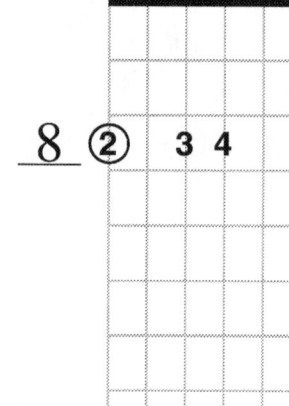
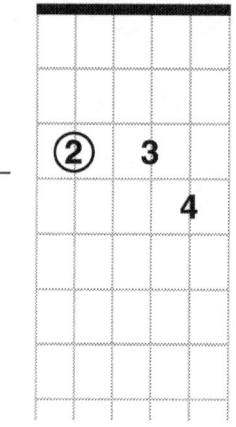

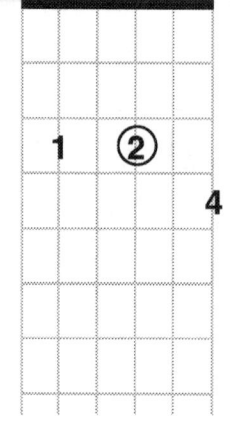
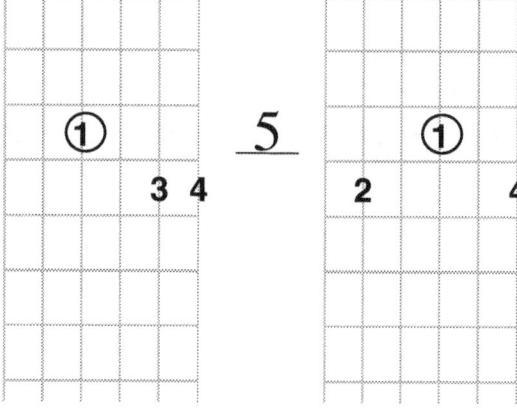

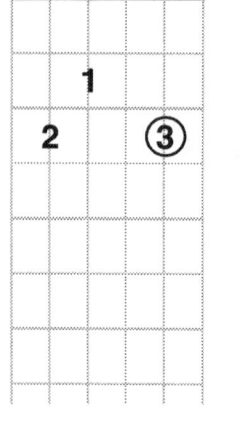
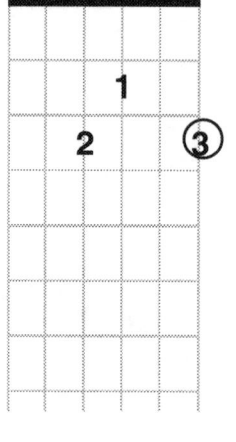
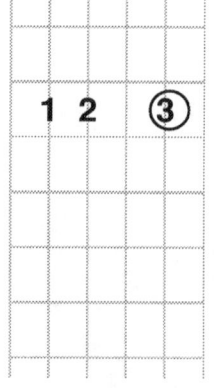
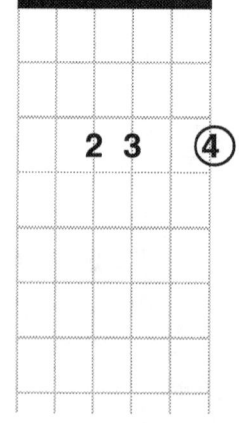

C-m⁷-D⁵   C-m⁷-P⁵

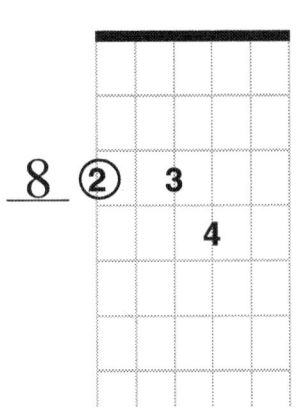 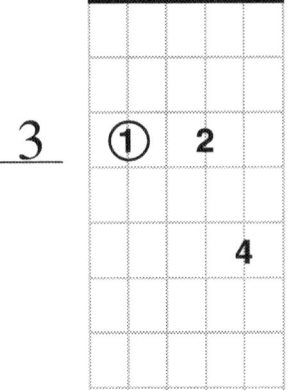 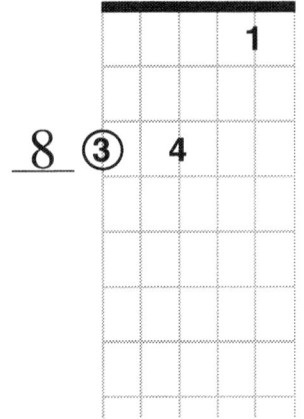 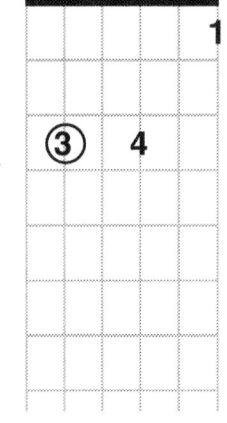

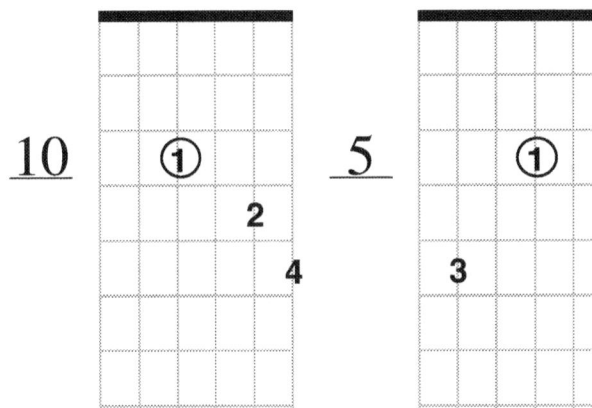 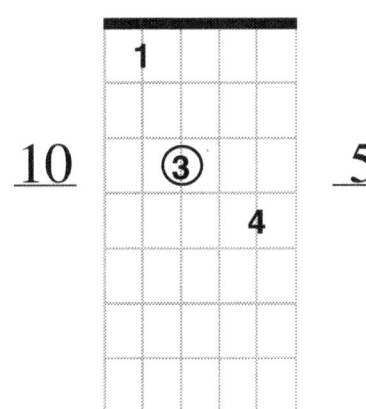 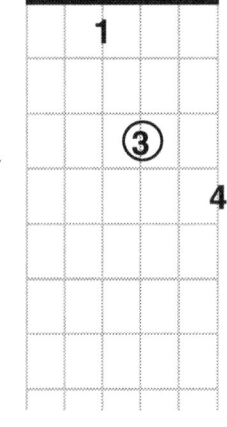

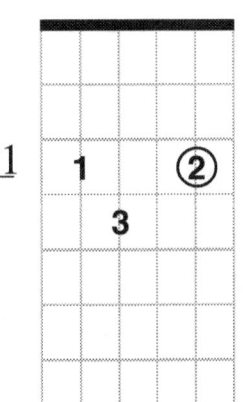 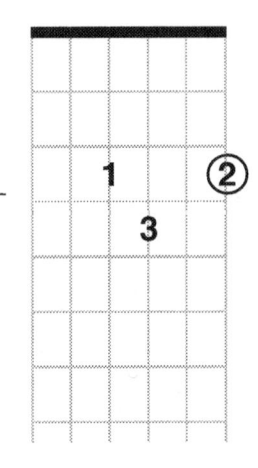 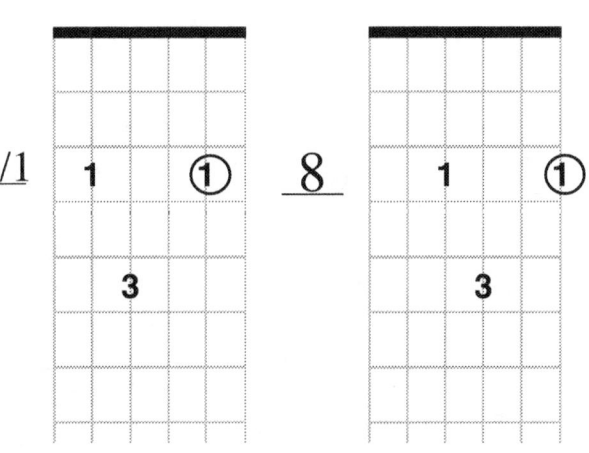

C-m^7-m^6 C-m^7-M^6

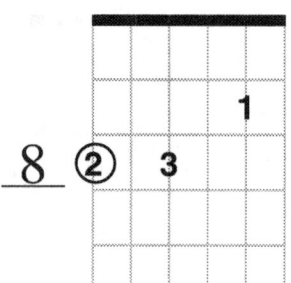
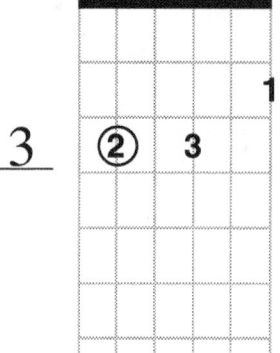
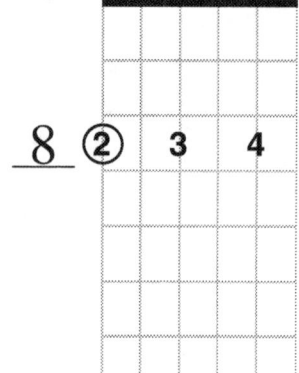
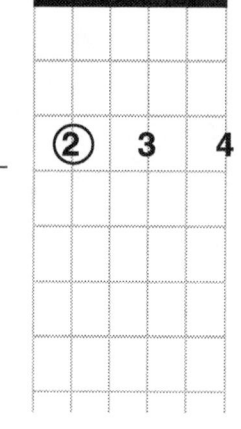

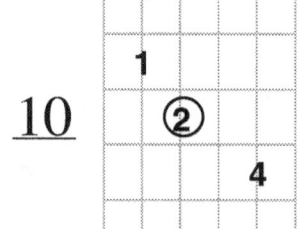
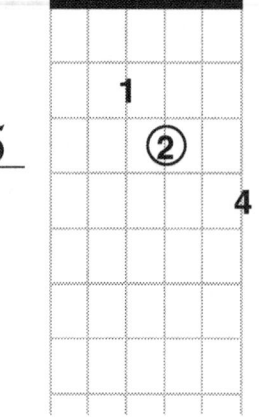
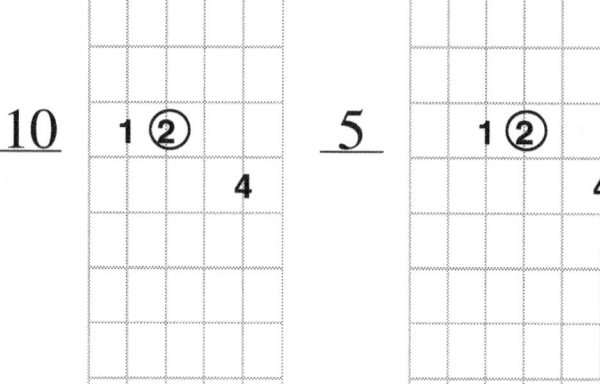

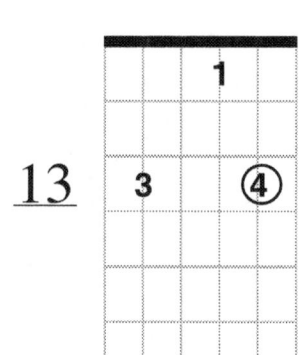
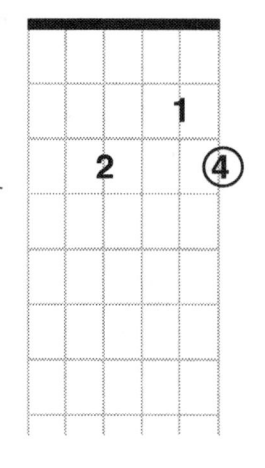
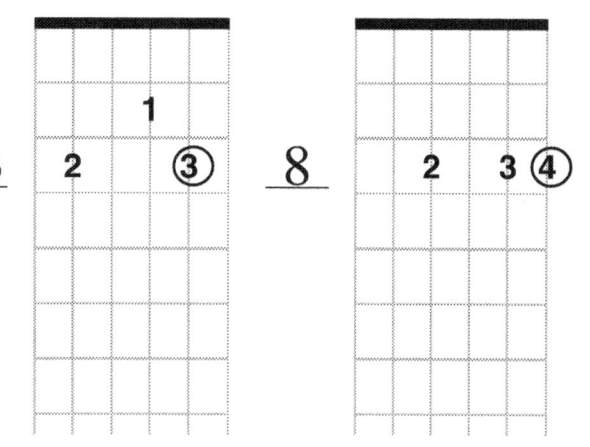

C-M²-m³+   C-M²-M³+

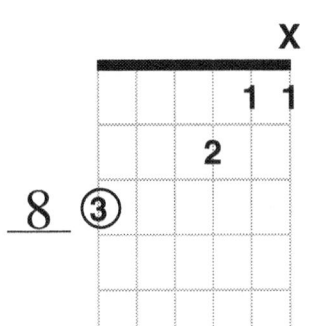
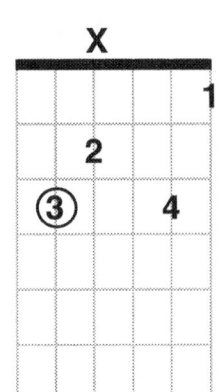
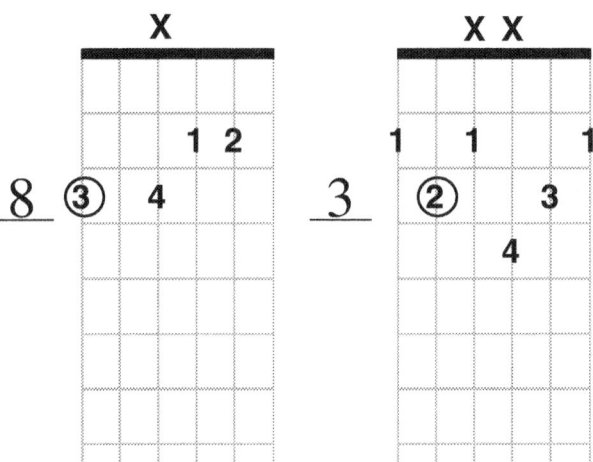
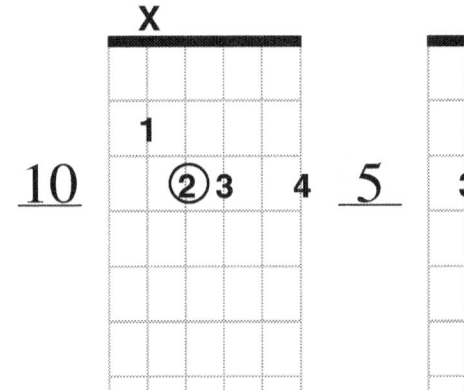
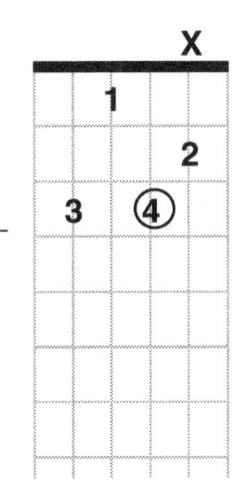
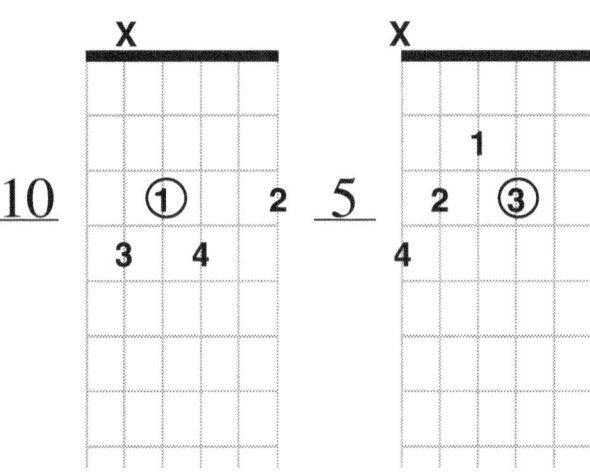
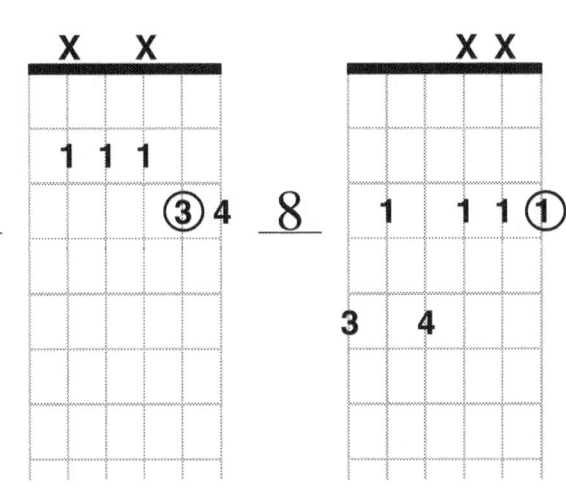
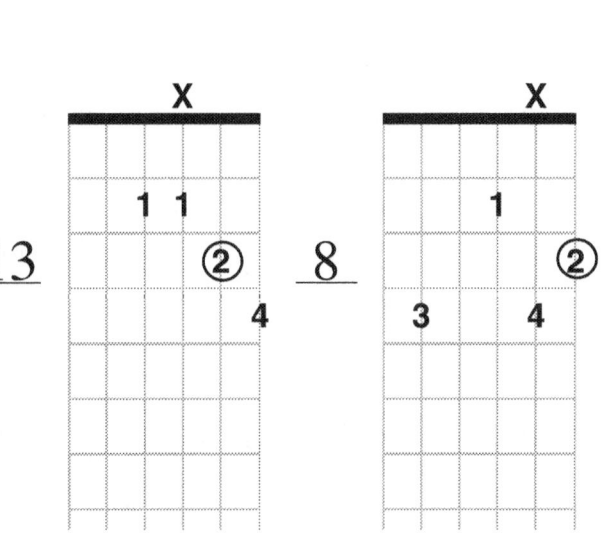

$C\text{-}M^2\text{-}P^4+$ $C\text{-}M^2\text{-}D^5+$

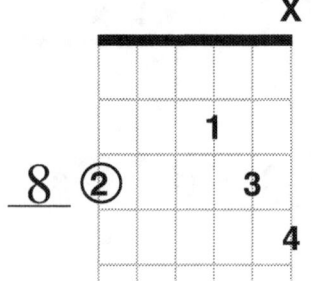
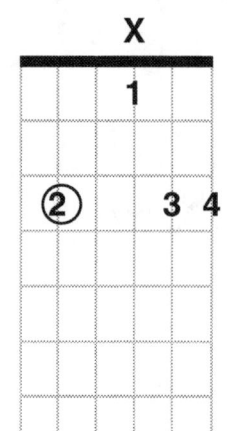
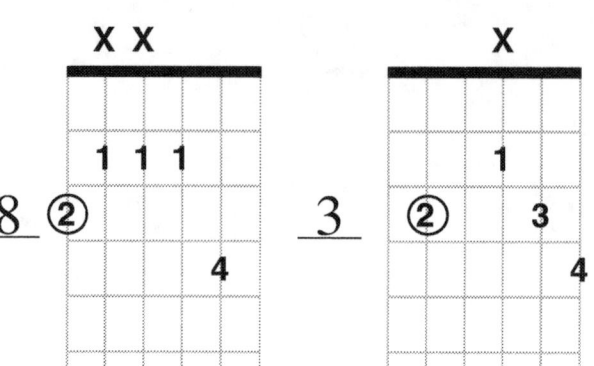
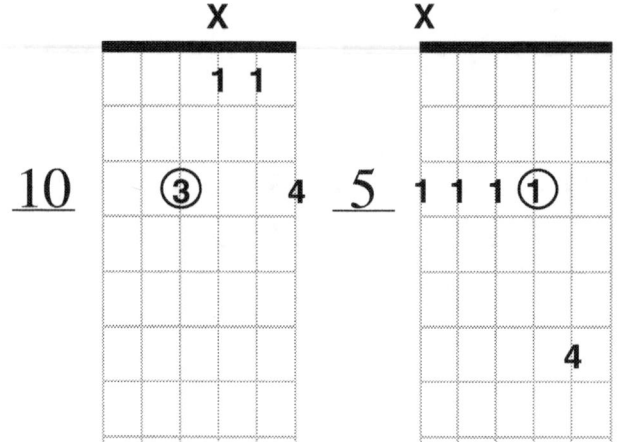
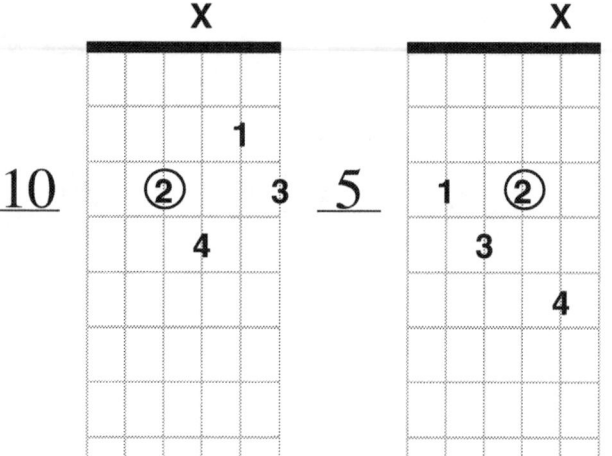
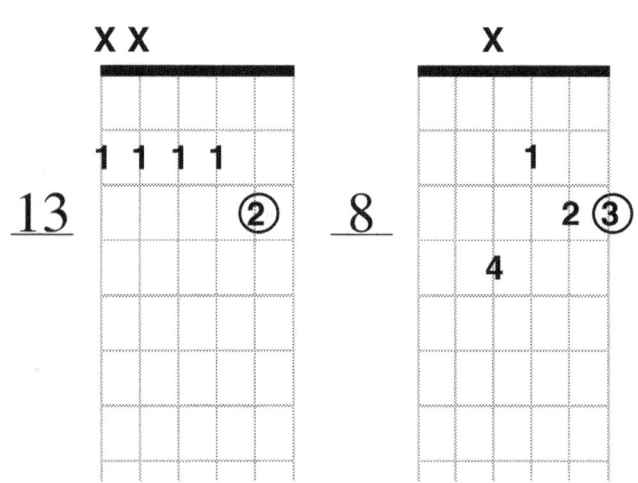
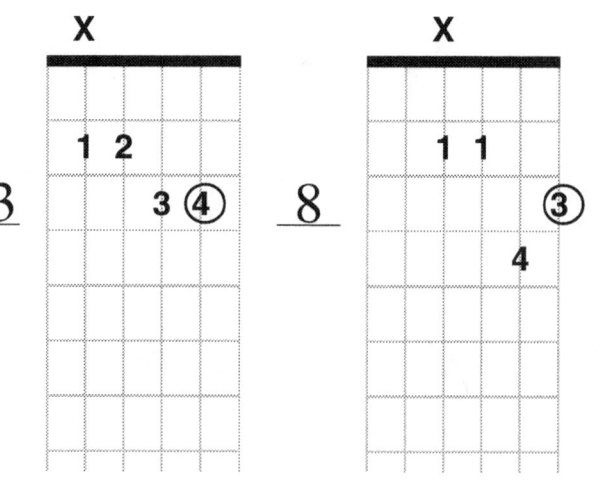

$C\text{-}M^2\text{-}P^5+$ $\qquad$ $C\text{-}M^2\text{-}m^6+$

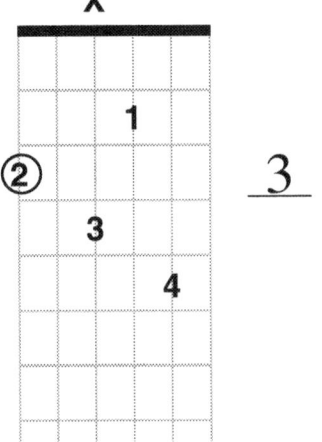
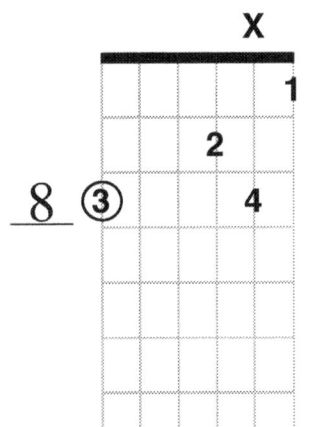
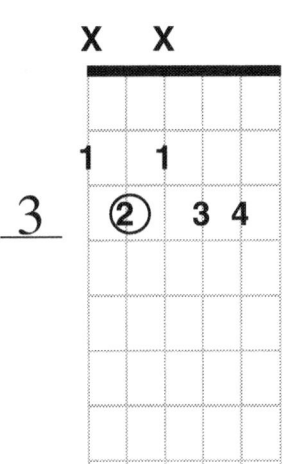

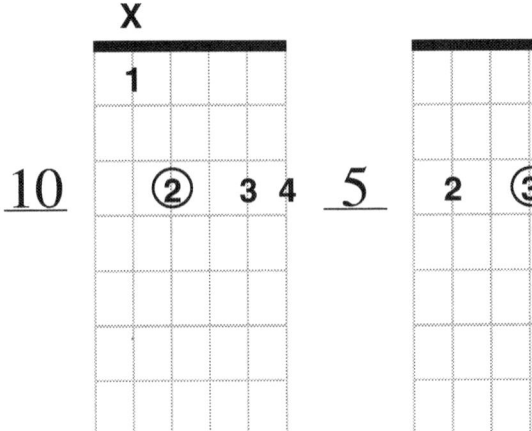
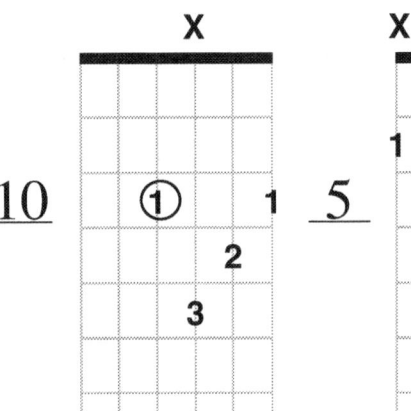
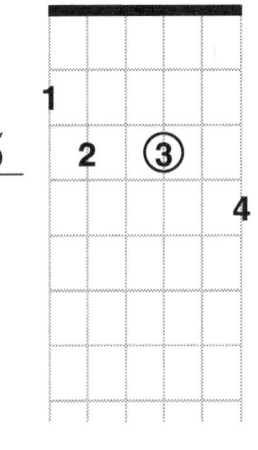

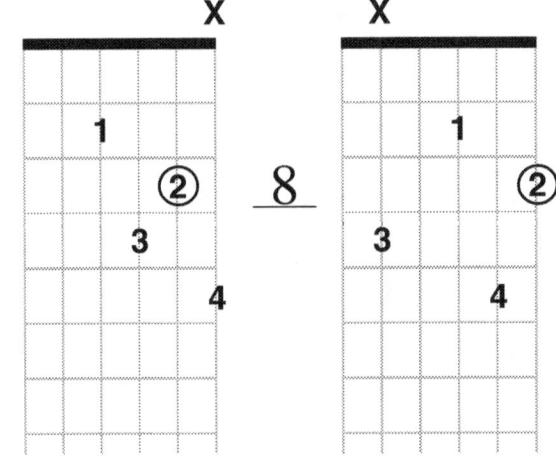
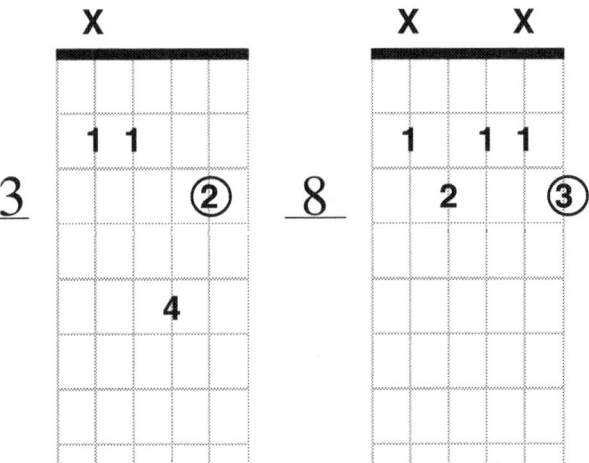

$C-M^2-M^6+$ $\qquad$ $C-M^2-m^7+$

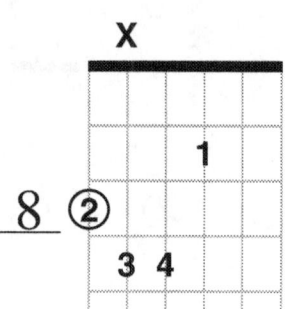
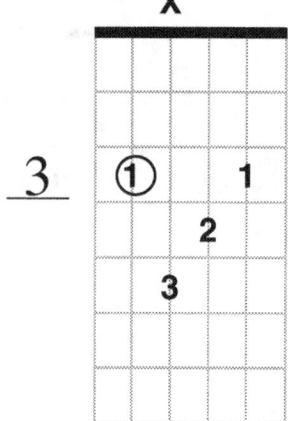
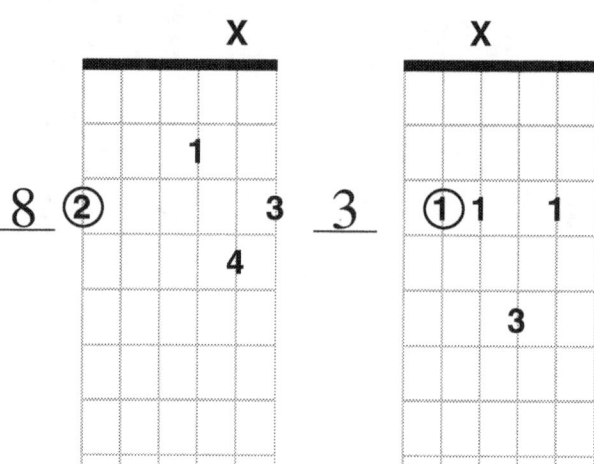

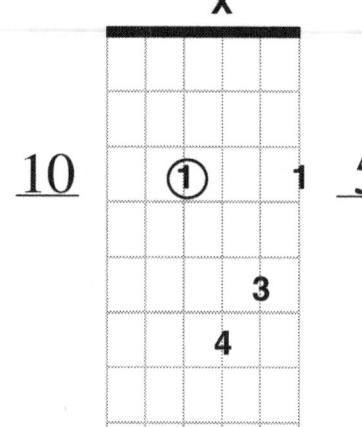
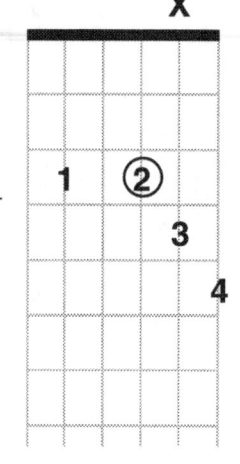
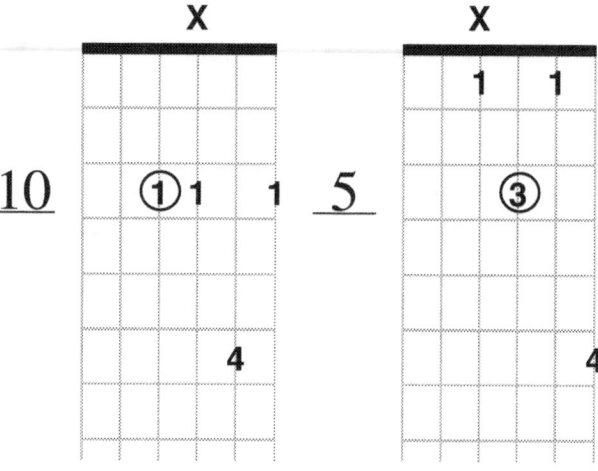

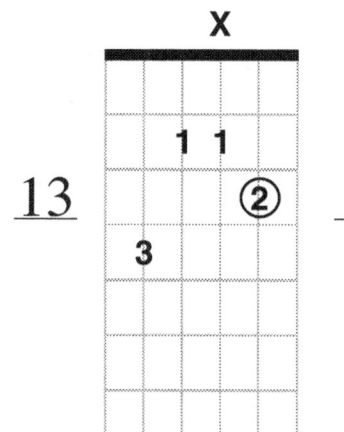
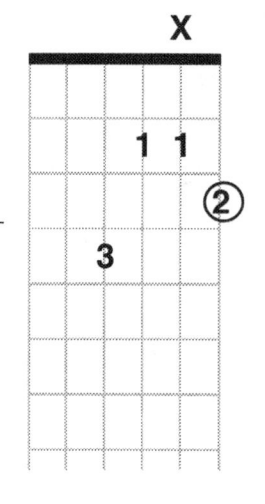
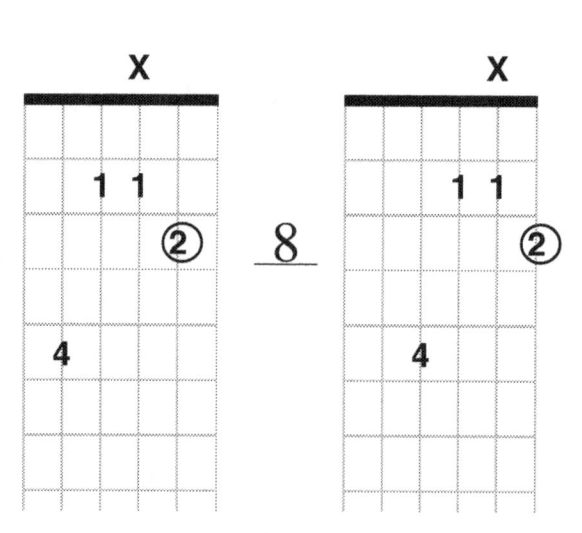

$C\text{-}M^2\text{-}M^7+$

$C\text{-}m^2\text{-}m^3+$

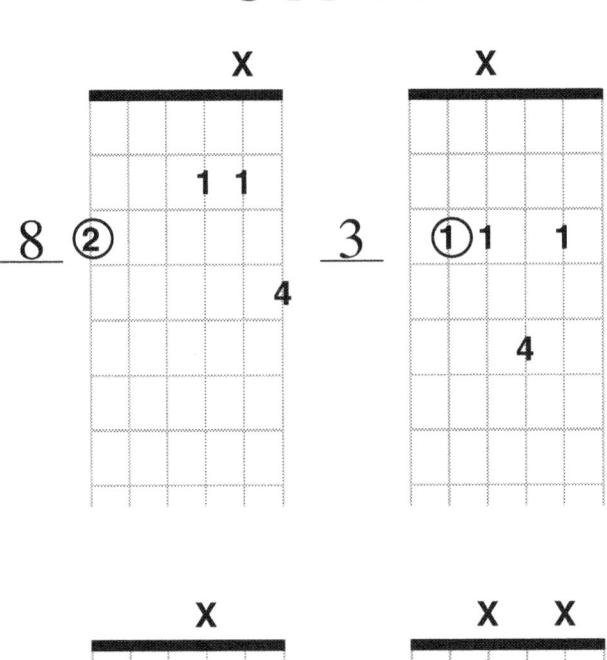
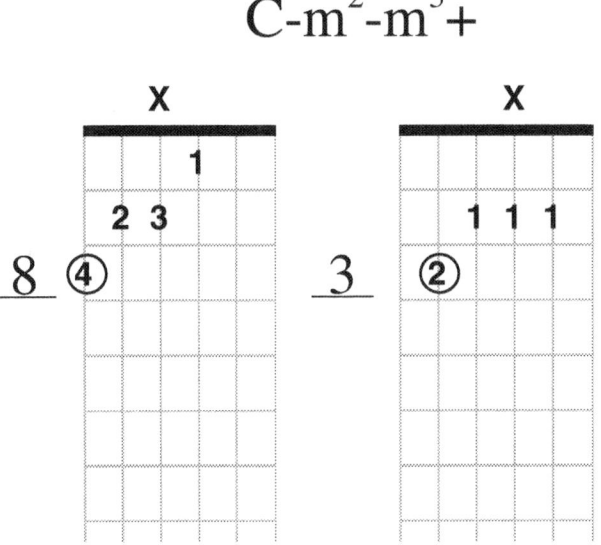
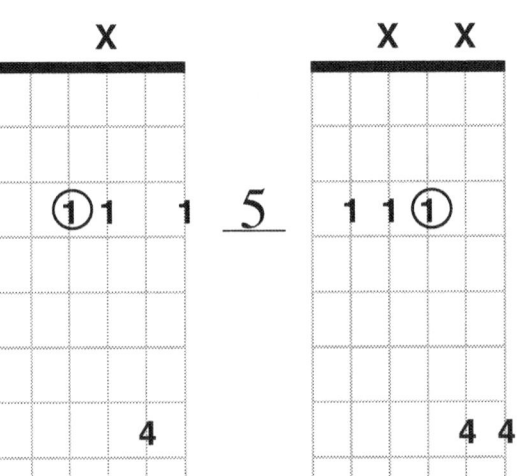
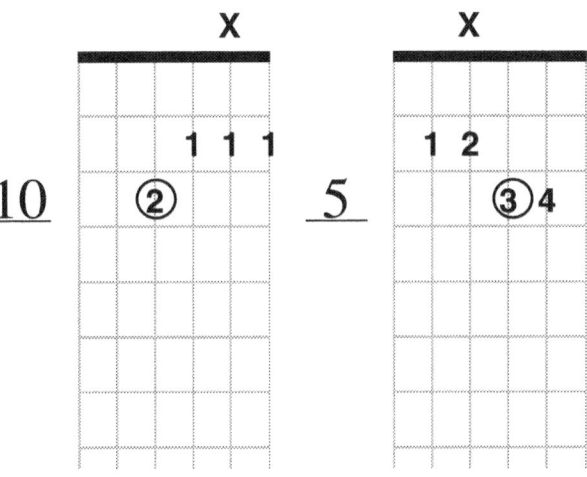
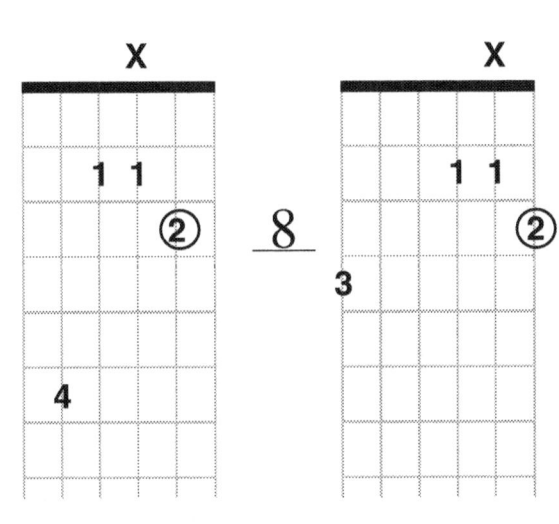
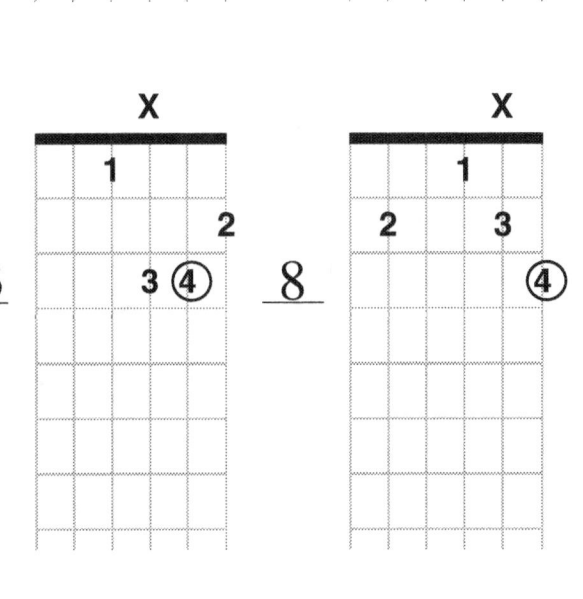

$C\text{-}m^2\text{-}M^3+$ $\qquad$ $C\text{-}m^2\text{-}P^4+$

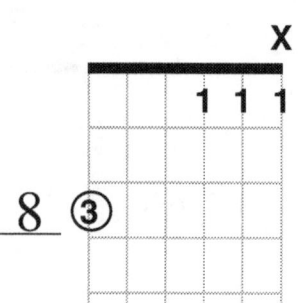
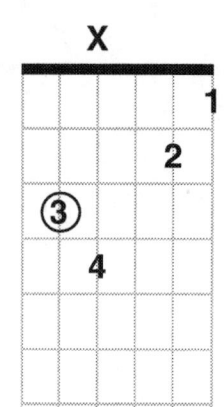
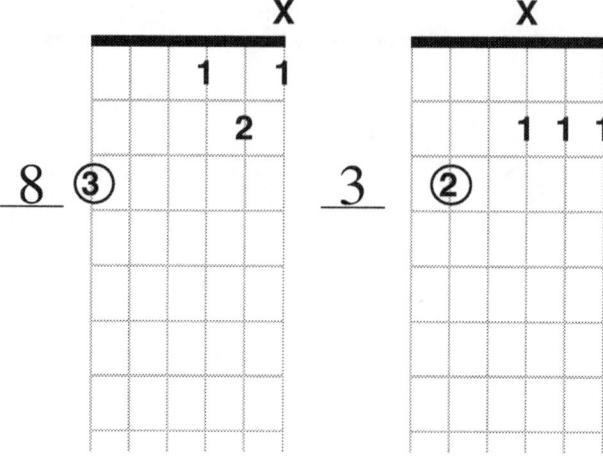
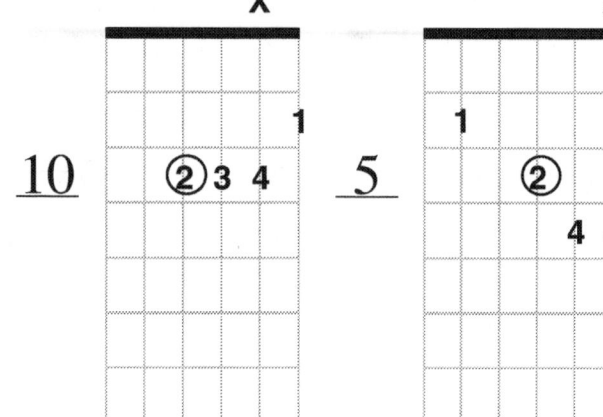
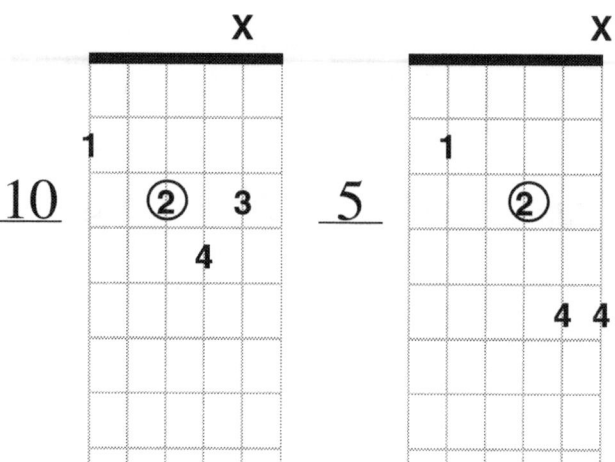
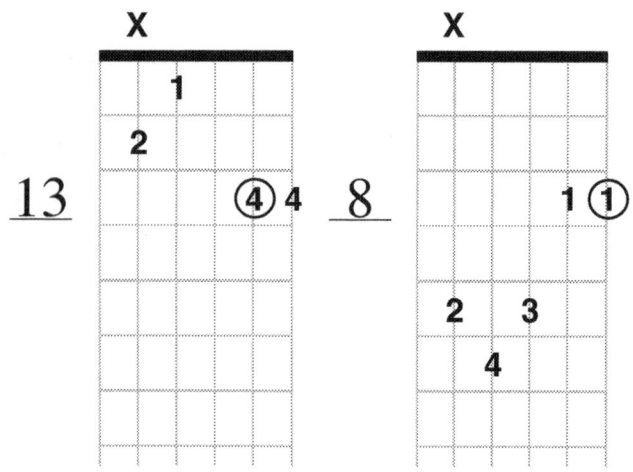
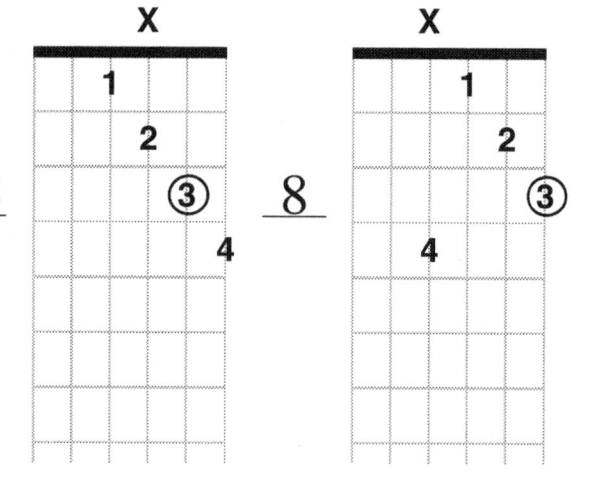

$C\text{-}m^2\text{-}D^5+$ $C\text{-}m^2\text{-}P^5+$

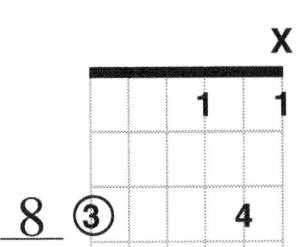
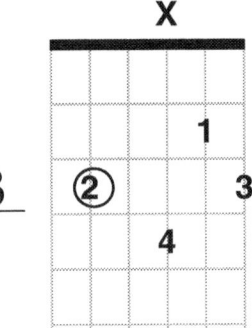
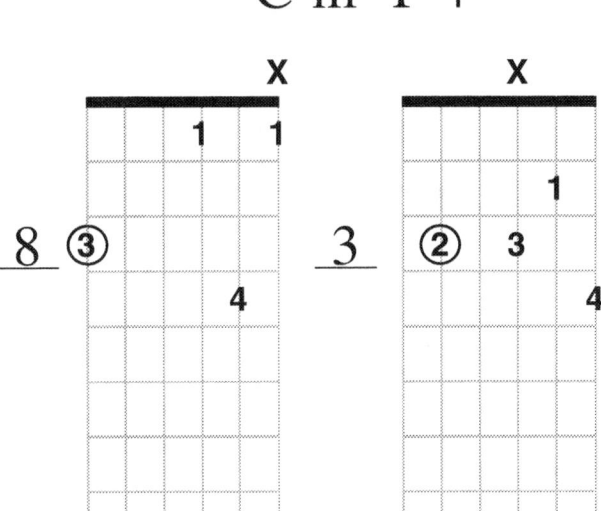

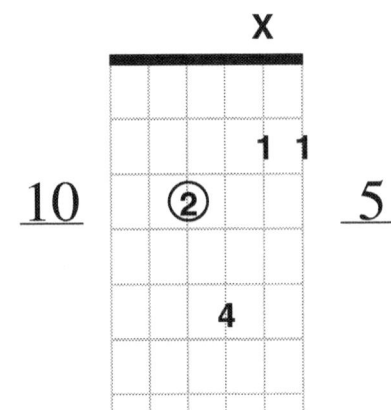
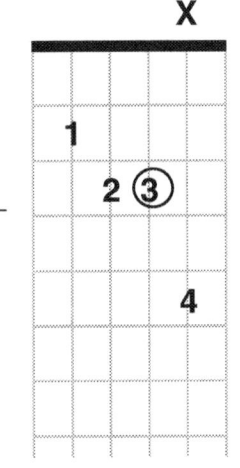
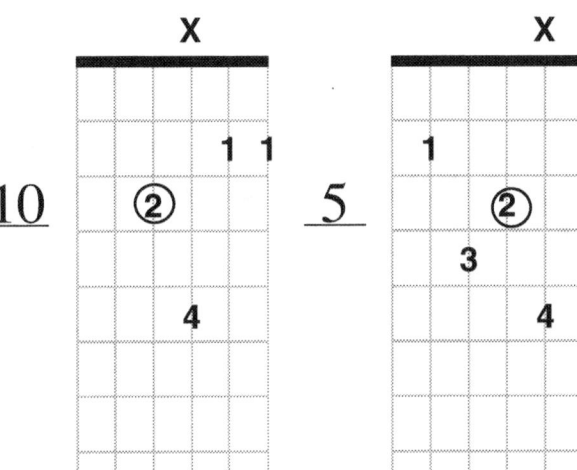

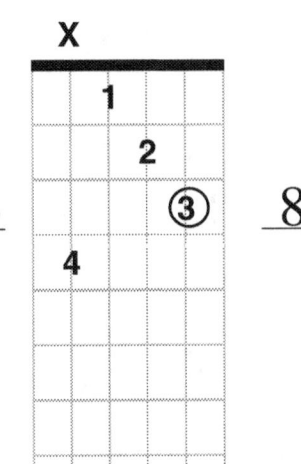
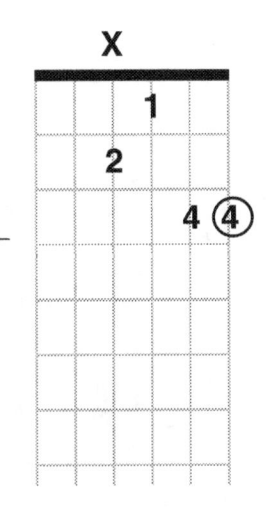
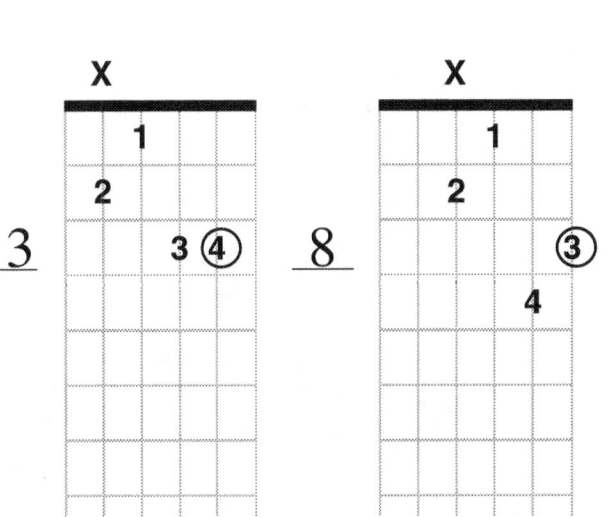

$C\text{-}m^2\text{-}m^6+$ $\qquad$ $C\text{-}m^2\text{-}M^6+$

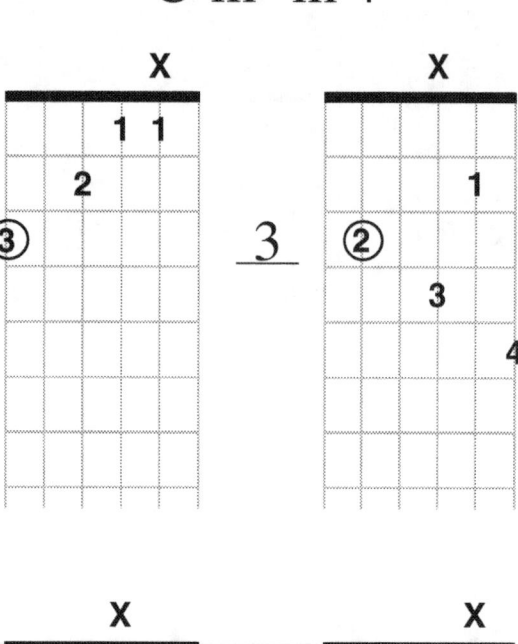
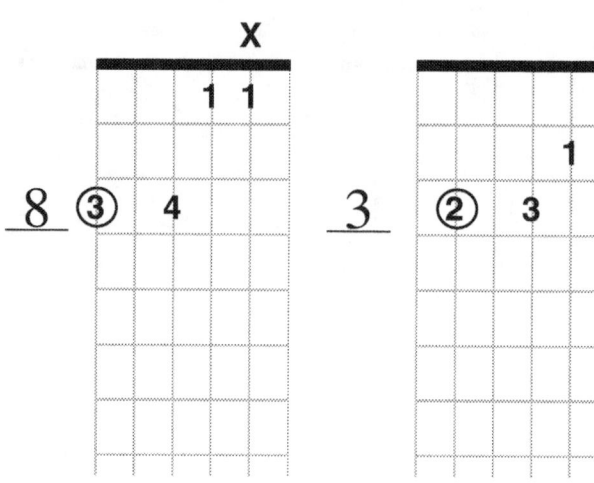
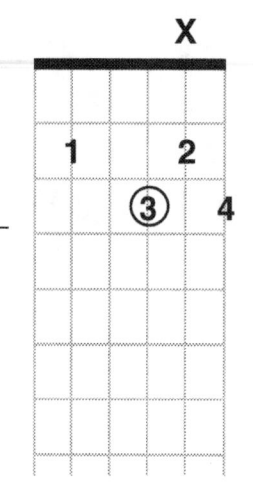
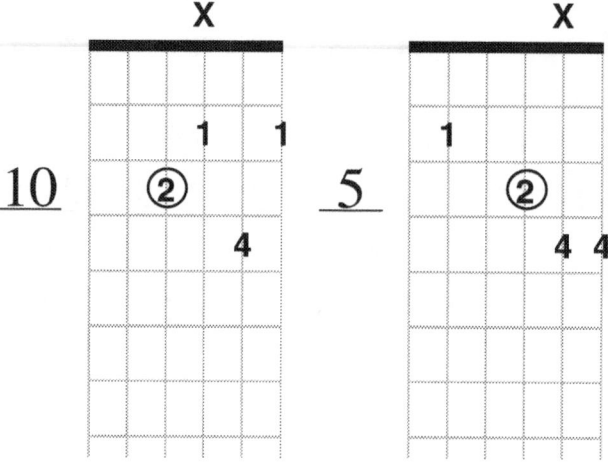
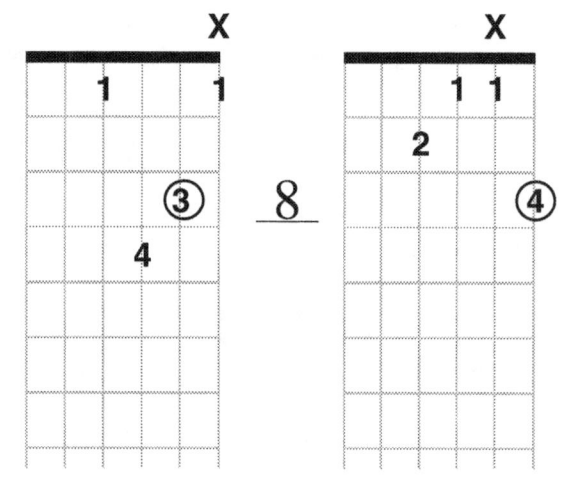
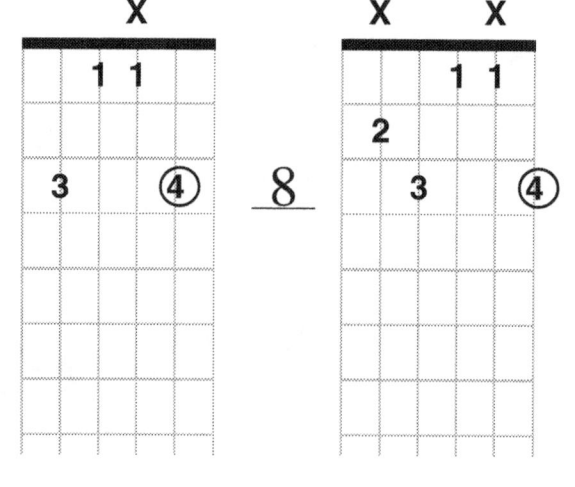

C-m^2-m^7+   C-m^2-M^7+

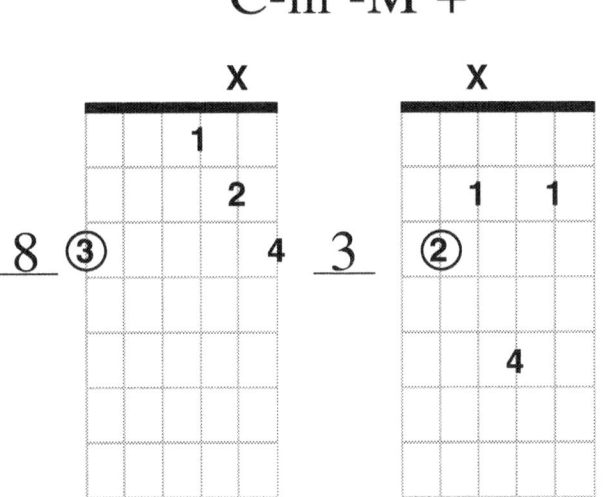
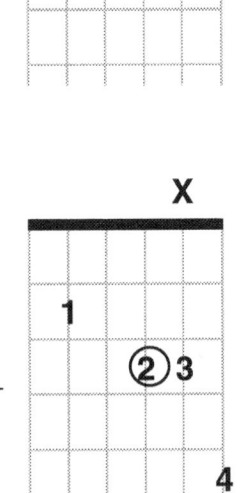
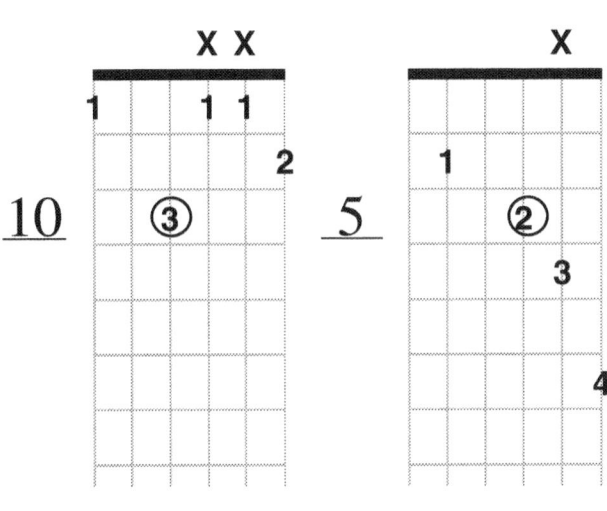
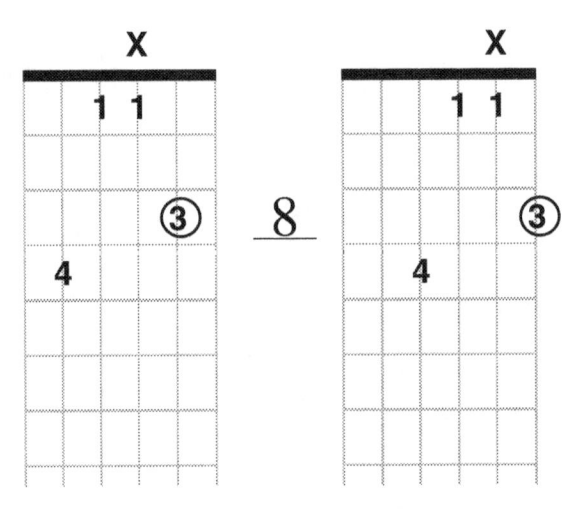
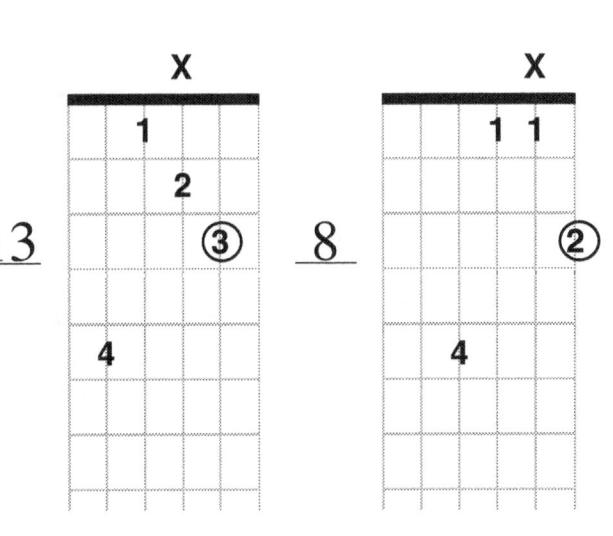

C-M³-m²+   C-M³-M²+

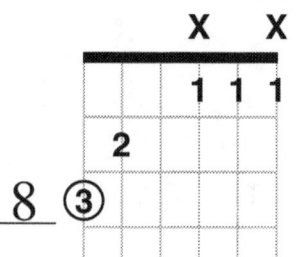
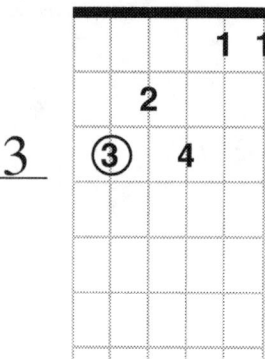
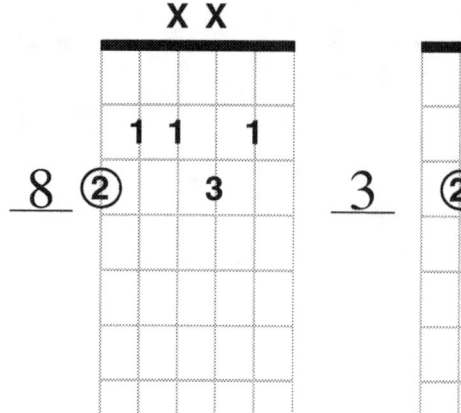
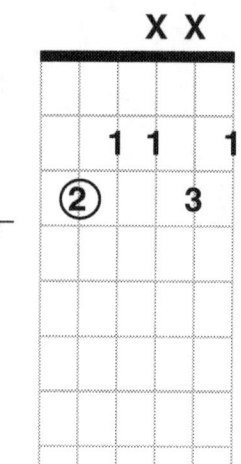

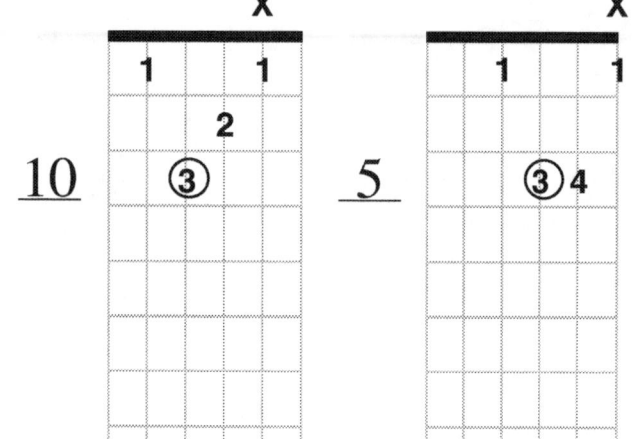
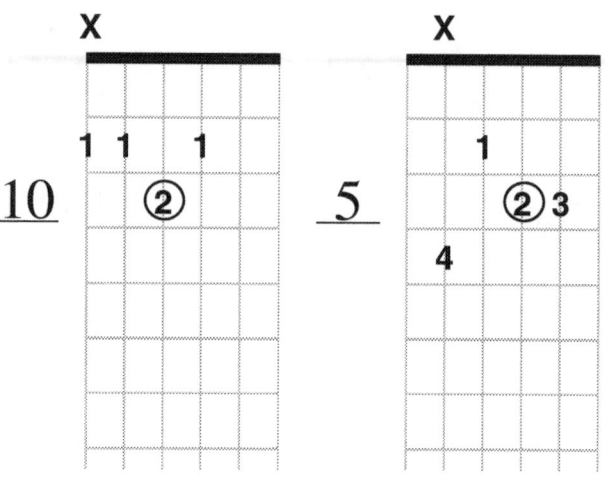

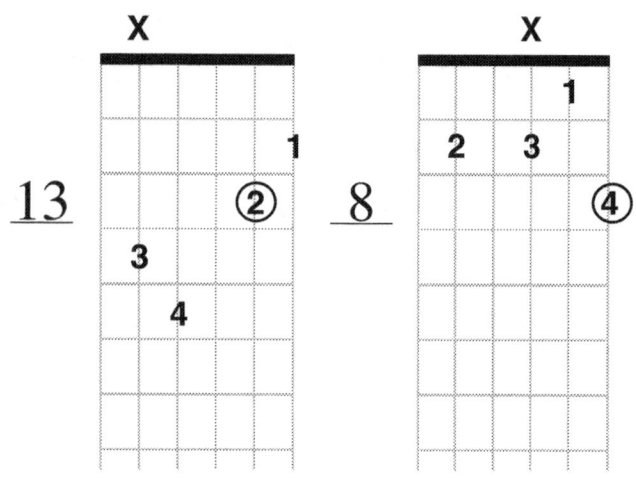
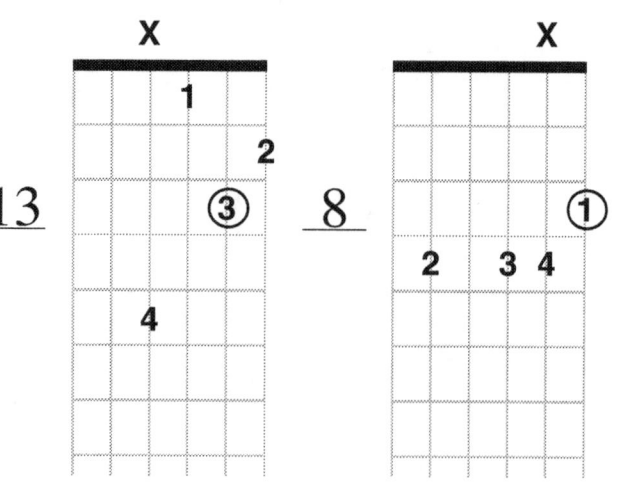

$C\text{-}M^3\text{-}P^4+$ $C\text{-}M^3\text{-}D^5+$

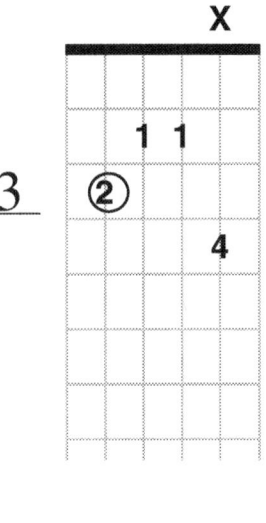
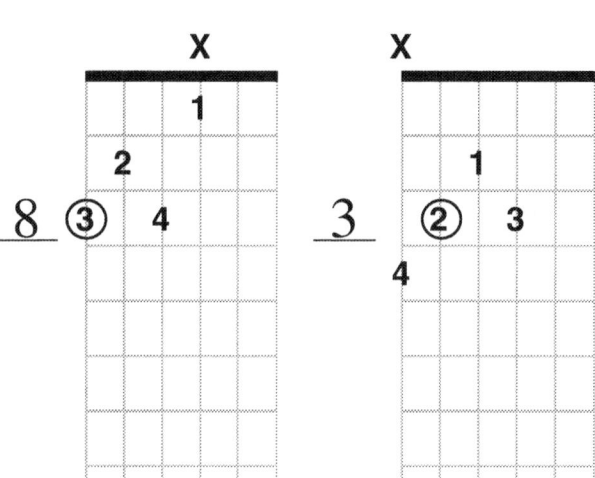
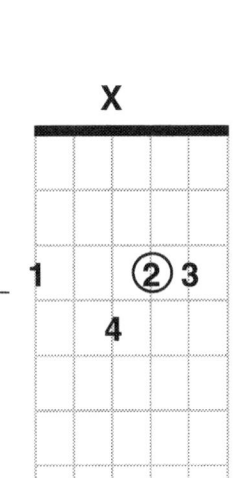
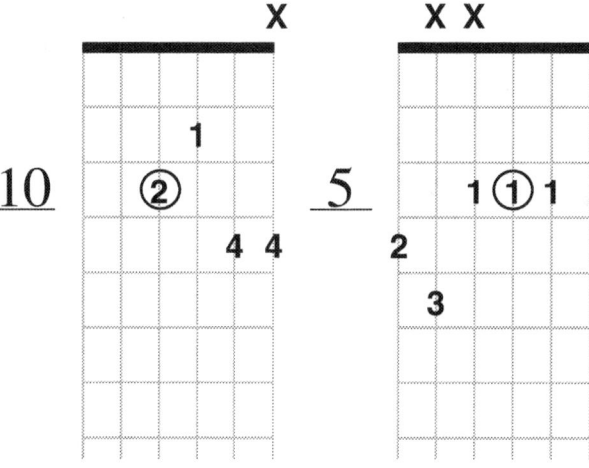
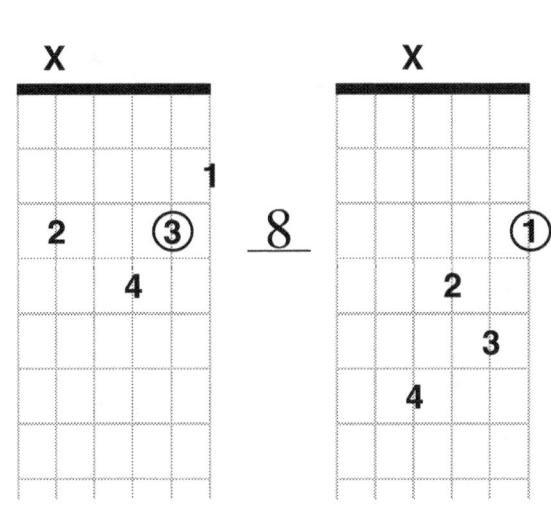
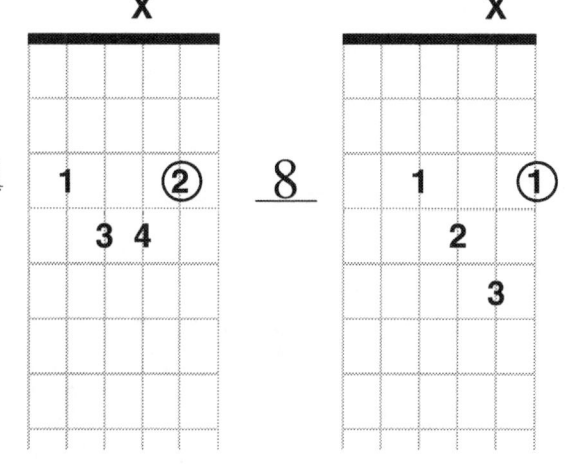

$C\text{-}M^3\text{-}P^5+$ $C\text{-}M^3\text{-}m^6+$

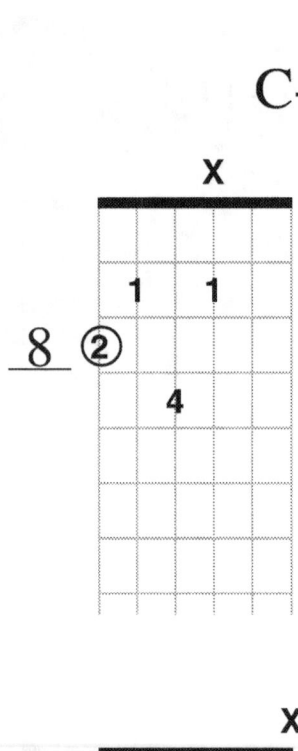
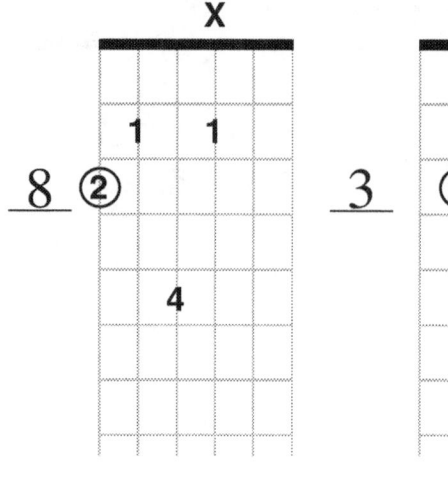
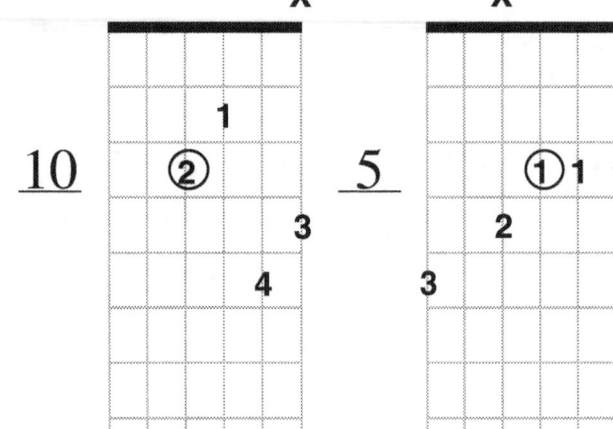
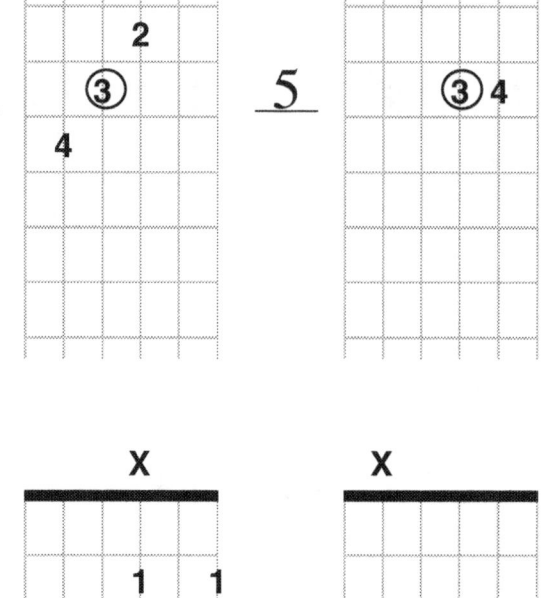
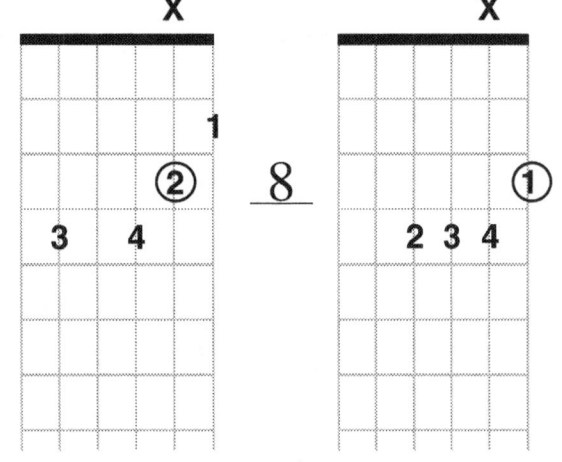
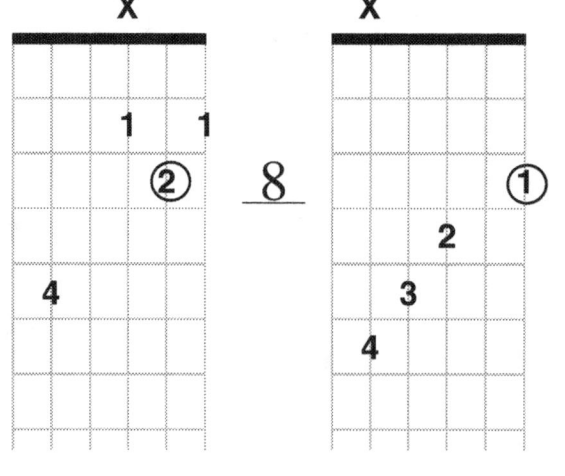

C-M³-M⁶⁺   C-M³-m⁷⁺

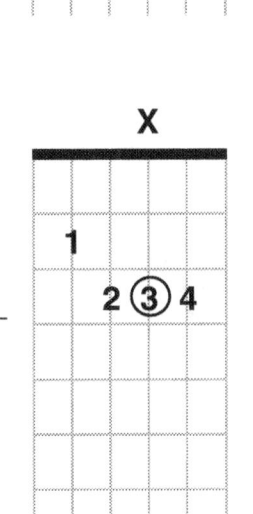
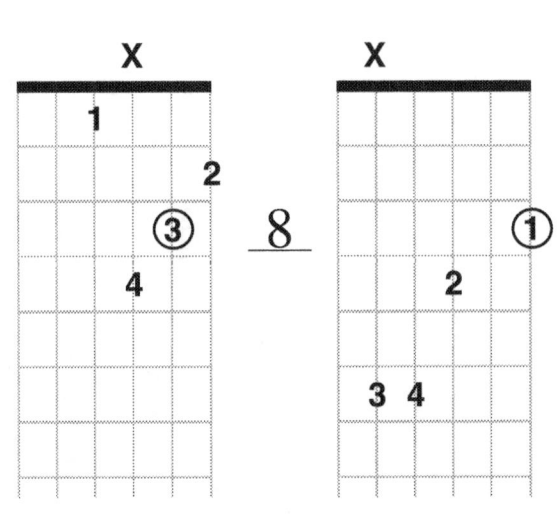
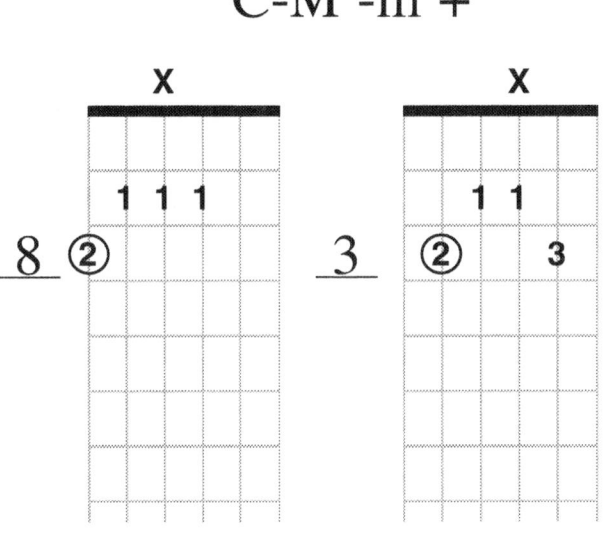
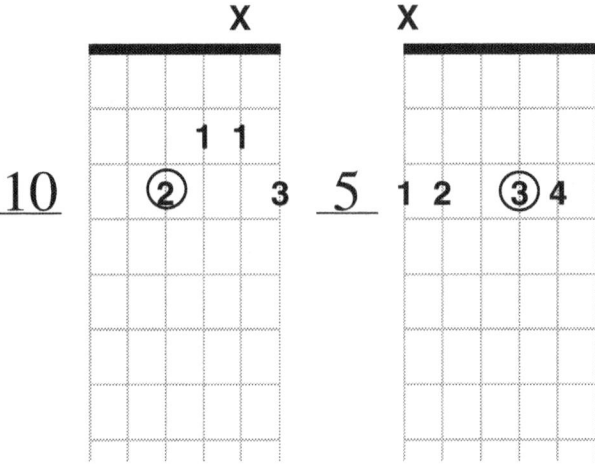
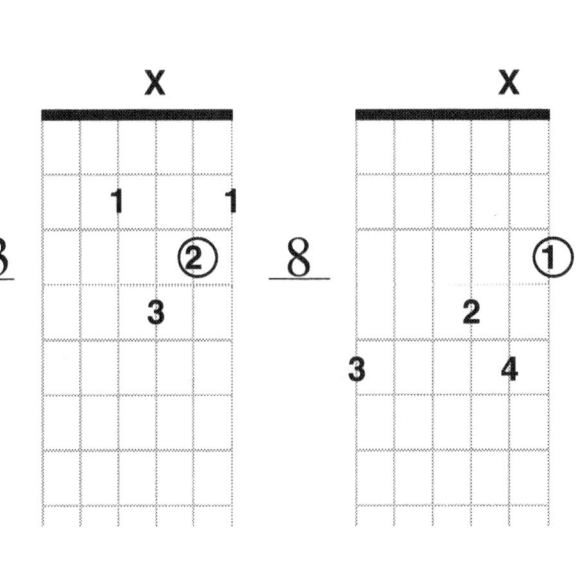

C-M³-M⁷+   C-m³-m²+

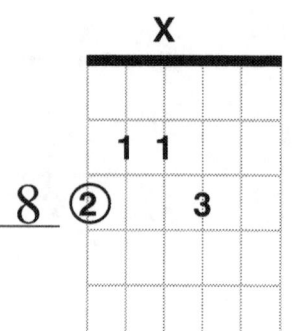
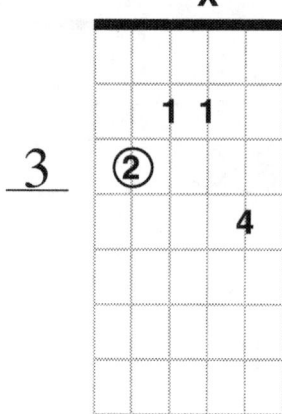
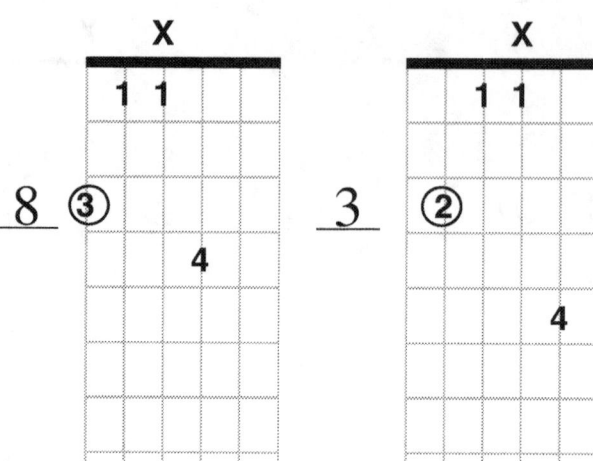
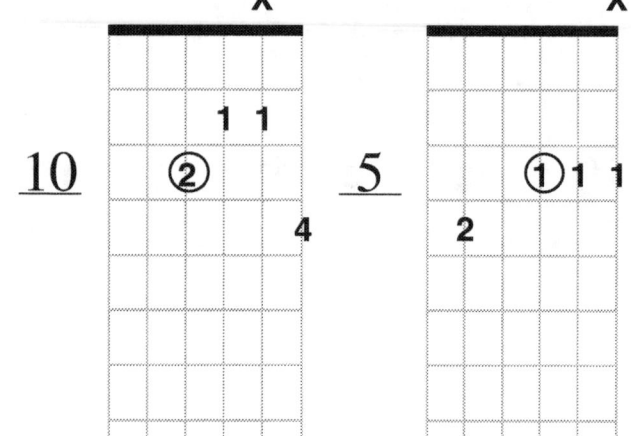
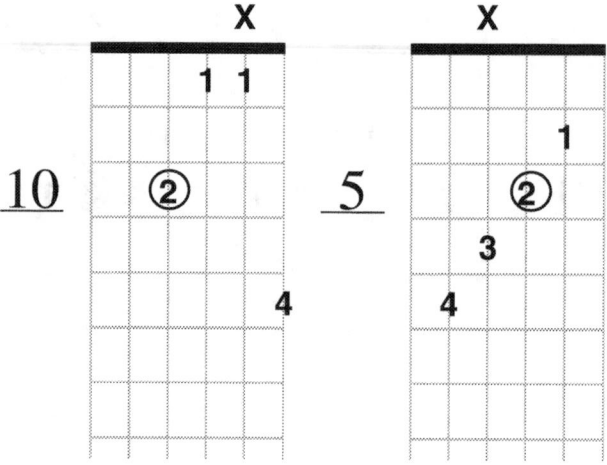
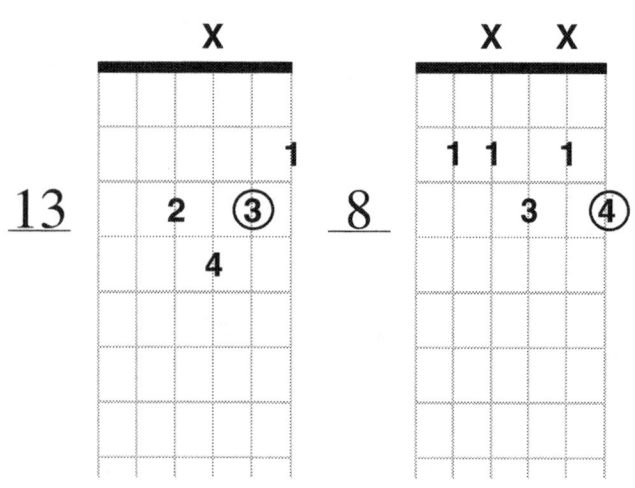
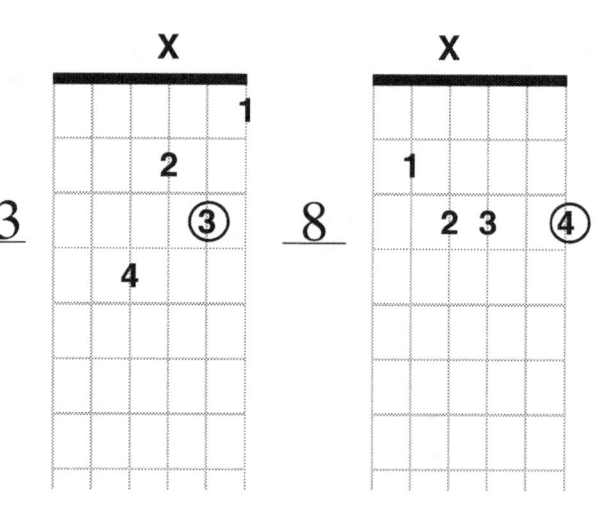

$C\text{-}m^3\text{-}M^2+$

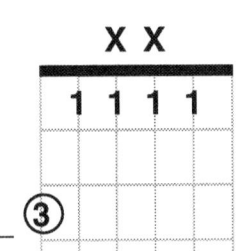
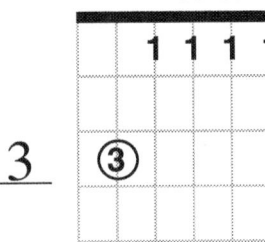
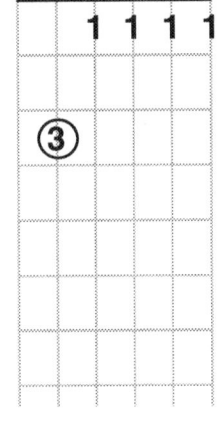
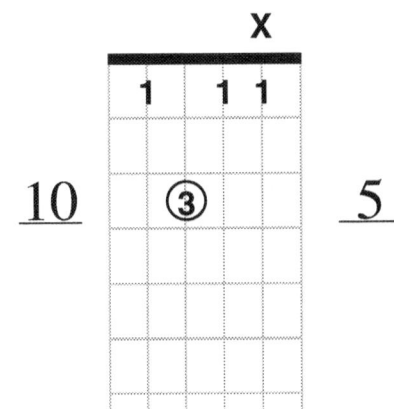
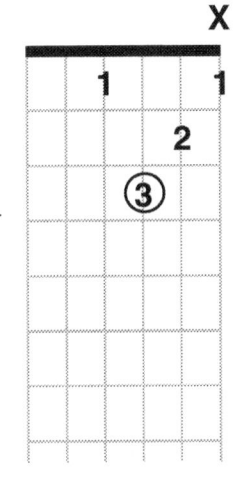
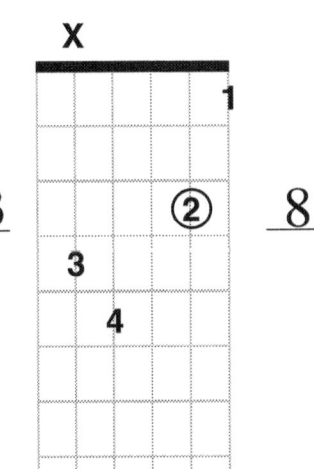
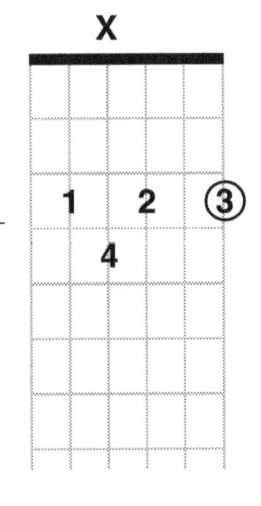

$C\text{-}m^3\text{-}P^4+$

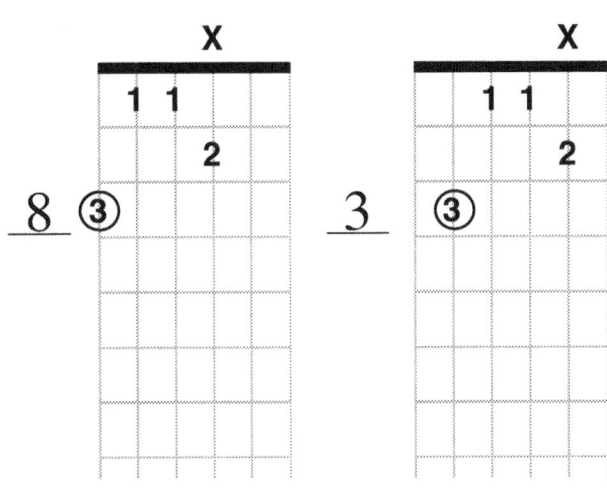
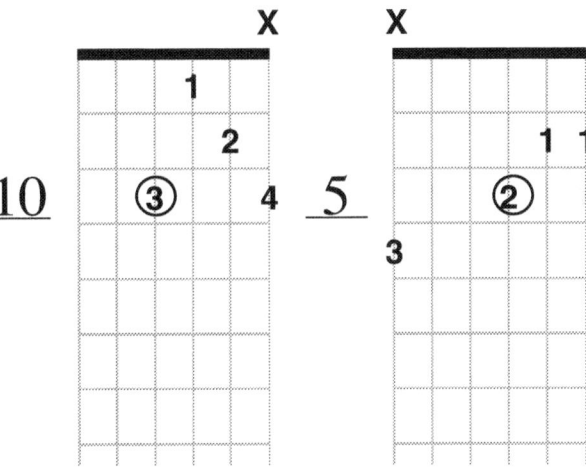
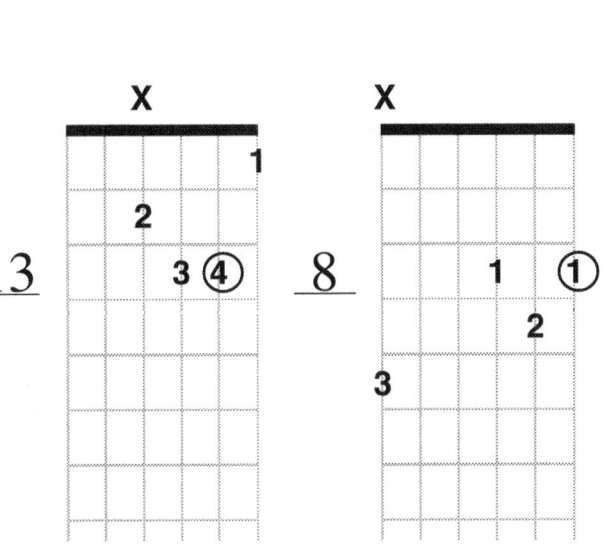

$C\text{-}m^3\text{-}D^5+$ $\qquad$ $C\text{-}m^3\text{-}P^5+$

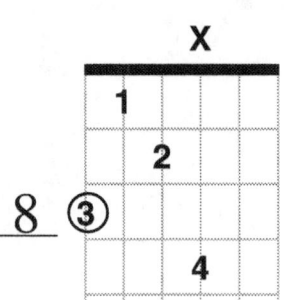
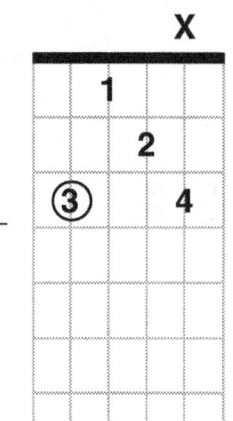
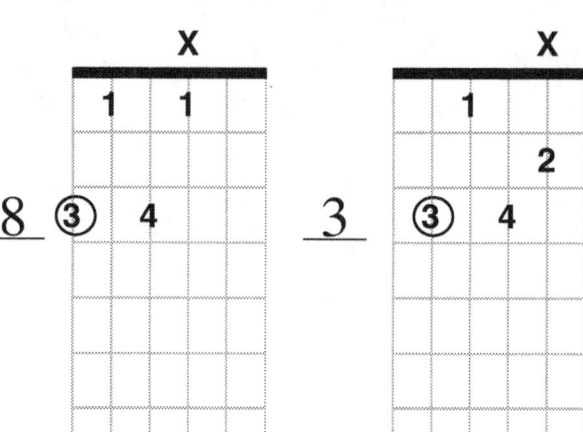
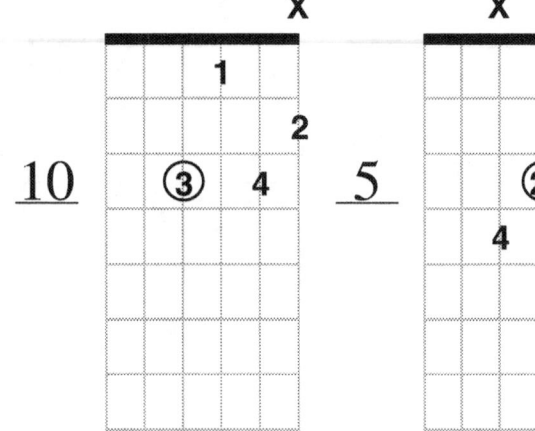
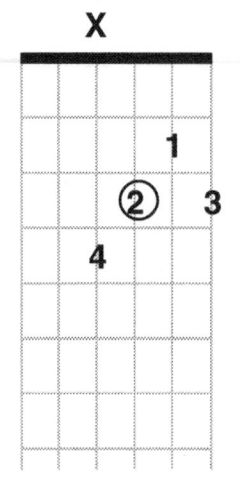
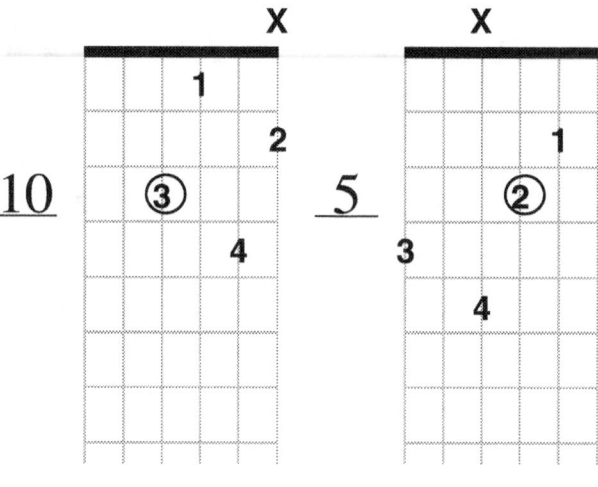
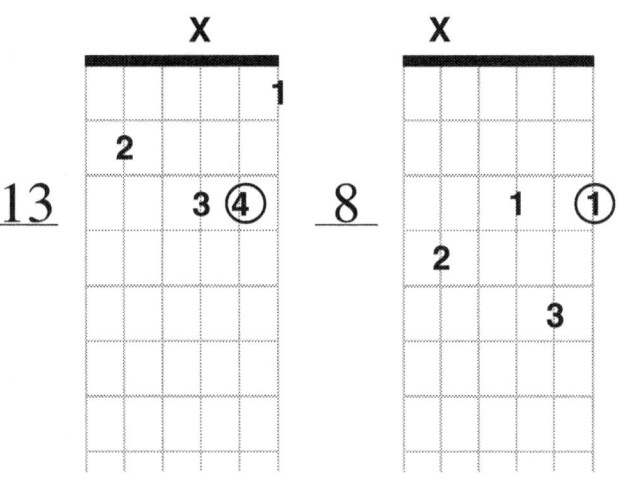
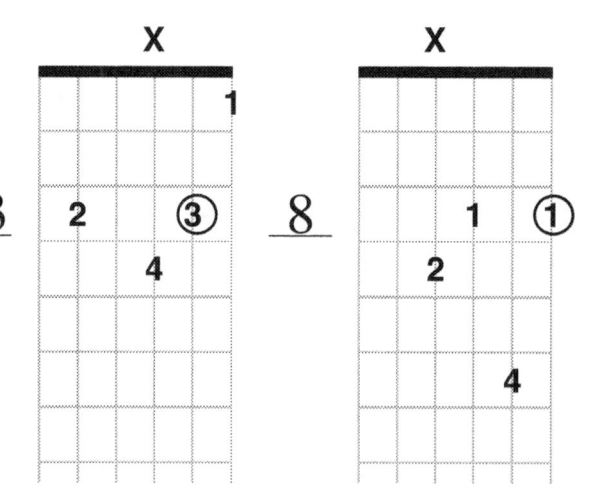

C-m³-m⁶+   C-m³-M⁶+

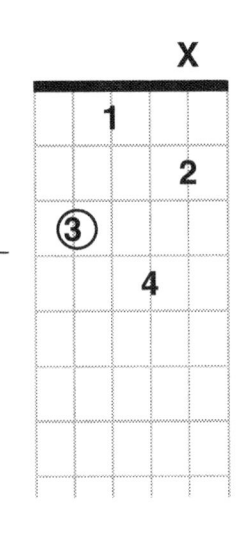
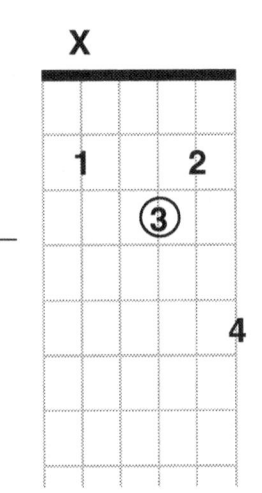
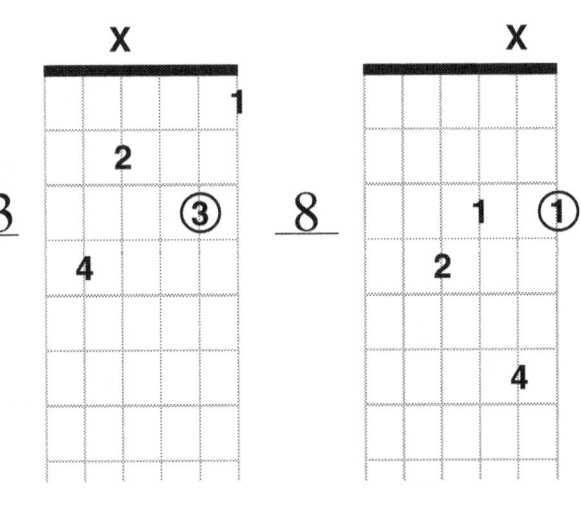
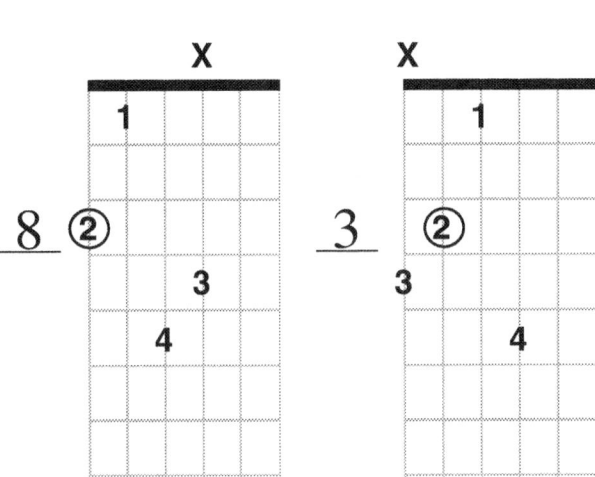
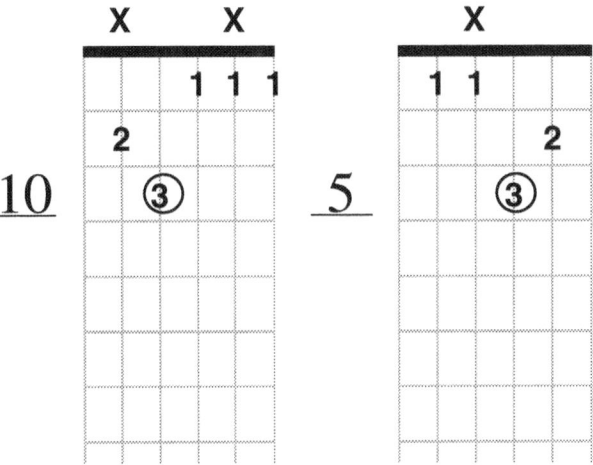
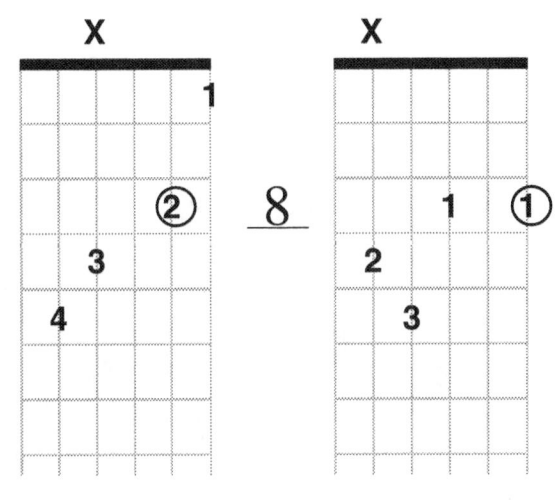

$C\text{-}m^3\text{-}m^7+$ $C\text{-}m^3\text{-}M^7+$

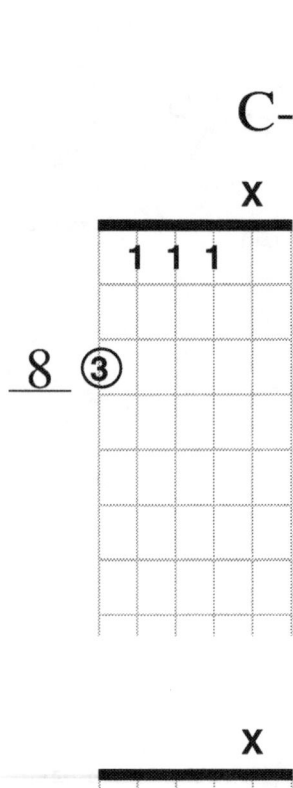
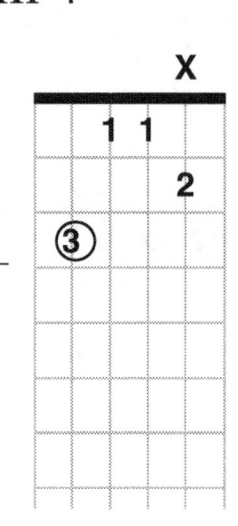
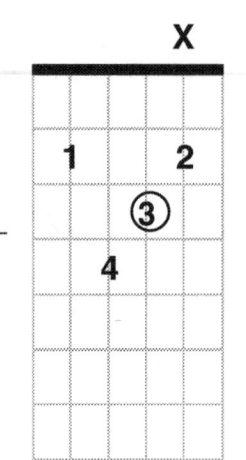
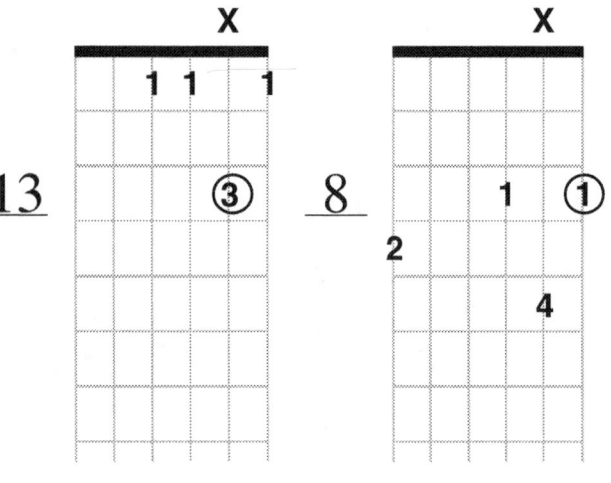
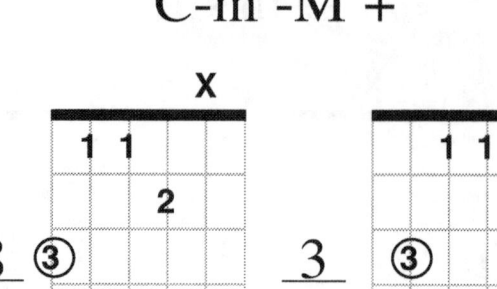
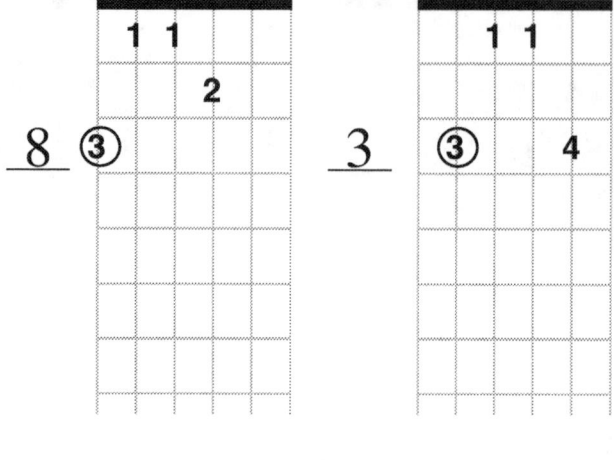
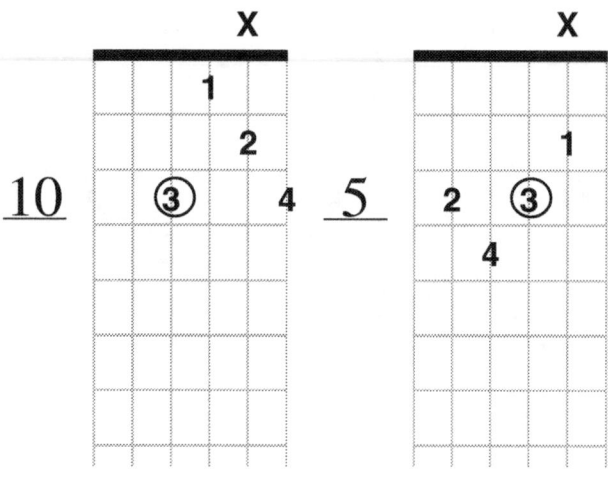
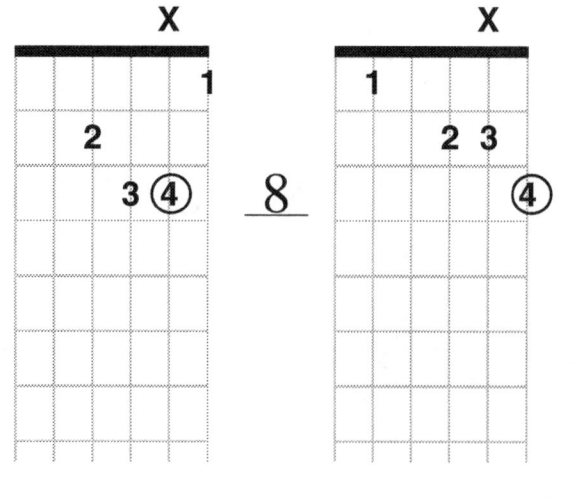

C-P⁴-m²+   C-P⁴-M²+

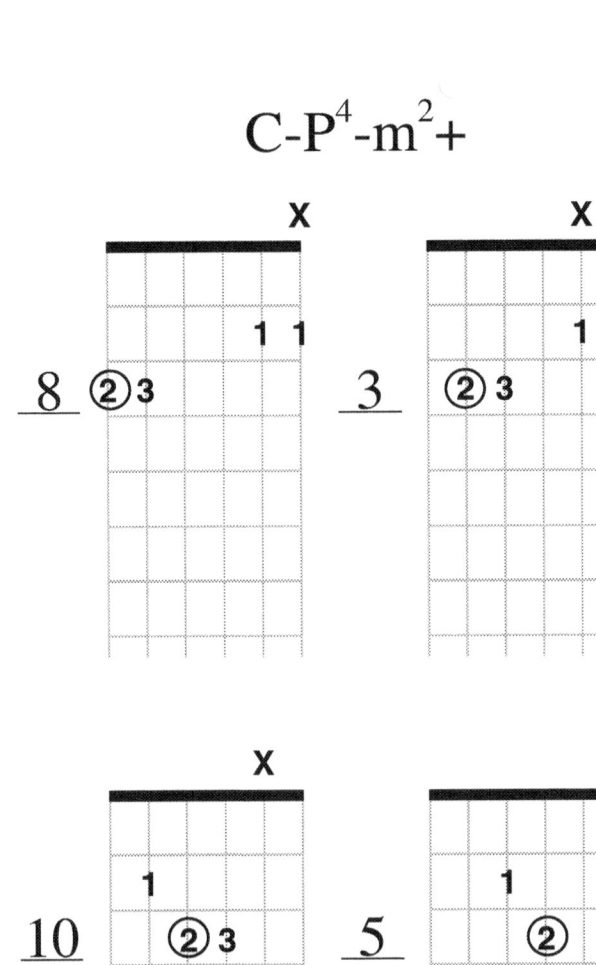
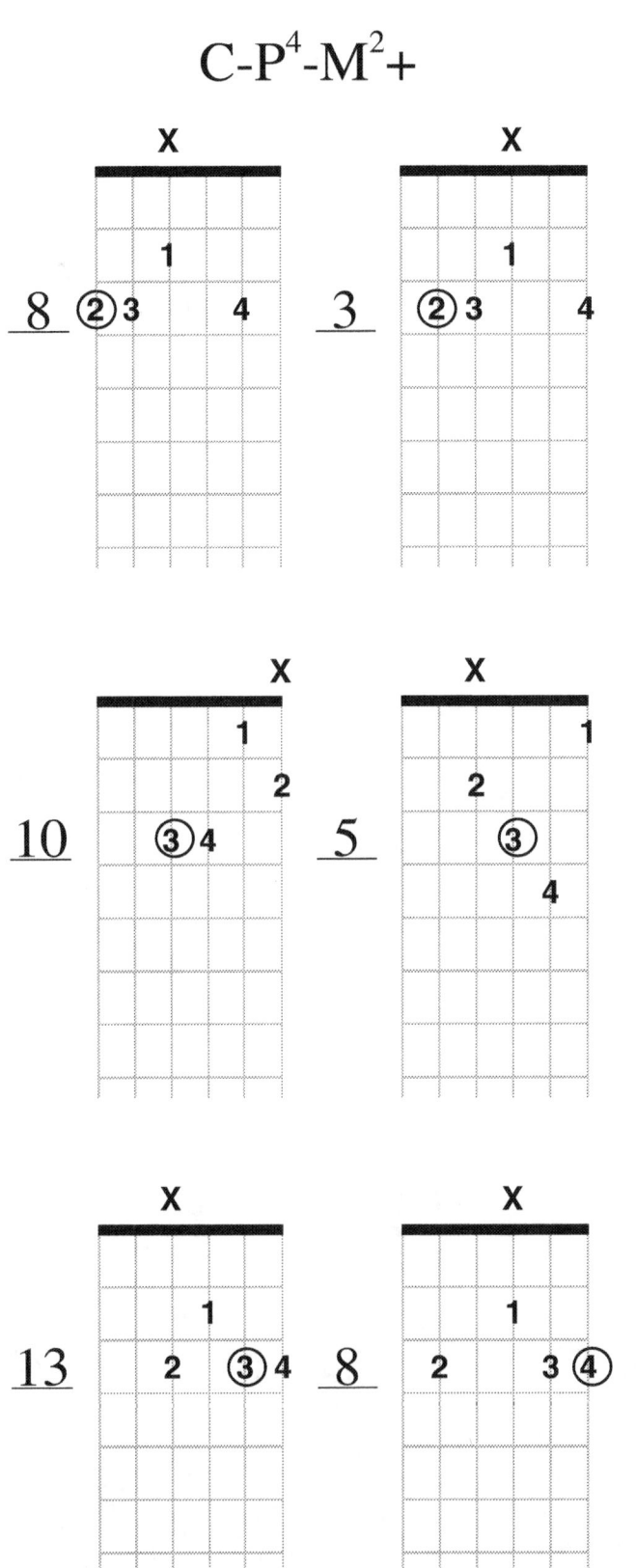
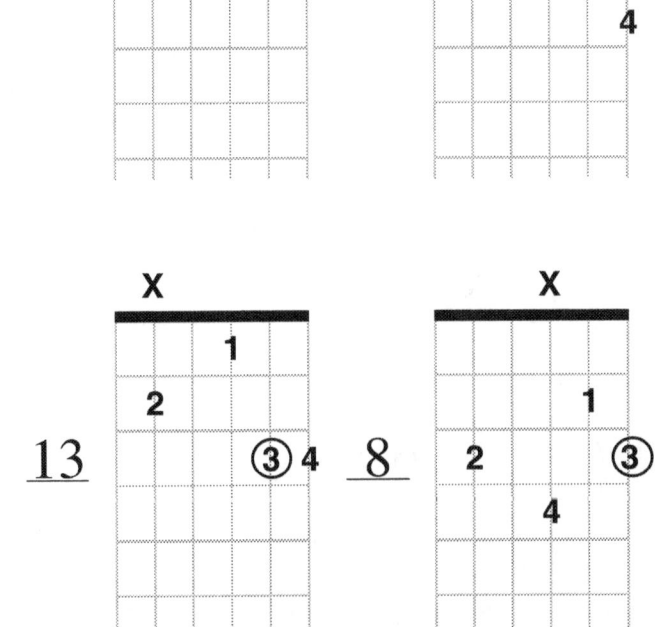

$C-P^4-m^3+$ $C-P^4-M^3+$

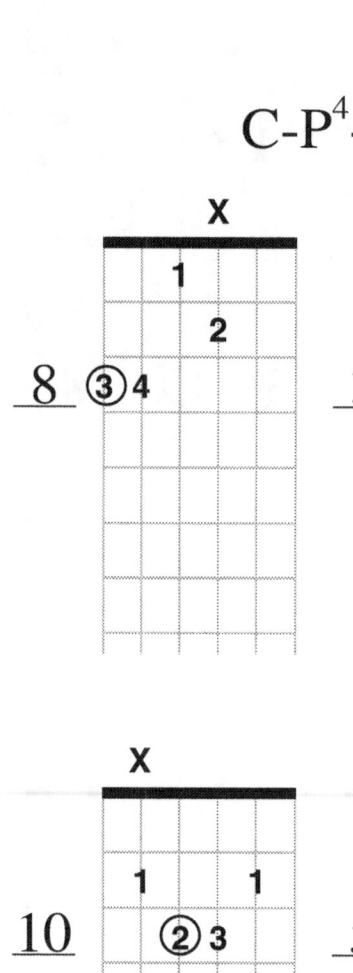
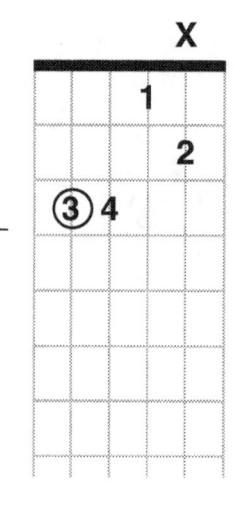
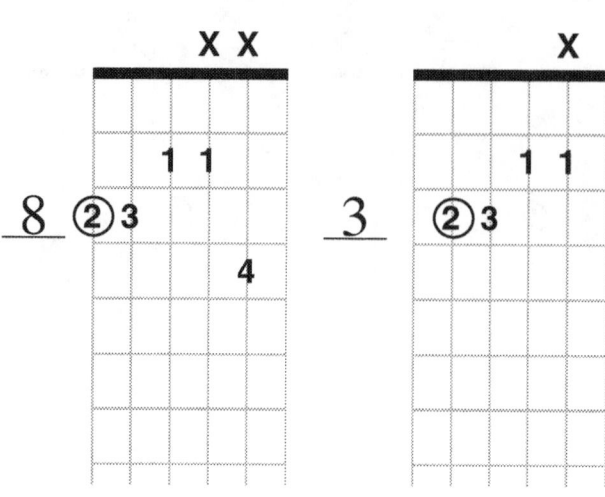
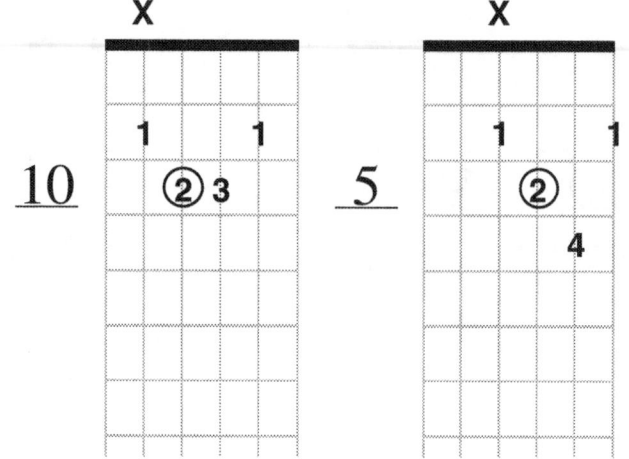
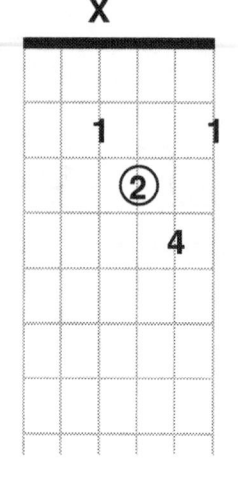
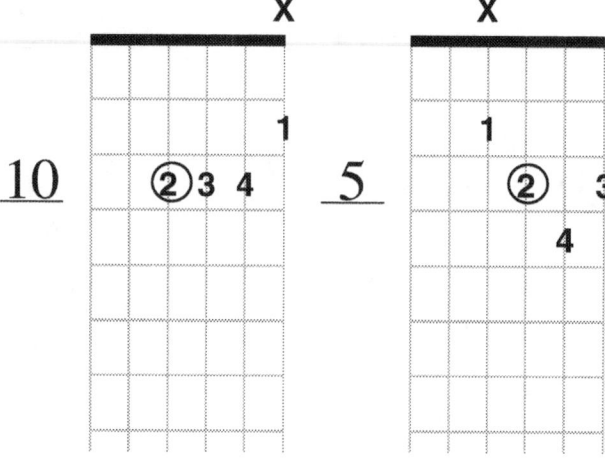
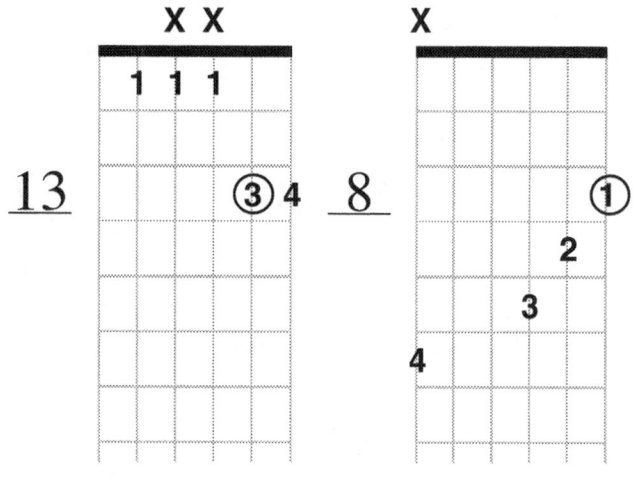
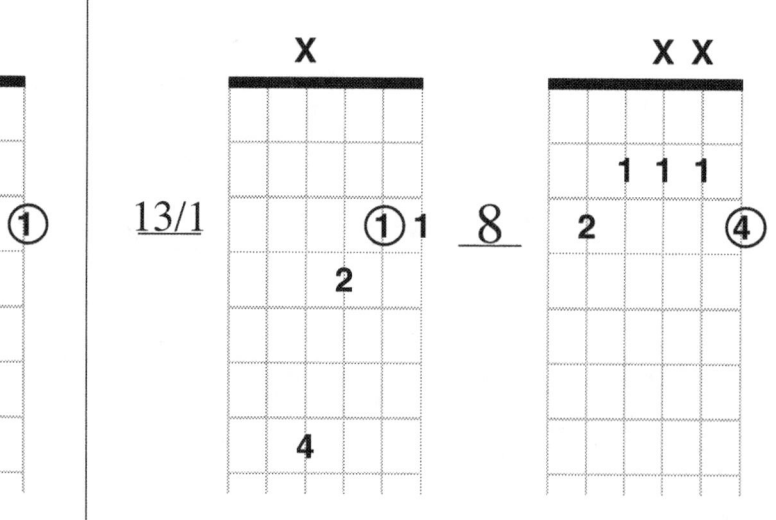

$C-P^4-D^5+$ $C-P^4-P^5+$

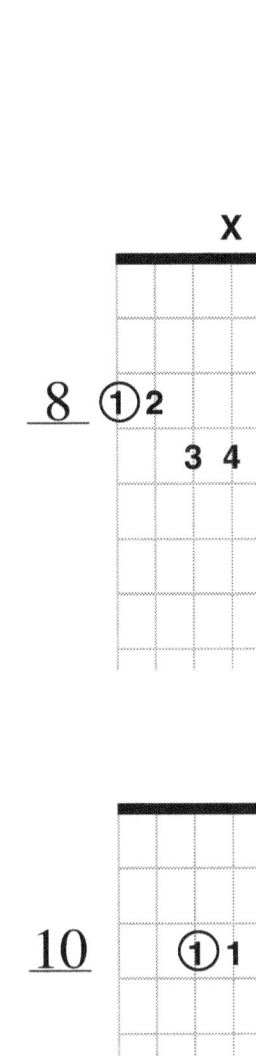
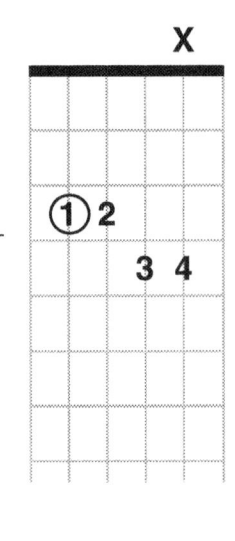
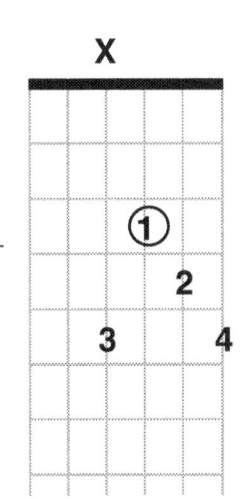
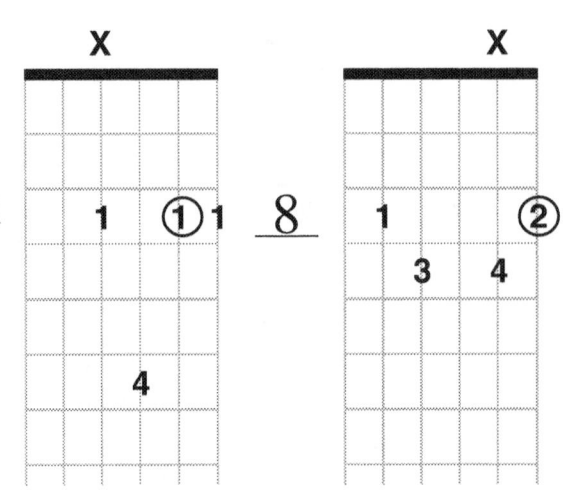
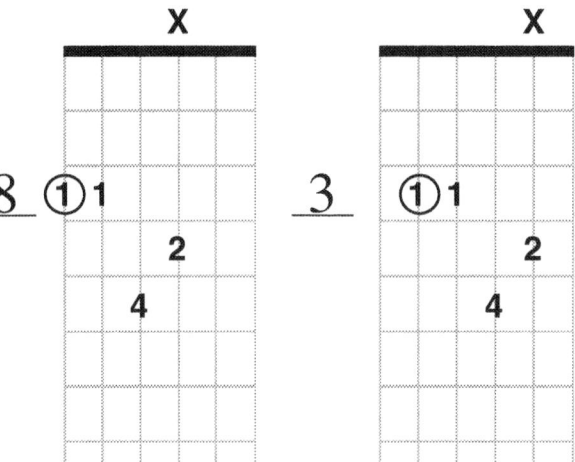
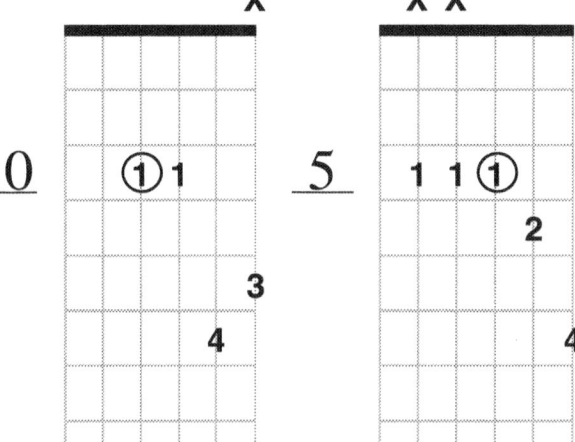
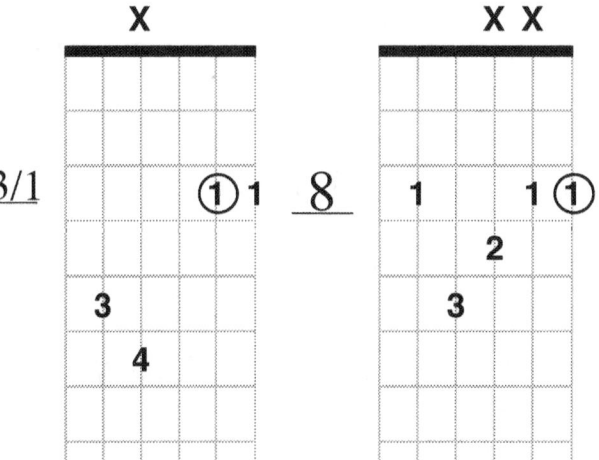

$C\text{-}P^4\text{-}m^6+$ $C\text{-}P^4\text{-}M^6+$

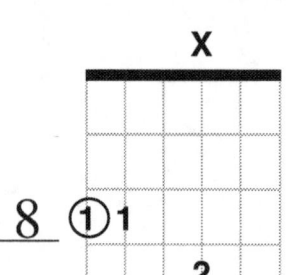
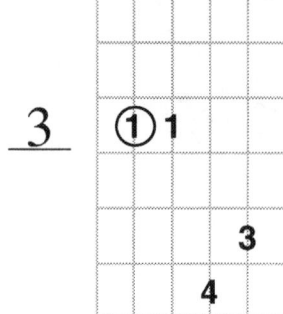
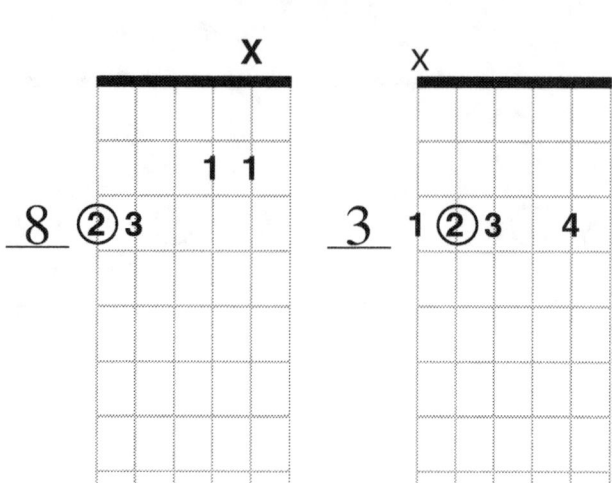

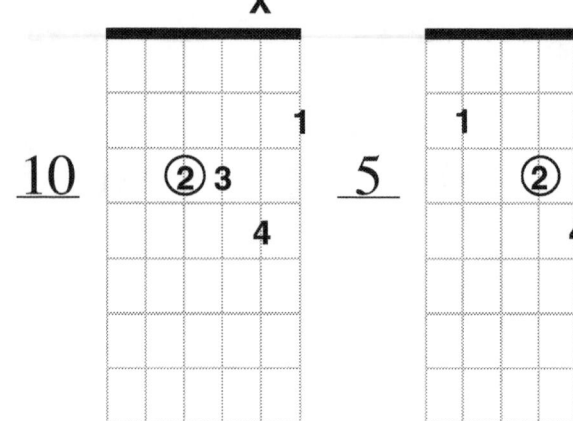
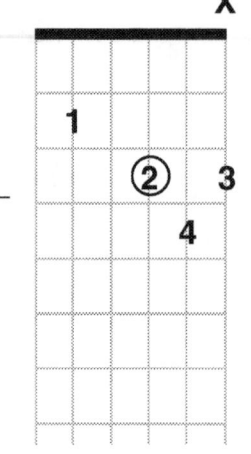
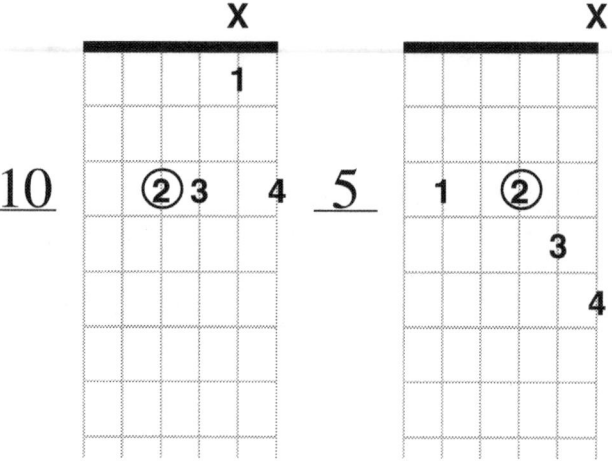

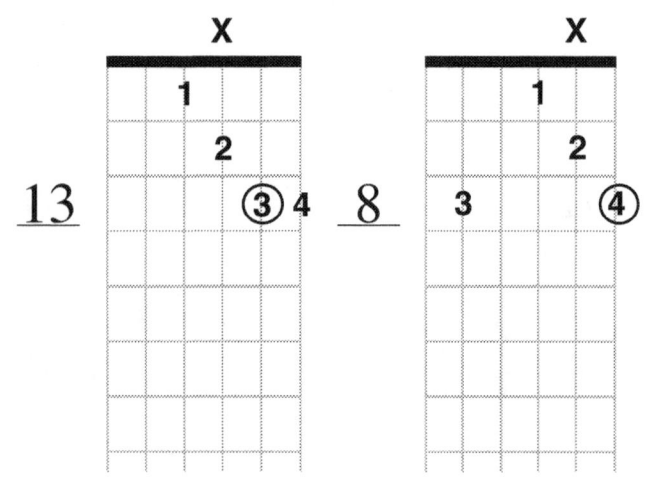
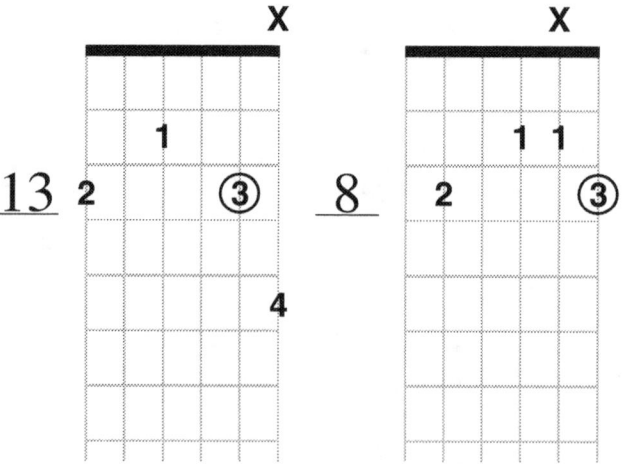

$C\text{-}P^4\text{-}m^7+$ $C\text{-}P^4\text{-}M^7+$

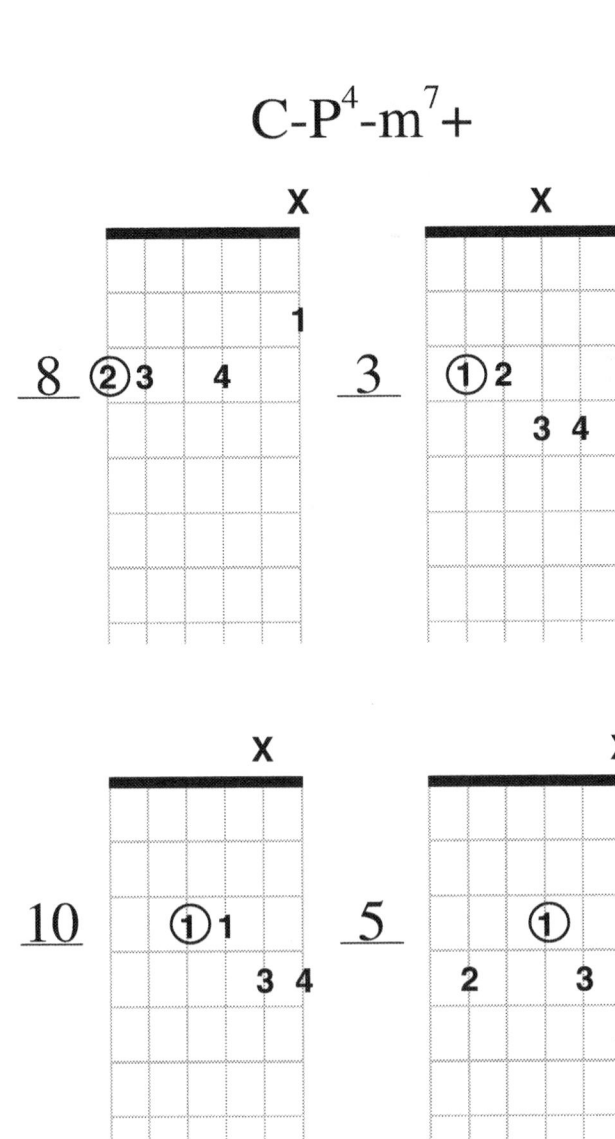
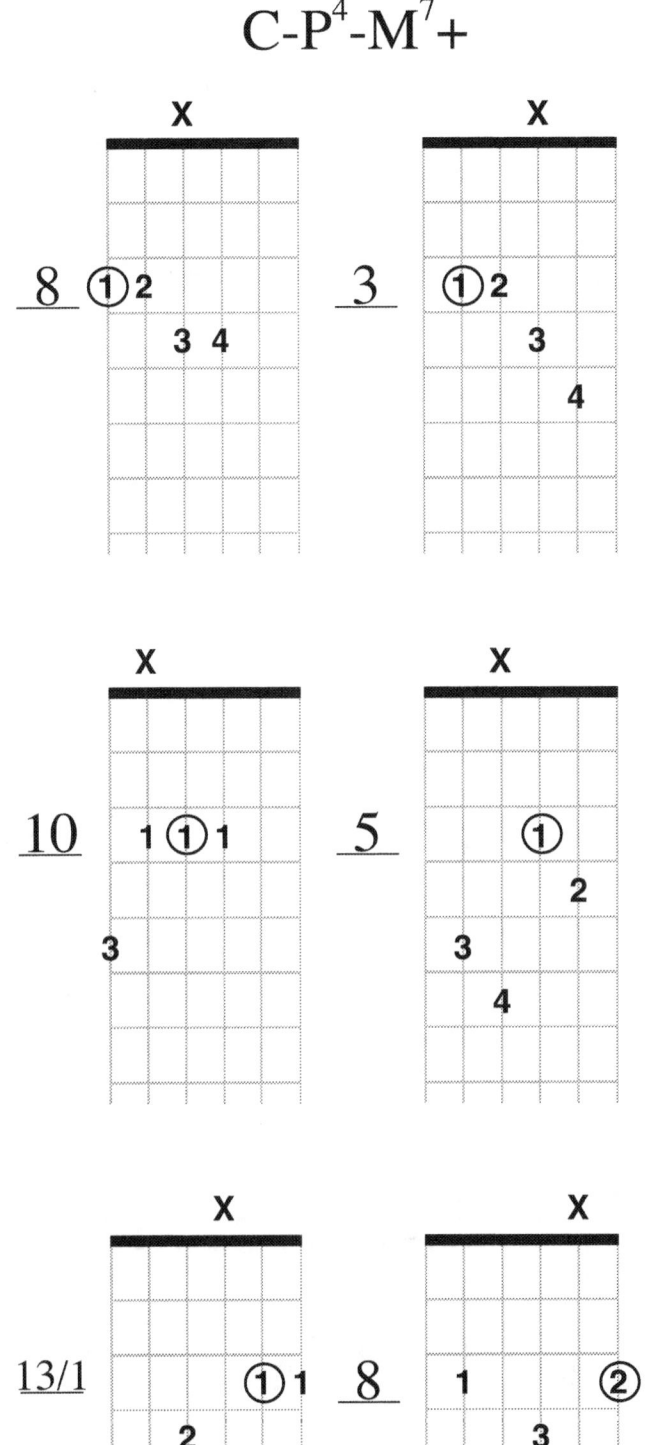
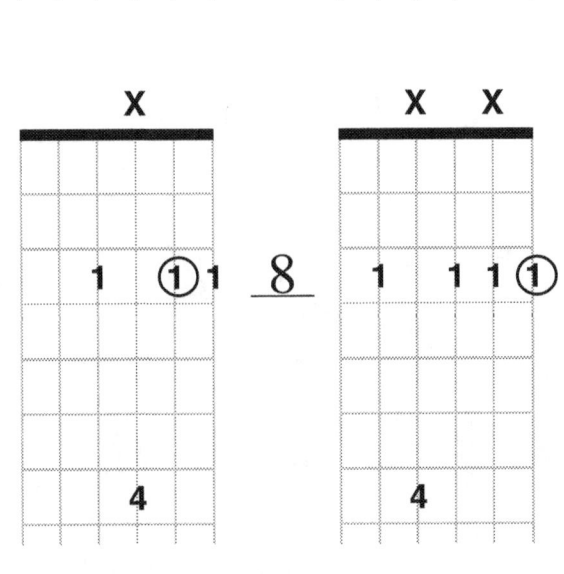
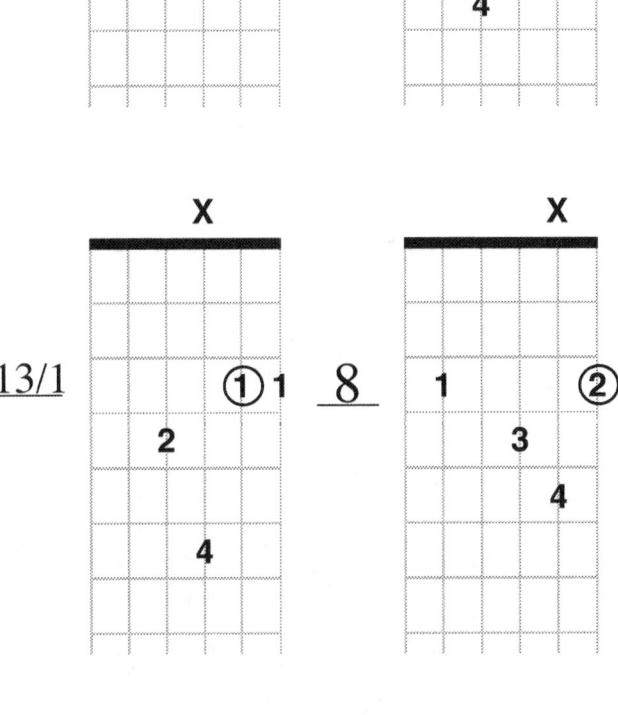

$C\text{-}P^5\text{-}m^2+$ $\qquad$ $C\text{-}P^5\text{-}M^2+$

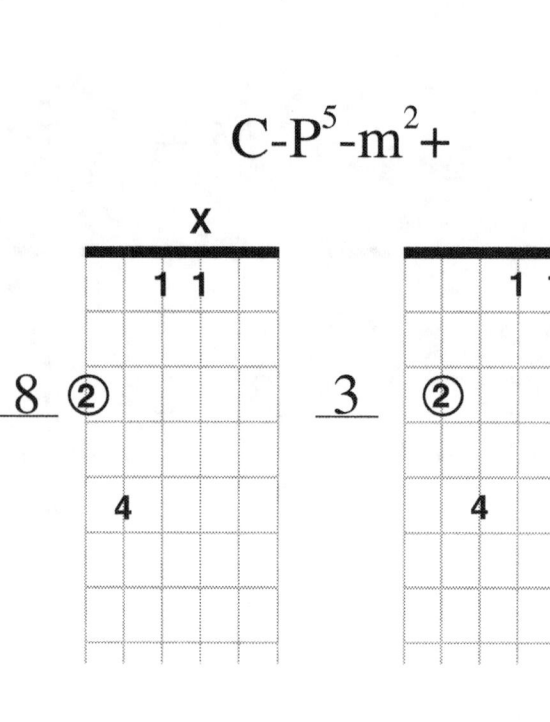
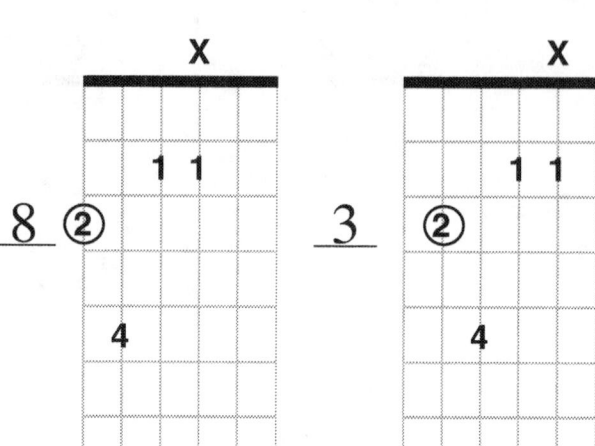
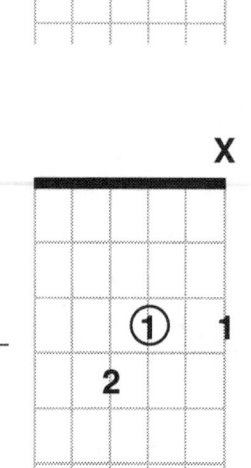
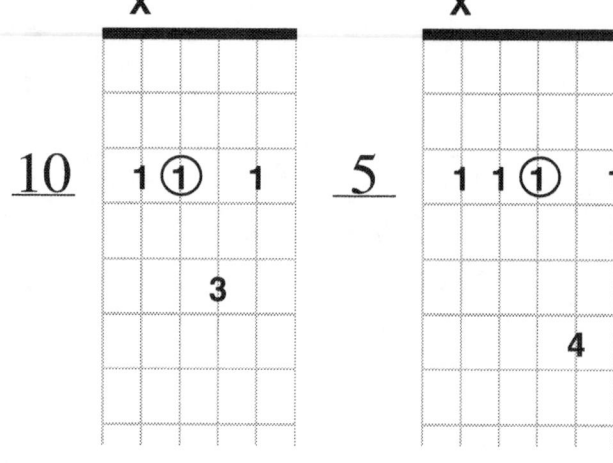
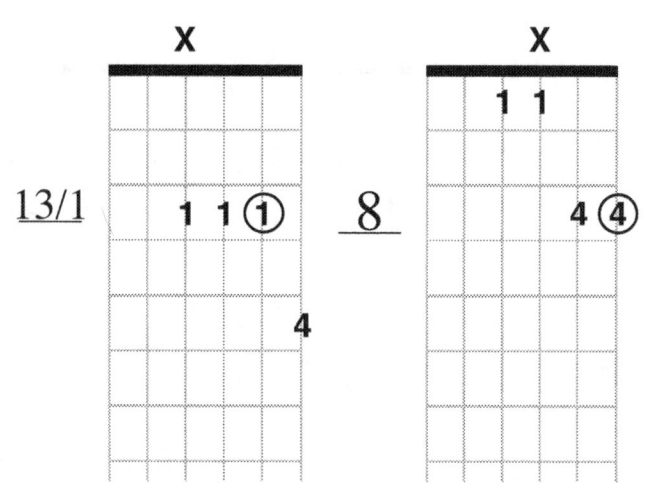
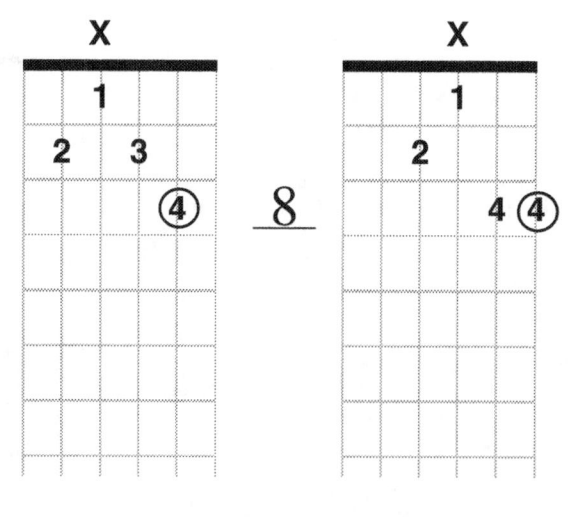

C-P^5-m^3+   C-P^5-M^3+

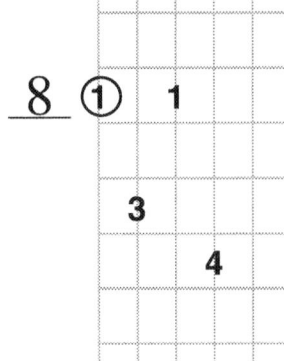
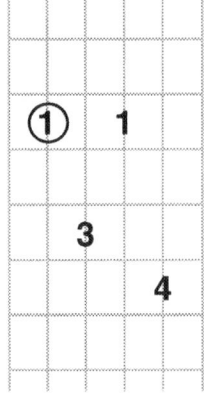
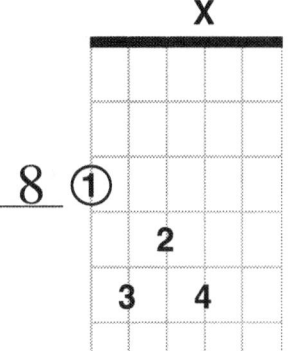
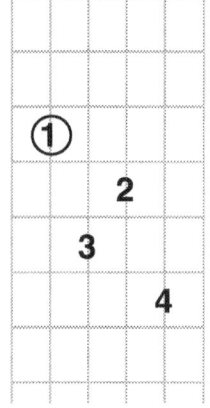

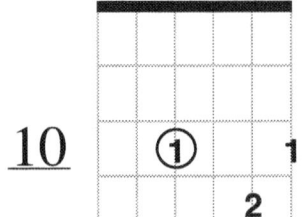
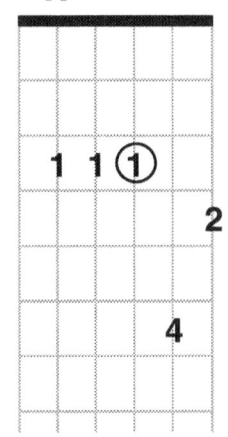
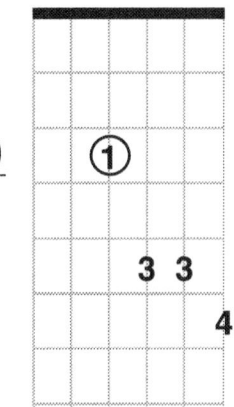
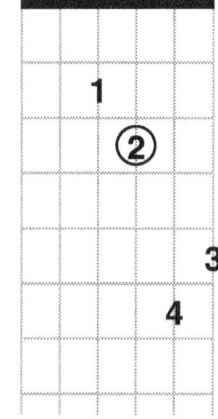

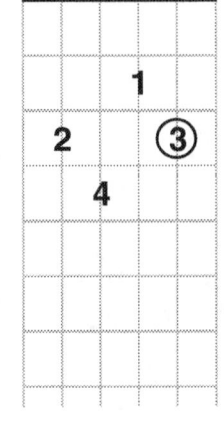
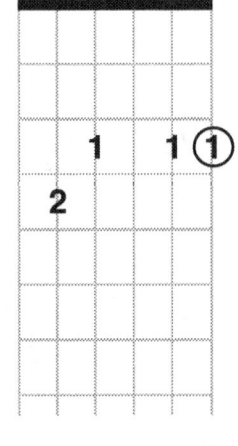
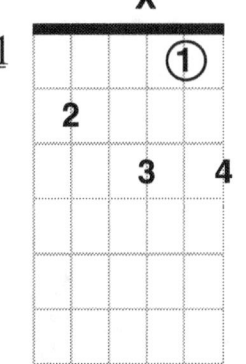
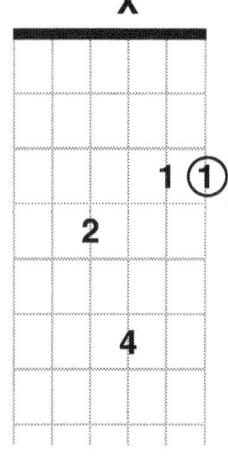

$C\text{-}P^5\text{-}P^4+$ $\qquad$ $C\text{-}P^5\text{-}m^6+$

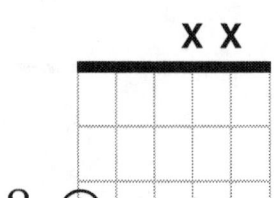
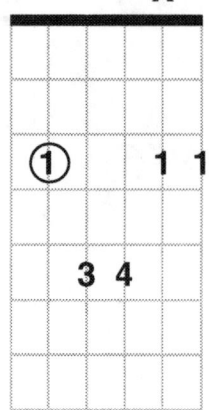
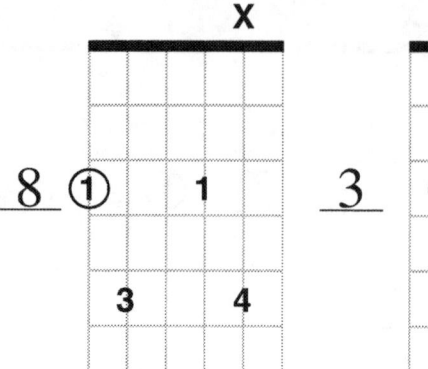
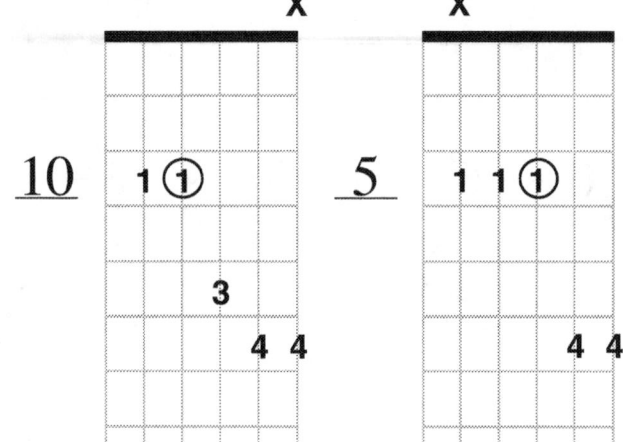
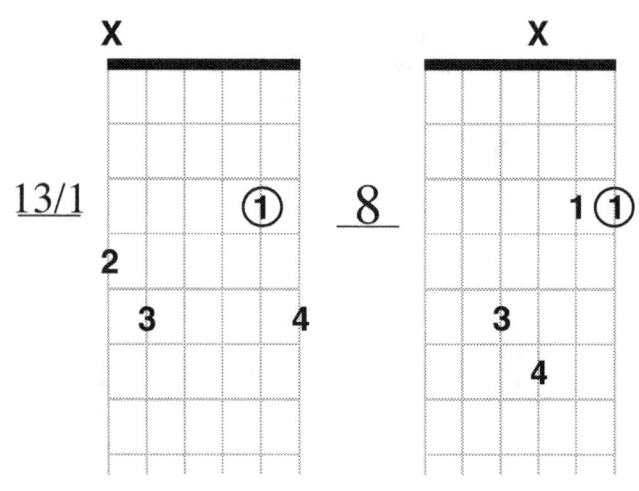
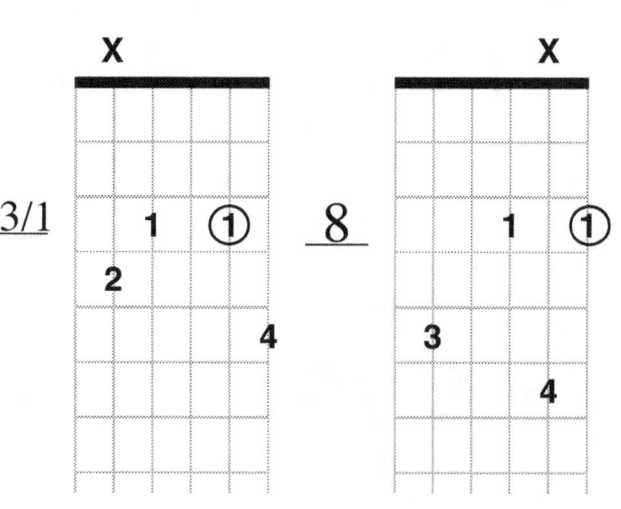

C-P^5-M^6+   C-P^5-m^7+

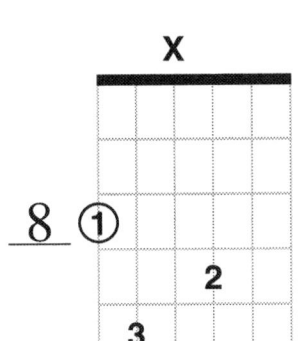
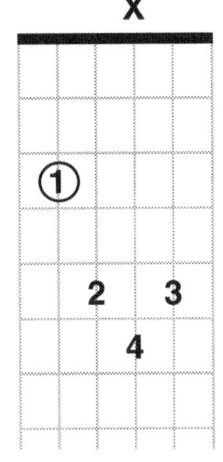
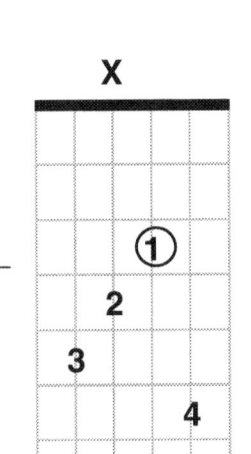
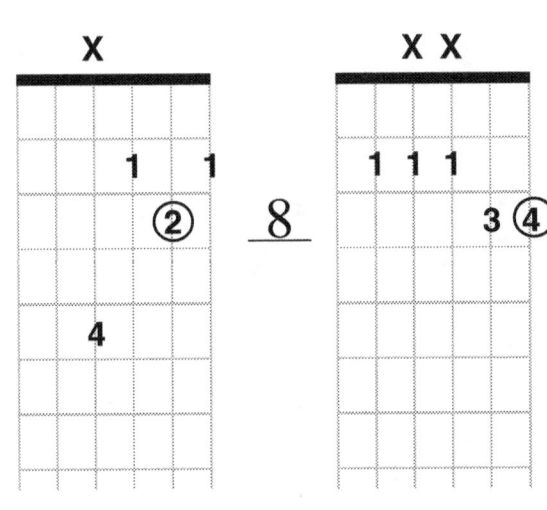
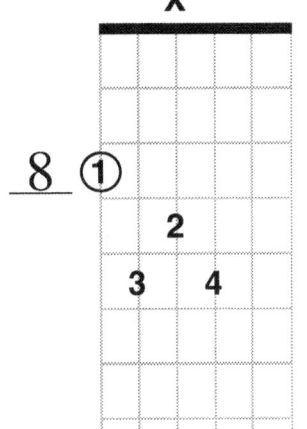
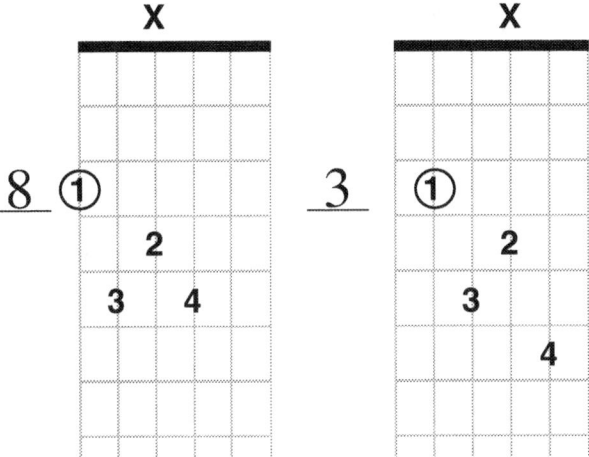
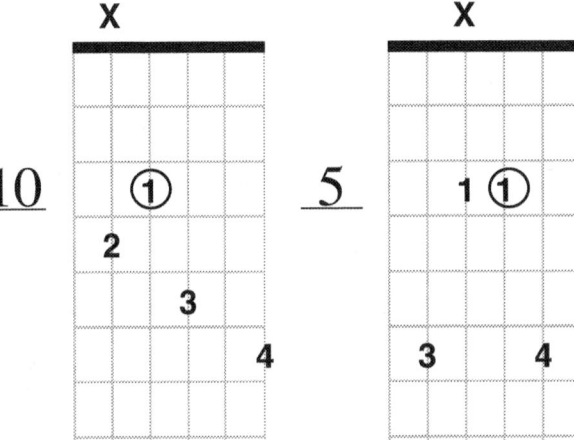
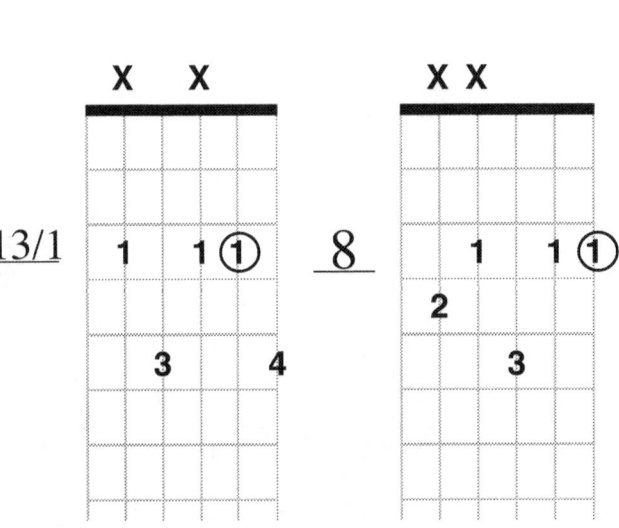

C-P^5-M^7+ 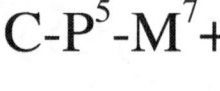   C-D^5-m^2+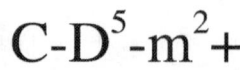

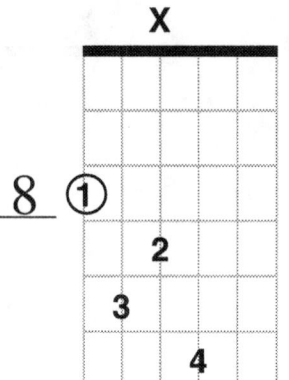 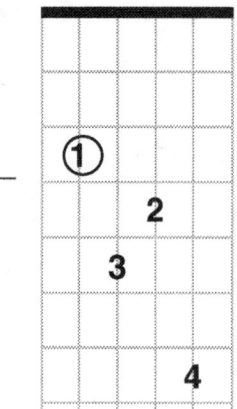 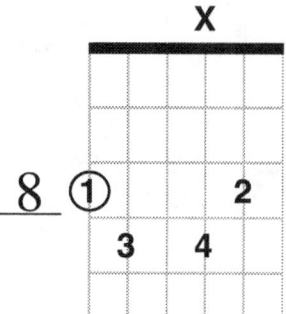 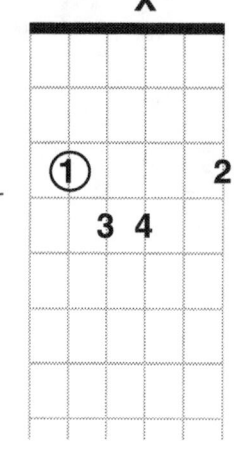

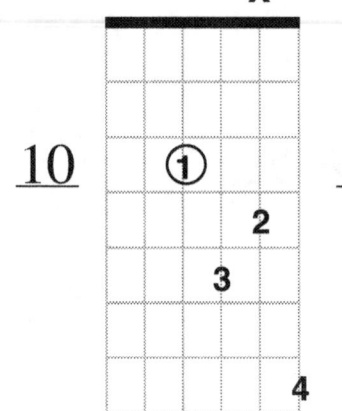 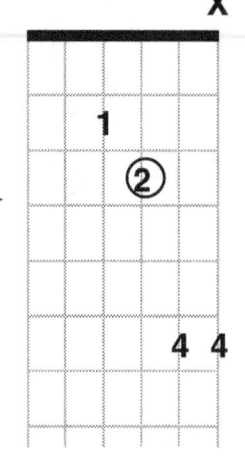 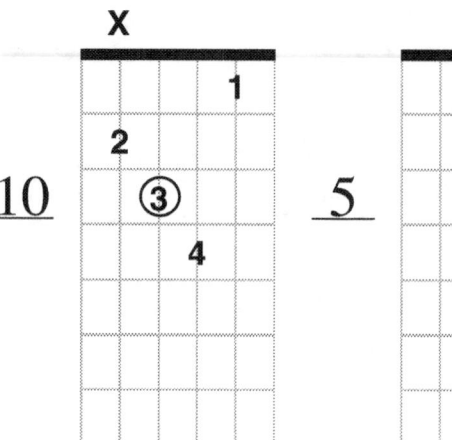

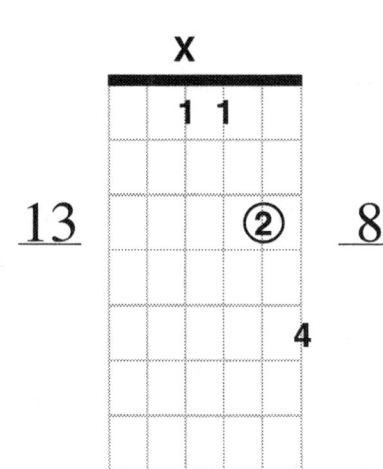 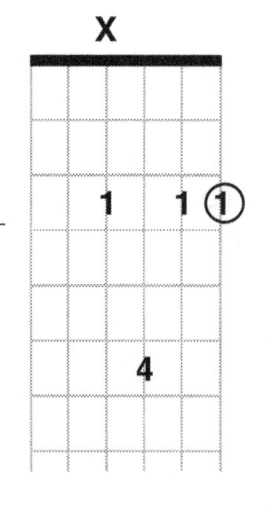 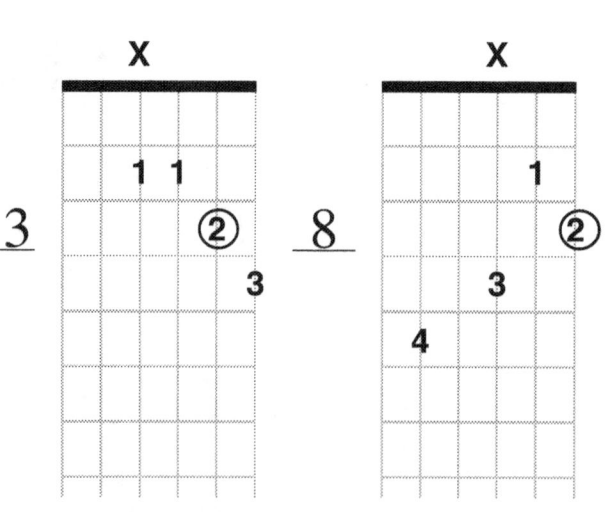

C-D^5-M^2+   C-D^5-m^3+

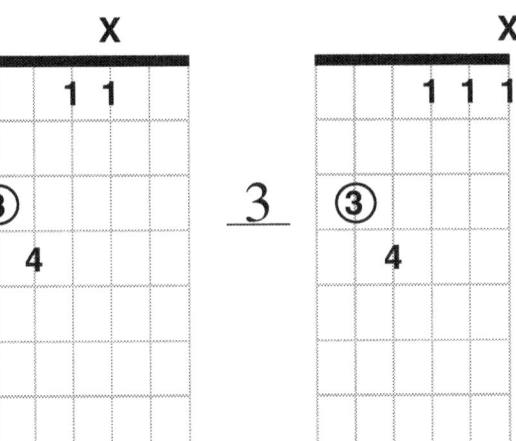
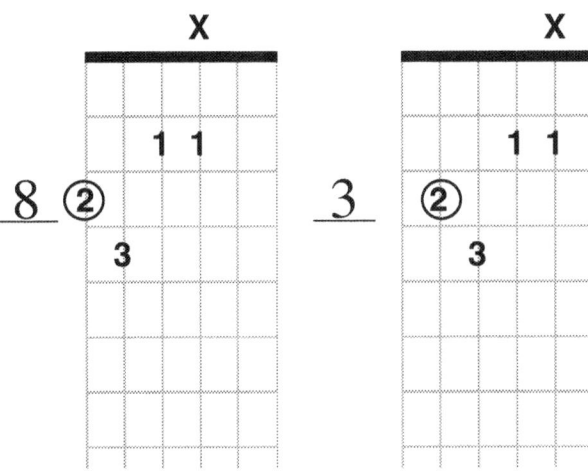
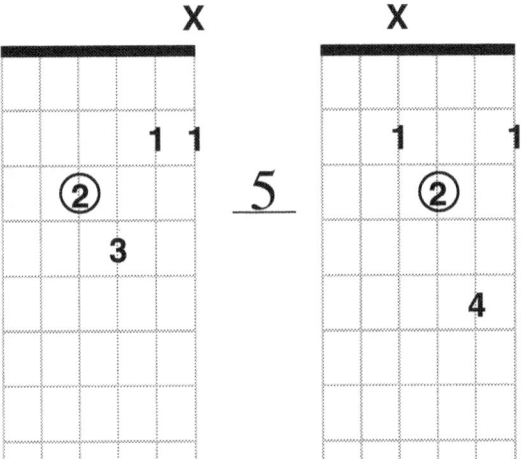
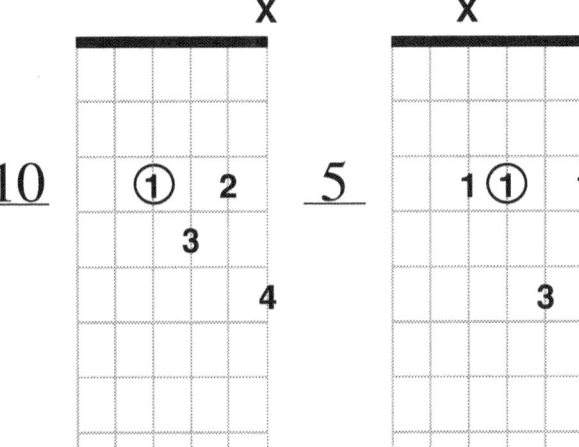
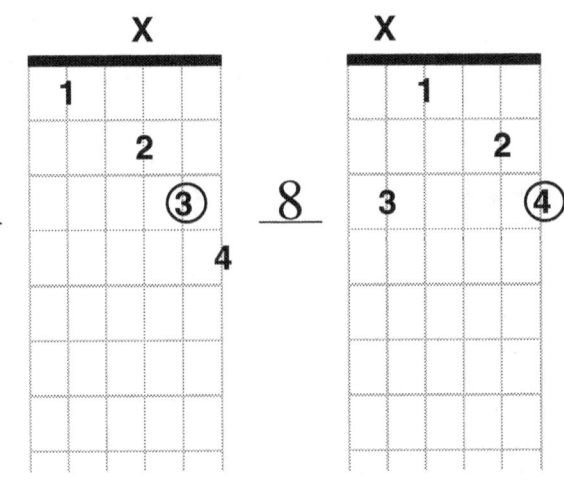
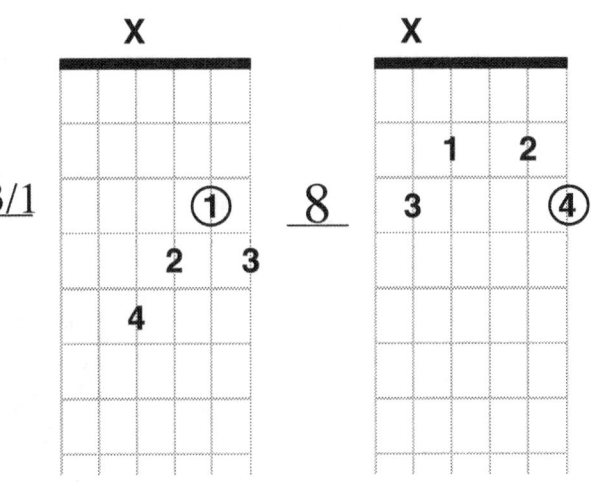

C-D^5-M^3+   C-D^5-P^4+

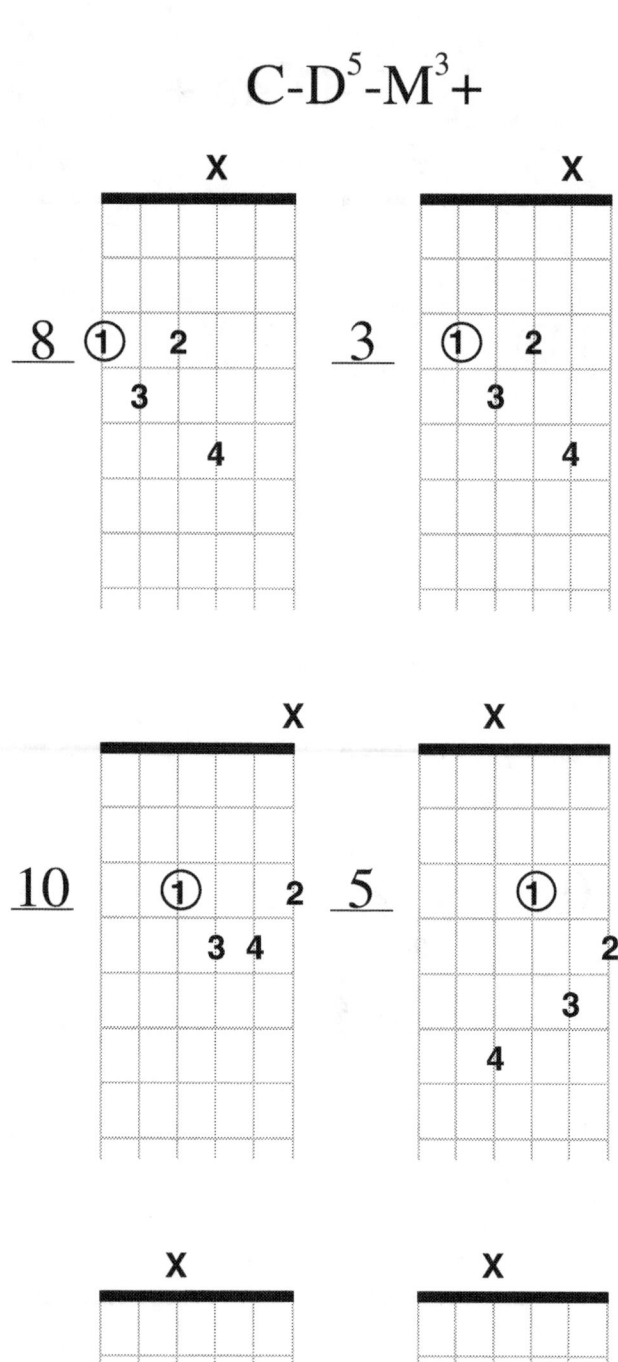
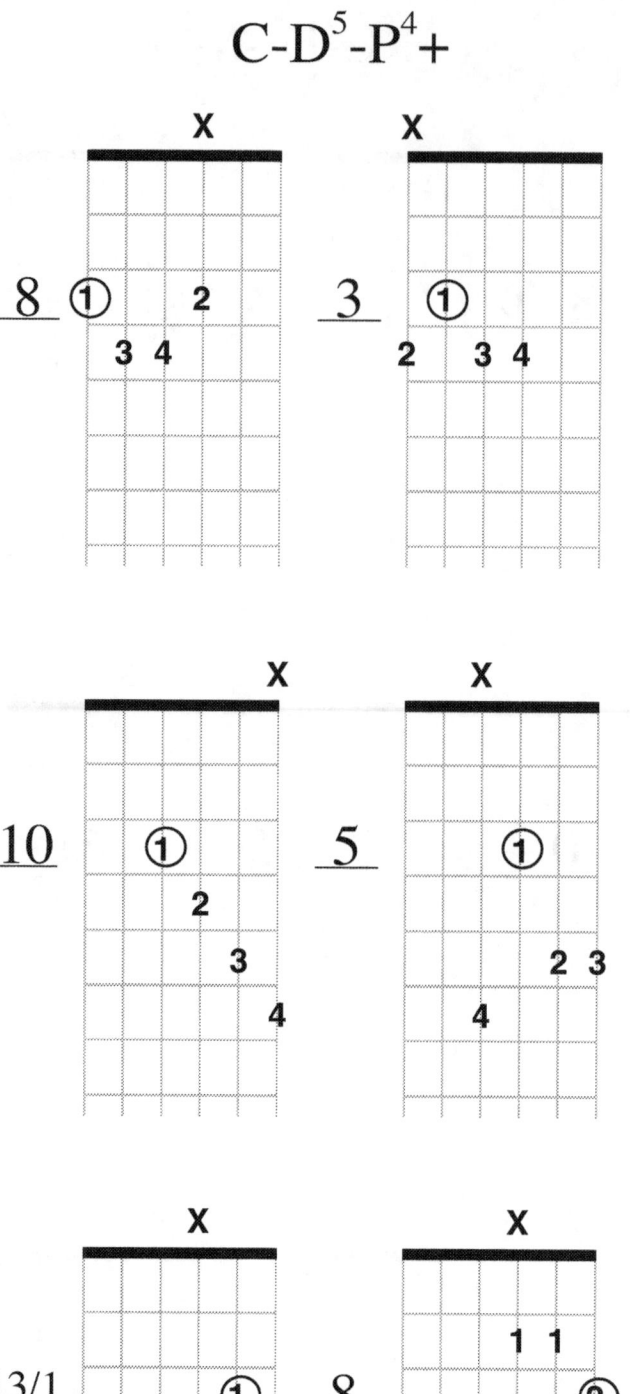
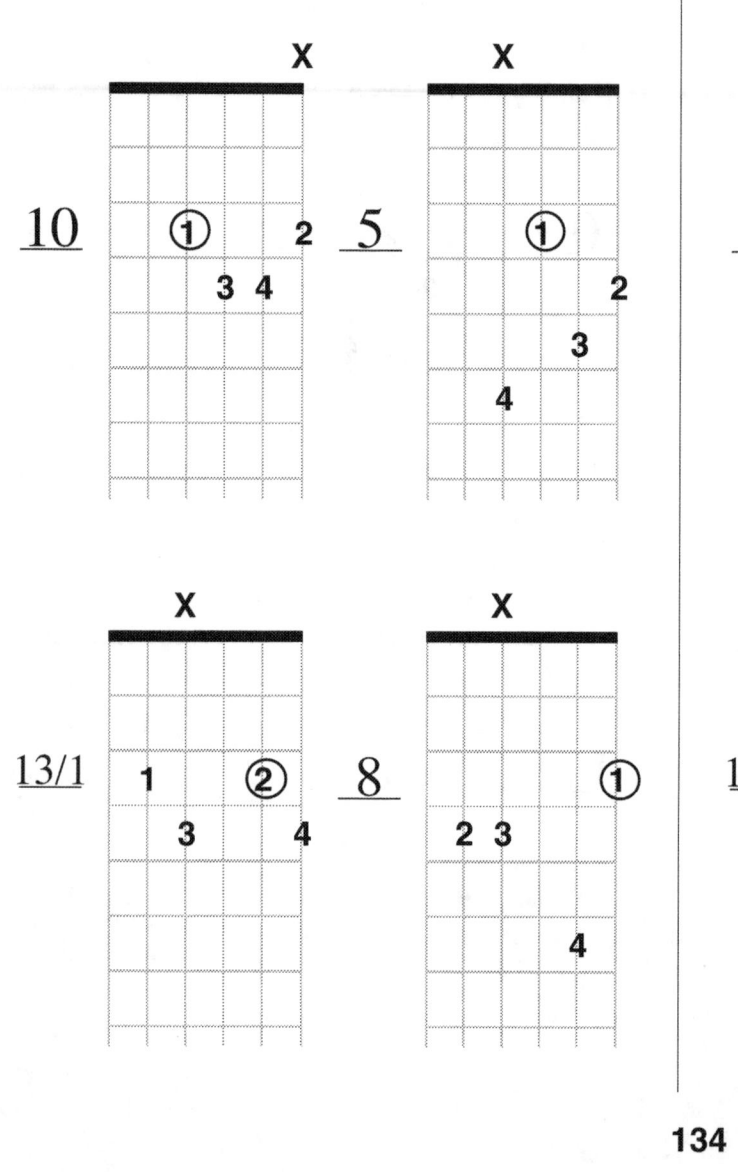

C-D^5-m^6+   C-D^5-M^6+

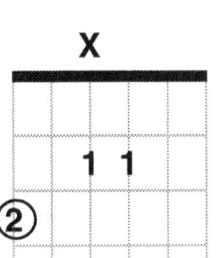
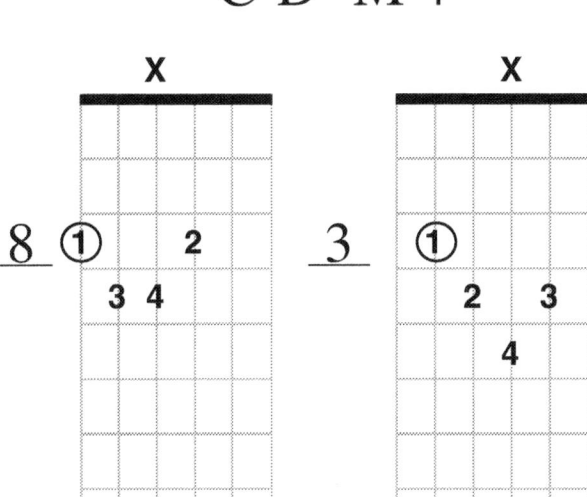
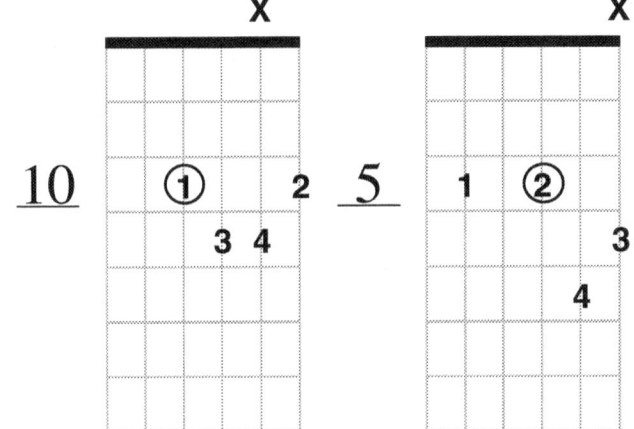
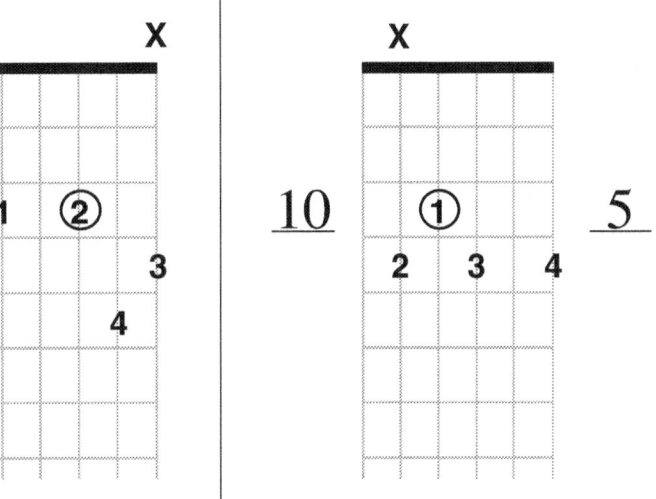
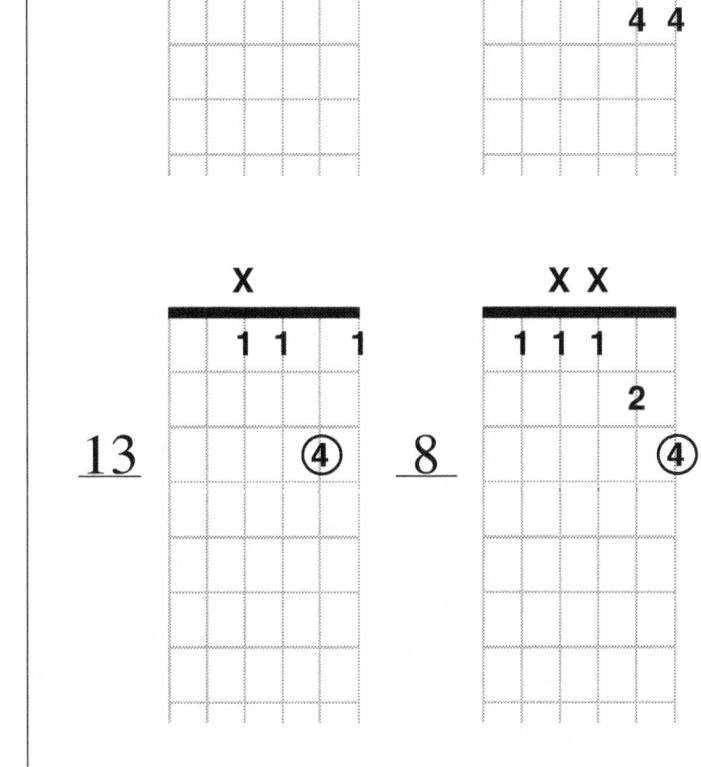

C-D⁵-m⁷+   C-D⁵-M⁷+

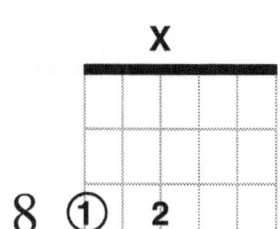
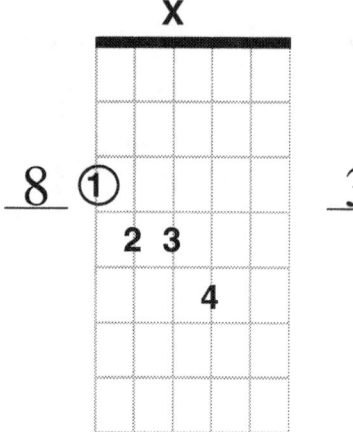
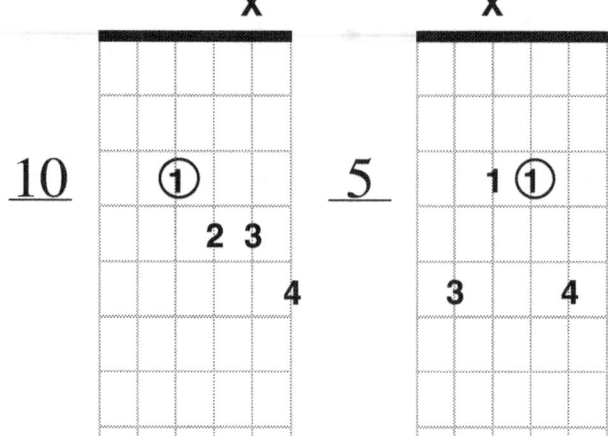
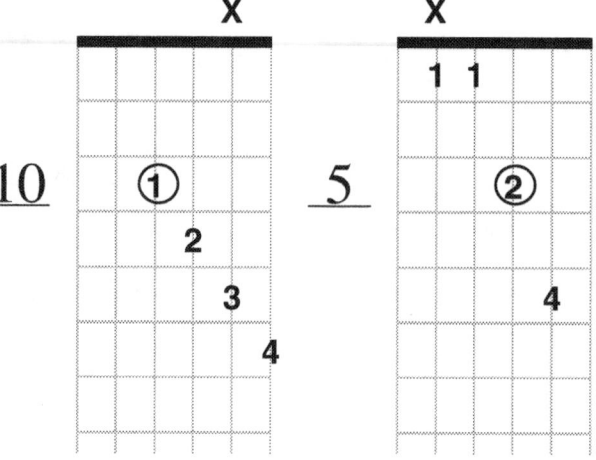
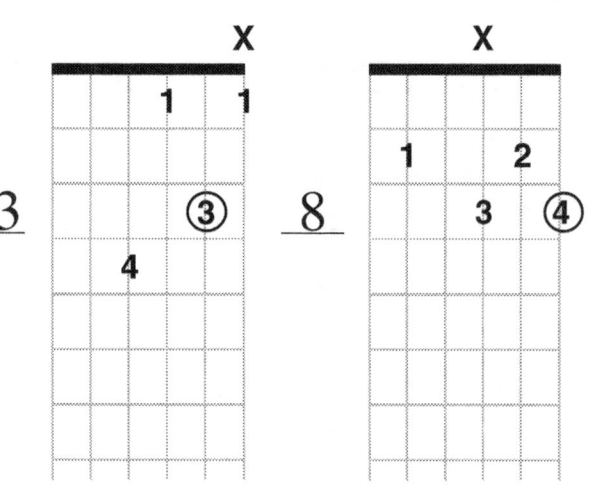
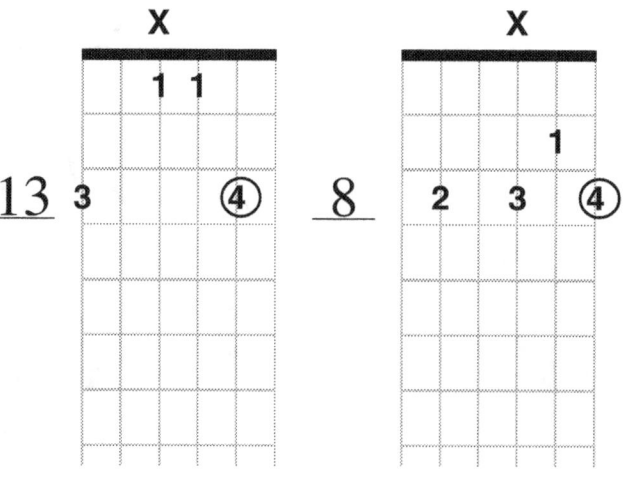

C-M⁶-m²+   C-M⁶-M²+

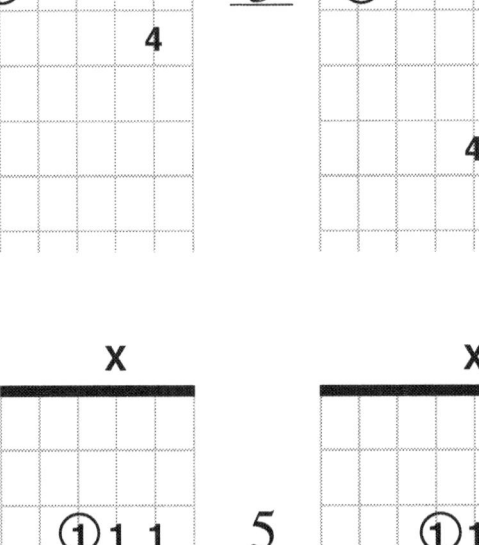
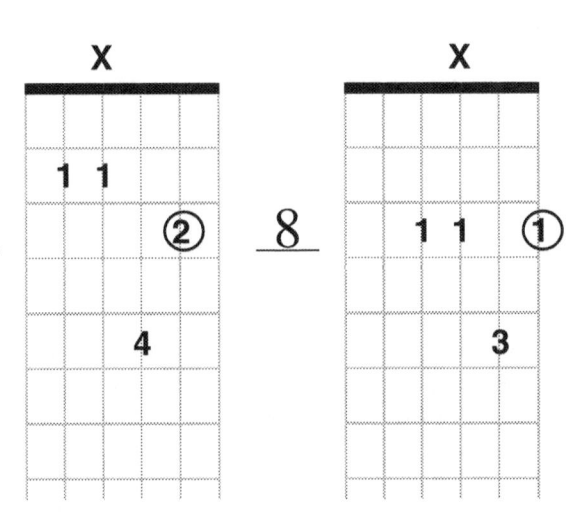
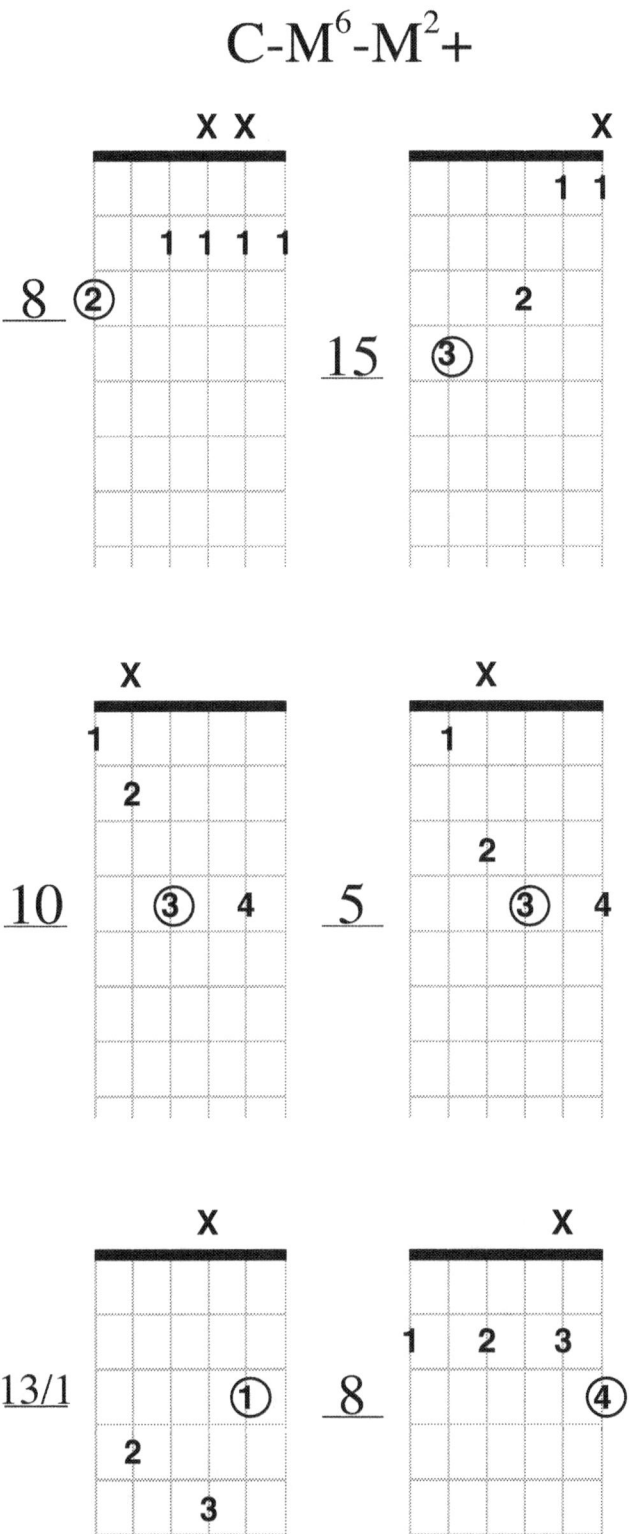

C-M⁶-m³+   C-M⁶-M³+

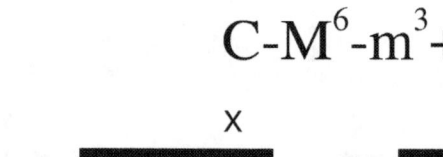
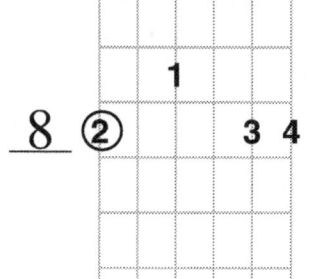
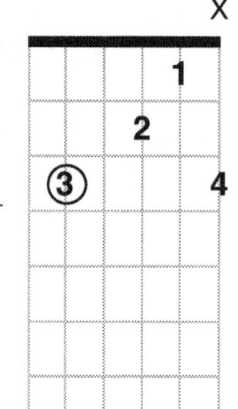
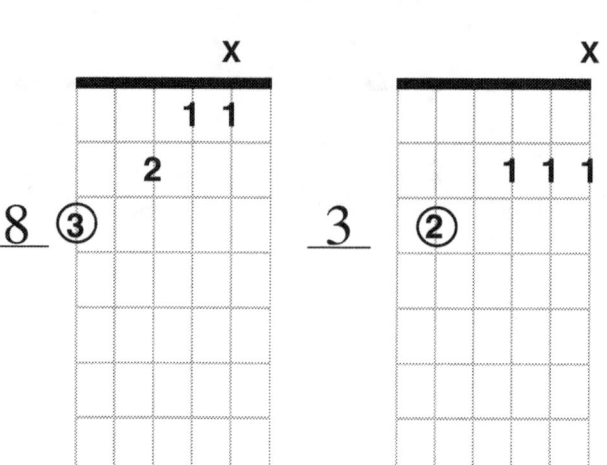
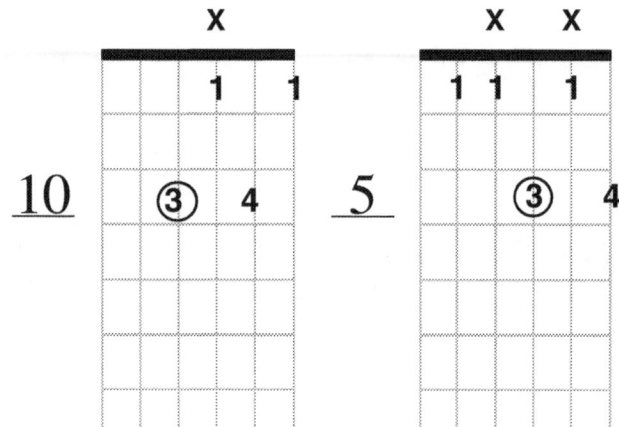
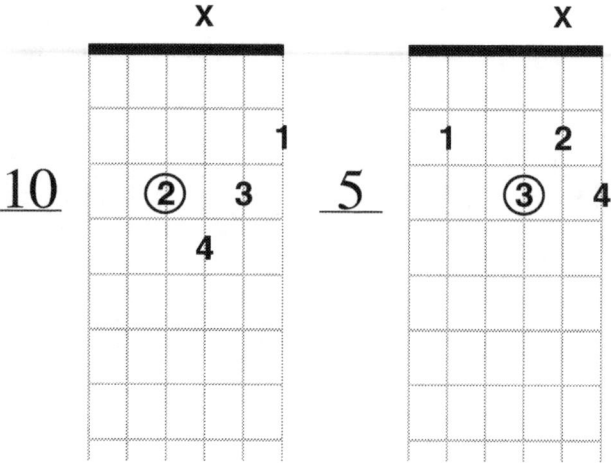
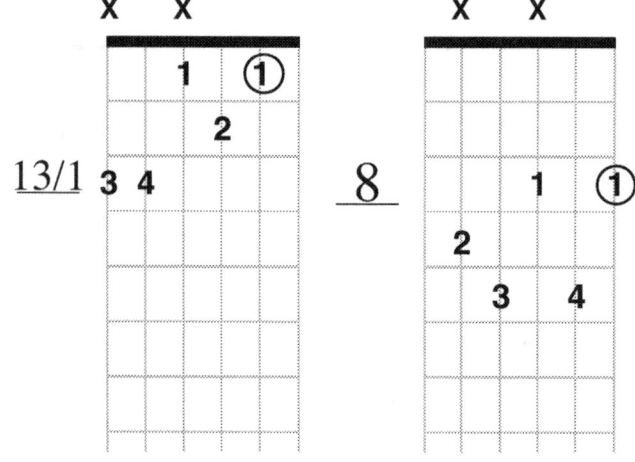
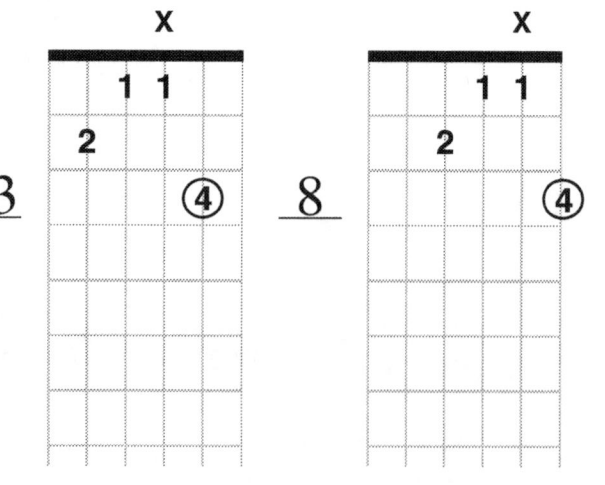

C-M^6-P^4+ | C-M^6-D^5+

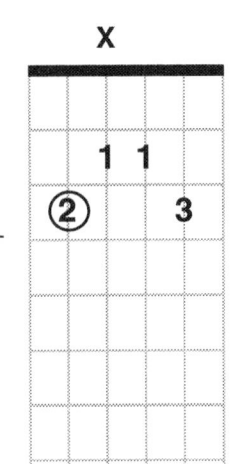
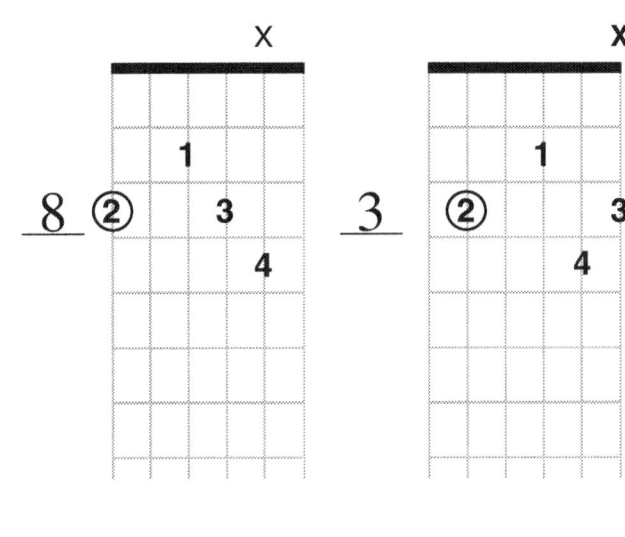
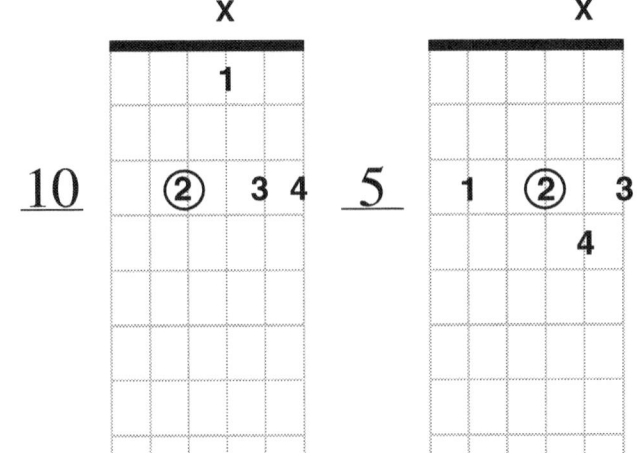
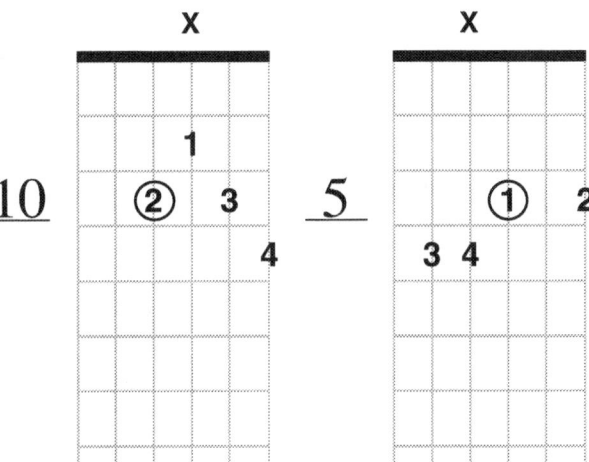
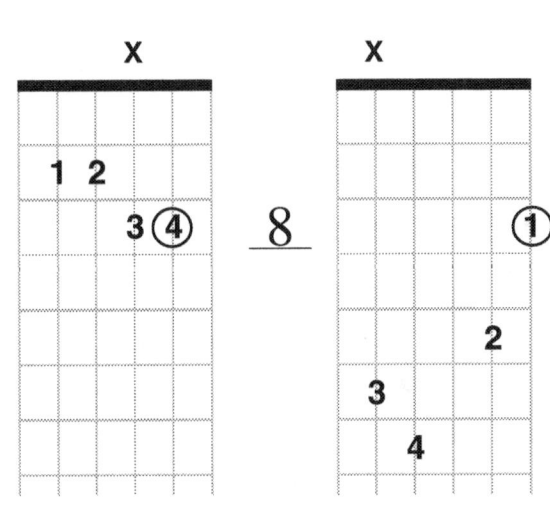
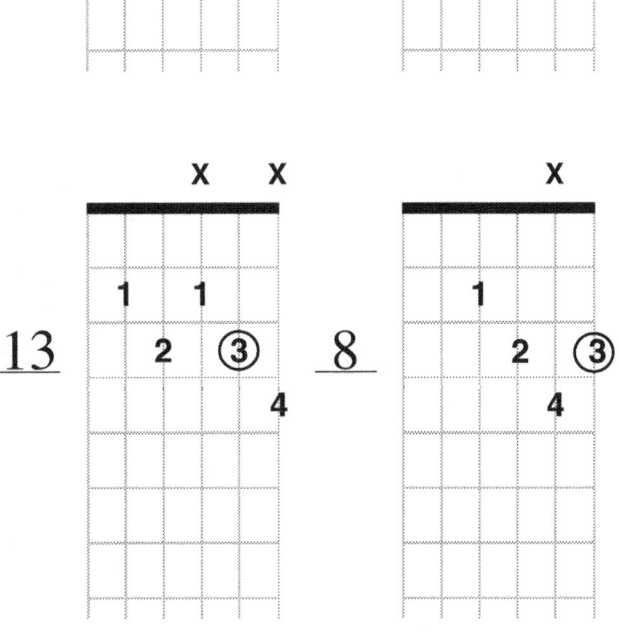

C-M⁶-P⁵+   C-M⁶-m⁷+

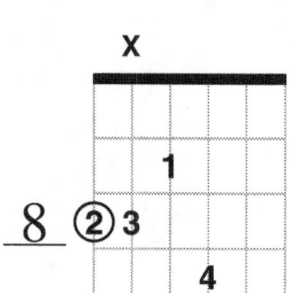
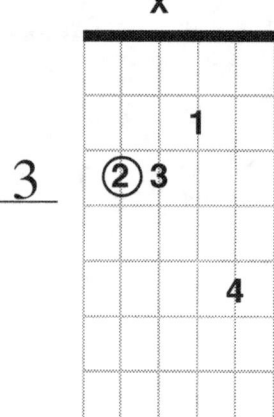

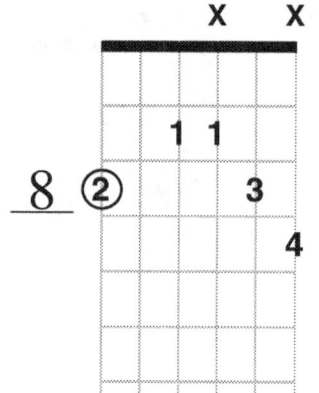
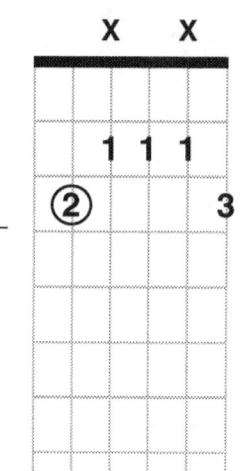
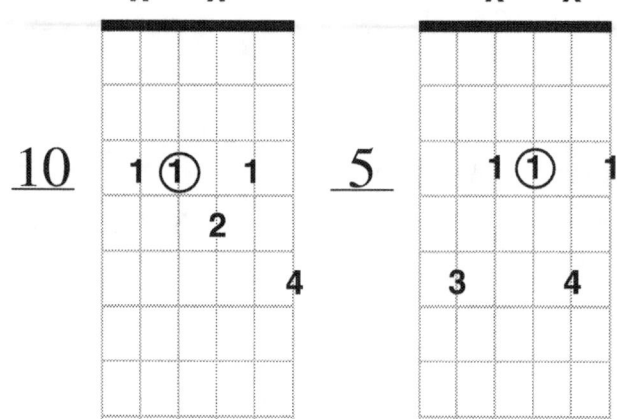
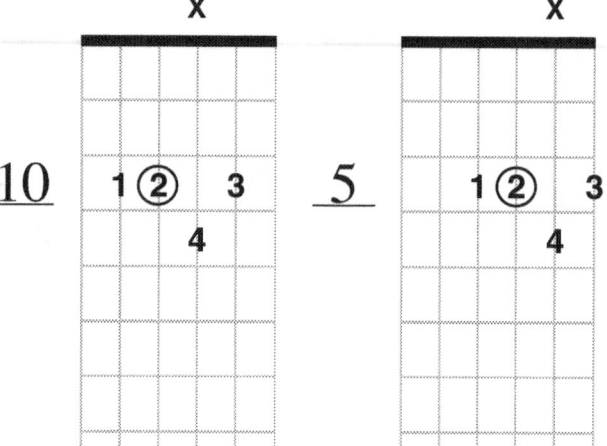
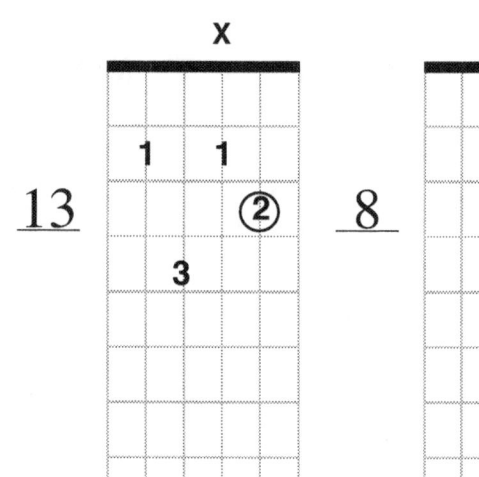
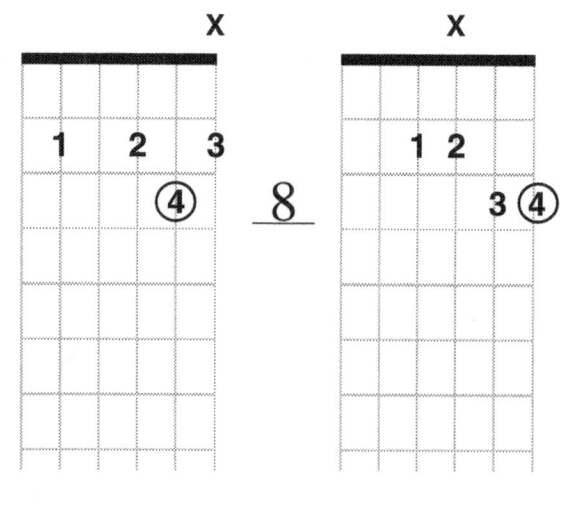

$C-M^6-M^7+$ $C-m^6-m^2+$

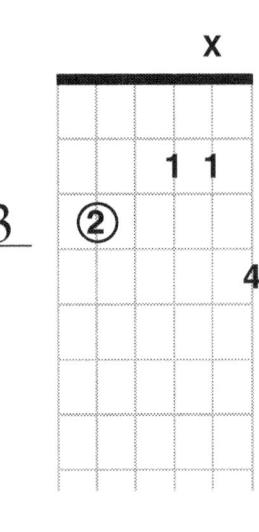
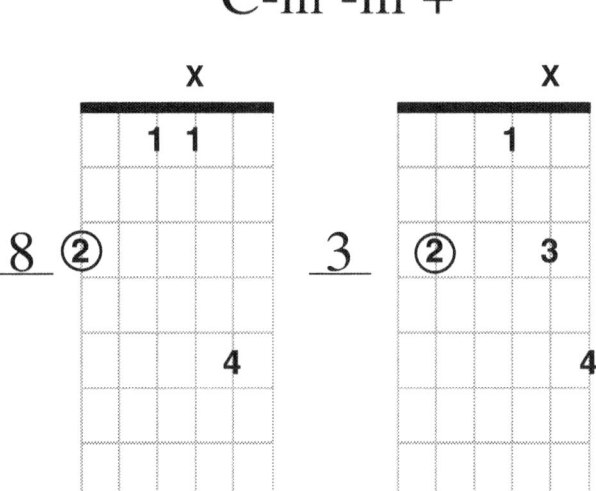
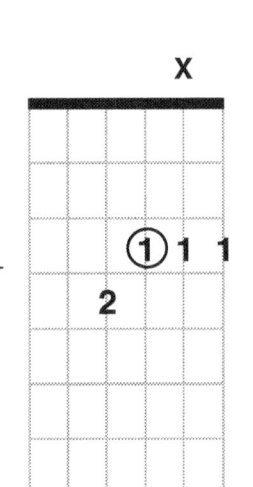
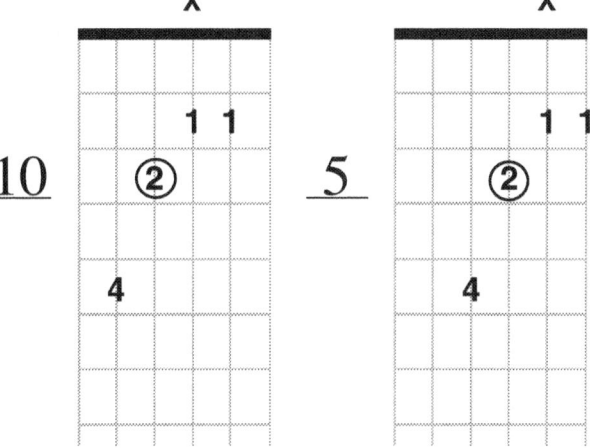
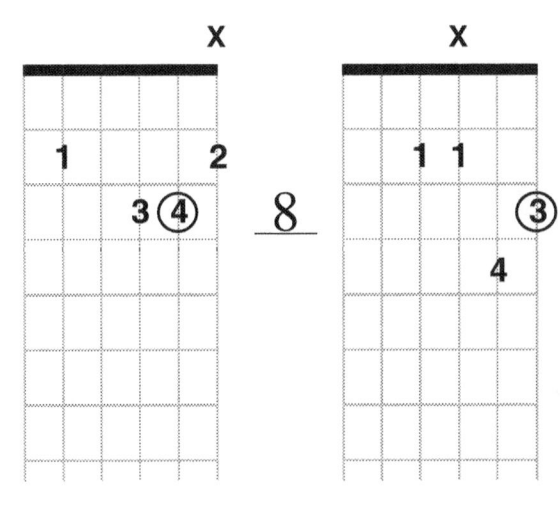
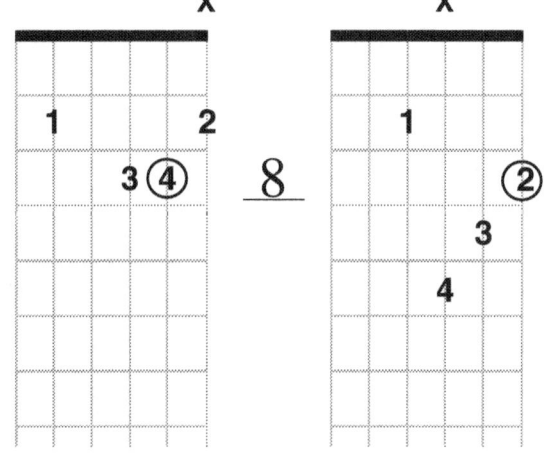

C-m^6-M^2+   C-m^6-m^3+

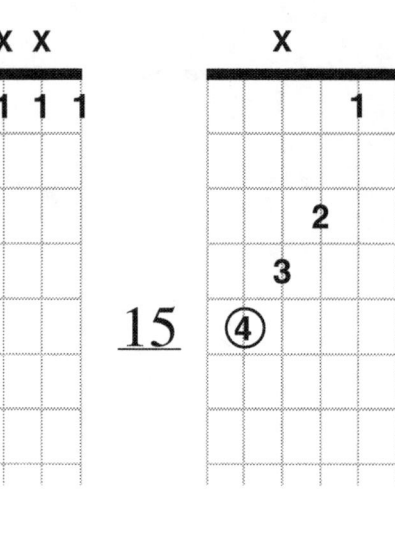
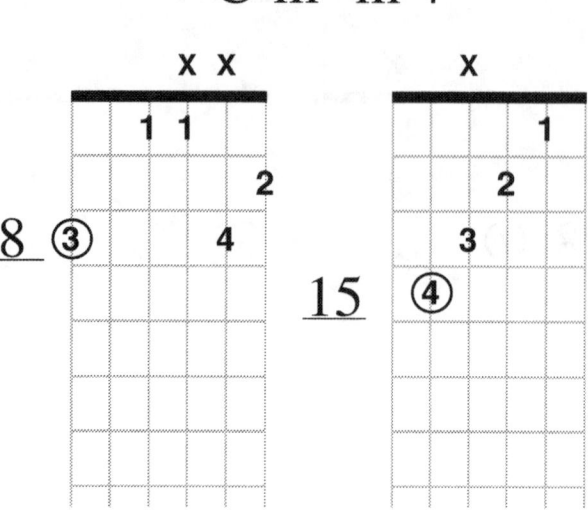
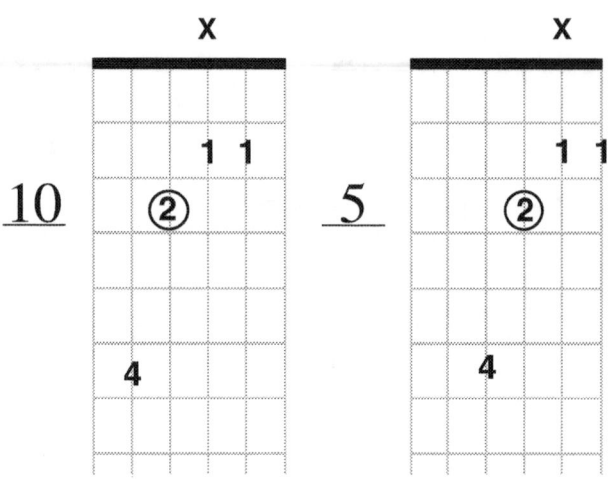
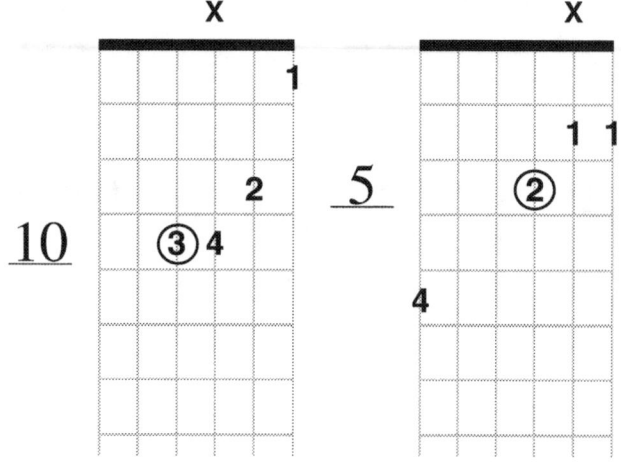
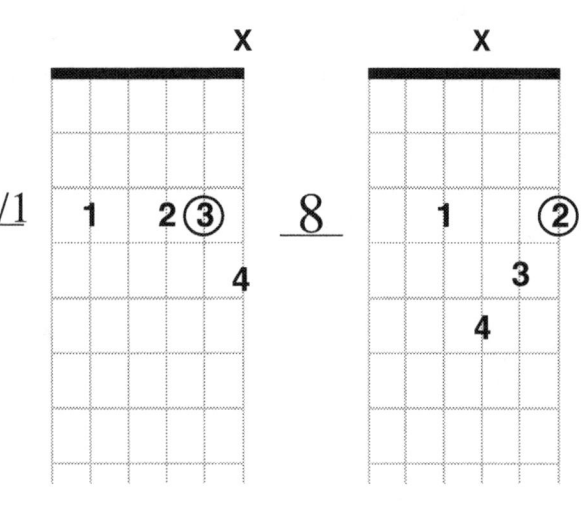
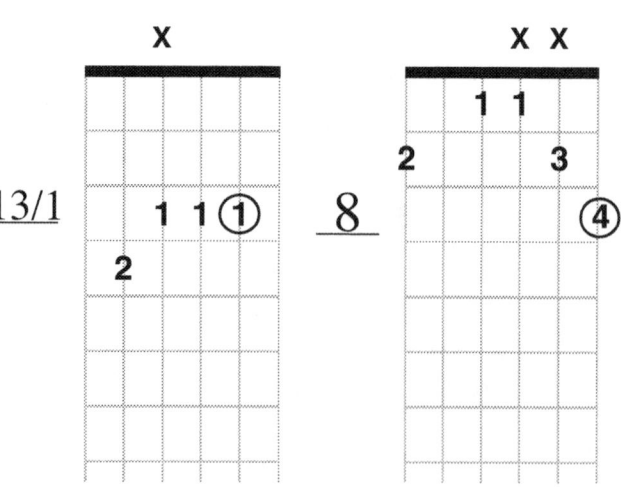

C-m^6-M^3+   C-m^6-P^4+

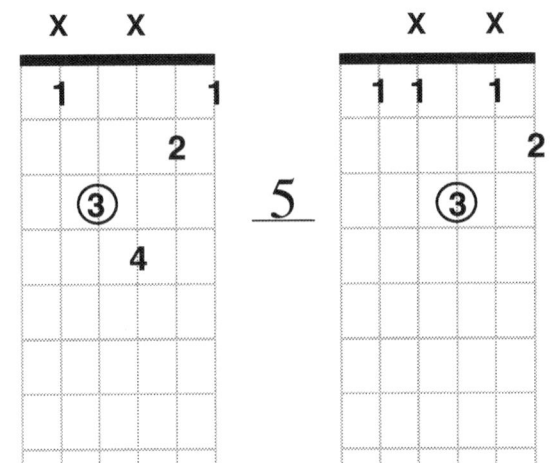
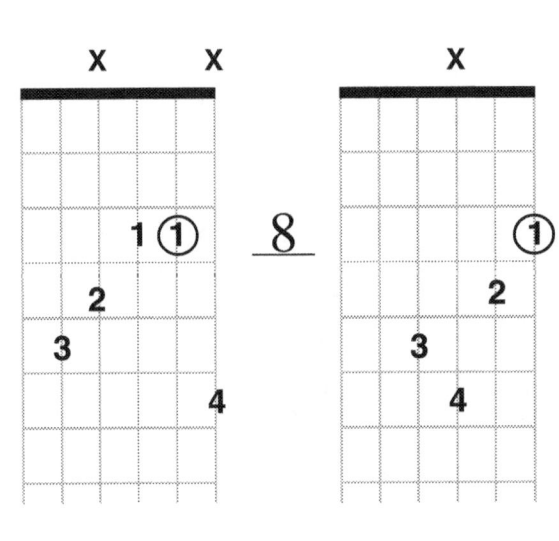
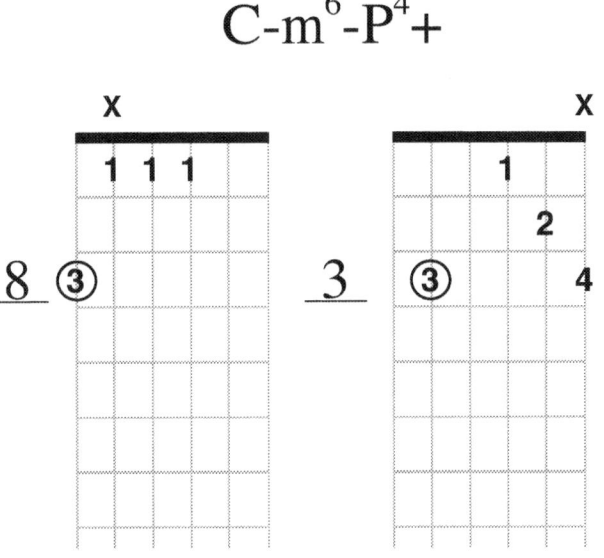
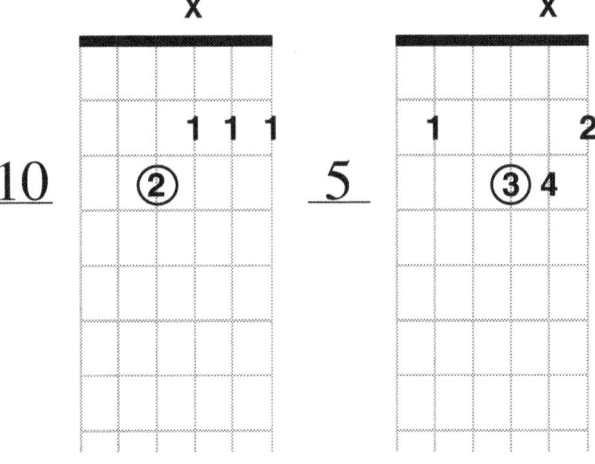
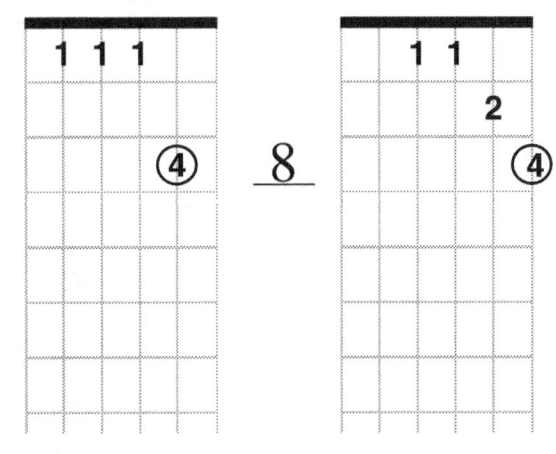

C-m⁶-D⁵+   C-m⁶-P⁵+

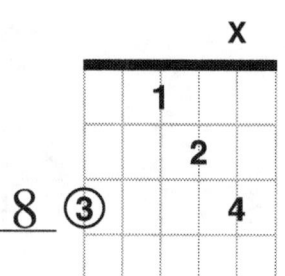
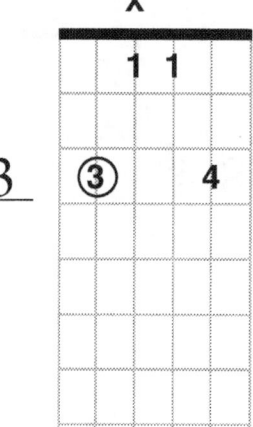
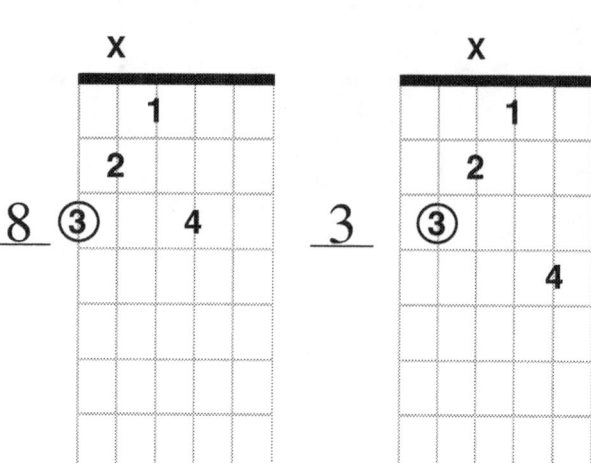

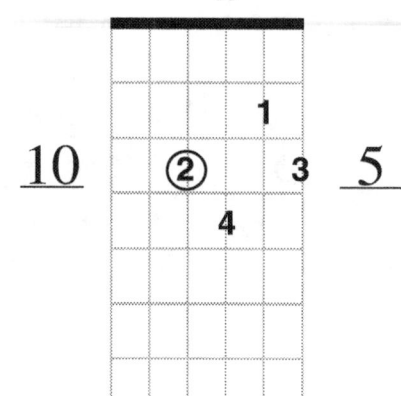
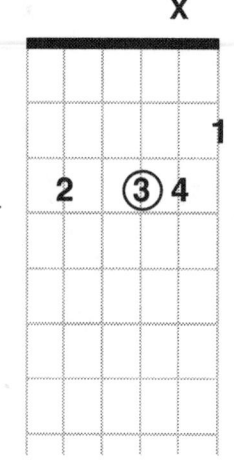
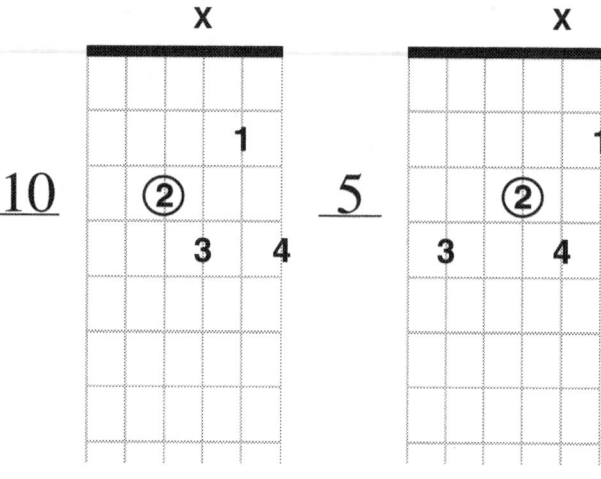

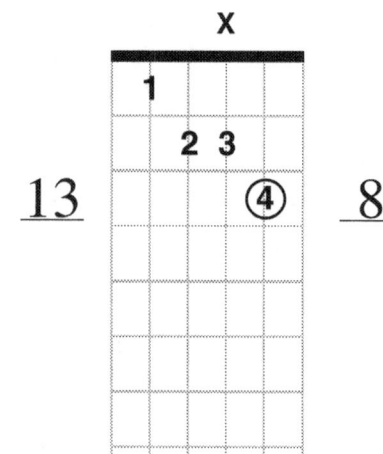
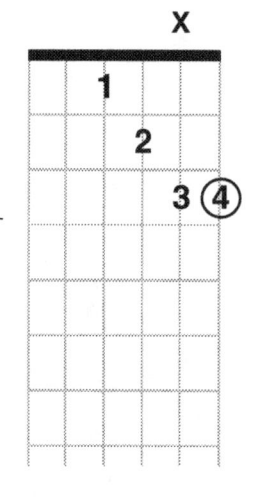
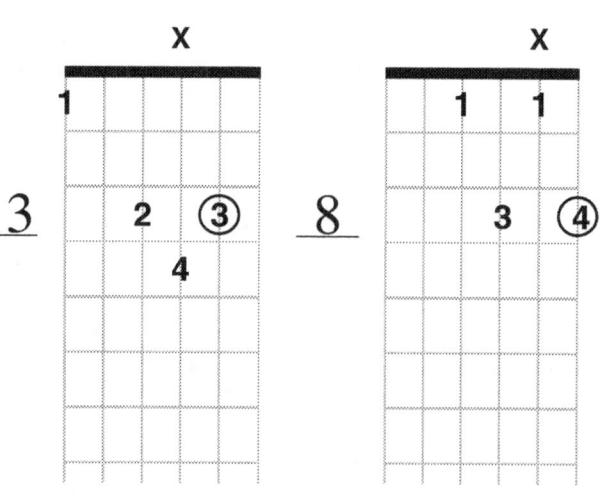

$C\text{-}m^6\text{-}m^7+$ $C\text{-}m^6\text{-}M^7+$

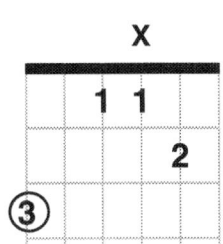
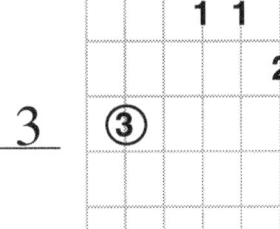
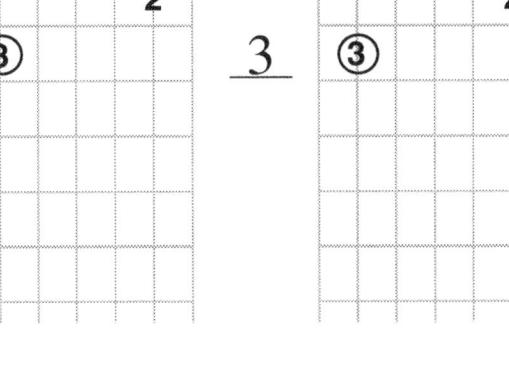
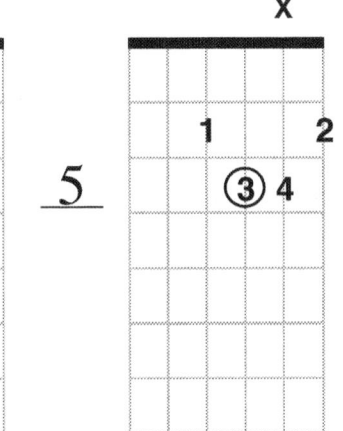
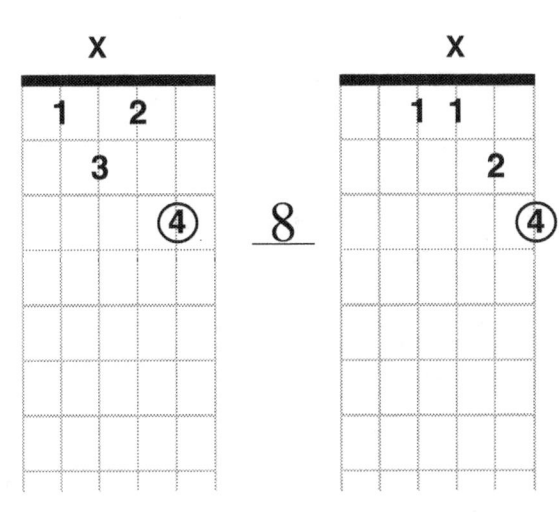
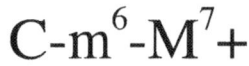
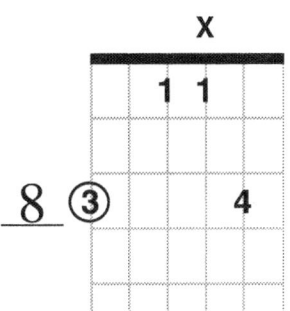
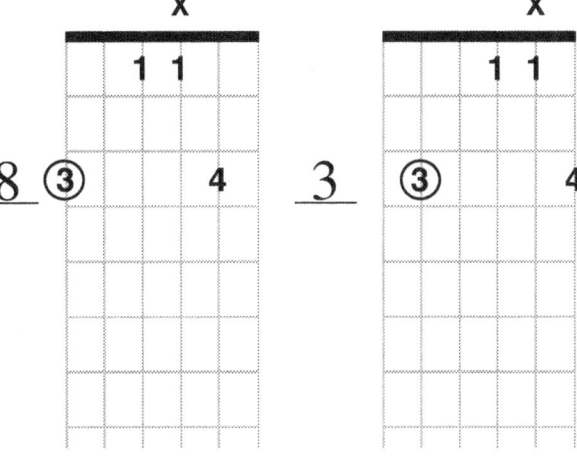
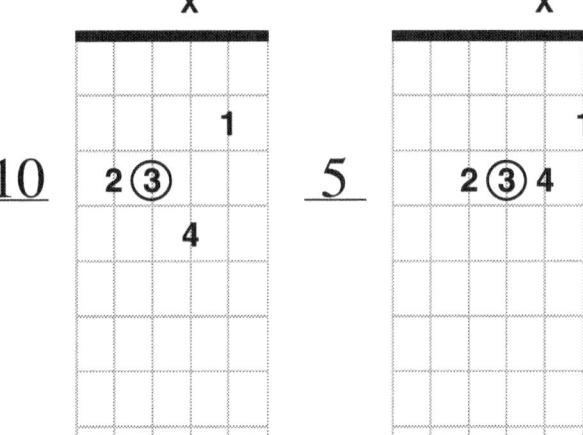
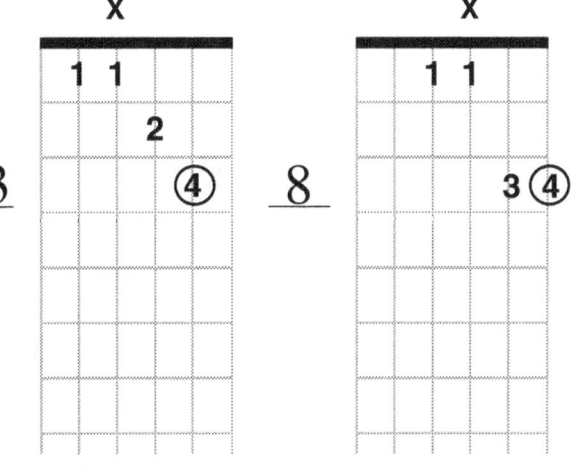

C-M⁷-m²+   C-M⁷-M²+

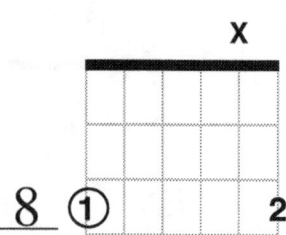
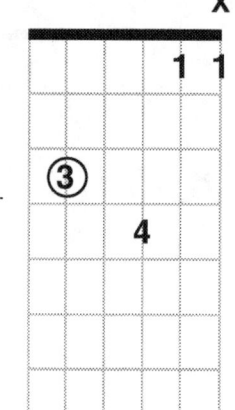
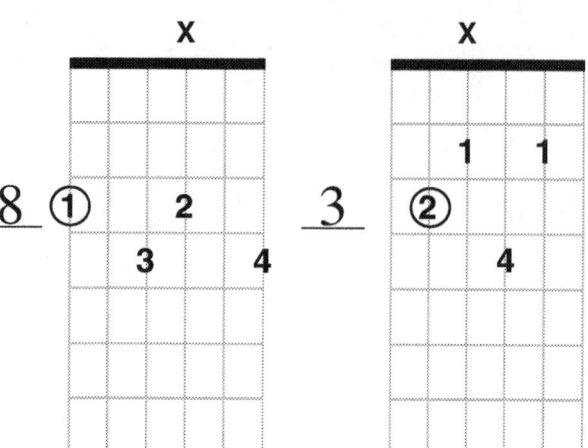
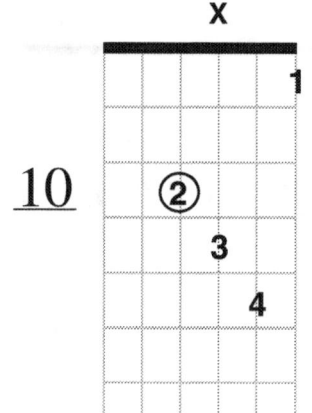
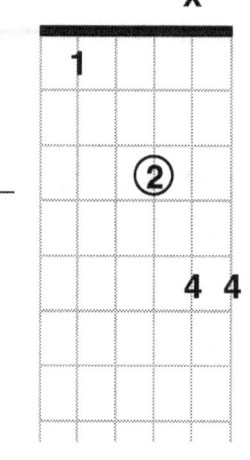
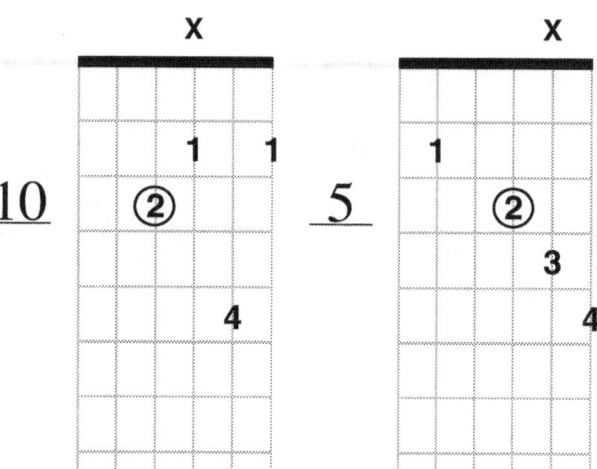
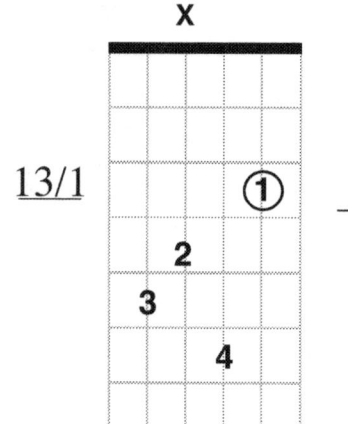
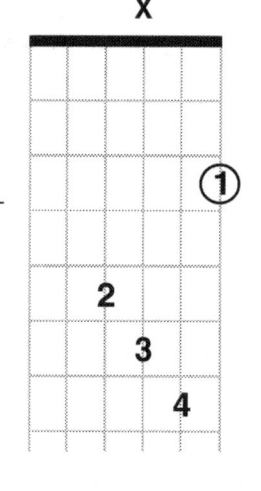
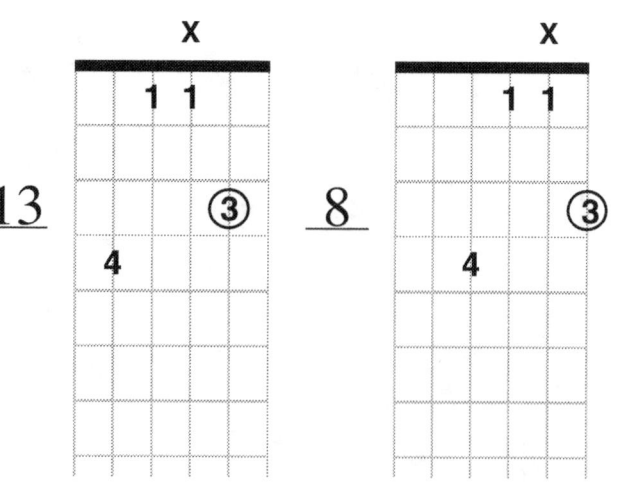

$C\text{-}M^7\text{-}m^3+$ $C\text{-}M^7\text{-}M^3+$

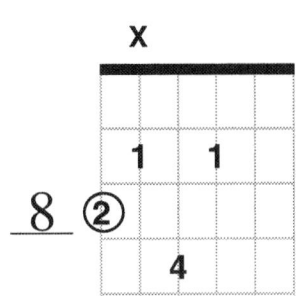
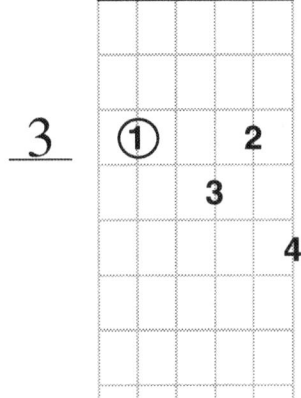
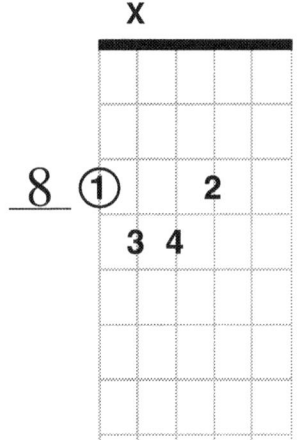
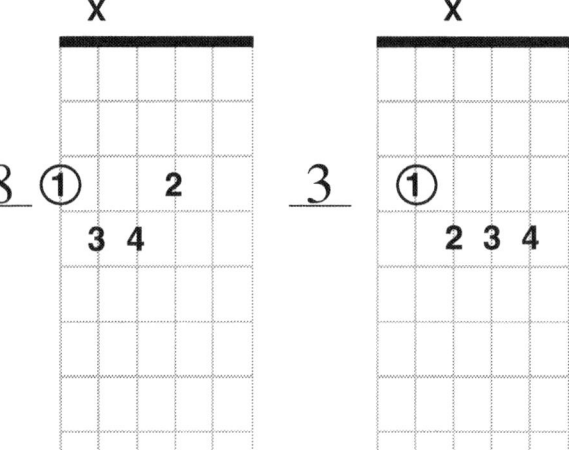
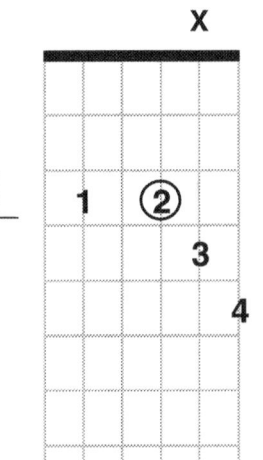
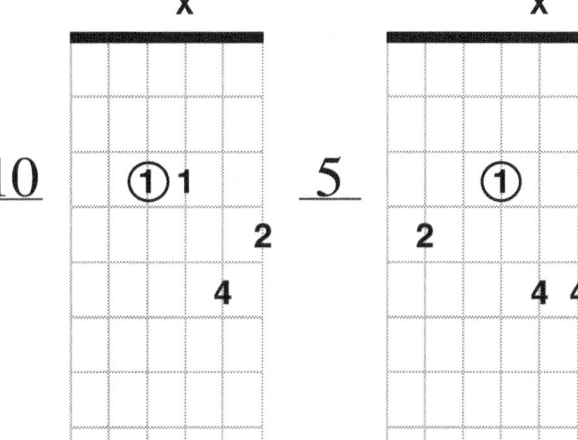
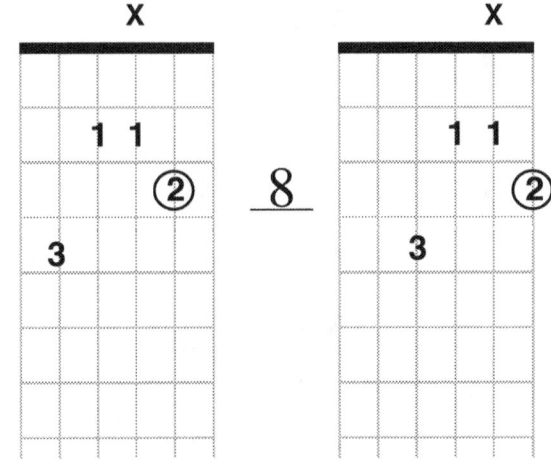
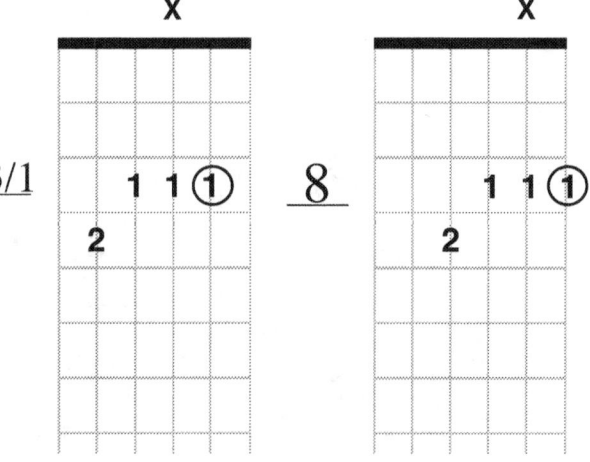

C-M^7-P^4+   C-M^7-D^5+

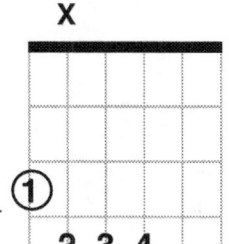
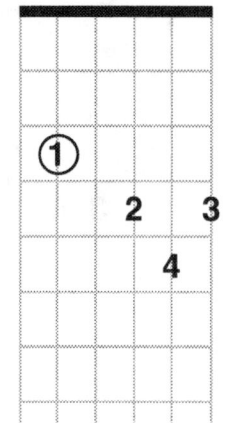
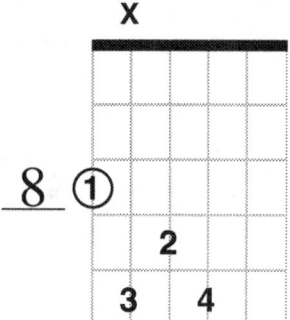
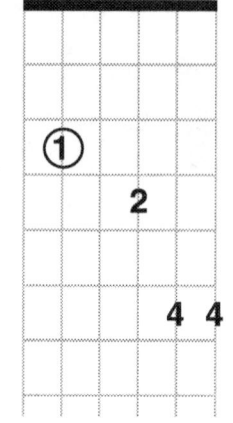
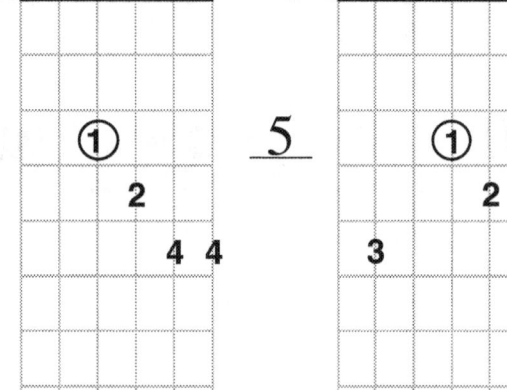
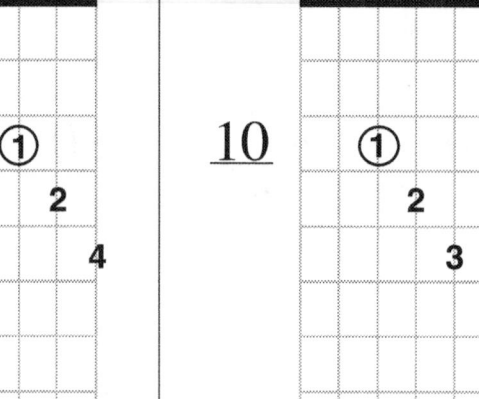
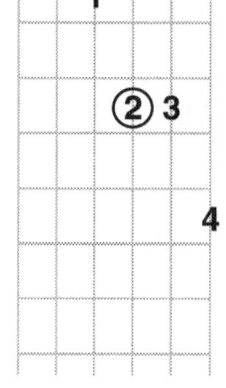
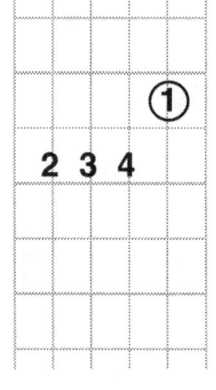
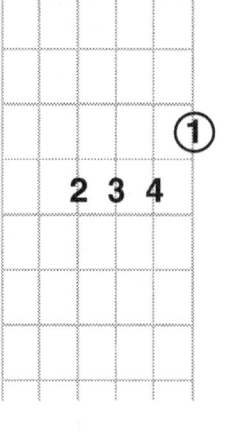
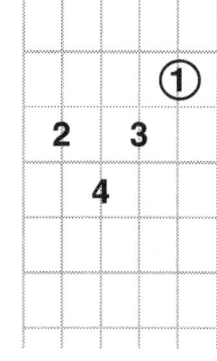
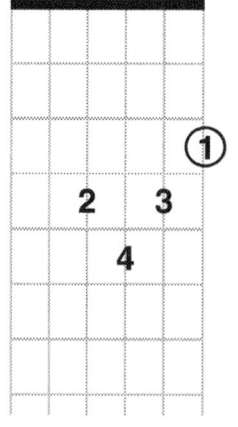

C-M^7-P^5+   C-M^7-m^6+

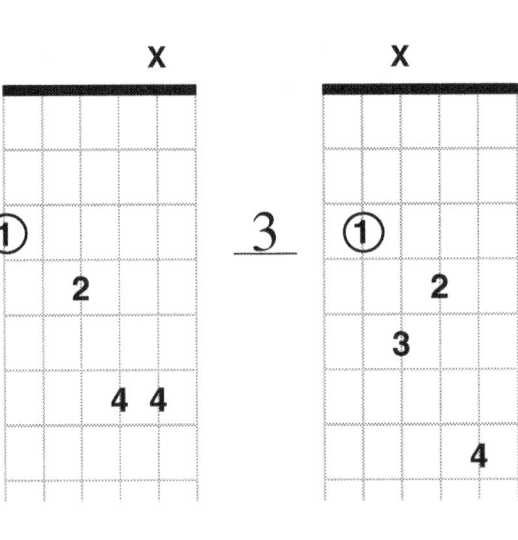
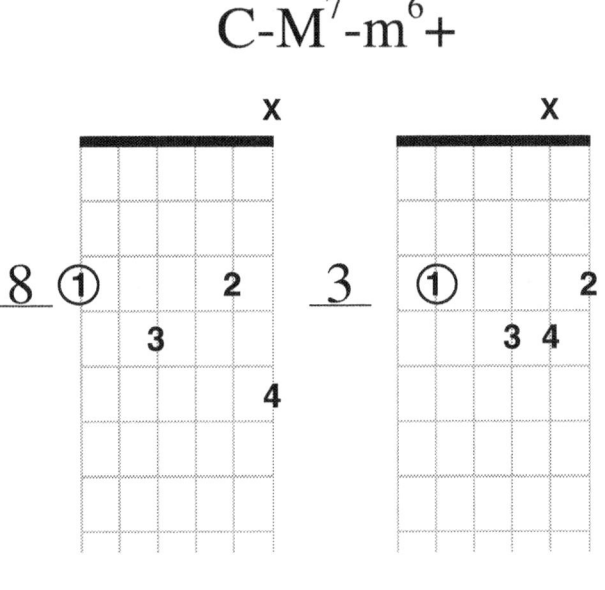
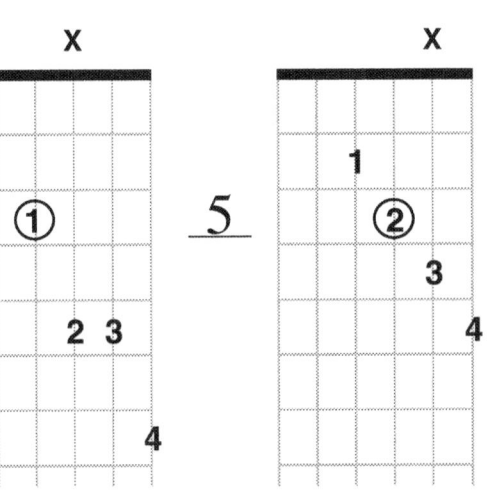
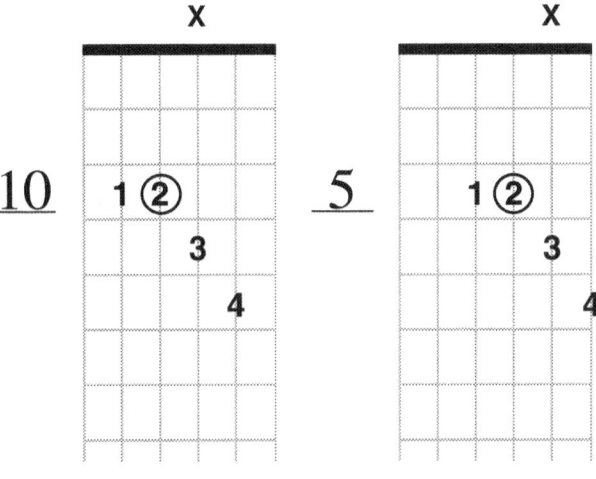
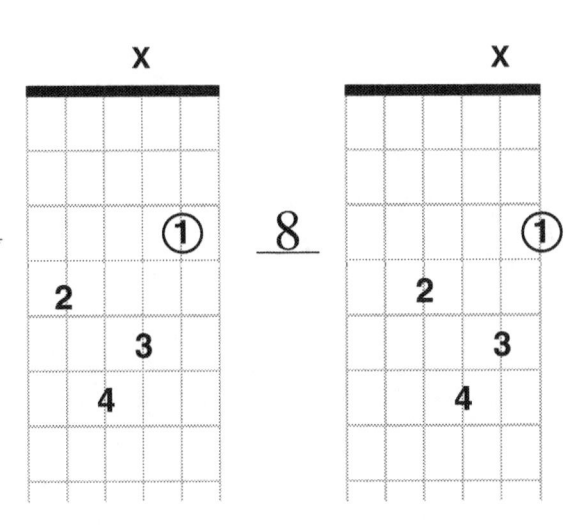
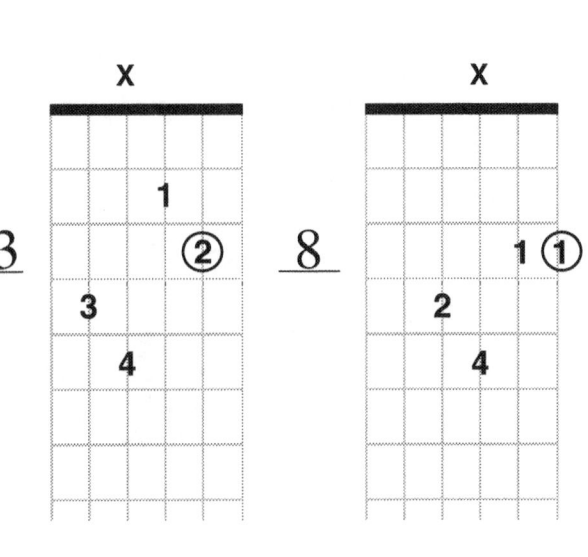

C-M⁷-M⁶⁺

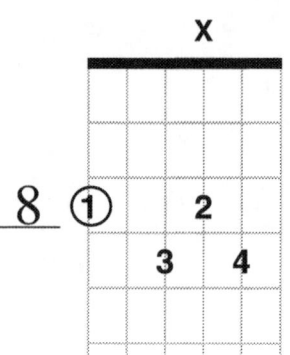
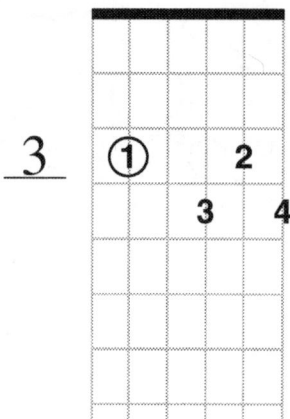
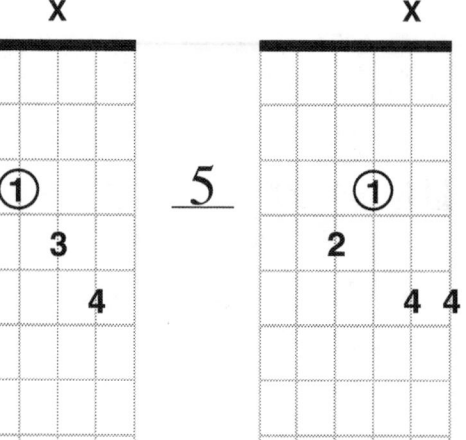
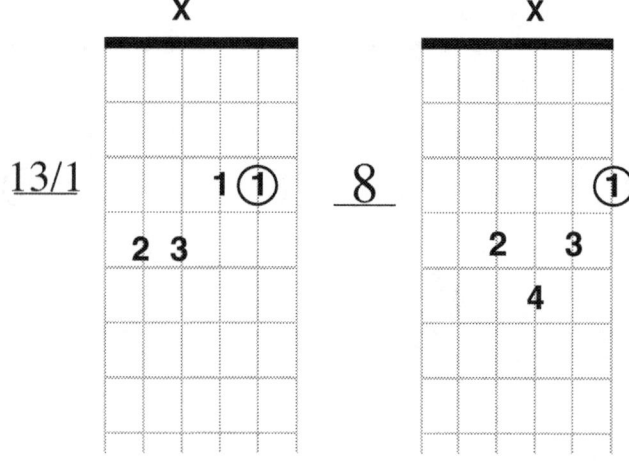

C-m⁷-m²⁺

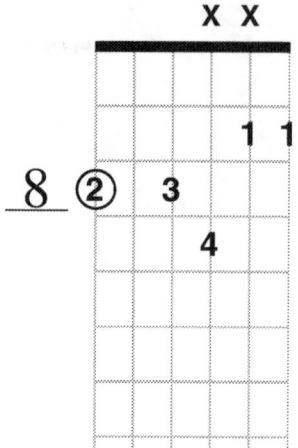
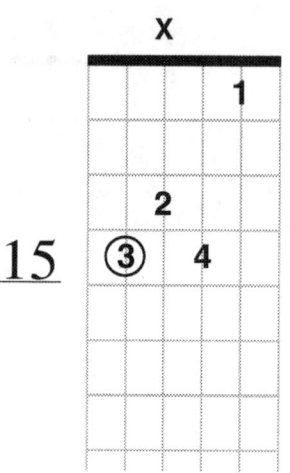
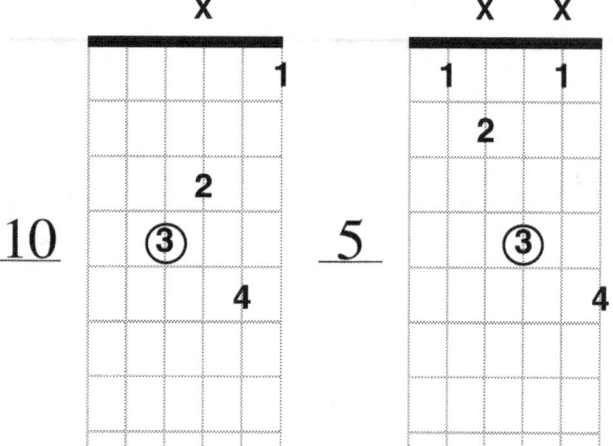
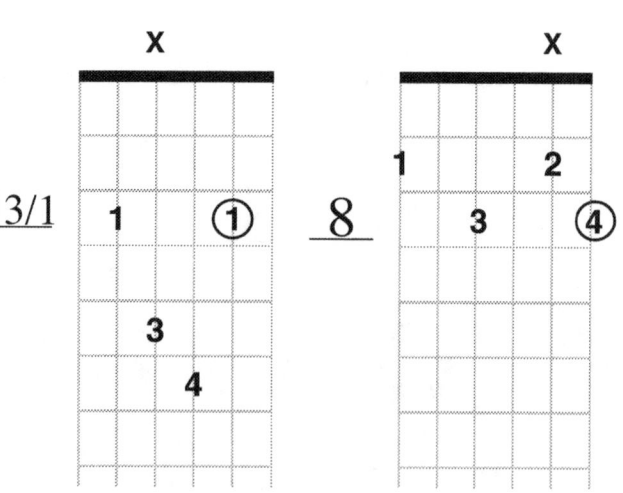

$C\text{-}m^7\text{-}M^2+$ $C\text{-}m^7\text{-}m^3+$

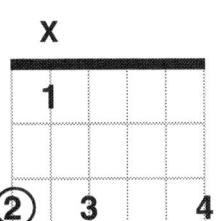
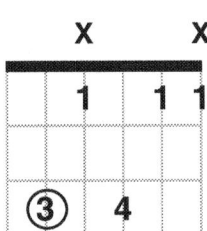
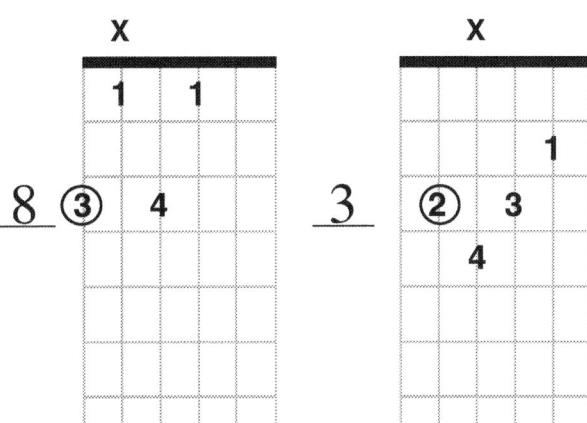

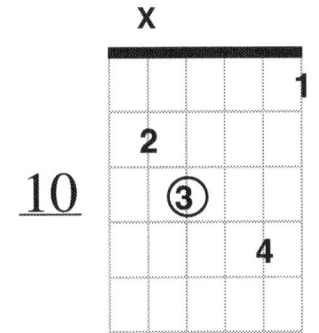
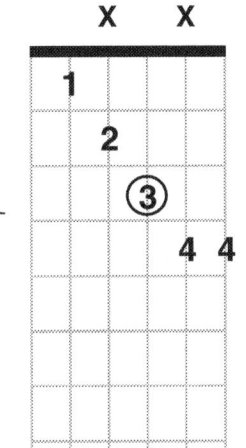
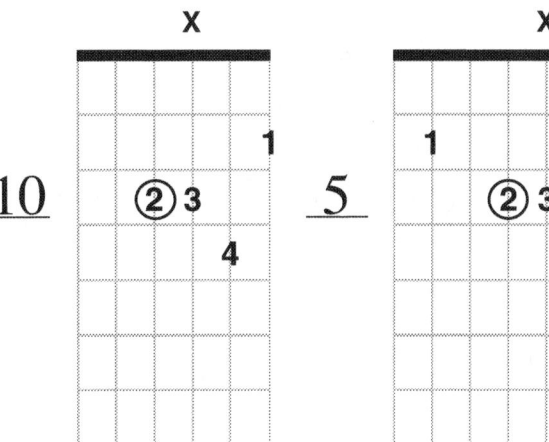

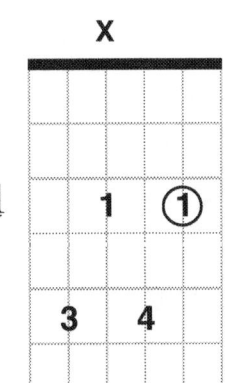
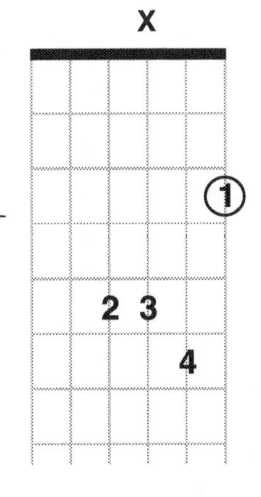
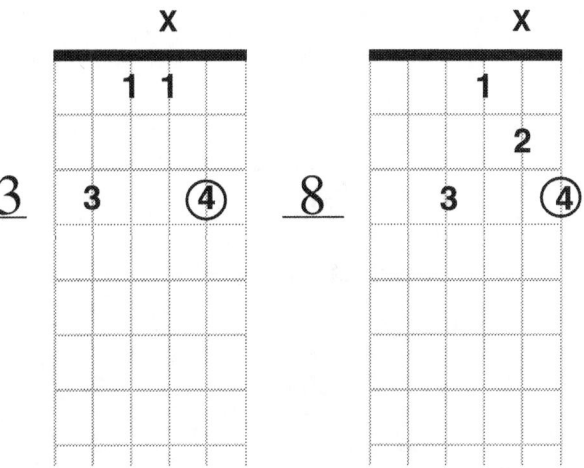

C-m⁷-M³+   C-m⁷-P⁴+

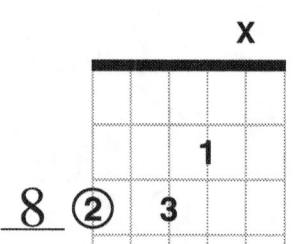
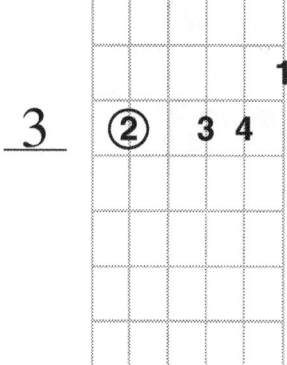
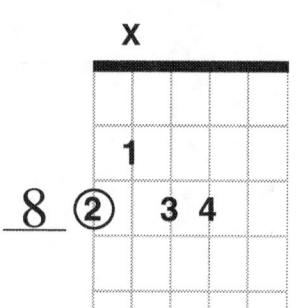
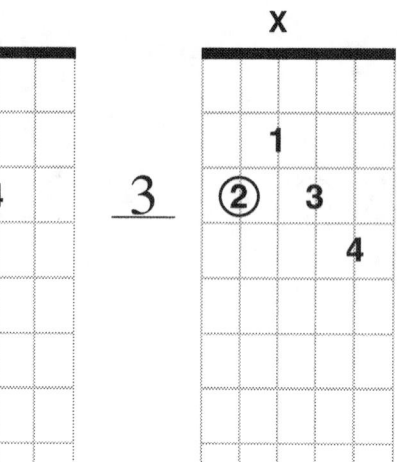
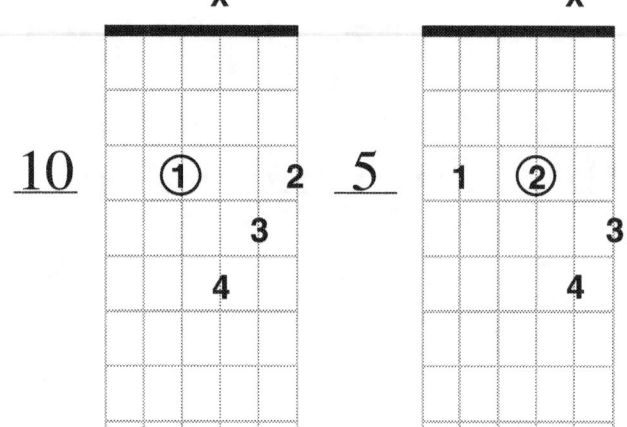
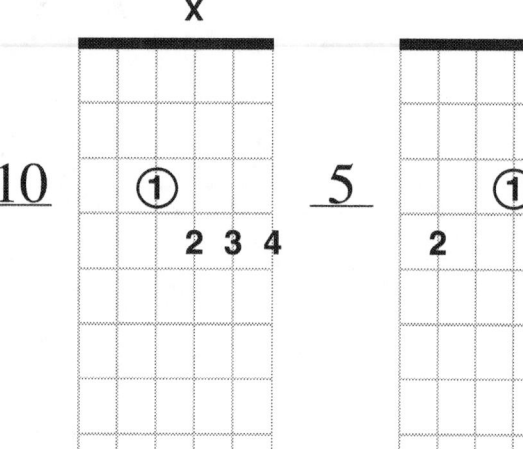
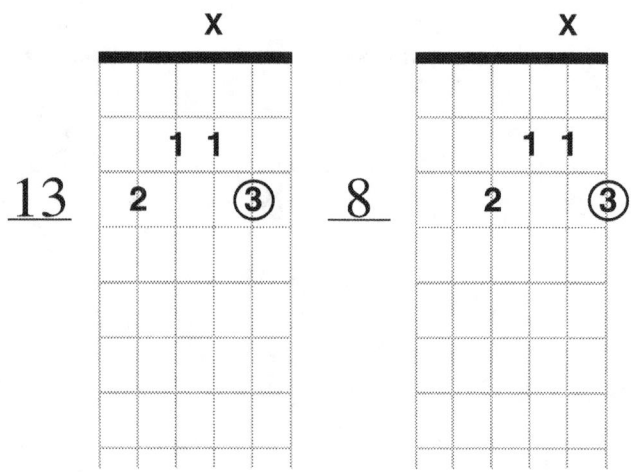
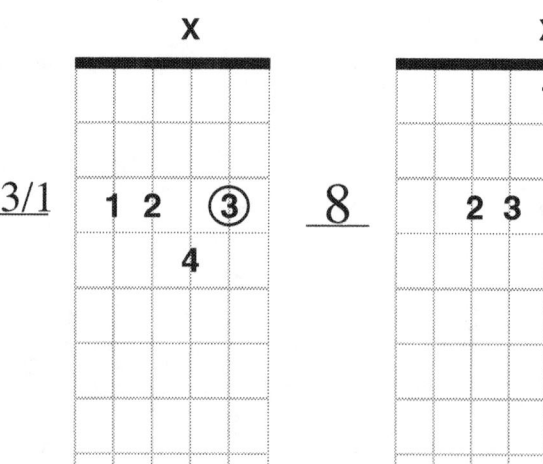

C-m^7-D^5+   C-m^7-P^5+

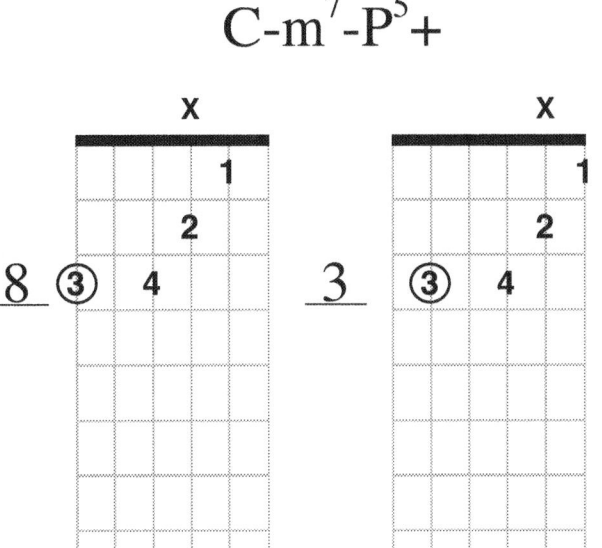

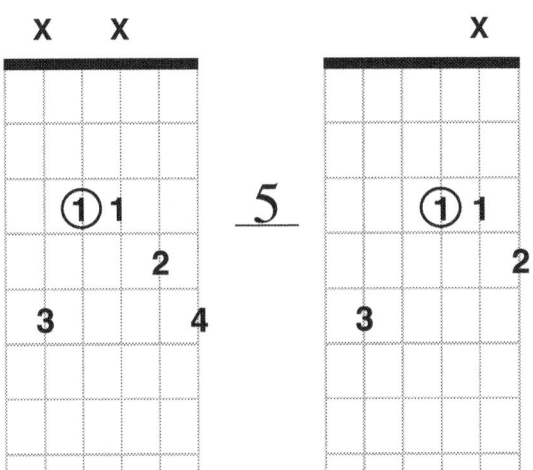
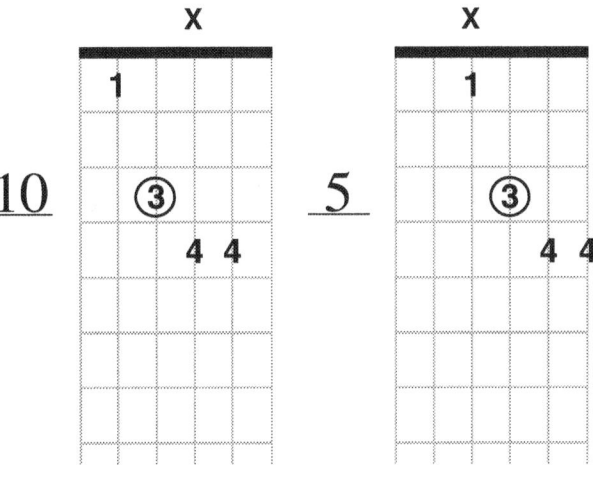

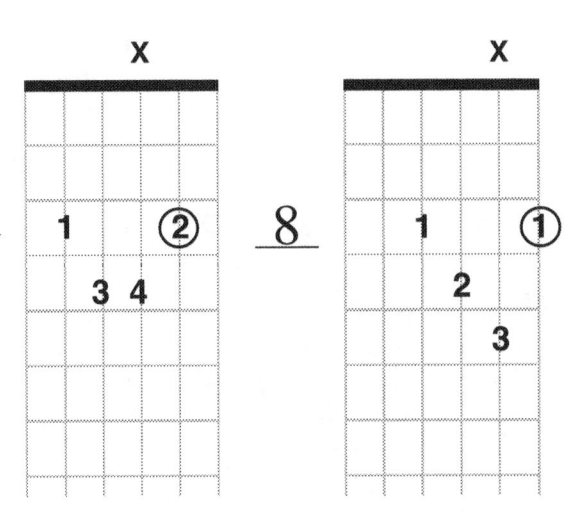
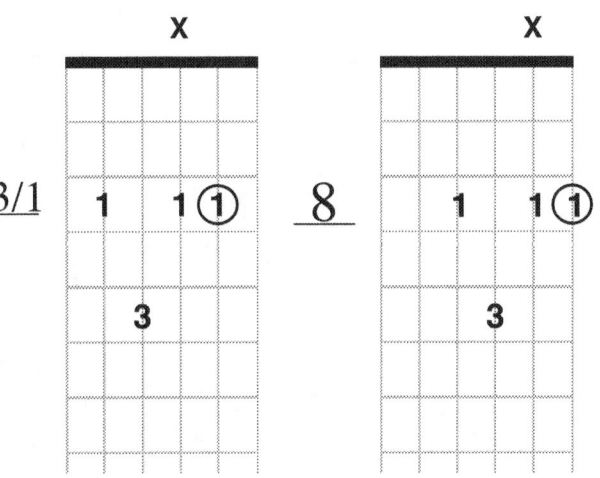

C-m⁷-m⁶+   C-m⁷-M⁶+

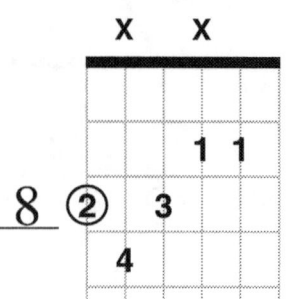
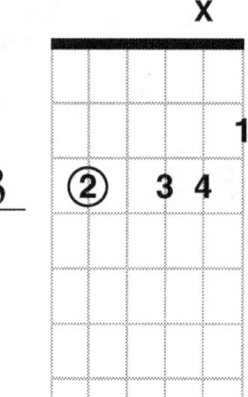
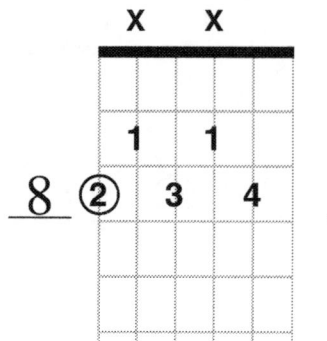
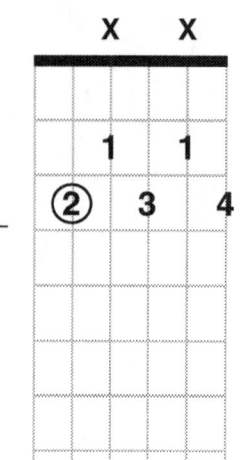
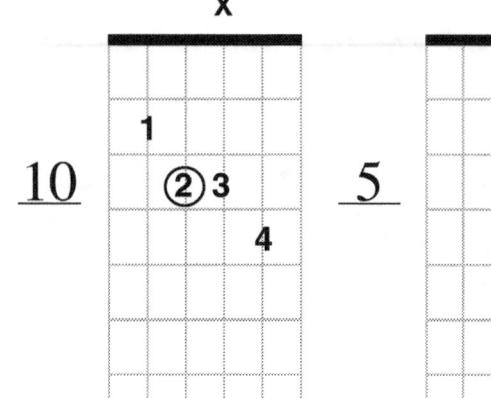
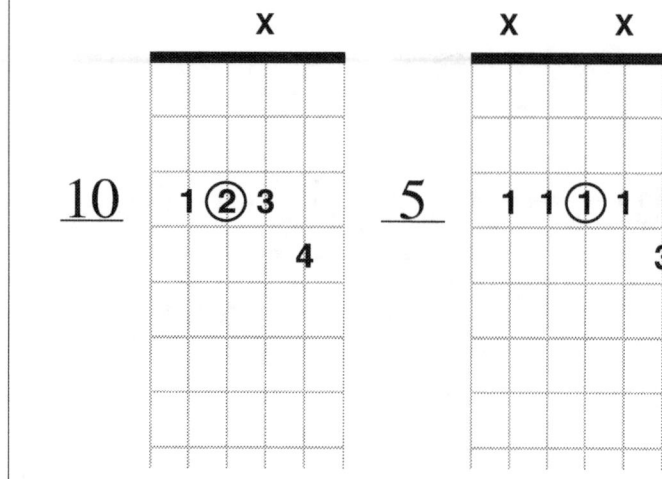
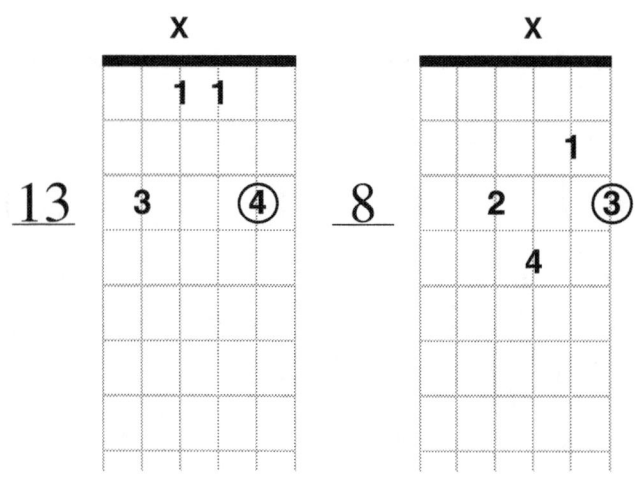
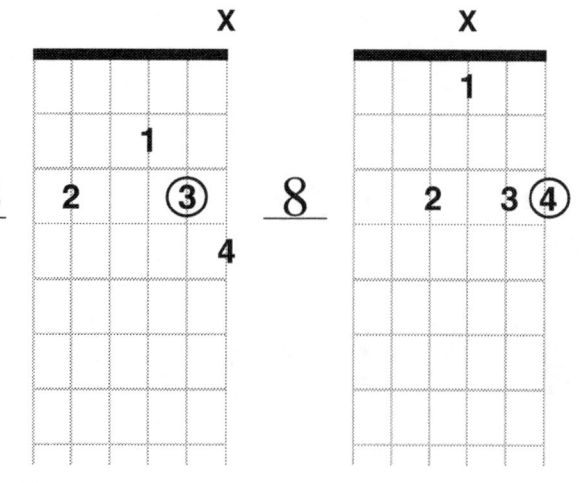

FREEDOM: GUITAR CHORDS AND PROGRESSIONS FOR THE 21ST CENTURY

The vast majority of chords and chord progressions used by today's guitar player are both derived and grounded in the theory and composition techniques used in the 18th and 19th Centuries. Now that we've arrived in the 21st Century, it's time to take advantage of the vast reservoir of material developed during the 20th Century.

Composers have moved beyond chords built on the interval of the third (Major, Minor, Augmented, Diminished - 6th, 7th, 9th, 11th, 13th, etc.) in search of new tonal colors. Not only have the chords been altered, but the manner in which they move and relate to each other has been drastically changed.

Now is the time to open yourself to these resources - becoming truly free and not just a copy of the past and present, by employing a gate into the future. This book not only gives you over 20,000 chords, but also outlines various 20th Century techniques for their use - all adapted for the guitar. The chords in this book will let you create music unlike anyone else's. For the first time you can be totally unrestrained.

Of these 20th Century chord structures, I have selected and fingered the most practical and feasible on the guitar fingerboard. There are 308 chord types, each in six inversions, creating a total of 1,848 chords for each of the twelve tones in music, creating a total of 22,176 chords.

CHORD CONSTRUCTION AND NAMES

The chords in this book have been created by combining different types of intervals: major, minor, diminished and augmented 2^{nds}, 3^{rds}, 4^{ths}, 5^{ths}, 6^{ths}, 7^{ths}, and octaves. Since these chords do not fall into traditional categories, they will be named by the intervals used to form them. For example, a chord created by combining a consecutive Major 2nd and minor 3rd on the root note "C" will be labeled $C-M^2-m^3$.

By using this method of chord construction we will obtain 3- and 4-note chord forms, which then may be used "as is" or as foundations on which 4-, 5-, and 6-note chords will be built (added-note chords – Ex. $C-M^2-m^3+$; the plus sign stands for an added note chord). Remember, an important technique in the composition of truly interesting music is the constant change in the textural fabric of a work – in other words, moving through chords of varying size: 2 (power chords), 3, 4, 5 and 6 notes.

ADDED-NOTE CHORDS

During the 20th Century, various notes were added into chords in order to create new and different shaded colors of sound along with varying degrees of calm and tension (Ex. C_6, $Cmaj_7$, C_7, C_7-9, etc.). The interaction of tension and calm, along with the constant ebb and flow of tonal colors, propels music through time and space. I have taken the basic chords in this book and, in similar fashion, introduced one or more notes into each chord formation – altering its density, color and tension (all added-notes are marked with an "x"). However, you shouldn't take these choices as the only ones possible. Experiment by adding your own open or closed notes into either the basic or added-note chords.

Remember, freedom to create chords and music that's uniquely your own is the primary goal of this book.

TRANSPOSITION

Each chord form will be shown on the root note "C" in 6 different positions. Each position is determined by the location of the chord's root on one of the 6 strings (the root will be circled). As the chord form is moved up the fingerboard its name will change accordingly.

A. Chords with root on the 6th string:

Fret	1st	2nd	3rd	4th	5th	6th	7th	8th	9th	10th	11th	12th
Chord	F	G♭	G	A♭	A	B♭	B	C	D♭	D	E♭	E

B. Chords with root on the 5th string:

Fret	1st	2nd	3rd	4th	5th	6th	7th	8th	9th	10th	11th	12th
Chord	B♭	B	C	D♭	D	E♭	E	F	G♭	G	A♭	A

C. Chords with root on the 4th string:

Fret	1st	2nd	3rd	4th	5th	6th	7th	8th	9th	10th	11th	12th
Chord	E♭	E	F	G♭	G	A♭	A	B♭	B	C	D♭	D

D. Chords with root on the 3rd string:

Fret	1st	2nd	3rd	4th	5th	6th	7th	8th	9th	10th	11th	12th
Chord	A♭	A	B♭	B	C	D♭	D	E♭	E	F	G♭	G

E. Chords with root on the 2nd string:

Fret	1st	2nd	3rd	4th	5th	6th	7th	8th	9th	10th	11th	12th
Chord	C	D♭	D	E♭	E	F	G♭	G	A♭	A	B♭	B

F. Chords with root on the 1st string:

Fret	1st	2nd	3rd	4th	5th	6th	7th	8th	9th	10th	11th	12th
Chord	F	G♭	G	A♭	A	B♭	B	C	D♭	D	E♭	E

CHORD MELODY*

A world of possibilities opens up if we approach the construction of a chord progression as a melody in its own right. In this procedure the sound of each individual chord is vitally important, not only to the moment it sounds, but as to its role in the overall construction of the entire work. Each chord may be thought of as one forward step in the creation of a melody. This melody of chords may be used as a background to a work in any musical style or a solo unto itself. Each chord in the progression should be chosen carefully with regard to its individual tonal color and to the amount of tension contained within the chord. In addition, each chord's relationship to the adjacent chords – and subsequently to the entire work – must be taken into consideration. Architecture and planning is of crucial importance in all forms of music.

As the rules of traditional harmony govern the role and use of chords and keys, the chords of this book offer the guitarist unlimited freedom and a definite need for logical methods governing the choice of chords and how to move them.

The following ideas offer direction and guidance for the use of these 21st Century chords. The possibilities are limitless and, as stated in the Foreword, offer you the capability to be truly *free*, never at a loss for inspiration, and never having to sound like anyone else.

*In the jazz idiom, the solo styling of harmonizing some or all of the notes of a song with supporting chords. In this book we are expanding the term to signify the concept chords as melodic steps.

SUGGESTED IDEAS

1. **Substitution:**
   One method of chord choice is to simply replace some or all of the chords in a traditional progression or song with the chords from this book using your ear and imagination as a guide. For example, any chord in this book may replace a C major chord.

2. **Melody as a Guiding Force:**
   a) Create a melodic line that will then act as a foundational bass line, an inner voice, or a melody on which to build your chords. You may stay within a particular scale or move between them: major, minor, modal, synthetic, chromatic or 12-tone row.

   b) Let each note in this melody act as the root of a particular chord.
   Ex.: melody notes = C, E^b, F, G may be harmonized with one category of chord type.
           Ex.: C-PP^5, E^b-PP^5, F-PP^5, G-PP^5, or with mixed types,
               Ex.: C-MM^2, E^b-mM^3, F-PPP^{4+}, G-P^4-D^5

c) The choice of harmonic rhythm (speed at which chords change) depends on the sound and effect you are after. As a general rule, a solo chord passage would be more active rhythmically and contain more chords than a background progression. In fact, as a background it is generally accepted that the chord rhythm would fall into a continuum (a recurring pattern that creates an expectation on the part of the listener) with slight variations for variety. This is especially important if you're layering multiple parts against the chords (melody, countermelody, fill-ins, harmony parts, bass lines, drum parts, etc.) so as to keep each layer identifiable, separate, and, above all, clearly defined in its role in the overall architecture – *planning is everything*.

3. **Tension and Calm:**
   The interplay of tension and calm (release) is an essential force in moving music from one point to another. Although relative to each person's musical experience and surrounding (cultural) influence, the following outline gives a general guide to the degrees of tension generated by certain interval combinations. Since these combinations form chords, you're the judge of the total effect. Remember, all of this is part of the 20th Century – the fundamental belief in the freedom of each individual to be unique, creative and totally free.

   General Guide:

   Minor 2nd, Diminished 5th, Major 7th = strong dissonance (other notes in chord will either reinforce or soften interval effect)

   Major 2nd, Minor 7th = soft dissonance

   Minor 3rd, Major 3rd, Minor 6th, Major 6th = consonance

   Perfect 4th, Perfect 5th, Octave = open consonance

4. **Cycles:**
   The 20th Century has seen chord progressions based on cyclic motion:

   Ex. Cycle of Perfect 4^{ths}:
   C-mA^3+, F-MA^6, B^b-M^7-m^3, E^b-P^5-P^4, A^b-PP^5, etc.

   Cycle of Perfect 5^{ths}:
   G-mA^3, D-Am^7+, A-P^5-M^6, E-ma^7+, etc.

5. **Ostinato:**
An ostinato pattern, traditionally in the bass, is a constantly repeated pattern of notes or chords that creates feelings of expectation and tension within a type of hypnotic lull that draws the listener deeper and deeper into the work. A perfect example of this procedure is Nirvana's *Smells Like Teen Spirit* (one of the most influential songs in the history of Rock) in which the use of a 4-chord circular progression acts as the foundation upon which all else is built.

6. **12-Tone Row as the Guiding Force:**
During the early part of the 20th Century, Arnold Schoenberg developed a manner of composition based on the equality of the 12 tones of the chromatic scale. I suggest you investigate this study, but for now we can adapt the principle of the row to build a foundation upon which to create an infinite number of chord families, each containing 12 chords.

   Sample Row (12 tones – no repeats)

   $B^b - C - E^b - F - D - D^b - A - G^b - E - G - B$

   Once you form row, choose chords (sound, tension, color, etc.) and add harmonic chord rhythm.

7. **Aleatoric (music by chance):**
Devise any method imaginable to relate one chord to another. For example:

A	B^b	B	C	D^b	D	E^b	E	F	G^b	G	A^b
1	2	3	4	5	6	7	8	9	10	11	12

Roll dice to choose order of notes on which to build chords.

8. **Bi and Tri-Tonal Groupings:**
With a fellow guitarist, recorder or sequencer, experiment with moving various chord forms against each other with different rhythms. Remember, each layer should have its own chord type and rhythm to set it apart from the rest.

9. Pedal Tones:

In all styles of music the use of a single note (pedal tone) held or repeated against a series of chords has been a very important and widely used compositional technique. With the use of pedal tones you can devise innumerable background pads upon which to compose melodies, improvise solos, or create chord melodies. As the pedal tone is sounded, the chords (traditional or 21st Century) will pass under, through, or over it. The resulting effect is one of shifting tonal colors and varying degrees of tension as each chord interacts with the pedal tone. On the guitar, open strings offer great potential for truly colorful pedals. The following examples illustrate the use of pedal tones set against a mixture of traditional and 21st Century chords.

Suggested Guidelines:

1) Play example as written in whatever rhythm you prefer.

2) Choose groups of 2 or 3 chords and improvise various progressions, letting each chord's sound color dictate direction and duration.

3) Use our own favorite traditional chords with various pedal tones in similar fashion.

4) Combine 21st Century and your own traditional chords into various progressions over, under, or through pedal tones.

5) Let your ear and imagination guide you.

6) Achieve freedom.

PEDAL E – 6th STRING

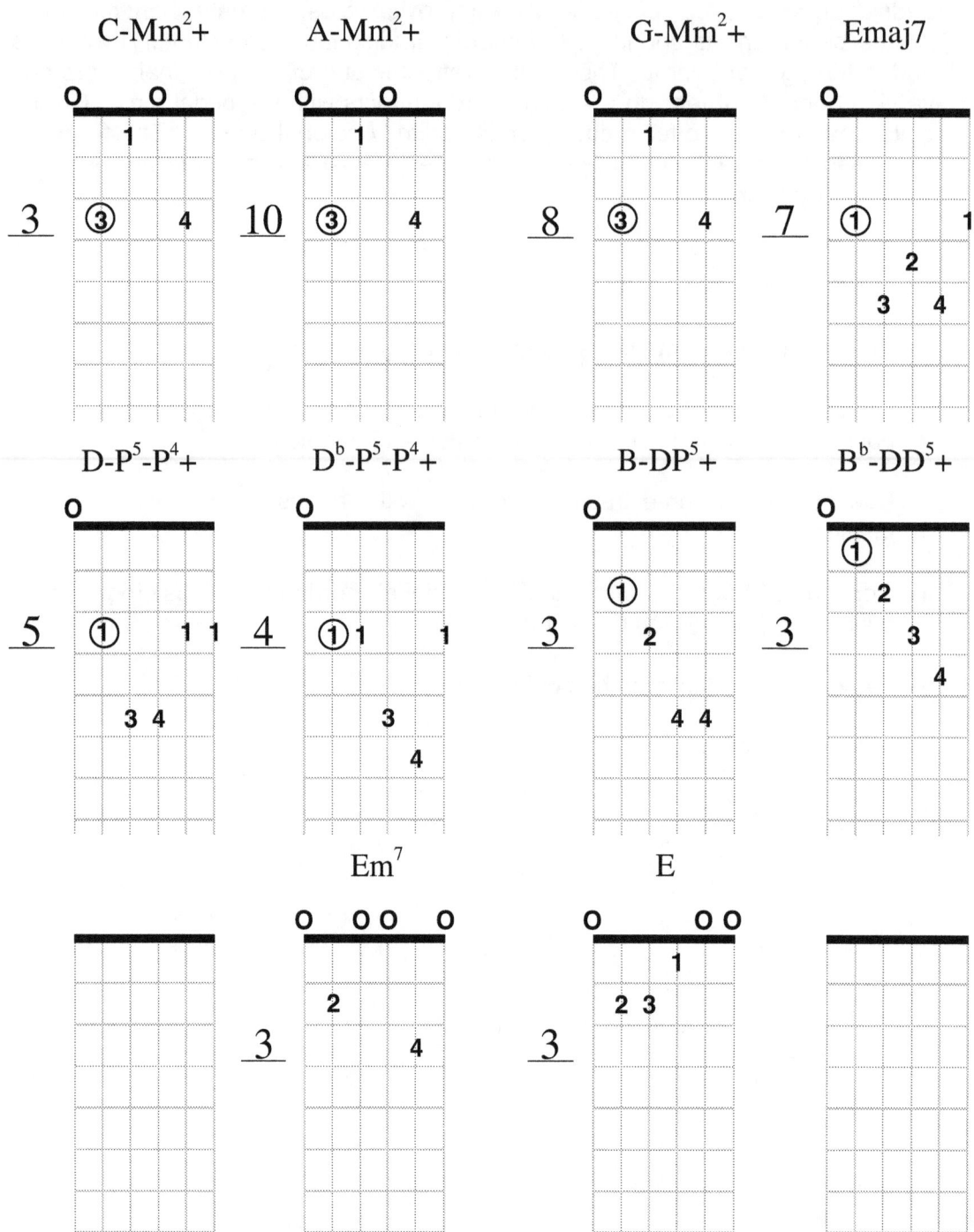

PEDAL G – 3rd STRING

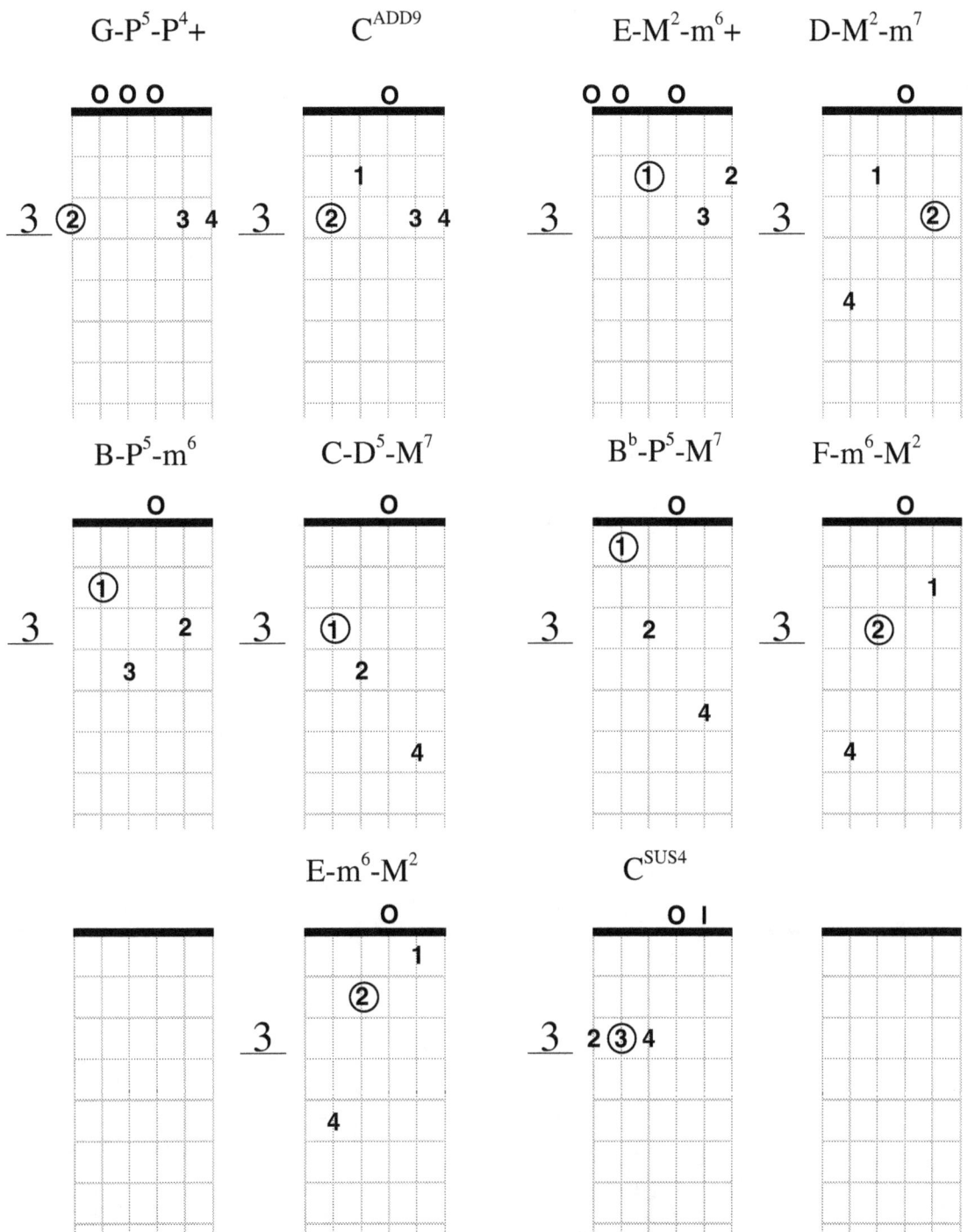

PEDAL E – 1st STRING

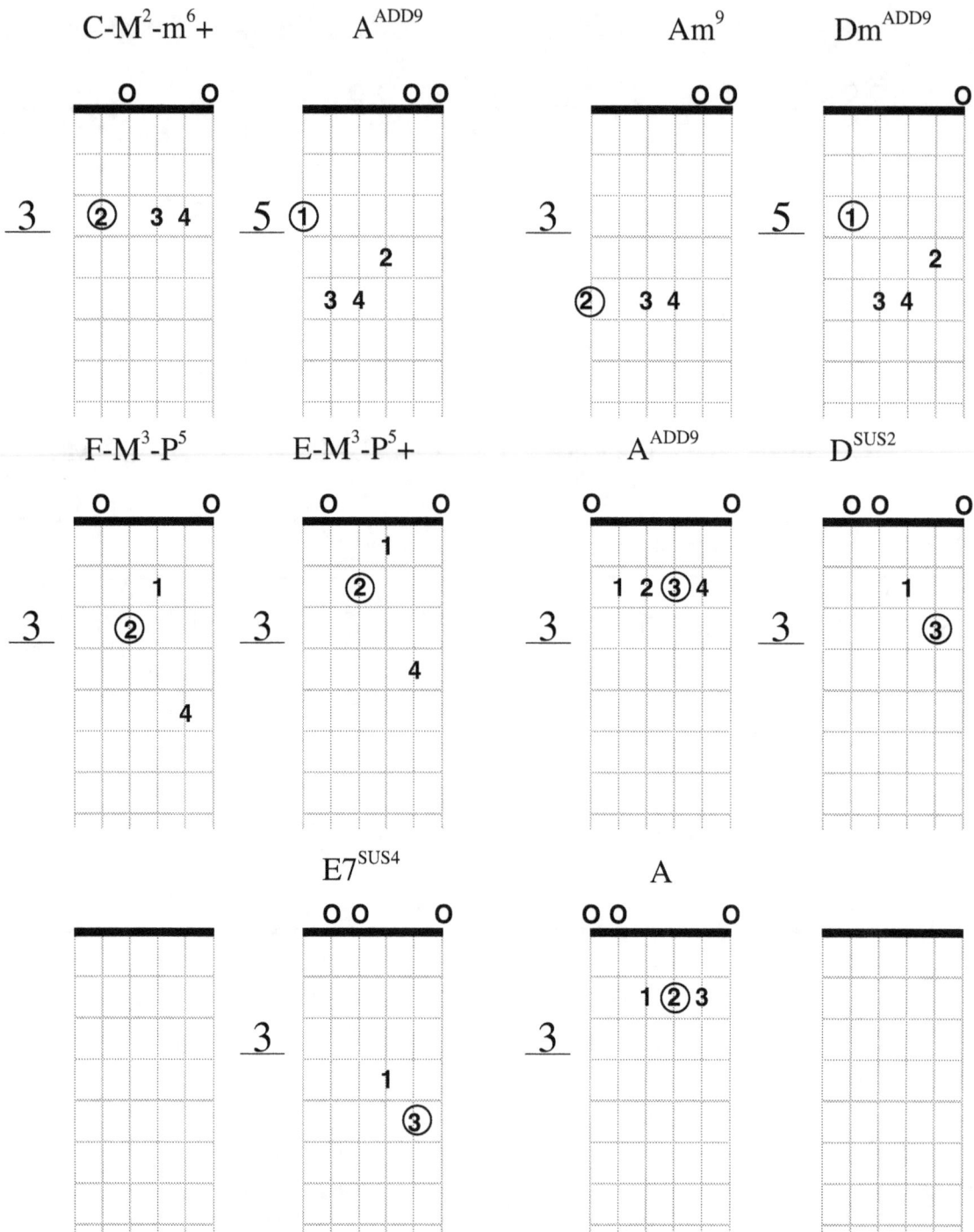

10. Parallel Chord Movements:

A technique especially suited and extremely colorful on the guitar comes from the music of Claude Debussy. A single chord form is moved across the fingerboard creating parallel motion as the chords glide from one to another. If pedal tones are added to this technique a whole new set of colors emerge.

PARALLEL MAJOR 7th OVER PEDAL A

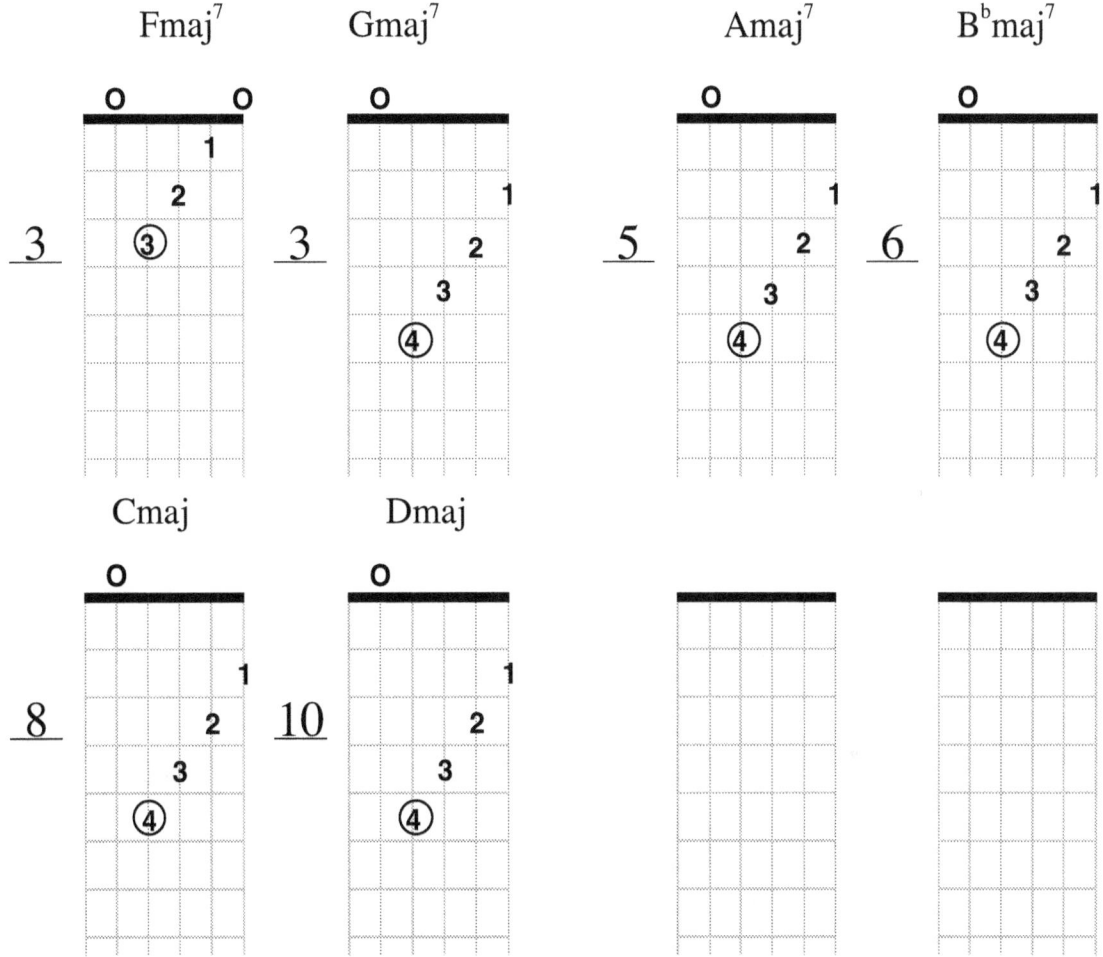

21stCenturyChords.com

The official web site for 21st Century Chords, with new lessons each month, information about other books by Joe Lilore, links to useful sites, and more! Check us out on the web at *www.21stcenturychords.com*.